JUSTICE and PEACE

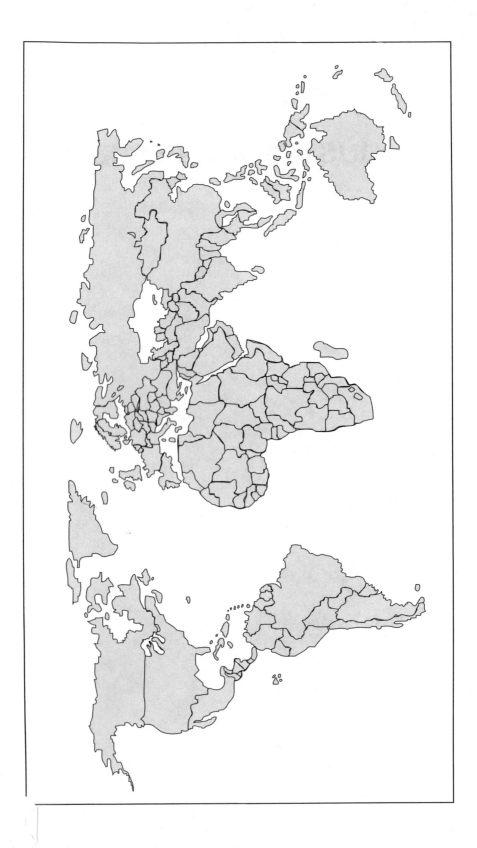

JUSTICE and PEACE

A Christian Primer

SECOND EDITION
Revised and Expanded

J. Milburn Thompson

ORBIS BOOKS
Maryknoll, New York 10545

Seventh Printing, September 2009

Copyright © 2003 by J. Milburn Thompson

This is a substantially revised edition of *Justice and Peace: A Christian Primer* © J. Milburn Thompson, Maryknoll, N.Y.: Orbis Books, 1997. Published by Orbis Books, Maryknoll, NY 10545-0308. Manufactured in the United States of America.

Permissions: Excerpt from *The Great Ascent: The Struggle for Economic Development in Our Time* by Robert L. Heilbroner, copyright © 1963, reprinted with permission of HarperCollins Publishers. From *The Fate of the Earth* by Jonathan Schell, copyright © 1982, by Jonathan Schell. Reprinted by permission of Alfred A. Knopf, Inc. and Jonathan Cape (U.K.). Originally appeared in *The New Yorker*. Figure 4.1 from "Moral Claims, Human Rights, and Population Policies," by the Yale Task Force on Population Ethics, copyright © 1974, reprinted with permission of *Theological Studies*. Table on "America's Political/Economic Choices," from *Peace and Change* in a review by Seymour Melman, copyright © 1993, reprinted with permission of Blackwell Publications Company.

Library of Congress Cataloging-in-Publication Data

Thompson, Joseph Milburn, 1947–
    Justice and peace : a Christian primer / J. Milburn Thompson.—2nd ed.
        p. cm.
Includes bibliographical references and index.
    ISBN 1-57075-461-6 (pbk.)
    1. Christianity and justice.   2. Social justice.   3. Peace—Religious aspects
—Christianity.   I. Title.
    BR115.J8 T46 2003
    261.8—dc21

                                                            2002155948

Contents

Introduction

"Peace is both a gift of God and a human work. It must be constructed on the basis of central human values: truth, justice, freedom, and love."[1]

"The life and words of Jesus and the teaching of his Church call us to serve those in need and to work actively for social and economic justice. As a community of believers, we know that our faith is tested by the quality of justice among us, that we can best measure our life together by how the poor and the vulnerable are treated."[2]

The almost universal response to the September 11 terrorist attacks was, "This changes everything." The way Americans and others looked at the world did indeed change. In perspective, such changes are the rule, not the exception. The world changed dramatically, for example, with the collapse of communism in Europe, symbolized by the dismantling of the Berlin Wall in 1989. Such dramatic changes generally mean that humanity is faced with different problems, rather than fewer problems.

Dramatic changes in global politics call for innovative thinking and imaginative analysis. Now is a good time for Christian citizens to take a fresh look at international relations and foreign policy.

OBJECTIVES AND AUDIENCE

This is a starter book, a primer. It is written for college students, thoughtful Christians, and anyone who is concerned about global issues and wants to learn more. It is intended for budding scholars, not established experts. It strives to be scholarly in the sense of being well-researched, accurate, and balanced in seeking the truth. The scope of this text precludes any pretense of making major contributions to the understanding of or the solution to the myriad problems it reviews. Indeed, there is a certain amount of hubris involved in even attempting a book that addresses such diverse disciplines and so many controversies. No author can pretend to be competent in history, economics, politics, ecology, international relations, ethics, and theology. Rather, the goal is to inform citizens well enough that they can be active participants in public policy debates and catalysts for constructive change in the contemporary world. Participation and transformation are the responsibilities of all citizens in a democracy, and certainly of Christian citizens.

This is therefore a getting-started book as well.[3] Information, understanding, and rigorous critical analysis are necessary first steps for creating a more just and peaceful world. Analysis, however, is not sufficient; society needs to be changed.

Public policy primarily reflects values and interests. For example, should the alleviation of global hunger be a goal of foreign policy or is national self-interest its only objective? Should a particular piece of legislation serve the basic needs of the poor or the welfare of corporations? These are fundamentally questions about values and interests. Once one decides which values public policy should serve, the process of translating those values into appropriate policies remains complex and often controversial. However, citizens can and should participate in the discussion and in the development of policies and systems. When citizens "leave it to the experts," they simply ensure that the expert's values and interests become policy.

Any analysis of American foreign policy and of the global situation must be undertaken from some perspective. Every analyst, whether located in the Pentagon, a university, or the local cafe, brings assumptions, values, goals, and objectives to debates about international relations. This particular book brings a *Christian perspective* to bear on the world situation.

A Christian perspective is grounded in the conviction that God is sovereign and that God's rule is loving and just. By creating human beings in God's own image, God has bestowed upon each and every person an intrinsic dignity and an infinite value. This human dignity is nourished and developed in community. Humanity is God's people—a family—called to love and care for one another and for the earth. As co-creators with God, human beings are responsible for creating a just community conducive to the flowering of each person's potential.

Such a perspective means that an analysis of the contemporary global situation is important. Christians are called to care for brothers and sisters, near and far. Christians should be concerned about what public policies do for and to people. There should be no gulf between faith (our relationship with God) and everyday life.[4] Christians are called to live their faith in the world, and this means that politics, economics, and social policy are significant.

This study will operate on three interrelated levels. The first level focuses on the reality of the situation. The first step is to ask what ethicist Daniel Maguire calls "reality revealing questions."[5] What is going on? Who is doing what to whom? The goal here is to seek information and gather the facts.

The second level involves analysis and evaluation. The task now is interpretation. One's perspective is brought to bear on the facts, seeking insight and surfacing possible solutions. What are the causes of this problem? What are the objectives and consequences of various solutions? Analysis is complex, and there will be differences of opinion. Often these disagreements are rooted in the values and interests that are brought to the analysis. For example, nearly everyone agrees that terrorism should be prevented and resisted. The differences in the proposals regarding terrorism are rooted both in different values and goals—to take revenge on evil terrorists or to reconcile them into a just community, for example—and in different analyses of the causes of the problem and the consequences of various solutions.

The third level moves to commitment and action. Reasonable solutions must be sought and implemented; strategies for change need to be devised and deployed. This, too, is complex, difficult, and often frustrating. Sometimes creative solutions fail to be realized. Other times solutions fall short of resolving the problem or bring with them new problems. There are times, too, when remedies work, and real progress can be celebrated. Obviously this process of reflection and action is ongoing, as Christians move in faith and hope toward the Kingdom God has promised.

There is a spiritual dimension that corresponds to this conceptual and ethical framework. Peace activist Ammon Hennacy once wrote:

> Love without courage and wisdom is sentimentality, as with the ordinary church member. Courage without love and wisdom is foolhardiness, as with the ordinary soldier. Wisdom without love and courage is cowardice, as with the ordinary intellectual. Therefore one with love, courage, and wisdom is one in a million, who moves the world, as with Jesus, Buddha, and Gandhi.[6]

The Eastern Christian tradition repeats the Jesus Prayer, "Lord Jesus Christ, Son of the living God, have mercy on me a sinner," as a form of centering mantra. An alternative, based on the quote from Ammon Hennacy, might be, "God, my mother, teach me the compassion, the wisdom, and the courage of your heart."

These three virtues correspond helpfully to the three levels of social analysis. A *compassionate heart* is essential for seeing those who are poor and suffering in our midst. Without compassion a statistic such as "one in every six American children is poor" elicits only indifference and apathy. Compassion is essential, but not sufficient. Unless we pause to seek *wisdom*—to gather information and interpret it carefully—we may do more harm than good. And without the *courage* to raise our voices and to get our hands dirty in the struggle to change society, compassion is mere sentimentality, and wisdom is academic in the worst sense of the word. Compassion, wisdom, and courage give a spiritual dimension to the seeing, judging, and acting[7] that are essential for social analysis.

This book, then, is an introduction to the obstacles to justice and peace posed by the contemporary world.[8] It seeks to inform the reader through a critical analysis of the pressing problems facing humanity at the dawn of the twenty-first century and to transform both the reader and the world.

The book begins by tracing the major trends in the development of the contemporary world—colonialism, the industrial/technological revolution, and the Cold War and its aftermath. Succeeding chapters focus on the obstacles to a more just and peaceful world: the gap between the rich and the poor, the population explosion and environmental destruction, violations of human rights, war and conflict, weapons of mass destruction and the trade in arms, and an inadequate theory of international relations as well as a nebulous foreign policy. The final chapters of the book reflect directly on the Christian perspective and on the meaning of Christian citizenship. Resources for action on behalf of justice and peace and for further study are suggested. Although the book focuses on global issues and foreign policy, it also attends to related domestic issues.

This organization of the book makes sense, but the chapters could easily be organized differently. The penultimate chapter on the Christian perspective could come first or second. While it makes sense to read the historical chapter before the chapters on issues, the latter could be re-arranged in many different ways. Although those chapters are somewhat interconnected, each could stand on its own, and the reader (or teacher) might want to impose his or her own order on these topics. Not only is humanity interdependent, but the issues facing humanity are deeply interrelated. Each of the issues addressed here, for example, is a genuine "security" issue, a threat to peace. The words of Pope Paul VI point to the interrelated themes of the book, "If you want peace, work for justice."

The study questions after each chapter aim to stimulate further discussion of the issues raised in the text rather than test comprehension of the material. The "For Reflection" sidebars in the text are also to provoke reflection and discussion.

REVISIONS TO THE FIRST EDITION

A book on global issues inevitably needs to be updated. The first edition of this book was written in 1996 and published in 1997. Two of the major trends since then are the globalization of the world's economy and the expansion of terrorism. A response to these themes has been woven into the book, but a significantly re-worked chapter 2 addresses globalization more directly and chapter 5 considers a moral response to terrorism. There has been a concerted effort to bring the statistics and situations throughout the book up-to-date (to the end of 2002).

There are other changes worth noting, especially for those who have used the book in teaching. The "Christian Citizenship" section formerly in chapter 8 has been combined with "Resources for Involvement and Information" and forms a new chapter 9. In the first edition an appendix with several tables gave historical and demographic information and economic and social indicators and indices for the countries of the world. These have been eliminated in the revised edition, but chapter 9 tells the reader where to find current information on the countries of the world on the world wide web. The section titled "Is Humanitarian Intervention Justified?" has been moved to chapter 5 from chapter 7. In the first edition, chapter 5 included five in-depth case studies of ethno-nationalist conflict. This edition tries to give an overview of the new landscape of conflict throughout the world. The case study on Haiti that was in chapter 4 has been eliminated.

ACKNOWLEDGMENTS

Teaching and learning is a communal activity. I have presented this material in the classroom for over twenty-five years. The responses of students have refined these ideas and transformed me again and again. I extend my thanks to all those students, and my appreciation to those who presented this material to me—my teachers and academic colleagues. I hope this book will be as good a teacher as those books and articles I have read in researching it. I look forward to the responses of colleagues and students, to continuing the conversation.

When I wrote the first edition of this book, I was teaching at Saint Joseph College in West Hartford, Connecticut. Since then I have moved to Bellarmine University, which is located in my hometown, Louisville, Kentucky. I want to thank Saint Joseph College for the incentive to write this book and, more importantly, for giving me time to write it. I received a sabbatical leave during the fall 1996 semester, in part through the generosity of my colleague Dorothy Keller, making it possible to complete this project. My friends in the Religious Studies Department at Saint Joseph College—John J. Stack, Ann Marie Caron, and Joan M. Kelly—supported and encouraged me. Father John Stack, in particular, has been a wonderful mentor. I am also grateful to my new colleagues in the Theology Department at Bellarmine— George Kilcourse and Clyde Crews—old friends from our graduate studies at Fordham University—for their support in working on the revised edition.

Two political scientists, John Kikoski and Kenneth J. Long, read and commented on virtually the entire text of the first edition, and this is a much better book because of their suggestions. Several colleagues commented on various chapters of the first edition: Rosemarie Gorman, Jean M. Graustein, Michael Hovey, Peter Markow, Harold T. McKone, Shyamala Raman, Ruth Rosenbaum, John J. Stack, and Kathryn Wrinn. Several of my new colleagues at Bellarmine have been conversation partners on topics related to the revised edition: Curt Bergstrand, Derek Curtis, Ira Grupper, Charles Hatten, Robert Lockhart, Margaret Miller, Barry Padgett, Frank Raymond, Hank Rothgerber, Julie Schrader, Frank Slesnick, Lee Thomas, and Tim Welliver. Each of them has contributed to the clarity and accuracy of the text, and I appreciate their time and ideas. I have too often stubbornly resisted the wise counsel of these many colleagues.

Various members of the staff at Saint Joseph College assisted in finding research materials or in generating the graphics for the first edition of the book: Deborah Ahl, Donald Gustafson, Kathleen Kelley, Bonnie Merk-Birman, Dorothy O'Dwyer, and Patricia Senich, as well as my friend, Paul Doherty. Their assistance is much appreciated.

I did significant work on the revised edition at the library of Saint Martin's College in Lancaster, England, during the summer of 2002. I am grateful to Principal (President) Christopher Carr for his hospitality, to Head Librarian David Brown and his fine staff for their help, and to Hilary Alcock, Director of the International Office, for paving the way. The library staff at Bellarmine University, ably directed by Marquita Breit and Joy Hatch, has also provided valuable assistance. Michele Thomas, secretary for the Humanities at Bellarmine, has been extremely helpful, as was her predecessor, Susan Merryweather.

My editor at Orbis Books, Susan Perry, has been wonderful. She was receptive to the idea of this book, confident that I could actually write it, painstaking in her critique and corrections, and patient with my struggle to revise it without the benefit of a sabbatical leave. My wife, Mary Ann, who teaches Community Health Nursing at Bellarmine University, is the first to read and critique the drafts of my writing. She is at once a tough critic and a strong advocate.

Finally, I re-dedicate this book to my parents, Joe and Dorothy Thompson. When my father died in 1999, I lost an important conversation partner about global issues and faith. (He thought this book was too idealistic.) I am happy that one of my brothers, Bart, has continued the conversation. I have been fortunate to have loving parents and a functional family, and I am grateful.

CHAPTER ONE

The Twenty-First Century:
How Did We Get Here?

". . . [T]he most fundamental task is for our community of faith to understand and act on two fundamental ideas. The first is drawn from the Beatitudes: 'Blessed are the peacemakers, they will be called children of God.' The second is the familiar call of Pope Paul VI: 'If you want peace, work for justice.'' These two deceptively simple statements outline the key elements of our mission: To be Christian is to be a peacemaker and to pursue peace is to work for justice.[1]

On September 11, 2001, our world changed. The terrorist attack that destroyed the World Trade Center in New York City and damaged the Pentagon in Washington, D.C., killing three thousand ordinary people, was so brutal as to be incredible. As an act of terrorism it was brilliant. There are no better symbols of American (and Western) economic and military power than the World Trade Center and the Pentagon, and the coordination, skill, and sophistication of this new type of suicide bombing and the commonplace character of its victims did indeed terrorize a complacent American populace. Why would someone hate America so much as to forfeit his life to kill thousands of average Americans? Is there a moral response to such a violent and immoral act?

World politics had already changed dramatically at the beginning of the last decade of the twentieth century (1989–91) with the collapse of communism in Eastern Europe and the Soviet Union. This positive political development, however, had little practical effect on realities such as global economic inequality, population pressures, or environmental destruction. Poverty has bedeviled humanity from its origins, but modern economic systems, the global economy, and ecological concerns are relatively new. Violence has always been a scourge for humankind, but today we seem to be combining medieval brutality with hi-tech sophistication. The aim of this chapter is to trace the three major trends or historical movements that set up the current economic, political, and environmental situations.

Obviously, this is a look at the big picture. Understanding these historical megatrends is very important if humanity is to overcome the obstacles to a more just and peaceful world. Trying to remedy a problem without addressing its history is like trying to rid a yard of dandelions without pulling up their roots. It doesn't work.

The three historical movements that have produced the contemporary world are colonialism, the industrial/technological revolution, and the trends that characterize the latter half of the twentieth century—the Cold War and globalization. Each will be examined in turn.

COLONIALISM

Commemorating Columbus

In 1992 the peoples of the Americas commemorated the 500th anniversary of Columbus landing in what we now call the Caribbean. There was much controversy about this anniversary. While earlier generations in the United States might have unabashedly danced in the streets in honor of this cinque-centennial, and some wished to do so, many people were too aware of the ambiguities for a wholehearted celebration. This paragraph's first sentence was carefully crafted to attend to some of the politically sensitive issues raised by this anniversary, and dissecting that sentence can introduce those issues.

"The peoples of the Americas": Contrary to the assumptions of some Americans, Columbus did not find the United States, but the Americas— North, South, Central, and so on. He first landed in what is today the Dominican Republic, and he explored the Caribbean on subsequent journeys. Columbus thought he was in India, so he called the people who were here "Indians."

"Landing," not discovery. As the comedian and social commentator Dick Gregory used to say, "How do you 'discover' a land that is already occupied?" Yet in elementary school I learned that Columbus discovered America in 1492. There is a good deal of hubris and more than a touch of racism in the notion that until Europeans set foot in a place, it does not really exist. The Americas were a "New World" for the Europeans, but these lands were already home for the indigenous people.

"Caribbean": The Carib people were found on many of the islands in the sea named after them when Columbus arrived. The Carib people are now extinct. They were wiped out by the diseases and the swords brought over by the Europeans. When whites arrived in the Americas there were about 100 million aborigines in the hemispheres. Within about a century that number was reduced by nearly 90 percent. This "demographic disaster has no equal in history, not even the Black Death."[2]

"Commemorate": It is, in part, because we are acutely aware of the fate of native peoples, resulting from Europeans coming to the Americas, that we remembered, rather than celebrated, this anniversary. The European "settlement" of the Americas was a mixed tragedy. From the perspective of the aboriginal peoples the settlement was a conquest that led to the exploitation of their labor and resources, the loss of their land and freedom, and their death.

The next chapter in the story is the enslavement of Africans to work on the plantations in the Caribbean and North and South America. This is surely one of the most tragic stories of exploitation and oppression in all of human history. There were, of course, winners and losers in this sad saga. Europe and some Europeans benefited immensely from the exploitation of the resources of the Americas, and there was a mutual enrichment that developed from the mingling of these cultures and peoples. But despite benefits that may have accrued for the overall good of humanity from colonialism, the central story line is one of inhumanity and injustice. Basically white people from Europe exploited the people, lands, and resources of black, brown, red, and yellow people all over the globe. That is the story and the legacy of colonialism.

Thus far, the tale of colonialism has been introduced through the prism of the commemoration of the 500th anniversary of Columbus landing in the Americas. It is beyond the scope of this book to explore colonialism in detail, but it is important to communicate the breadth of European colonialism and a sense of what it meant to those who were colonized.

Europe Colonizes the World

The colonial period began around 1500 and lingers into the present, although nearly all colonies have now gained political (but not economic) independence. During this period only a handful of countries escaped direct colonization, most notably China, Japan, and Turkey.[3] No country, however, escaped the impact of European military and economic power. Indeed, these exceptions avoided direct colonization principally because of the balance of power among contending European colonizers.

In the case of China, for example, the European powers and the United States agreed on an Open Door policy after the British navy defeated China in the Opium Wars of 1839–1842. This agreement was designed to block Russia and Japan from actually annexing Chinese territory, thereby keeping the wealth, technology, and resources of China open to the exploitation of all. Through its victory, Britain won the "right" to profitably export deadly opium *into* China.[4]

Another set of figures indicates the extent of European colonial control. "In the year 1800, Europe, its colonies, and its former colonies already covered 55 percent of the world's land surface. By 1914, that figure reached an astonishing 84 percent of the land surface."[5] Given the indirect colonial control of countries like China and Turkey, virtually every people on earth has experienced the domination or influence of Europeans.

Phase One—1500–1815

The colonial period of European expansion can be divided into two phases.[6] The first phase, from 1500–1815, was characterized by exploration and trade. Spain and Portugal, and later the Netherlands, were the dominant powers during this period.

As Marco Polo learned, the crafts and goods of the Orient were at first superior to those of Europe. By the sixteenth century, Europe was beginning to trade on a more equal basis with the East. The goal of the European powers regarding the East was to establish trading posts and trade routes, and to compete favorably with each other for the goods of the Orient. The Europeans found Africa to be inhospitable for settlement because of disease, climate, and terrain. Thus, they tended to establish heavily armed forts in African ports for the sake of trade. In Central and South America, however, Spain and Portugal established colonies. Here the environment was amenable and the natives were easily conquered because the Europeans had swords, guns, and horses. The Europeans came in and took over. Mexico provides a good example of what happened in this first phase of colonization.

Mexico. When Hernán Cortéz landed on the coast of Mexico in 1519 with perhaps 600 soldiers, he encountered the Aztec empire that had swallowed Mexico during the seventy-year rule (1427–1496) of its great leader Tlacaelel. The Aztecs were themselves foreign conquerors of the various peoples in Mexico. They had demanded onerous tribute from the indigenous people, and sacrificed tens of thousands of them to their gods. The Aztec empire was no Garden of Eden.

The Aztec capital, Tenochtitlan, on the site of today's Mexico City, with its streets of water and huge market, was superior to the stinking burgs of medieval Europe. "It could boast archives of bark books, a magnificent calendar, and priests versed in math and astronomy. All Aztec children went to school."[7]

The sophistication of the Aztec civilization, however, did not include metals, horses, or the wheel. When Cortéz brandished his sword, fired his blunderbuss and cannons, ran his horses, and declared himself a god, he found a willing reception among the oppressed indigenous people and a woefully ill-armed opponent in the Aztecs. Cortéz conquered the capital and melted down the exquisite jewelry in the Aztec treasury into gold bars. The Spanish soldiers raped the women, took the land, and enslaved the people. Angered by human sacrifice, the Spanish killed the Aztec priests and scribes, and burned their bark books, reducing this pre-Columbian culture to smoke. In their sadistic cruelty and their single-minded search for wealth, the Spaniards managed to make the Aztec tyranny pale in comparison.

The Indians dropped from overwork in the mines and on the plantations, despaired because of the destruction of their culture, and died from the diseases brought by the Europeans—smallpox, malaria, influenza, measles, typhoid, dysentery, etc.—to which they had no resistance. "The net result of this ruthless exploitation was that the native population declined from seventeen million in 1522 to a mere one million by 1608. Here, surely, is a piece of genocide that rivals any in history!"[8]

By the seventeenth century, Spain had set up a system of "trade" with its colonies that was enshrined in law. The colony sent gold and silver, sugar and tobacco to Spain, and the "mother" country sent back consumer goods. "Bales of tobacco leaves floated to Seville; the Spanish worked these into cigarettes and returned them to Mexico City."[9] Manufacturing was a monopoly of Spain and strictly forbidden to the colonies. All trade was required to use Spanish ships. Thus did colonization cripple the economies of the colonies with economic dependency.

Spain set up two systems within its colonies that have left a lasting legacy throughout Latin America—the hacienda and a three-tiered caste structure. The hacienda was a large, nearly self-sufficient plantation growing sugar, cotton, or, later, coffee (an import from Africa, via the Middle East, to the New World). The hacienda was owned by a landlord and worked by indebted peasants under the supervision of a foreman. This pattern of a landed elite and impoverished landless peasants still endures throughout Latin America and in much of the Two-Thirds World. A 1975 World Bank survey of eighty-three former colonies found that, typically, only 3 percent of landowners controlled 79 percent of farmland.[10]

Intermarriage between the Spanish and the Indians created a three-tiered caste system in most of Latin America. At the top were the "pure" Europeans, often well-educated and wealthy, called *creoles*. Next were the *mestizos*, or mixed bloods, who occupied a middle role. At the bottom were the Indians or indigenous peoples, who continue to be the poorest people in the lowliest positions. In some countries, such as Brazil, Cuba, and Puerto Rico, the slave trade added Africans to this mix. Caste, color, and class continue to present problems of justice in much of Latin America.

Along with the sword came the cross. In Mexico, at least, the first Franciscans and Dominican missionaries tried to convert the Indians and to protect them from the murderous and greedy soldiers. Bartolomé de las Casas, for example, boldly denounced the inhumane treatment of the Indians to some temporary effect. After Juan Diego's vision of the dark Virgin of Guadalupe in 1531, Indians flocked to the church. By the beginning of the seventeenth century, however, the early missionaries had moved on to other parts of Central America and California. They were replaced by bishops, appointed by the King of Spain, and secular priests from Spain who were often aristocrats seeking their fortune in Mexico. Now the church became a direct agent of Spanish imperialism and itself a large landowner in the hacienda system. The religious message to the peasants was that the Lord would reward their humble obedience in the next life. Through the power of the church, Spain was able to rule for almost three centuries with barely an army present.[11]

The sixteenth through the eighteenth centuries established the global dominance of Europe and the economic patterns that endure to the present. The basic pattern was that Europe got wealthy and the colonies became impoverished. This happened because the colonizers established the rules of the game to benefit themselves. The colonial relationship was lopsidedly exploitative. Europe stole the rich resources of the colonies and then used the colonies as a market for European goods. This plundered wealth strengthened Europe for even greater plunder. Within the colonies a similar system prevailed. The wealthy elite, who now possessed the land, became richer through the labor of the peasants under their control. Whether one's perspective is global or domestic, the rich became richer and more powerful because they developed a system that exploited others for their benefit. Here lie the roots of injustice in the contemporary world.

Phase Two—1815–1945

The nineteenth century was the zenith of the British Empire. In 1815 Great Britain defeated Napoleon. With France subdued and Spain in decline, Britain ruled the seas. "By 1914, fully one-quarter of all humanity was under the rule of this relatively tiny island state, and it was literally true that the sun never set on the British Empire."[12]

The wealth garnered from the colonial system fueled the Industrial Revolution, which in turn strengthened the power of the colonial system. "It was in part the cash of Liverpool, centre of the triangular trade in slaves, cotton and rum between West Africa, the West Indies and Britain, that financed the mills of South Lancashire, the cradle of the industrial revolution."[13] The British plunder of the Bengal region of India in the mid-eighteenth century provided London with enough capital to be midwife to the birth of the Industrial Revolution. In turn the Industrial Revolution gave the European states, and especially Britain, a considerable technological advantage. This commercial and military advantage quickly converted mutual trade relations with the East into the lopsided exploitation which characterized the colonial system. In other words, the colonial powers *caused* the underdevelopment of the colonies. British economic policy in India is one example.

India. Before Britain arrived in India, there was a thriving textile industry based in small shops. When this inexpensive cloth began to compete with the developing textile mills in England, Britain imposed export restrictions (such as a 75 percent tariff) on Indian goods. This diminished cotton exports to Britain in the period of 1815–1832 by a factor of thirteen. In Bengal, the British went so far as to deliberately break the little fingers of thousands of Indian weavers so they could no longer practice their craft. This ruthless policy resulted in massive unemployment.

> The net effect of this policy of enforced complementarity of the British and Indian economies was that the non-agricultural population decreased from 45 percent of the whole in early 1800 to only 26 percent by 1940. Simply put, India had been well on its way toward becoming an industrial, diversified economy. This was reversed by the British.[14]

Through such practices, Britain underdeveloped India.

British trade policy toward its colonies worked as follows. The colony could only export to or import from Britain, using only British ships. The manufacture of certain goods that might compete with those produced in Britain was forbidden, and the whole protectionist system was buttressed by tariffs.[15] It was such policies that caused the British subjects who had relocated to the North American colonies to revolt. For example, at one time, no wool or cloth could be produced in the colonies except for local use, and steel furnaces and rolling mills were forbidden. Goods often had to be shipped to

England even if their destination was the colony next door. And, of course, there were the taxes and tariffs that burdened the colonials. In North America there was a successful revolt. In Asia and Africa these policies stood.[16]

Africa. Although Britain was the dominant power in the nineteenth century, it was not without rivals. In Africa the competition became so sharp that the European powers gathered at the Congress of Berlin in 1884 and carved up the map of Africa into zones of control. The countries created at Berlin bore no resemblance to the natural frontiers or the historical boundaries of various tribes and peoples. Traditional enemies were often lumped together in one state, while in other instances, single tribes were divided into two or three different countries. The casual arrogance of the Congress of Berlin continues to reap a bitter harvest of ethno-nationalist conflict and political chaos in contemporary Africa.[17]

The Congress of Berlin acknowledged Great Britain's control of Uganda and Kenya. Britain was interested in East Africa, and especially Kenya, in part, to protect its trade routes to Asia through the Suez Canal. The colonial administrators decided that Kenya, with its fertile highlands, should produce corn, coffee, wheat, and sisal for export to England. To that end, it created plantations for white settlers by moving the Masai and Kikuyu tribes from their lands and into reservations.

Providing cheap labor for the white settlers, however, turned out to be a problem. The Kikuyu and Masai peoples were self-sufficient and saw no need to work for money. Thus, to meet the need of white settlers from Britain and South Africa for cheap labor, the colonial administration had to adopt measures to undermine native economic independence and to force the local people to depend on a paid labor market for their needs.

First, the colonials instituted a hut tax that had to be paid in cash. Thus the natives would have to earn money to stay out of jail. Next, officials reduced the size of the reservations so that there was not enough land to meet the needs of the tribe. They also taxed the few commodities used by Africans, which raised prices. Finally, they instituted a passbook system and required tribal leaders to produce a quota of workers or be replaced. While the few thousand whites in Kenya received full government services and assistance, the four million blacks were neglected.

Not surprisingly the black population decreased from 4 million to 2.4 million in the first two decades of the twentieth century. Many whites expected that the blacks would simply die off. "As Kenya's colonial commissioner commented in 1904, after he had pushed the Masai and many other tribes further back into preserves, 'There can be no doubt that the Masai and many other tribes must go under. It is a prospect which I view with equanimity and a clear conscience.'"[18] Thus did the colonial plantation system come to Africa.

In dozens of other ways the colonial system skewed the development of the colonies. For example, the capital cities in colonies often were not established in the best place to administer the country, but in the spot that gave easiest access to the outside world. Thus, twenty-eight African capitals are in port cities, while those in Chad, Niger, and Mali are all in the extreme southwest corner of these vast countries.[19] The plantations produced cash crops for export—sugar in the Caribbean, coffee in Brazil, tea in Sri Lanka— instead of subsistence crops for local consumption—corn, beans, or rice. The frequent result was a local economy skewed to cash export that was dependent upon the "mother" country and vulnerable to the fluctuations of the international market, while local people often went hungry.[20] Economic dependency and underdevelopment are two of the legacies of colonialism. It can be said that the colonial powers created the Third World.

The church, by now Protestant and Catholic, continued to play an ambivalent role in the process of colonization. Missionaries were certainly sincere in their belief that they were bringing a saving truth to peoples who had not heard the Gospel, that they were saving souls.[21] The idea that Europeans were bringing Christianity and civilization to primitive cultures and heathen peoples was used to justify European expansion and colonial domination. In hindsight, this appears to be a smokescreen for a pattern of exploitation that is directly contrary to the Gospel. But there were surely many people who sincerely thought they were doing what was right. Anglican Archbishop Desmond Tutu, who won the Nobel Peace Prize for his nonviolent resistance to apartheid in South Africa, reflects on the connection between Christianity and colonization from the African perspective: "They used to say that the missionaries came to Africa and they had the Bible and we had the land. And then they said, 'Let us pray.' And when we opened our eyes, we had the Bible and they had the land!"[22] Although having the Bible may be a good thing, using the Bible to steal the land and dominate the people is diametrically opposed to the Bible's teaching.

Education soon became a primary activity of the missionaries, but this too was ambivalent, if not insidious. "The colonial education system was geared to building a class of unimaginative but obedient administrators and concentrated on Westernizing the most able of the indigenous people."[23] Education communicated the so-called superior values of the colonial masters to the elite among the indigenous people and created a cadre of dutiful bureaucrats to carry out the ruler's orders.[24] This fostered a "colonial mentality," that is, a cultural inferiority complex that becomes a self-fulfilling prophecy. An exploited people begin to internalize the stereotypical characteristics born of the prejudices of their exploiters. The result is a dependence that is rooted not only in economic and social structures but in a psychic sense of inferiority. It is no wonder, then, that when Mahatma Gandhi, aware of events like the British maiming of Bengali weavers and the massacre at Jallianwalla Bagh,[25] was asked by a British reporter what he thought of Western civilization, he replied, "I think it would be a good idea." The deleterious effects of colonialism were not only economic and social, but also cultural and psychological. Colonialism was an assault on human dignity, perpetuated by Western Christians. Colonial peoples have experienced this and generally understand this history, but colonial powers often manage to deny or rationalize or forget what happened.

The importance of the history of colonialism for relations among people today was driven home to me by an Irishman I once met on a ferry from France to Ireland. He told me that in his worldwide travels people often mistook his accent to be British, as had I. He said that once he set them straight, people welcomed him with generous hospitality. He could tell that his anecdote had puzzled this naive American, so he explained: "The British have oppressed people all over the globe, but the Irish have never had an empire. Lots of people dislike the British, but they love the Irish, because we have a lot in common with them." I now know the difference between a British and an Irish accent, and the difference it can make.

Phase Three—The United States Emerges as a Neo-Colonial Power in the Twentieth Century

As the power of Portugal and Spain declined in the first part of the nineteenth century, their colonies in Latin America won their political independence. In the twentieth century the remaining European powers and the emerging powers in Asia spent themselves in two world wars and in efforts to maintain their empires against colonial rebellions. During the twentieth century, and especially in the period after World War II, most colonies in Asia, Africa, and the Caribbean gained their political independence. The economic structures established during colonial rule, however, have allowed the North to continue to exploit the South. This pattern of economic domination, in the absence of direct political rule, is called neo-colonialism. The United States emerged as the pre-eminent neo-colonial power in the twentieth century.

Because the United States freed itself from colonial rule, one might think it would be in sympathy with anti-colonial sentiment, and in solidarity with those trying to shake the shackles of a colonial past. Indeed, in the 1950s, Ho Chi Minh, having read the U. S. Declaration of Independence, wrote to the U. S. President asking for assistance in Vietnam's struggle for independence from French colonial rule. But by the beginning of the twentieth century, as the European powers declined, the United States stepped in to fill their boots, militarily and economically—as Ho Chi Minh discovered. The United States first supported France and then took France's place on the battlefield in Vietnam in the 1960s.

In 1898, the United States occupied Cuba, Puerto Rico, and the Philippines as part of the spoils from the Spanish-American War. Puerto Rico, some would argue, remains a colony of the United States. In the Philippines, the United States inherited the Filipino rebellion against Spanish colonial rule and crushed it.[26] American textbooks tend to call this episode the Philippine Insurrection. Filipino historians refer to it as the Philippine-American War.

President William McKinley captured the American mindset toward the world at the beginning of the twentieth century in a personal revelation to a group of Protestant missionaries who were visiting him at the White House. McKinley told the visitors how he had agonized and prayed about what to do with the Philippines. Then late one night it came to him:

(1) That we could not give them back to Spain—that would be cowardly and dishonorable; (2) that we could not turn them over to France or Germany—our commercial rivals in the Orient—that would be bad business and discreditable; (3) that we could not leave them to themselves—they were unfit for self-government—and they would soon have anarchy and misrule over there worse than Spain's was; and (4) that there was nothing left for us to do but to take them all, and to educate the Filipinos, and uplift and civilize and Christianize them, and by God's grace do the very best we could by them, as our fellow-men for whom Christ also died.[27]

First, of course, the United States had to subdue the Filipinos, already a deeply Catholic people, who were fighting for the very self-government that McKinley thought they were incapable of achieving.

Americans thought of themselves as benevolent colonizers, trying to remake the Philippines in our image through education and a market economy.

But the U. S. performance in the Philippines was flawed. The Americans coddled the elite while disregarding the appalling plight of the peasants, thus perpetuating a feudal oligarchy [imposed by Spanish colonial rule] that widened the gap between the rich and the poor. They imposed trade patterns that retarded the economic growth of the islands, condemning them to reliance on the United States long after independence. The American monopoly on imports into the Philippines also dampened the development of a native industry. At the same time the unlimited entry of Philippine exports to the United States bound the Archipelago inextricably to the American market. Economically at least, the Filipinos were doomed to remain "little brown brothers" for years—though many, despite their nationalist rhetoric, found security in the role.[28]

Despite American pretensions of a more relaxed attitude and benevolent intentions, American colonialism seems indistinguishable from European colonialism.

With the exception of these three countries that were the spoils of the Spanish-American War, the United States did not have direct colonial relationships. Instead of imposing political control, the United States usurped economic influence and control over former colonies as the power of European countries declined and its own power rose during the twentieth century. This economic influence was backed up by military power. The Philippines illustrates this very clearly, but it is hardly a singular case.

Since the Spanish-American War, the United States has intervened militarily in the Caribbean and Central America over twenty times. Early in the twentieth century the United States created the country of Panama so we could build our canal. The most recent U. S. intervention in Panama was in 1989. The United States occupied Haiti from 1915–1934, the Dominican

Republic from 1916–1924, and Nicaragua from 1926–1933. The United States intervened in the Dominican Republic in 1965 to prevent a constitutionally elected president, who had been overthrown, from returning to power, and in Haiti in 1994 to return an elected president to power (a better idea). The United States sponsored a rebellion in Nicaragua throughout the 1980s. It has supported brutal despots in Haiti, Nicaragua, Guatemala, the Dominican Republic, and Panama.[29]

The rationale for this intervention has been a mixture of economic and strategic interests. The Caribbean, after all, is perceived by America to be its backyard, as president after president has repeatedly proclaimed in justifying these interventions.[30] The United States brought to these adventures the same condescending domination that characterized its relationship with the Philippines. Americans have been surprised to find that even if we start schools and build roads, people deeply resent being controlled by, or dependent on, others.

America's backyard, according to the Monroe Doctrine, extends well beyond the Caribbean into South America. In the early years of 1970, Chile, a stable and relatively prosperous democracy, elected a socialist president, Salvador Allende, who won a plurality of votes in a three-way contest. When Allende began to nationalize the copper industry, depriving American companies of their lucrative profits, he was overthrown and killed in a CIA-aided coup that resulted in a military dictatorship under General Augusto Pinochet.[31]

United States influence in Latin America, however, has generally been economic, rather than overtly military. The perpetuation of the economic domination of the Third World by the First World after the colonies achieved political independence is simply a new form of colonialism—neo-colonialism. The domestic and global structures of injustice usually did not change when Europe ceded or lost direct political control of the colonies. Theologically this systematic injustice is social sin. The global economic inequity, that is, the widening gap between the rich and the poor (the topic of chapter 2), is rooted in the patterns and structures established under colonialism.

THE INDUSTRIAL REVOLUTION

The interplay between colonialism and the Industrial Revolution has already been noted. The wealth amassed from colonialism fueled the Industrial Revolution which, in turn, further consolidated the power of Europe over the colonies. The point of this section is to try to communicate a sense of how technology has shaped the modern world and of what that means in terms of justice and peace.

When Britain Was the World's Workshop

The Industrial Revolution is a phenomenon of the nineteenth century. It began in Britain and by the end of the century had spread to Europe and the United States. The development of science and the scientific method during the Enlightenment (eighteenth century) prepared the way. Science seeks to understand the way things work; technology applies science to practical problems. The last three centuries have produced an explosion of scientific knowledge and technological advances. Since we are at the crest of this historical wave, we forget how far and how fast the industrialized nations have come. It is important to appreciate the amount and the rate of change that has occurred.

The impact of the Industrial Revolution is dramatized at the Welsh Folk Museum near Cardiff, Wales. The museum has reproduced replicas of the same family cottage, furnished in a typical fashion for a working-class family, at fifty-year intervals from 1650 through 1950. Thus, there were seven identical houses in a row. The inside of the house hardly changed from 1650 through 1850. A wooden table and chairs stood on a rough hewn wooden floor. The family had few and simple possessions. Suddenly in 1850 there was a dramatic change. There appeared curtains and rugs, table settings, a stove for heat and cooking, even knickknacks decorating the room. Life was becoming progressively more refined and more cluttered. By 1950 the house itself hardly seemed adequate for a family. Where does one put the bathroom? refrigerator? bedrooms?[32]

> **For Reflection**
> William Manchester titled his bestselling book on the Middle Ages and the Renaissance *A World Lit Only By Fire* (Boston: Little, Brown & Co., 1992). No electricity, only candles. No steamships, only sailing ships. No engines, only horsepower. What a very different world that was.
>
> Yet, when traveling in remote areas in the Philippines, I encountered villages "lit only by fire." There are different worlds in our contemporary world.

Historians now talk of a First Industrial Revolution, primarily in Britain, from 1750–1871, and of a New or Second Industrial Revolution throughout the developed world from 1871 to 1960. The development of an industrial economy in nineteenth-century Britain was preceded by social and technological innovations in agriculture that dramatically increased the productivity of the land. A confluence of other social and technological changes seem to have erupted in the Industrial Revolution: the transition from a feudal to a market economy, developments in textile production, improvements in iron and steel manufacture, and the creation of the steam engine. All this led to the rapid transition from crafting by hand to producing by machine, thus multiplying the productivity of labor a hundredfold. In the nineteenth century the Gross National Product of Great Britain increased by an astounding 400 percent.

The Industrial Revolution increased other things as well: human misery, pollution, and population. An economy based on industry more than agriculture meant the movement of people from rural areas to overcrowded cities where they worked long hours for low wages in dangerous mills or mines. The industrialists increased their profits by exploiting the labor of children, women, and men. Unemployment was a constant worry in a rapidly changing economy. The cities were ill-prepared to handle the influx of so many people. It is the condition of working people that Dickens would dramatize, Marx would decry, and Pope Leo XIII would address in the first social encyclical, *Rerum Novarum: The Condition of Labor* (1891).[33]

Industry produced more goods, but its byproducts fouled the air and polluted rivers and lakes, harming the health of humans and the habitats of animals. The increase in productivity and wealth came at a terrible cost to the environment.

In the late eighteenth century there was a surge in the population in Europe and even in countries as far removed as the United States and China. The causes of this population boom are not clear. There were improvements in public health and in the food supply and diet, and women were marrying younger. Whatever the exact reasons, there were suddenly many more "have-nots" crowding into major cities and stuffed into rural hovels. This increasing labor force would fuel the Industrial Revolution as much as the coal and the steam it ran on and the steel it produced.

At first, however, the Industrial Revolution produced the prospect of a mismatch between the number of people and the resources of a finite earth to sustain them. In 1798 Thomas Robert Malthus, an English country curate, expressed this concern in his now famous *Essay on Population*. Malthus noted that population increased geometrically, like interest on a savings account. If the annual population growth rate is 2 percent, then the population will double every 35 years. Britain's population was doubling every 25 years. Malthus thought it inconceivable that the productivity of the land could keep pace with this growth in population. He predicted that population would be kept in check only by widespread famine, disease, and/or war. Malthus's pessimism was out of step with the optimism of the intellectuals of his day who were anticipating the perfectibility of humanity and who engaged Malthus in critical debate.[34]

In the nineteenth century Malthus's dire predictions proved to be wrong. Three escape hatches prevented the Malthusian trap from closing on the British people. The first was emigration. Between 1815 and 1914 around 20 million Britons left the country and settled in the United States, Canada, Australia, and southern Africa. Nearly half of Britain's population emigrated. The second was the remarkable improvement in agricultural productivity. Not only did Britain itself produce considerably more food, it was also able to import food from the lands its subjects were settling. In the nineteenth century the power of the land was able to match the power of population. The third and most significant development was the Industrial Revolution with its leap forward in productivity and in wealth. "During the nineteenth century as a whole, the British population grew *fourfold*, whereas the national product grew *fourteenfold*."[35] Human ingenuity, then, was key to avoiding the Malthusian trap.

Thus, "the power of population" was answered, not so much by "the power in the earth" itself, but by the power of technology—the capacity of the human mind to find new ways of doing things, to invent new devices, to organize production in improved forms, to quicken the pace of moving goods and ideas from one place to another, to stimulate fresh approaches to old problems.[36]

Moreover, the Industrial Revolution led to social changes that decreased population growth. Thus, Britain went through a demographic transition that stabilized population over time.

It is important to note, however, that not every country escaped the Malthusian trap in the nineteenth century. Ireland and India, two countries under British domination, experienced famine. These famines, however, like most famines, were caused more by oppressive political and economic policies rather than by simple Malthusian scarcity. War, in the form of the social turbulence of the French Revolution and the attempt at imperial conquest under Napoleon Bonaparte, served to vent France's population pressures.[37]

In the twenty-first century, Malthus's predictions pose an acute problem. The earth's population continues to explode—6 billion in 1998, around 8 billion by 2025—and the growth is happening primarily in the developing countries, which lack the wealth and technology to cope with the increase. The escape hatches open to Britain are closing or closed today. In this century Malthus may prove to be right after all. (Chapter 3 will further discuss this problem.)

Future Shock

Change, more and faster, has characterized the New Industrial Revolution in the twentieth century. Technology, now powered by coal, oil, and nuclear energy and converted into electricity rather than steam, produced an astounding array of inventions that dramatically altered patterns of human life and the arrangements of human society.

My maternal grandmother was born in 1900. A brief reflection on her life can serve to illustrate the amount and rapidity of change that humans have experienced in the twentieth century. Mamie Allen was born on a farm outside Louisville, Kentucky, and she married a farmer and local sheriff, John Reinhardt, when she was sixteen. Her husband built the house she would live in nearly all of her life. In that house she gave birth to two boys and a girl. When her daughter, Dorothy, married Joseph Thompson, the Reinhardts gave the couple a piece of land next to their home as a wedding present. Thus I grew up next door to my grandmother, my grandfather having died when I was very young.

> **For Reflection**
> Interview someone who is 75 or older about how much change they have experienced in their life and how they have coped with it.

It is instructive to think of all the changes that occurred as Grandma's life marked the progress of the century. Electricity was one of the first improvements. It had to be added to the house when the electric lines made their way into the environs of Louisville. With it would eventually come a multiplicity of appliances—refrigerators, stoves, washers, dryers, vacuum cleaners, fans, air conditioners—that would lighten the burdens of everyday life. I remember when the pipes for natural gas were laid in our neighborhood and the huge coal furnace in Grandma's rough basement was converted to gas. This meant that on cold winter mornings she could simply adjust the thermostat rather than trudge down into the basement to start a fire.

Plumbing—running water and a bathroom—had been added to the house before I came along, but the old outhouse was still standing during my childhood. So was a stable where the horse used to be kept. Grandma never learned to drive. She never flew on a plane. In fact, she seldom traveled at all. Her grandson, on the other hand, has lived in Baltimore, New York City, and Hartford, and has traveled throughout Europe and the Philippines and to the Middle East and the Caribbean. Human beings have been to the moon and back, a feat Grandma refused to believe. Mobility was one change that Grandma decided to do without. The telephone, however, was a device she found exceedingly useful. Perched on a chair in her kitchen she would talk for hours with her family and friends. Every afternoon she could be found watching soap operas on the TV, another invention she enjoyed, along with the radio prior to that. She never went out to movies; she was in a nursing home when video cassettes came along. Her grandson has thus far stubbornly resisted the compact disc innovation in music and video. Photocopy machines, faxes, and computers are foreign even to her children, but the stuff of life for her grandchildren.

Although Grandma didn't own one, the automobile, as she always called it, radically changed her life by making suburbs possible. Eventually she sold the farm to a developer, and a subdivision was built around her house. This led to a small shopping center across the street and a McDonalds on the corner. The city had arrived. Henceforth our dogs would have to be tied up.

Grandma was married during World War I, her son and son-in-law fought in World War II, her grandsons are of the Vietnam generation, and her great-grandchildren were eligible for the Gulf War, Somalia, Haiti, Bosnia, and Afghanistan. She was lucky not to lose any of her progeny to war, given the developments in destructive power over her lifetime and the frequency of their use.

When the doctors decided she needed a pacemaker for her heart, she decided that "no one was going to cut her open," and none of us could persuade her otherwise. Amazingly, that so-called weak heart sustained her through her eighty-ninth year. The modern health care system did prevail upon her to have a different lifesaving operation at a later point in her life, but it could do little to stave off the diminishment she suffered from Alzheimer's disease.

Along with the technological changes came profound social change. Grandma was a traditional, even old-fashioned, woman whose life centered on home and family. Yet she was a very independent woman. She never grasped my sister's commitment to a career, yet the independent model that Grandma provided has surely been a part of my sister's success.

The depth of change that has characterized the twentieth century is captured by Kenneth Boulding, an eminent economist and imaginative social thinker: "The world of today . . . is as different from the world in which I was born as that world was from Julius Caesar's. I was born in the middle of human history, to date, roughly. Almost as much has happened since I was born as happened before."[38] Alvin Toffler, the author of *Future Shock*, suggests that if the last 50,000 years of human existence were divided into lifetimes of approximately 62 years each, there have been about 800 generations. The overwhelming majority of all the goods we use in daily life have been developed in this the 800th lifetime. If agriculture was the first wave of economic development and nineteenth-century industrialism the second, then we have already moved into the third stage, the service or information economy. There are some countries, however, which are representative of each of these stages of economic organization.

Until the Industrial Revolution the speed of travel was limited to about twenty miles-per-hour—the speed of a horse-drawn coach or a sailing ship. Trains and steamships increased our speed dramatically, but in the 800th lifetime cars and planes have made everyday travel rapid and accessible while space shuttles and rockets travel much faster.

Now more books are produced *each day* than were produced in a year prior to the modern era. Most of what we know about science and technology has been discovered and developed in this 800th lifetime.[39]

People who move into another culture often experience culture shock. Familiar patterns and rituals do not work, and they are unfamiliar with the ones that do. This experience is the basis of Toffler's notion of future shock. The scope and speed of change can make it difficult for individuals and societies to cope or adjust. The skills a person has developed over a lifetime may suddenly be useless. Machines make it possible for women to take on new roles. The experience of successive generations can be so different as to make it difficult for parents and children and even siblings to understand each other and communicate. The pace of life tends to accelerate beyond endurance.

In the developed world, the blessings of technology have been real, but ambivalent. There is less drudgery in everyday life, and yet paradoxically less time to enjoy life. Geographical and social mobility are surely beneficial, yet mobility can fragment families and fracture communities. Answering machines may facilitate communication, but they reduce the number of real conversations. Miracles of healing take place in acute-care hospitals, yet some children are not vaccinated against common diseases, and we seem to have forgotten how to die well. The energy that fuels the modern economy also pollutes the environment. Technology has given us nuclear energy and nuclear medicine as well as nuclear bombs. The Industrial Revolution has at once been a blessing and a curse.

A few years ago three people from rural Nicaragua were brought to Hartford on a speaking tour. Their hosts took them to Sturbridge Village, a tourist site in Massachusetts that re-creates life in eighteenth-century America. There the Nicaraguans discovered a lifestyle comparable to their own.

The Industrial/Technological Revolution characterizes the world and experience of people in the developed countries of the North. It is a basis of their wealth and power. But the experience of the majority of people in the less developed countries of the South seems that of another century, another age. The lack of technology is a basis of their poverty. This gap between the rich and the poor raises profound questions of justice.

TRENDS AT THE BEGINNING OF THE TWENTY-FIRST CENTURY

Colonialism and the Industrial Revolution help us understand the great divide between the North and the South and point to the source of wealth and power in the contemporary world. If we are seeking justice and peace, it is also important to have a sense of recent history. The Cold War dominated politics and international relations from the end of World War II in 1945, until around 1990, when it abruptly ended. It is also important to note the rise of democracy and the fall of tyranny in many places around the world since 1986, and the economic and cultural trend that is called globalization. This is a time in history ripe with opportunity to create justice and make peace.

Great Powers and Empire

The Modern Era, from 1500 to the present, can be understood as a competition among large powers for empire. Indeed, imperialism is nearly synonymous with colonialism, and industrialization enabled a country to gain the economic and military power necessary to join the competition for empire.

As we have seen, from the sixteenth through the nineteenth centuries, the large powers were all European. Each, in turn, tried to dominate the others. Spain was the dominant power at the beginning of the seventeenth century. The Treaty of Westphalia in 1648 concluded the Thirty Years' War in Europe between the alliance of Spain and Austria versus most of the rest of Europe. Spain's defeat marked the decline of its hegemony and the rise of the power of The Netherlands. The Treaty of Westphalia confirmed the notion of sovereign states engaged in a balance of power relationship with each other. At the end of the eighteenth century France sought to dominate Europe, but Napoleon was ultimately defeated by an alliance led by Great Britain. The nineteenth century was the century of the British Empire.

In the twentieth century two non-European powers—the United States and Japan—entered the competition, and different countries in Europe—Germany, Russia, and Italy—began to jockey for power. The First World War (1914–1918) was a horrific contest between European alliances led by Britain and Germany. Germany lost after the United States entered the war in 1917 on the side of Britain. Germany resented the punitive conditions imposed by the Treaty of Versailles in 1919. In Eastern Europe, the Russian Revolution of 1917 enabled Russia to incorporate its neighbors into the

Union of Soviet Socialist Republics (U.S.S.R.) under Russian control. The Soviet Union represented the establishment of a Russian Empire.

In the 1930s, Japan, which had already occupied Taiwan and Korea, conquered China. In Europe, Germany, under the leadership of Hitler, was gaining ascendancy and gobbling up its neighbors. The German invasion of Poland in 1939 marked the beginning of World War II. Hitler signed a nonaggression pact with Stalin's Soviet Union, which allowed him to quickly overrun France. Then he double-crossed Stalin and invaded the Soviet Union. After Japan destroyed much of the U. S. Pacific Fleet in a surprise attack on Pearl Harbor in late 1941, the United States entered the war, first against Japan, then against Germany. The Second World War brought the inhumanity of warfare to new lows through the attempted genocide of the Holocaust, the firebombing of enemy cities, and the introduction of nuclear weapons in the destruction of Hiroshima and Nagasaki.[40]

The Cold War

World War II decimated the great powers of Europe and Asia. The United States emerged relatively unscathed and with a robust economy. Of the 60 million deaths in World War II, by far the greatest share was suffered by the Soviet Union. Yet the Soviet army had repulsed the German invasion and by the end of the war controlled Eastern Europe and East Germany. When Churchill (U.K.), Roosevelt (U. S.), and Stalin (U.S.S.R.) met at Yalta in 1945, they agreed that Eastern Europe would remain under Soviet influence and that Germany would be split into four sectors, each controlled by one of the allies. Berlin, the German capital, deep within the eastern, Soviet sector, was also divided among the four allies—the United States, Britain, France, and the Soviet Union. Thus, what Winston Churchill called the Iron Curtain, dividing the West from the East, was established in Europe. In the early 1960s the Soviet Union turned Churchill's metaphor into a literal wall that divided West and East Germany and West and East Berlin. West Berlin became a capitalist and democratic island in the midst of Communist East Germany.

The Second World War thus dissolved into the Cold War, a continuous, yet relatively stable, conflict between two superpowers—the United States (the West) versus the Soviet Union (the East)—and the ideological, political, and economic systems they represented—capitalist democracy versus socialist communism. Each developed a network of alliances—the North Atlantic Treaty Organization (NATO) led by the United States and the Warsaw Pact led by the Soviet Union—and struggled to retain Third World clients and to enlarge their spheres of influence. While this was a global struggle between West and East fought on many fronts—Korea, Vietnam, the Caribbean and Central America, Africa, the Middle East, Afghanistan—the main fault line ran through Europe. The great fear of the West was that the Soviet Union would overrun Western Europe, thus consolidating the whole Eurasian landmass from Siberia to Ireland under a Communist Russian empire. And the Soviet Union feared yet another invasion from Western Europe.

The United States adopted a foreign policy of "containment," which sought to halt and oppose Soviet and Communist expansion throughout the globe by whatever means possible—military, political, economic, ideological. The Soviet Union joined the fray. The two superpowers and their allies engaged in a massive arms race in both conventional and nuclear weapons in service of containment. Thus, anti-communism became the single, overriding goal of U. S. foreign policy during the Cold War. Anti-communism justified gargantuan defense budgets, a massive arsenal of doomsday weapons, wars, proxy wars, interventions, coups, counterinsurgency, foreign aid, and support of anti-Communist dictators. While the Cold War led to several wars and civil wars throughout the Third World, it did not result in a direct confrontation between the two superpowers, in part because they were deterred by the threat of "mutually assured destruction" by nuclear weapons.

It is not that these two superpowers and the systems they represent are of equal moral value. Communism is a totalitarian system that denies fundamental human rights and that deserves condemnation and committed opposition. Still, during the Cold War period, *both* sides too frequently practiced the dubious ethic of the end (winning the conflict) justifying the means, *any* means. The single-mindedness of the policy of containment may also have blinded U. S. policy-makers to the complexity of global situations and to the ambiguity of their own intentions and actions. Thus the Cold War led to many debates and divisions within the West about the ethics of foreign policy.

The End of the Cold War

After 45 years of conflict and tension, the Cold War ended with the collapse of communism in the West, first in Eastern Europe, then in the Soviet Union itself. In 1985 a reform-minded leader, Mikhail Gorbachev, rose to power in the Soviet Union. In 1989, when the Solidarity movement in Poland directly challenged the Communist government, the Soviet Union sat back and allowed the government to fall. Soon refugees from Eastern Europe were pouring into Western Europe through gaping holes in the Iron Curtain. On November 12, 1989, Germans from East and West began chipping away the Berlin Wall with sledgehammers, wishing, as one of them quipped, that it had not been Germans who had built that wall. The fall of the Berlin Wall symbolized the collapse of communism in Eastern Europe. Within a year Germany had formally re-united and Communist governments throughout Eastern Europe had been replaced by fledgling democracies. Except in Romania this "velvet revolution" was accomplished nonviolently.

Gorbachev hoped that domestic reform would save the Communist system within the Soviet Union, but he could not hold back the tide of change. By the end of 1991 democracy had swept aside communism in the Soviet Union itself, and the 15 republics of the U.S.S.R. were becoming independent. World maps were being revised to include new nations with unfamiliar names such as Belarus, Georgia, and Kazakhstan. It was a remarkable transformation.

Analysts differ on why the Cold War suddenly ended. Some argue that the Reagan arms build-up in the 1980s forced the Soviet Union into bankruptcy as it tried to keep pace. Others believe the Soviet system collapsed from economic stagnation and bureaucratic corruption. One thing is clear: Communism did not work. In retrospect, Russia now is exposed as virtually a Third World economy with a genuinely frightening nuclear weapons capability, a respectable space program, and a large but ineffective military that has been unable to subdue the rebel province of Chechnya. Russia's transition to a market economy and a democratic polity remains halting and precarious.

A Wave of Democracy Sweeping the Globe

The democratization of Eastern Europe and the Soviet Union can be seen as part of a wave of democracy sweeping the globe.[41] Beginning in 1986 dictators throughout the world began to topple like dominoes. In the Philippines the People Power Movement swept Cory Aquino into power, replacing the "conjugal dictatorship" of Ferdinand and Imelda Marcos.[42] On the heels of rapid economic growth, South Korea made the transition from a repressive government to a representative one. Baby Doc Duvalier was overthrown in Haiti, although the transition to democracy there has been a halting process. Nicaragua changed government by ballot. South Africa began the transition to majority rule, and several of the countries in southern Africa experienced positive political changes. By the end of the 1980s nearly every country in South America was, at least formally, a democracy. United Nations peacekeeping missions have supported positive change in Cambodia and El Salvador. The early years of the 1990s saw constructive developments in such seemingly intractable conflicts as the Middle East and Northern Ireland, although progress in Northern Ireland remains perilous, and Israel and the Palestinians have regressed to violence and reprisals. Genuine democratization generally signals political progress, but politics is only part of the picture.

Globalization

The last few years of the twentieth century and the beginning of the twenty-first century have been characterized by globalization. Much has been written about this phenomenon, but it remains difficult to define. In its most positive sense, it refers to the increasing interdependence of the peoples on earth and to a vision of global harmony and unity. Amazing advances in communications technology have fueled globalization. Capital can be transferred anywhere in the world by the touch of a "send" key, and consumer goods can move rapidly from country to country, continent to continent. Labor can also migrate to where it is needed, but more slowly. Capitalism, with its profit motive, now dominates the world economy. Not surprisingly, this has resulted in winners and losers, progress and pitfalls.

Since the beginning of the Industrial Revolution, there has been a tendency to exploit workers, to concentrate wealth in the hands of a few, and to plunder the earth of its natural resources. Transnational corporations now scour the earth in search of the cheapest labor, the laxest environmental regulation, the lowest taxes, and the greatest profit. The poor are often oppressed and the earth polluted in this process. Yet, paradoxically, this process also represents the opportunity for economic progress and a better life for many—as did the Industrial Revolution.

Globalization also tends to homogenize the diverse cultures of the world into a monoculture dominated by Western values. Religious fundamentalism, an often violent rejection of the modern world, represents a backlash against the experience of powerlessness and cultural fragmentation produced by globalization.

CONCLUSION

The end of the Cold War did indeed present the global community with a ripe opportunity to create a world that is more just and that lives in peace. The Kingdom of God, however, has not yet come. The gap between the rich and the poor continues to widen. Ethno-nationalist conflict has volcanically risen to the surface all over the globe in places such as Bosnia and Kosovo, East Timor, Rwanda and Burundi, Sri Lanka, Chechnya, and Canada. Terrorism has become a terrible tool for the disillusioned and the displaced. Human rights are universally recognized, but widely violated. Nuclear weapons still hang over humanity's head like the sword of Damocles, and conventional weapons continue to spread like a plague. Environmental damage may threaten the planet itself and thus all of its inhabitants.

These are some of the obstacles to justice and peace in the beginning of the twenty-first century. Now that we have a sense of how humanity arrived at this promising but precarious point in history, we are ready to address these issues.

STUDY QUESTIONS

1. How do you think Columbus Day should be commemorated?
2. The first phase of colonialism was dominated by Spain and the second phase by Great Britain. What similarities and differences do you see in the colonial rule of these two powers and in the legacies and consequences of their colonial reigns?
3. There is no doubt that colonialism is exploitative and oppressive, yet it may also have some benefits. Do you think the European colonizers brought any benefits to their colonies? How did Europe benefit from the exchange with their colonies?
4. What injustices in the contemporary world are based in colonialism?
5. There have been other countries besides Europe that have colonized their neighbors or their region. The Incas, for example, had colonized Mexico by the time Cortéz arrived. China and Japan have tried to exercise hege-

mony in the Far East at various times, and various tribes (nations) in Africa have developed empires at one time or another. While colonialism is always exploitative, is it possible to rank some colonial regimes and their legacies as worse than others?

6. Is the United States an imperial power?
7. The condition of labor during the Industrial Revolution gave rise to the critique of Karl Marx and to the critique of Pope Leo XIII in his encyclical *On the Condition of Labor (Rerum Novarum)*. Compare and contrast these critiques. Is industrial capitalism inherently exploitative of labor? Why does there seem to be a decline in the union movement today? (For an historical perspective, see the film *Matewan* [1987] directed by John Sayles.)
8. Is the globalization of the economy a new phase of the Industrial Revolution? Who are the winners and losers in the Industrial Revolution? in the globalization of the economy?
9. What justice and peace issues in the contemporary world are based in the Industrial Revolution?
10. Why did communism in Eastern Europe and the Soviet Union collapse?
11. Does the collapse of communism mean that socialism is not a viable economic system? Is there any alternative to capitalism in the contemporary world? What problems are there with capitalism?
12. It would seem that the end of the Cold War presents the world community with an opportunity for peace. Do you think this is true? What are the obstacles to peace? How could the world take advantage of this historical moment?
13. Is some form of democracy (participative or representative government) necessary for a just society? Are most of the world's states becoming genuinely more democratic? How can the process of democratization be aided?

CHAPTER TWO

Poverty and Development

"Blessed are you who are poor, for the kingdom of God is yours. Blessed are you who are now hungry, for you will be satisfied. But woe to you who are rich, for you have received your consolation. Woe to you who are filled now, for you will be hungry." (Luke 6: 20–21, 24–25)

"Central to the biblical presentation of justice is that the justice of a community is measured by its treatment of the powerless in society. . . . The way society responds to the needs of the poor through its public policies is the litmus test of its justice or injustice."[1]

Poverty is the bane of humankind. It is not a new problem, but the gap between the rich and the poor is widening and worsening today. This is ironic, tragic, and unjust, because, perhaps for the first time in human history, there is enough wealth on Earth to meet the basic needs of every person. Until the misery and degradation of billions of brothers and sisters is alleviated there will be no justice, and there will be no peace.

This chapter explores the gap between the rich and the poor among nations, within nations, and within the United States. It begins by recounting personal experiences that have made me aware of the reality of global poverty and have stirred compassion. Then it analyzes the economic gap between the North and the South, examines the promise and peril of globalization, and focuses on key issues in the debate about economic development. The final section of the chapter explores two issues related to poverty in the United States.

THE HUMAN FACE OF POVERTY

In 1990 I traveled widely throughout the Philippines, visiting small Christian communities in urban and rural settings. Trying to understand and experience the problems faced by a developing country was a transforming experience. The United States has pockets of poverty in the midst of wealth; most Americans never see the stark conditions in inner cities or the hollows of Appalachia. The Philippines has isolated islands of wealth in a sea of poverty; human destitution is public, omnipresent, and pitiful. It is a different world.

Bishop Antonio Fortich of Bacolod, an advocate for the poor, called the Philippine island of Negros a "social volcano."[2] Sugar cane covers the island in a coat of green; everywhere it is planted right up to the edge of the road. The land is owned by a few, but worked (when there is work to be had) by the many landless peasants. In the late 1980s not even the plantation own-ers were making a profit on sugar, and the poor were desperate. Some of them joined an underground resistance group, the New People's Army, to fight for a different society. The Philippine military struck back with even greater repression.

On Negros I visited a settlement of people who had been dislocated from their village by the military. Their rural village had been destroyed, and they were afraid to return. One of the women recounted how her son had been captured and beheaded by the military. Several other mothers told of sons who had "been disappeared." So these internal refugees had moved to this remote, uninhabited spot, and they were working to plant in the rocky ground and to build simple shelters. There was no electricity. A nearby stream provided water. The church in Bacolod was trying to supply them with rice until they could harvest their own, and we had brought supplies in the jeepney we hired for the visit. On our return to Bacolod some women with sick children came with us. As we bumped our way through the rocky field and then the rural roads, I meditated on the listless, pale children with brown, patchy hair nestled in the arms of their mothers. Mothers and chil-dren were all malnourished, and had little hope of finding adequate health care or better nourishment in the city. This is the sad human face of poverty. The plight of these children and their families still haunts me.

There is a section of Manila called Smokey Mountain. It is the garbage dump, a mountain of refuse adjacent to Manila Bay. At the time of my visit, several thousand people inhabited Smokey Mountain, eking out a living by selling scraps from the dump. To a visitor the stench was overpowering. This abject poverty, unknown to most Americans, is all too pervasive in the Two-Thirds World.

One out of every six persons on earth (1.2 billion people) lives on less than $1 a day, and nearly half (2.8 billion) live on less than $2 a day.[3] "Every three seconds, somewhere in the world, a child dies as a result of malnutri-tion. That's over 1,000 every hour, 30,000 every day, 10 million every year."[4] It is as if every morning Camden Yards, the baseball stadium in Baltimore, was filled with children and by evening all were dead. What is wrong with the world that such suffering can exist?

By and large these are not the children we sometimes see on TV or in news magazines with distended stomachs and arms and legs like toothpicks, vic-tims of *famine* in Ethiopia or Somalia. Some people do starve to death, but even famine, the extreme of hunger, is usually the result of war or social upheaval along with adverse weather conditions. Such was the case in Ethiopia, Somalia, and southern Africa. Most often, however, the poor die of disease after being weakened by *chronic malnutrition*. People are mal-nourished, not because there is not enough food, but because they cannot afford to buy food because of their poverty.

Poverty means that people are not able to meet their own basic needs. Poverty means being hungry and malnourished; drinking unsanitary water; having no access to even basic health care such as immunizations against childhood diseases; living in crowded, unsafe, inadequate or no shelter; having no shoes or shirt to wear; being illiterate. The poor are anxious and fearful, constantly struggling to survive. Poverty means breaking your back for twelve hours in the hot sugar cane fields only to go deeper in debt to the landowner, or sweating over a sewing machine for ten hours and still not being able to afford three simple meals a day. At least two out of every three people on Earth live in poverty. They represent the "Two-Thirds World."

If poverty demeans human dignity and stunts human potential, its antidote is development. *Development* means changing the whole social system so that every person has the opportunity to fulfill his or her full human potential and live a dignified and productive human life. Development is more than an economic concept; it is a human concept. Three core values are

---

For Reflection

It is difficult for a middle-class American to walk in the sandals of a poor Kenyan or Pakistani or Guatemalan. Economist Robert Heilbroner suggests a thought experiment of transforming a typical suburban American family into a typical family in the Two-Thirds World to convey the point:

"We begin by invading the house of our imaginary American family to strip it of its furniture. Everything goes: beds, chairs, tables, television sets, stereos, lamps. We will leave the family with a few old blankets, a kitchen table, a wooden chair. Along with the bureaus go the clothes. Each member of the family may keep in his or her "wardrobe" the oldest suit or dress, one pair of jeans, a shirt or blouse. We will permit a pair of shoes for the parents, but none for the children.

We move to the kitchen. The appliances have already been taken away, so we turn to the cupboards. The box of matches may stay, a small bag of flour, some sugar and salt. A few moldy potatoes, already in the garbage can, must be hastily rescued, for they will provide much of tonight's meal. We will leave the family with a handful of onions, and a dish of dried beans. All the rest we take away: the meat, the fresh vegetables, the canned goods, frozen foods, the crackers, snacks, candy.

Now we have stripped the house: the bathroom has been dismantled, the running water shut off, the electric wires taken out. Next we take away the house. The family can move to the toolshed. [The cars, of course, exit with the garage]. . . .

Communications must go next. [No phone. No Internet.] No more newspapers, magazines, books—not that they are missed, since we must take away our family's literacy as well. Instead, in our shantytown we will allow one radio.

Now government services must go. No mail delivery. No garbage pick-up. No fire protection. No water. No sewers. There is a two-room school, three miles away. There are, of course, no hospitals or doctors nearby. The nearest clinic is ten miles away and is tended by a midwife. It can be reached by bicycle, provided the family has a bicycle, which is unlikely. Or one can go by bus—not always inside, but there is usually room on top.

[There are no banks, no ATMs, no credit cards.] We will allow our family a cash hoard of five dollars. . . ."

Source: Robert Heilbroner, *The Great Ascent: The Struggle for Economic Development in Our Time* (New York: Harper & Row, 1963), pp. 33–35, slightly edited.

included in the meaning of human development: *sustenance*—the ability to meet basic needs, including food, shelter, health, and protection; *self-esteem*—a sense of worth and self-respect; and *freedom*—the ability to participate in significant personal and social choices. Since poverty precludes the attainment of these values, development aims to establish economic conditions and structures conducive to the realization of human potential and dignity. Generally, economic development requires economic growth and the reduction of inequality. "Rising per capita incomes, the elimination of absolute poverty, greater employment opportunities, and lessening income inequalities therefore constitute the *necessary* but not the *sufficient* conditions for development."[5]

Before addressing some of the issues involved in economic development, it is important to understand the economic inequalities that characterize the contemporary world.

THE GAP BETWEEN THE NORTH AND THE SOUTH

Specialists in international relations often divide the Earth into nine regions:

1. North America (Canada and the United States);
2. Latin America (Mexico, Central America, the Caribbean, and South America);
3. Western Europe;
4. Russia and Eastern Europe (Eastern Europe, Russia, and the 15 republics of the former Soviet Union, sometimes referred to as the Commonwealth of Independent States or CIS);
5. The Middle East and North Africa (the countries on the southern and eastern shores of the Mediterranean Sea and the Persian Gulf, often referred to as simply the Middle East);
6. Africa (Sub-Saharan Africa);
7. South Asia (from Afghanistan through Indonesia);
8. China;
9. Japan and the Pacific (including Australia and New Zealand).

These designations will generally be used in this book, but it is important to note that other terms and other divisions are used, especially regarding Asia. East Asia usually refers to China, Korea, and Japan. Southeast Asia refers to the countries from Myanmar (Burma) through Indonesia and the Philippines. South Asia sometimes includes Southeast Asia, and sometimes it does not. These regions are artificial divisions, but they do reflect commonalities of politics, economics, culture, and religion among the countries in the different regions.

In terms of economics, the most important division is between the wealthy, technologically developed countries of the "North"—North America, Western Europe, and Japan and the Pacific—and the poor, less technologically developed countries of the "South"—Latin America, Africa, most of the Middle East, and Asia.[6]

The South has been called the "Third World," an unfortunate and out-dated term. The term mixes the "apples and oranges" of economics and politics. The difference between the developed countries of the First World and the Third World is primarily economic—wealth vs. poverty, technological development vs. the lack thereof. The Second World, a term seldom used now, referred to the Communist countries, the East vs. the West, distinguished more by their politics than their economic development. Except for China, Cuba, and North Korea (politically worrisome exceptions to be sure), the Second World is no more. Russia and most of the former republics of the Soviet Union and Eastern Europe are making the transition from a socialist to a capitalist economy, and from a totalitarian to a democratic polity. They are classified as middle-income, rather than high-income, countries.[7] The economies of all of these countries have declined significantly, causing much hardship and suffering. Their economic and political transition is difficult and precarious. Economically, they are teetering between the North and the South. Among these countries, Poland, the Czech Republic, Slovakia, Slovenia, Croatia, Estonia, and Lithuania seem to be moving up instead of sliding down.[8]

Even before the end of the Cold War, the Third World was a problematic designation. It tends to be a pejorative term. The First World is the winners; the Third World, the losers. It is important to remember that the term refers only to economic and technological development and *not* to cultural development or human development. India, for example, is one of the world's centers for spiritual development, and Filipinos are undoubtedly among the world's most hospitable people. Nor does the term Third World capture the diversity of economic development found in the less industrialized countries. The economies of Niger, Nepal, and Haiti, which are among the poorest in the world, should not be lumped together with those of Algeria, South Korea, and Costa Rica, for example, which are much more economically developed. The First and Third designations also gloss over the history of colonialism and imperialism that is the background for the current situation, and more than a hint of racism lurks within the terms.

It is difficult, however, to find more adequate language for highlighting the global reality that a minority of the countries of the world, with a minority of the world's population, enjoy a high standard of living, while most of the people on Earth struggle to meet their most basic needs. The notion of the "Two-Thirds World" at least captures the idea that the poor greatly outnumber the rich, and the use of "North" and "South" points to the reality of rich and poor countries in a helpful way.

The gulf between the poor and rich in the world is becoming wider and the South and North are becoming polarized into two very different worlds. The poorest 20 percent of the world's people saw their share of global income decline from 2.3 percent to only 1 percent in the last forty years, while the share of the richest 20 percent rose from 70 percent to 86 percent. "The income gap between the fifth of the world's people living in the richest countries and the fifth in the poorest was 74 to 1 in 1997, up from 60 to 1 in 1990 and 30 to 1 in 1960."[9] Even more striking is the concentration of wealth at the very top among the ultra-rich. In just four years, from 1994 to 1998, the assets of the world's 200 richest people increased from $440 billion to more than $1 trillion, an amount more than the combined income of the poorest 41 percent or about 2.4 billion people. "The assets of the three richest people were more than the combined GNP of the 48 least developed countries."[10]

MEASURING POVERTY AND DEVELOPMENT

The meaning of poverty—its human reality and global prevalence—is almost beyond our comprehension. Certainly any compassionate and just person, when made aware that over a billion brothers and sisters on planet Earth are hungry, will care enough to want to right this wrong. The causes of global poverty, however, are complex and controversial, as are the solutions. Indeed, it is even hard to measure poverty.[11] In order to address the global issue of poverty, it is important to understand some economic terms and the ways that poverty, economic inequality, and development are measured.

The most common measure of poverty is *income analysis,* which is based on the annual *gross domestic product* (GDP)—the value of all goods and services produced within a country's borders—and/or *gross national product* (GNP)—GDP plus net income from abroad—divided by the number of people in the country to yield the *per capita* GDP or GNP. While per capita GDP (or GNP) can give some sense of the economic well-being or standard of living of a country's average resident, it does not tell us anything about the distribution of income within the country. If a country has ten people, for example, one of whom is enormously wealthy and the rest destitute, the per capita GDP may look fairly healthy even though most of the people are desperately poor. In countries with a rich elite and a multitude of poor, there is no average resident. The *Gini coefficient* is used to gauge the economic inequality of a nation. It ranges from 0 (exact equality) to 1 (one person owns everything). The higher the Gini coefficient the greater the inequality of wealth and income within a country.[12]

Until recently the per capita GDP of various countries was compared based on the official exchange rates of the countries' currencies. These market exchange rates, however, may not reflect a currency's true purchasing power at home. Thus, since about 1992 some economists have begun making the comparison on the basis of *purchasing power parity* (PPP), that is, how much of a common "market basket" of goods and services each currency can purchase locally. In general, PPP comparisons produce slightly lower per capita GDP figures in wealthy countries and higher ones in poorer nations.[13]

A different measure of poverty is a *basic needs approach,* which was described in the *Human Development Report,* first published in 1990. The United Nations Development Program (UNDP) argued that economic growth, as measured by GDP per capita, was a necessary, but not sufficient, measure of genuine human development. Thus the UNDP fashioned the *human development index* (HDI) in an attempt to measure a more holistic conception of human development. The HDI combines standard of living (real per capita GDP), life expectancy, and educational attainment. In 1999 the HDI ranking of 31 countries was more than 20 places higher or lower than their ranking by per capita income. Belize, for example, ranks 54 on the HDI, but 75 in per capita GDP, while Qatar is 48 in HDI and 24 in per capita GDP. Although Belize has about a fourth of the per capita income of Qatar, it does better in meeting the basic needs of all of its people.[14]

GLOBALIZATION: PROMISE AND PERIL

In the first chapter we saw how the tremendous productivity of the Industrial Revolution (along with colonialism) allowed Britain (and then other countries) to attain remarkable economic growth. From about 1850 to 1920, the world experienced a first period of globalization. Since the end of the Cold War in 1989, the world is experiencing a second period of economic integration or globalization.[15] It is once again, as Charles Dickens says in the opening line of *A Tale of Two Cities* (1859), the best of times and the worst of times.

There can be no economic development without sustained economic growth, that is, unless a nation's economy registers a growth in GDP year after year.[16] Otherwise the population shares scarcity and will generally experience unemployment and declining income. Globalization, ushered in by the age of the world wide web, offers the promise of tremendous productivity and economic growth, but it is a brutal process when it is focused on profit and not on lifting up the poor. If it is to be good news for the poor it will need to be managed so that any economic growth benefits the poor. The poor need globalization that wears a human face.[17]

The collapse of communism in the Soviet empire effectively ended the debate between socialism and capitalism. The centrally planned economy offered by socialism did not work. Some version of free-market capitalism seems to be the only viable alternative left on the horizon. Capitalism offers a productive economic system that can generate the income necessary for economic development.[18] Globalization increasingly seems to be a fact of life. The challenge is to manage this new system to benefit the Two-Thirds World and to find a healthy balance between economic growth and the common good.

Globalization is integrating the world into one global market. It is facilitated by new communication technology—computers, the internet, cellular phones, and media networks. Capital roams the earth at lightning speed, to the tune of over $1.5 trillion a day in foreign-exchange trading.[19] Long-distance transportation has become more efficient (see the TV advertisements for UPS, DHL, and FedEx), and shipping costs have been reduced, in part because what is transported has often become lighter. Global trade is benefiting consumers and the producers who are most competitive. Labor too is migrating, but at a slower pace than capital, and in the face of many more restrictions. Often labor migration might be better described as social dislocation.

Thomas L. Friedman, a foreign correspondent and columnist for *The New York Times,* likens a country's entrance into the global market to putting on a "Golden Straitjacket." This means a country must adapt to the following rules:

> making the private sector the primary engine of its economic growth, maintaining a low rate of inflation and price stability, shrinking the size of its state bureaucracy, maintaining as close to a balanced budget as possible, if not a surplus, eliminating and lowering tariffs on imported goods, removing restrictions on foreign investment, getting rid of quotas and domestic monopolies, increasing exports, privatizing state-owned industries and utilities, deregulating capital markets, making its currency convertible, opening its industries, stock, and bond markets to direct foreign ownership and investment, deregulating its economy to promote as much domestic competition as possible, eliminating government corruption, subsidies and kickbacks as much as possible, opening its banking and telecommunications systems to private ownership and competition, and allowing its citizens to choose from an array of competing pension options and foreign-run pension and mutual funds. When you stitch all these pieces together you have the Golden Straitjacket.[20]

As a result of these policies a country's economy generally grows and its average income increases, but its politics shrink in that there is little choice but to abide by these rules or capital will flee the country.[21] The economic success of several countries in Asia in the mid-1990s illustrates how golden these policies can be, but the Asian crisis of the late 1990s also demonstrates how restrictive this straitjacket is. When Thailand's currency crashed in 1997, foreign investment vanished even faster than it had arrived, dealing a crushing blow to the economies of Thailand, South Korea, Indonesia, and Malaysia, and having negative consequences as far as Russia and Brazil. Indeed, even an economy as successful as that of the United States appears susceptible to shocks such as stock market slumps, terrorist attacks, and corporate corruption.

While globalization generally produces economic growth, it also has negative consequences. Capitalism tends to concentrate wealth and to widen the gap between the rich and the poor. Globalization is often accompanied by the spread of Western and American values and products, symbolized by the golden arches of McDonalds or the antics of "Friends." Many decry this loss of local identity, practices, and values. Increasing productivity also uses up the earth's resources and pollutes the atmosphere, the land, and rivers, lakes and oceans. The fast and greedy world of globalization seems to be leaving the poor behind, homogenizing culture, and speeding up environmental destruction. Thus, it is not surprising that there has been a backlash against globalization in the name of the poor, of cultural diversity, and of the earth itself. Anti-globalization protestors disrupted the World Trade Organization's meeting in Seattle in November of 1999 and the Group of 8 meeting in Genoa in July of 2001.

Before focusing on overcoming poverty and on the environment (in chapter 3), it is important to offer some general comments on the backlash against globalization. First, it must be said that the critics make valid points. Capitalism may produce increasing wealth, but it has no mechanism for distributing it fairly or to those whose need is greatest. And globalization has run roughshod over local cultures and exploited the environment. While free-market capitalism increases participation in society and tends toward democratization, the Golden Straitjacket paradoxically limits a country's and an individual's choices. The market can thrive in a democracy, but the market can also begin to dictate policy.[22] Globalization introduces serious problems.

It makes little sense, though, to be anti-globalization, to try to destroy the system. There does not appear to be a realistic and viable alternative, and globalization offers the productivity that is necessary, but not sufficient, for overcoming poverty. It seems better to attempt to manage the system so that it meets the basic needs of all people, respects local cultures, produces sustainable growth, and enhances participation in society. The goal is "to ensure that globalization works for people—not just for profits."[23]

The system itself can often be directed toward conserving the environment or culture. It is easier to preserve a forest if the loggers can be provided with realistic economic opportunities tied to conservation, such as harvesting the forest for medicines or creating an eco-park that draws tourists. Multi-national corporations can be shown that environmental responsibility pays in the end. Tourism can be a strong incentive for preserving a nation's historical landmarks and cultural symbols. Often there are marketplace solutions to market-based problems.[24]

Globalization has paradoxically empowered its critics to be more effective agents of change. The internet is a wonderful tool for information not only about the stock market, but also about environmental atrocities and human tragedies. It has allowed organizers to create a transforming groundswell of concern about issues such as land mines and the Multilateral Agreement on Investment.[25]

Finally, a free market does not mean an unregulated market. Globalization with a human face means finding the rules and institutions that can govern global markets in a way that protects workers, preserves community and culture, conserves the earth and its resources, and enhances participation without losing the advantages of competition. Entrepreneurs know they must work within the rules of the game. It is the responsibility of citizens and the leaders they choose to construct and enforce rules and regulations that result in human flourishing, sustainable growth, and the common good. "The fundamental moral criterion for all economic decisions and policies is this: they must be at the service of all people, especially the poor."[26]

OVERCOMING POVERTY

If globalization is going to work for the poor, what must be done? There are several issues that need to be addressed in response to this question: investment, foreign aid, trade, debt, and equity.

Multi-National Corporations and Investment

In order to enter the globalization expressway to economic growth, developing countries need an infusion of capital. Multi-national corporations (MNCs) are one source of this required investment.

Multi-national corporations or trans-national corporations are centrally organized, but have no real home. Many of them, such as Exxon, Toyota, and Daimler-Benz, originate in Organization for Economic Cooperation and Development (OECD) countries, which are high income, First-World countries, but some are now appearing in the Newly Industrialized Countries (NICs), such as Samsung and Hyundai in South Korea, and some in other developing countries, like Pemex in Mexico. Whatever its national origin, a MNC seeks to maximize its own interests and those of its shareholders rather than the interests of any country or of the poor. Although MNCs are not in the development business, their investment of capital, technology, and management skills, which can create jobs and foreign exchange for developing countries, can contribute to economic development. The question is: Whose interests does such private foreign investment serve?

MNCs are central actors in the globalization of the world economy. They are not the pawns of any state, rich or poor, but independent actors, influenced by a global market that they in large part create and manipulate, and from which they profit. The global economy has become fiercely competitive and unforgiving of inefficiency; it seems to transcend the control of even the most powerful governments or corporations.

In truth, however, the economy is a human reality, not one that transcends human control. The economy is a system established by human choices, which should serve human needs, and which can be changed by human decisions.[27] Undoubtedly some economic systems serve human needs better than others and an economic system can make it easier or harder for various actors in the economy to make ethical and just choices.

Corporations are also human realities. If their boards of directors and managers single-mindedly seek the maximization of profit without a thought for their workers, the environment, or the communities in which they are located, then that is a choice rather than the nature of a corporation. A corporation can also choose to seek a fair profit for its owners, to pay a fair wage to its workers, not harm the environment, and contribute constructively to the community. The tensions implied in these choices become particularly acute when powerful MNCs operate in poor countries.

One issue is the sheer wealth and power of MNCs in comparison with that of developing countries. As Table 2.1 indicates, in a ranking of countries and corporations according to the size of their annual product, over 40 percent of the top 100 consistently are corporations. Thus, countries in the Two-Thirds World are often at a disadvantage in negotiating with a MNC for needed investment and jobs. This is especially so if the MNC is subcontracting with a foreign-owned factory in a free enterprise zone in a developing country. If, for example, the cost of labor rises in Indonesia, or if Indonesia raises taxes or strengthens regulations such as its minimum wage or environmental or safety laws, a company such as Nike can move its operations to Vietnam. Nike simply terminates one contract, for example, with a Taiwanese-owned factory in Indonesia, and enters into another contract with a Korean-owned factory in Vietnam.[28] Workers and communities are often at the mercy of MNCs.

Too often the end result of this global economic system of investment and trade is not the economic development of poor countries, but a net transfer of more wealth from the South to the North—typically about $43 billion a year flows from the Two-Thirds World to the First World.[29]

MNCs argue that they invest large amounts of capital in developing countries and bring sophisticated technology and management skills, which create jobs, produce goods and services, and increase economic growth. Critics contend that the MNCs *control* capital and technology, introduce inappropriate technology (tractors instead of tillers), manipulate markets, and crush cultures through advertising (for example, infant formula instead of breast milk, Coca-Cola instead of fruit juice), and in the end take the profits home.[30] Critics call this neo-colonialism.

While MNCs are not always good for developing countries, in a globalized economic system, investment, technology, and economic growth are essential, but not sufficient, for integrated development. MNCs are not going to go away, and countries in the Two-Thirds World often need what they can bring. The challenge is to make sure MNC investment in the South results in genuine development, not exploitation.

International codes of conduct as well as reasonable national regulations such as minimum wage requirements that provide at least a subsistence wage for a family, standards of safety, prohibition of child labor, the right to organize unions, environmental protections, and so on can be helpful. In a competitive business environment a level playing field allows corporations to be fair and ethical. If, for example, there is no minimum wage or environmental restrictions, then the corporation that pays its workers well or controls its emissions is at a competitive disadvantage, at least in the short term. Obviously independent monitoring and vigorous enforcement of corporate compliance is as important as the regulations themselves.

In spring 1996 there was a public debate on the responsibility of MNCs toward workers in developing countries. TV personality Kathy Lee Gifford, who was also the celebrity sponsor of a fashion line for Wal-Mart, was fingered by Charles Kernaghan of the National Labor Committee, at a congressional hearing, for turning a blind eye to labor abuses in Honduras where the clothes were made. Ms. Gifford had been honored for giving $1 million of her clothing line's $9 million in annual profits to the Association

Table 2.1
100 Largest Economic Entities

COUNTRY/CORP.	GNP/REVENUES ($ BILLIONS)	COUNTRY/ CORP.	GNP/REVENUES ($ BILLIONS)
1. United States	9,837	51. Egypt	98
2. Japan	4,841	52. Total Fina Elf	94
3. Germany	1,873	53. Ireland	93
4. United Kingdom	1,414	54. Nippon Telegraph/Telephone	93
5. France	1,294	55. Singapore	92
6. China	1,080	56. Itochu	91
7. Italy	1,074	57. Malaysia	89
8. Canada	687	58. Allianz	85
9. Brazil	595	59. Intl. Business Machines	85
10. Mexico	574	60. ING Group	82
11. Spain	558	61. Colombia	81
12. India	457	62. Volkswagen	79
13. Rep. of Korea	457	63. Siemens	77
14. Australia	390	64. Sumitomo	77
15. Netherlands	364	65. Philippines	74
16. Argentina	285	66. Philip Morris	72
17. Russian Federation	251	67. Marubeni	71
18. Switzerland	239	68. Chile	70
19. Sweden	227	69. Verizon Communications	67
20. Belgium	226	70. Deutsche Bank	66
21. Wal-Mart Stores	219	71. E.ON	66
22. Turkey	199	72. AXA	65
23. Exxon Mobil	191	73. U.S. Postal Service	65
24. Austria	189	74. Credit Suisse	64
25. General Motors	177	75. Hitachi	63
26. BP	174	76. Nippon Life Insurance	63
27. Saudi Arabia	173	77. American Int'l Group	62
28. Denmark	162	78. Carrefour	62
29. Ford Motor	162	79. American Electric Power	61
30. Hong Kong, China	162	80. Pakistan	61
31. Norway	161	81. SONY	60
32. Poland	157	82. AT&T	59
33. Indonesia	153	83. Duke Energy	59
34. Enron	138	84. Royal Ahold	59
35. DaimlerChrysler	136	85. Boeing	58
36. Royal/Dutch Shell	135	86. Honda Motor	58
37. General Electric	125	87. El Paso	57
38. South Africa	125	88. BNP Paribas	55
39. Thailand	122	89. Matsushita Electric Ind.	54
40. Finland	121	90. Algeria	53
41. Toyota Motor	120	91. Peru	53
42. Venezuela	120	92. Home Depot	53
43. Citigroup	112	93. Aviva	52
44. Greece	112	94. Bank of America Corp.	52
45. Israel	110	95. Assicurazioni Generali	51
46. Mitsubishi	105	96. Fiat	51
47. Portugal	105	97. Czech Republic	50
48. Iran, Islamic Repub. of	104	98. Fannie Mae	50
49. Mitsui	101	99. J.P. Morgan Chase & Co	50
50. ChevronTexaco	99	100. RWE	50

Sources: GDP 2000 from *Human Development Report 2002*. "Fortune's Global 500—The World's Largest Corporations," *Fortune* (July 22, 2002), pp. F-1, F-2. Revenues are for 2001

to Benefit Children, which opened shelters for crack-addicted children and children with AIDS. Ms. Gifford, who was embarrassed and repentant, called on Wal-Mart to monitor subcontractors in the Two-Thirds World regarding fair treatment of workers. When Michael Jordan, a $20 million-a-year spokesperson for Nike, was similarly criticized for Nike's treatment of workers in Indonesia, he dodged responsibility, passing the ball to Nike.[31]

As usual the issues here are complex and controversial. Critics of the MNCs contend that the *maquiladoras,* as the assembly factories in Central America are called, make exorbitant profits by exploiting poor workers. Mexico's minimum wage varies from region to region, but in 1999 it was about $25 per week. The take-home pay of a garment worker in Tehuacan, Mexico, was $25 to $50 a week. In 1999 a basic food basket for a family of five cost about $69 a week. Thus workers earning Mexico's minimum wage cannot even feed their families. This is not a subsistence wage, much less a just or living wage, as called for in Catholic social teaching. It would take about a day's pay for a worker to purchase a Big Mac, coke, and fries at the local McDonalds.[32] The girls and young women who make Nike sneakers in factories in Vietnam received $1.60 a day, but three meals of rice and vegetables cost $2.10.[33]

In *maquiladoras* that produce clothes under contract for The Gap, J.C. Penney, Sears, Eddie Bauer, and so on, the cost of labor is often less than 1 percent of the retail purchase price of the finished product. A Honduran woman is paid 16 cents to produce a shirt that The Gap sells for $20.00. A pair of Nike sneakers sells in the United States for more than a month's pay of the Indonesian workers who produce it.[34] It would seem that corporations could easily afford to pay workers better wages. In 1994 Allied Signal corporation paid Lawrence Bossidy, its CEO, $12.4 million, but paid its entire Mexican workforce of 3,810 only an estimated $7.8 million.[35]

Philip Knight, the billionaire chief executive officer (CEO) of Nike, argues that Nike subcontractors in Indonesia pay, on average, double the minimum wage there and provide free meals and subsidies for housing, health care, and transportation. MNCs do bring desperately needed jobs to developing countries. However, if corporations do not seek the lowest possible wage they cannot stay competitive and often fail; then no one has jobs. Mr. Knight points out that real wages have actually risen 55 percent in Indonesia since 1990.[36]

It is worth noting, however, that Nike posted a record $298 million profit in 1993, and that Nike's earnings nearly tripled in five years. In 1995 the average hourly wage paid in athletic footwear factories in Indonesia was 18 cents. Generally, less than 3 percent of the cost of a Nike sneaker goes for labor.[37]

When *New York Times* reporter Larry Rohter visited the free enterprise zone in Honduras—the site of the criticism of Ms. Gifford—he found that conditions in the apparel factories varied widely. Some were unionized; some did not allow unions. Some were clean and air conditioned; others were hot and squalid. Some plants abused their workers, requiring overtime, imposing unreachable production quotas, and firing pregnant workers to escape paying maternity benefits. But other plants respected worker rights, subsidized lunch, and provided free health care. Several Hondurans he interviewed considered their jobs in the *maquiladoras* a tremendous opportunity in comparison to the agricultural work they had been doing.[38]

Most of the factories in Honduras were Taiwanese- or Korean-owned subcontractors of American MNCs. The subcontractors generally pledge to follow a code of conduct respecting workers' rights adopted by MNCs, such as The Gap, but *monitoring* their compliance is essential. Indeed, consumer pressure, including a concerted effort by students at the College of Saint Catherine in St. Paul, Minnesota, resulted in The Gap agreeing to *independent monitoring* of the labor conditions in the *maquiladoras* in El Salvador and elsewhere.[39]

As incredible as it may seem, the issue of child labor in developing countries is also controversial. Worldwide, one in six children aged 5 to 17, nearly 250 million in all, are engaged in work that the International Labor Organization (ILO) thinks should be abolished. Over 8 million children are involved in appalling sorts of work, including forced labor, warfare, prostitution, pornography, and other illicit activities.[40] Who could support the practice of 10-year-olds working 10-hour days sewing soccer balls in Pakistan or rugs in India?[41] But what about a 14-year-old girl working six hours a day in an apparel factory in Honduras? Education for the majority of Hondurans ends with the sixth grade. Honduran law allows 14-year-olds to work six-hour days with permission from their parents. If teenagers are not allowed to work in the *maquiladoras* they will not be in school, but rather seeking more demanding work for even less pay in the fields.[42] In many parts of the world teen labor is different from child labor. Responses to child labor include compulsory schooling, monitoring compliance with the laws already established in developing countries, and, of course, saving children from the worst forms of labor that result in irreversible psychological or physical damage.

In response to the controversy about sweatshops in the 1990s, President Clinton established the White House Apparel Industry Partnership, a task force that included representatives of labor unions, human-rights groups, and industry powerhouses, to develop a Workplace Code of Conduct. Not surprisingly, the task proved to be difficult and contentious. In November 1998, the task force announced an accord in which apparel-makers who signed the Code of Conduct pledged to provide abuse-free factories, hire workers at least 15 years old, limit the workweek to 60 hours, pay at least the local minimum wage, and protect the right of workers to organize. The Fair Labor Association (FLA) was established to monitor the code.

However, many of the apparel unions such as UNITE and the Interfaith Center for Corporate Responsibility rejected the agreement because of two issues: the credibility of the FLA to monitor it and the definition of a living wage. Because the local minimum wage is not even a subsistence wage in countries such as Indonesia and Haiti, labor and human-rights representatives argued unsuccessfully that companies should commit themselves to pay a wage that could provide the basic needs for a family. Apparel companies and retailers insisted that a "living wage" could prove too hard to define and too expensive.[43]

At the beginning of the new century the anti-sweatshop campaign secured a firm foothold on many U.S. campuses through United Students Against Sweatshops (USAS). This student organization successfully lobbied administrations at many American universities to guarantee that university-logo garments and merchandise, a $2.5 billion industry in 1999, were not produced in sweatshops. It even established the Workers Rights Consortium (WRC) to monitor compliance with codes of conduct.[44] In the spring of 2002, a worker-owned cooperative called TeamX was established in California to produce a new brand—SweatX. TeamX received its start-up capital from The Hot Fudge Social Venture Fund set up by Ben Cohen after Ben and Jerry's Ice Cream was bought by a large corporation. TeamX is a unionized shop that is committed to paying a living wage, providing health care, a pension, a share of profits, and practicing a "solidarity ratio" in which no executive is paid more than eight times the wage of the lowest paid worker. It hopes to be a model for producing garments fairly and competitively.[45]

Although the efforts of the Apparel Industry Partnership, USAS, and TeamX give reason for hope, ending sweatshop labor is an uphill battle. A daunting problem is the size and mobility of the industry. In 1999, there were over 80,000 factories at work for the $180 billion U.S. apparel industry; subcontracting allows the industry to quickly move production from country to country. It is nearly impossible to monitor such a sizeable and slippery system. The essential keys to justice are "tough government enforcement of workers' rights and labor standards, and high levels of unionization."[46]

The exploitation of the worker has been a social justice issue since the beginning of the Industrial Revolution, and it continues to be a major concern as multi-national corporations comb the earth in search of cheaper labor and higher profits.

Multi-national corporations can make valuable contributions to the alleviation of poverty, but their single-minded drive for profits often blinds them to the common good and the needs of the poor. Worse, the power that accompanies their size and wealth enables MNCs to manipulate the system in their favor so that the rules of the game oppress the poor.

Foreign Aid

Another form of investment in developing countries consists of foreign aid from one government to another. Foreign aid has been unpopular among many Americans who think the United States should take care of its own poor and address its own social problems before helping others. This view is in tension with the theological notion that humanity is the family of God, brothers and sisters to one another, and that each person has an unearned value from being created in the image and likeness of God. According to this perspective a hungry child from Chad, China, or Colombia should elicit the same concern as a hungry American child. In justice, all deserve an opportunity to develop their full human potential. Indeed the greater need of brothers and sisters in the Two-Thirds World may invoke a greater responsibility from the more affluent in the human community. Moreover, as we have seen, there is at least an indirect connection between the wealth of the few and the poverty of the many on planet Earth. Our obligation to respond to the needs of the poor should be rooted more in justice than in charity.

This stinginess regarding foreign aid also goes contrary to the American perception of ourselves as a generous people. As the world's wealthiest country surely we can afford to assist the neediest. And many Americans think, incorrectly, that the United States is generous toward the Two-Thirds World. In one national opinion poll, 75 percent of Americans thought that the United States spent too much on foreign aid. When asked what percentage of the annual federal budget is spent for this, the typical guess was 15 percent, and 41 percent of Americans thought that foreign aid was the largest single item in the budget![47]

The facts indicate that foreign aid (or official development assistance [ODA]) was less than 1 percent of the federal budget in 2000, or nearly $10 billion. In 2000 the United States gave the lowest percentage of its GNP (0.10 percent) to foreign aid of the 22 developed countries.[48] Since the United States has the world's largest economy, it used to give the largest gross amount to foreign aid, even though it was the smallest percentage. No longer. Japan now consistently gives about a third more than the United States, even though its economy is about half the size, and in 1995 the United States was in fourth place behind Japan, France, and Germany.[49] The Scandinavian countries generally lead the list in percentage of GNP given for development assistance. In 1970, the U.N. General Assembly agreed on a goal of 0.7 percent of a country's GNP. In 2000, only 5 of the 22 developed countries met or exceeded that goal, and none of the rest gave 0.4 percent of their GNP. Foreign aid fell substantially during the 1990s, although Ireland bucked the trend by doubling its aid from 0.16 percent of GNP to 0.30 percent.[50] Perhaps the United States, which gives 0.10 percent, could follow Ireland's example. It would be a step down the road toward compassion and generosity.

The Cold War introduced some specific problems for the U.S. foreign aid program. Military aid and economic aid were lumped together (as they still are) and both tended to be used to fight communism and assist U.S. farmers and manufacturers, rather than assist in the development of the poor. Thus, if Georgia farmers had a surplus of peanuts (or, worse, of tobacco), the United States would purchase peanut butter to send to the Philippines, not because it was needed, but because the Philippines was a strategically placed, anti-Communist country. While this undoubtedly helped Georgia farmers (and the Philippine dictators), it actually had negative effects on the Philippine market and in the end hurt the poor.[51]

Israel and Egypt, strategic U.S. allies in the Middle East, are still by far the largest beneficiaries of U.S. assistance; together they receive about a third of the total, most in military aid.[52] Since September 11, 2001, U.S. aid to Pakistan has increased significantly, even though it is doubtful that Pakistan has the economic or political structure to be able to use the funds effectively to empower the poor.

Bilateral foreign aid (directly from one country to another) is often conditioned on the recipient purchasing American products, such as Ford tractors. This forces a foreign market to buy American products and parts, even though this might not be best for the recipient. Competitive bidding might result in getting less expensive tractors, if tractors are what the recipient really needs. Although much bilateral foreign aid today is in grants, some of it is in loans that contribute to the indebtedness of poor countries. Every college student knows the difference between a grant and a loan.

Too often foreign aid has been designated for projects that are economically or culturally inappropriate. For example, in 1981 Norway, with the best of intentions, built a state-of-the-art fish-freezing plant on the shore of Lake Turkana in tropical Kenya at a cost of over $20 million. This project made sense to Norwegians, but was comically disastrous in Kenya. The cost of operating the freezers in tropical weather exceeded the income from the frozen fish fillets. In addition, the Turkana people were herders who disdained fishing, and periodic droughts shrunk the lake so that the plant was no longer on the shore.[53] Clearly, a fish-freezing plant was not the best use of Norway's aid funds. Similarly, during the war to unseat the Taliban in Afghanistan in 2001, the United States airlifted food aid, including nutritious peanut butter, to Afghan refugees. The puzzled Afghans fed it to their camels and goats.

Foreign aid has too often fallen victim to corruption or been used for inappropriate, ostentatious, unwise, or even harmful projects. When the purpose of the aid was to support anti-Communist dictators, the donor turned a blind eye to corruption and waste. Now the war on terrorism is again tempting the United States in this direction, as in the case of General Musharraf in Pakistan. Enriching and arming dictators might create allies, but this is often at the cost of moral principles and greater suffering of the poor.

Although the end of the Cold War has eliminated the anti-Communist rationale for foreign aid, the United States still uses foreign aid primarily to serve its political and economic self-interest. It is perhaps unrealistic, and probably unwise, to think foreign aid should be blind to the interests of a nation's foreign policy, but its primary purpose should be humanitarian—to empower the poorest through assisting them in meeting their basic needs.

Developing countries need aid and assistance, but the way the United States gives foreign aid needs to be reformed if it is to improve the living standards of the poor. The following are suggestions for reforming U.S. foreign aid:

- The primary criterion for receiving development assistance should be need, but other considerations, such as the human rights record of the government and even U.S. strategic interests, can be considered.

- Development assistance should be separated from military aid. The former should increase; the latter decline. The United Nations suggests that its wealthy members give 0.7 percent of their GNP to development assistance, and this is a reasonable goal for the world's richest nation.
- In general, development assistance should be channeled through multilateral institutions (such as the United Nations) in order to increase the effectiveness of the aid for the recipient, rather than for the donor.
- Development assistance should be carefully aimed at countries with a genuine commitment to sound economic management, or it will be wasted. If a country does not have sound policies and institutions (related to the Golden Straitjacket), aid is likely to be stolen by the corrupt elite or to be ineffective in empowering the poor. If a country is badly run, it is better to pay for educating their best and brightest at universities in the global North, than to throw aid down a sinkhole.[54]
- There should be grassroots participation of the recipients in the design and implementation of projects. It seems that multi-million-dollar projects in developing countries almost always enrich the elite and harm the poor. Loans or grants in the tens of thousands of dollars range are generally much more likely to genuinely empower the poor. Such funds could ordinarily be channeled through community organizations, especially in situations where there is a corrupt government bureaucracy. Oxfam is a private organization that implements this model in its development projects. (See the Resources section in chapter 9 for information on Oxfam.)

In these ways foreign aid can become genuinely development assistance.[55]

Trade and NAFTA

Among those concerned for the economic development of poor countries, there has been an energetic debate about trade policy. Some have argued for *inward-looking development policies* (called "import substitution") that attempt to build indigenous industries and technologies appropriate for a country's resources through high tariffs and import quotas that protect domestic production. Others have fostered *outward-looking development policies* (called "export promotion") that welcome foreign investment and encourage free trade in the large global marketplace.[56]

The current consensus among development economists "leans toward an eclectic view that attempts to fit the relevant arguments of both free-trade and protectionist models to the specific economic, institutional, and political realities of diverse Third World nations at different stages of development. What works for one may not work for another."[57] It is important to attend to the specific situation of a developing country, but also to realize that fluctuations in the world economy can have a decisive impact on the success of a particular development strategy. An expanding world economy, for example, can assist an export-oriented policy, while a global recession can stifle it. Thus, the economic decisions taken by developed countries can have a devastating impact on developing economies.[58]

Four further insights can be garnered from the struggle for economic development during the past five decades:[59]

1. An inegalitarian power structure can turn either an export-oriented policy or an import-substitution strategy toward more inequality. It is not only trade policy that is important, but whose interests the policy is intended to serve.

2. Successful development seems to be linked to effective cooperation between the private and public sectors that share a commitment to a consistent and coherent development strategy. Consistent cooperation may be as important as the strategy itself.

3. The expansion of trade among developing countries (South-South trade and regional trading blocs) may have important benefits for development not found in trade between developed and developing countries (North-South trade). South-South trade may foster greater collective self-reliance among developing countries and reduce some of the export instability found in the world economy.

4. Trade barriers (such as tariffs and quotas) erected by developed countries against the exports of developing countries are a major obstacle to their efforts at diversification and trade expansion. Often these barriers are higher for processed products than for raw materials (higher for shirts than for cotton, for example), which adversely affects the terms of trade between developed and developing countries and hampers efforts at industrialization.

The income (26 percent of developing countries' GDP in 2000) that developing countries receive from trade (their exports) dwarfs that from either foreign investment (2.5 percent) or foreign aid (0.5 percent). Trade is vitally important for economic development. But global trade is a game rigged against developing countries through trade barriers and subsidies. The agricultural subsidies paid to farmers in developed countries amount to about $365 billion a year, or six times the $56 billion in foreign aid. "Eliminating trade barriers and subsidies in industrial countries that inhibit imports from developing countries is therefore an urgent priority, and a potential route to greatly accelerated development."[60]

Perhaps the North should move beyond free trade with the South toward trade arrangements that give a preference to developing countries that need assistance in becoming more competitive and whose egalitarian domestic policies indicate that economic growth will likely mean genuine development for the poor.[61] Either free trade or preferential trade will require assistance programs for displaced workers in developed countries.[62]

The North American Free Trade Agreement (NAFTA) has given some focus to this general discussion about the trade relationship between developed and developing countries. NAFTA was negotiated by the first Bush and the Clinton administrations and began on January 1, 1994. It binds Canada, Mexico, and the United States together in a free trade arrangement that gradually reduces import/export tariffs between them. It was opposed by U.S.

labor unions because of the fear of what third-party presidential candidate Ross Perot called a "giant sucking sound" of jobs going South to Mexico. The Clinton administration claimed that NAFTA would actually create jobs in the United States. The revolt of indigenous peasants in the province of Chiapas in Mexico on the day NAFTA went into effect dramatized their anxiety that they would not be able to compete with U.S. farmers in the production of corn and their long-standing grievances over not benefiting from the rich resources of their region.

It is very difficult to assess the results of NAFTA. Partisans in the debate tend to skew the data to benefit their position.[63] For example, in the first five years under NAFTA, 214,902 American workers registered with a U.S. government program to assist those displaced when companies moved to Mexico.[64] This seems an arresting figure at first, but it is a miniscule percentage of the American workforce, and nationwide unemployment in 1999 was below 5 percent—lower than many economists thought possible. Moreover, a displaced worker is often identifiable, while those who owe their high-paying jobs to free trade do not recognize that they have NAFTA to thank. Furthermore, many of the jobs moving to Mexico, some economists claim, would have moved somewhere else anyway because of the globalization of the economy. The U.S. economy is undergoing a structural transformation with or without NAFTA. Some argue that the challenge is not so much to protect outdated U.S. industry as to educate a workforce for the high technology economy of the twenty-first century.[65]

The same ambiguity pertains to NAFTA's impact on poverty in Mexico. NAFTA's critics proclaim that while Mexican productivity is up 36 percent, wages have dropped 29 percent, and that the poverty rate has almost doubled, from 34 percent to 60 percent, between 1994 and 1999.[66] Yet the *Human Development Report* indicates that Mexico's human development index is steadily improving and that the percentage of Mexicans living below the poverty line decreased from 34 percent in 1994 to 10 percent in 1999.[67] Although no one argues that NAFTA has solved all of Mexico's economic problems, trade between the United States and Mexico has expanded from $76 billion in 1993 to nearly $246 billion in 2000, with Mexico the net beneficiary.[68] Mexico has also become politically more democratic during the NAFTA years. Still, there is clearly much work to be done to secure labor rights and a higher standard of living for workers in Mexico and to address environmental issues, especially in the border region.

When President Clinton wanted to expand NAFTA into a Free Trade Agreement for the Americas, Congress refused to grant him "fast-track" authority whereby Congress agrees to vote yea or nay on trade agreements without amending them. After an uphill struggle, President George W. Bush received fast-track authority from Congress in August 2002. In theory at least, free trade between the countries in the Western Hemisphere could produce the economic growth necessary for economic development in countries in Latin America and benefit consumers everywhere. Nonetheless, it is not the only thing that needs to be done to raise the standard of living of the poor.

The Debt Crisis and Jubilee 2000

Debt is a daunting obstacle to economic development for most countries in the Two-Thirds World. Brazil and Mexico, the largest developing countries in the Western Hemisphere, have accumulated the largest debts. Brazil's external debt in 1997 was nearly $200 billion and Mexico's was nearly $150 billion. Nicaragua's $5 billion debt represents 305 percent of its annual GNP.[69] Most of the 41 countries with the worst debt burden, the "Heavily Indebted Poor Countries" (HIPC), are in Africa.

In the late 1980s the world experienced a *debt crisis* when Brazil, Mexico, and other countries threatened to default on their loans. Had they done so, the international banking system might have collapsed.

The debt crisis began in the mid-1970s when the Oil Producing and Exporting Countries (OPEC) were awash in petrodollars and banks were eager to lend money. Developing countries borrowed billions of dollars at low, but adjustable or floating, interest rates.

Borrowing capital can be sensible, even advisable, when the money is invested productively, such as in developing industry and infrastructure, because the profit can be used to repay the loan. Unfortunately, the ruling elites in many Two-Thirds World countries used the money for current consumption rather than productive investments. Huge chunks disappeared due to graft and corruption, as happened in the Philippines where Marcos and his cronies stole over $5 billion. Loans were used for showcase projects, like the Cultural Center in Manila that has been a dismal failure in attracting profitable international events. Some of the debt was incurred to pay for oil, which had become very expensive after 1973. Thus the Arab sheiks had their petrodollars returned to them to be loaned again. Perhaps 20 percent of Third-World debt was used to purchase weapons.[70] Using a loan for unproductive or unprofitable purchases leaves the borrower with no way to repay it. Note that the poor did not benefit from these loans, nor did the poor participate in the decisions about whether to borrow or how to spend the money.

Then in the 1980s interest rates moved upward dramatically. During the Reagan administration, the United States lowered taxes and increased military spending by borrowing heavily, which sent international interest rates skyrocketing. Even a 1 percent rate increase on a $1 billion loan increases the interest payment by $10 million. Interest rates doubled and tripled, pushing interest payments beyond the means of developing countries. At the same time, prices for raw materials (commodities) plummeted, leaving poor countries with even less income to service their debt. Thus Brazil and Mexico considered defaulting on their loans, in effect declaring bankruptcy.

Commercial banks, in conjunction with First-World governments, scrambled to re-negotiate loans to prevent default. Several years of this process alleviated the debt crisis. The commercial banks, which were seriously overextended, reduced their investment in developing countries and placed themselves on surer financial footing. Between 1982 and 1990 the poor nations of the Two-Thirds World transferred $418 billion into the coffers of First-World banks.[71]

Most First-World banks are now sound and secure; Third-World countries are not. They remain seriously indebted to developed countries and to the World Bank and the IMF.

If a large proportion of a family's income goes to pay off a mortgage, they will have less money to spend and have to stay at home most of the time. Likewise, if a country is deeply in debt, it will have less money to invest in social spending, such as education and health care. Thus it is no surprise that in the 41 HIPCs, which owe some $170 billion to foreign creditors, half of their 600 million people get by on less than a dollar a day.[72] This stark reality sparked anti-poverty activists to create an international anti-debt campaign called *Jubilee 2000* in the last years of the twentieth century. Inspired by the Jubilee principle articulated in Leviticus 15, which calls for the releasing of debt every fifty years, Jubilee 2000 pressed for the forgiveness of debts to mark the new millennium.

The anti-debt campaign resulted in the World Bank and the IMF launching the HIPC initiative in 1996. This initiative aimed to reduce the overall debt burden of the 41 most heavily indebted poor countries[73] to a sustainable level, if the countries recorded several years of sound economic policy. In 1999, at the behest of the G7 countries, which were being pressured by the anti-debt campaign, the HIPC initiative was accelerated and made more generous.[74]

Virtual bankruptcy of the world's poorest countries is morally untenable. Simply forgiving these debts, however, will not necessarily benefit the poor. The worry is that debt relief will simply benefit the incompetent, corrupt, authoritarian governments that racked up the debts in the first place and that this aid will disappear into a sinkhole.[75]

To qualify for the HIPC initiative, a country has to develop a "poverty reduction strategy" showing how it will use the savings from debt reduction to reduce poverty. The difficulty is that many of these countries can be described as "failed states," corrupt and decaying authoritarian regimes or anarchies riven with civil conflict. The corruption is often not only at the top, but penetrates throughout the society. Thus, even if more funds are allocated for health care, for example, the medicine is likely to be sold on the black market by health-care workers rather than distributed to the people in need. Many of these countries need considerable remedial help to develop programs aimed at reducing poverty and also need careful monitoring to make sure the programs are properly implemented. Such a process takes time, but the anti-debt campaign, out of well-intentioned concern for the desperate plight of the poor and skepticism about the foot-dragging and delaying tactics of the rich lenders, has insisted on speeding up the process of relieving debt.[76]

There are two other concerns about debt relief. Even as debt is being canceled, some of the same corrupt or incompetent governments are borrowing yet more money, in part because they have little choice—they are dependent on aid for income. There is also the concern that the cost of debt relief will cause the rich countries and their multilateral institutions, the World Bank and IMF, to reduce foreign aid.

The words of the "Our Father"—"And forgive us our debts, as we also have forgiven our debtors" (Mt. 6:12)—call Christians to an important ideal, but one that is difficult to practice in a way that effectively liberates the poor. Forgiving and relieving debt is an essential ingredient in reducing poverty, but unless it is carried out in combination with good economic policies, soundly administered, it is unlikely to benefit the poor.

Domestic Inequity and Human Development

Thus far this chapter has focused primarily on the gap between the North and South. Unfortunately, globalization often results in a "winner takes all" competition that can concentrate wealth at the top and leave the poor worse off and full of resentment.[77] A rising tide may lift all boats, but economic growth is not always like a rising tide. It is often more like a jungle where the fittest eats all the others. If economic growth is going to result in human development, it is essential that the poor be its beneficiaries.

Achieving economic growth is not easy for developing countries in a competitive global economy. The system is stacked against them. Steps such as the reduction or forgiveness of debt, MNCs' compliance with international codes of conduct, reformed development assistance, and free trade agreements can enable poor countries to achieve economic growth. But economic growth, though essential, is only half the battle. International or external economic reforms must be coupled with domestic or internal reforms focused on the poor. Indeed, without attention to equity in the distribution of goods and services, economic growth itself cannot be sustained.[78]

Equality (roughly equal incomes throughout a society) is not the goal of development, but equity (fair distribution) seems essential for genuine human development. The goal is to meet the basic needs of everyone in a society so that each person has the opportunity to flourish and to participate in and contribute to the community. The aim is not to bring down the rich but to remove the crippling obstacle of poverty so that everyone has enough. While wealth may be an obstacle to spiritual growth, as the Gospel clearly indicates, it is not in itself an obstacle to economic development. Increasing inequity in income, however, is often an indication that economic growth is not benefiting the poor or enhancing the common good.

A rich elite ruling over an impoverished majority is a legacy of colonialism in many developing countries. Brazil, for example, has Latin America's most unequal distribution of land, with 45 percent of the land owned by 1 percent of the population, but this is a familiar pattern throughout Latin America and much of the Two-Thirds World.[79] "Latin American and Caribbean countries have among the world's highest income inequality. In 13 of the 20 countries with data for the 1990s, the poorest 10% had less than 1/20 of the income of the richest 10%."[80] In the Two-Thirds World as a whole, the poorest 20 percent of the people receive only about 7 percent of the total income, but in Latin America they receive only 3 percent.[81] It should be the role of the government to distribute wealth so that all boats are indeed lifted up.

There is good evidence that there is a correlation between economic growth and income equity (fair distribution). Neither can be sustained without the other; economic growth and human development are mutually reinforcing.[82] This makes sense when one realizes that a growing economy needs more and better-educated workers and it also needs a larger market—meaning more consumers. It is social spending and fair wages within countries, and fair investment and fair trade among countries that produce these conditions for continued growth. Henry Ford was wise enough to pay his workers enough so they could afford to buy the cars they were producing; Nike, on the other hand, is not paying its Indonesian workers enough to feed their families, much less buy a pair of sneakers. There *are* clear strategies that governments can pursue to insure that economic growth results in genuine human development:[83]

1. A political commitment to increasing *job* opportunities and employment that pays a living wage. Success in lowering unemployment does not happen automatically, but it occurs more often when this is a central policy objective of the government. A country with a growing population and high unemployment should obviously seek patterns of growth that are labor intensive. Creating job opportunities in the private sector is generally preferable to establishing a large public-sector bureaucracy.

2. Social spending that enhances human capabilities, particularly *education* and *health*. Investment in human resources is a key to both human development and economic growth. South Korea, for example, has a literacy rate and an average years of schooling per child rating comparable or better than OECD countries.[84] "The Republic of Korea invests $160 per person a year in health and education, Malaysia $150. India, by contrast, invests only $14, Pakistan $10 and Bangladesh $5."[85] An educated and skilled workforce is essential to meet the needs of a high-technology economy.

3. Increasing access to productive assets, especially *land*, financial *credit*, and *technology*. Land reform is key to rural development, which is in turn essential to feeding hungry people and slowing the migration to the cities. Peasant families have worked the land for generations. Once it was their land, but at some point it was taken from them. It seems only fair to return it now. (Plantation owners, of course, usually take a different view.)[86]

The Grameen Bank in Bangladesh, founded by Muhammad Yunus, has demonstrated that small loans to poor women for micro-enterprises can significantly reduce poverty and make a profit for the bank. Since 1976 the Grameen Bank has made micro-loans to two million families in 35,000 villages in Bangladesh. The repayment rate exceeds 90 percent. Many of these loans have been the stimulus for enterprises that have enabled the poor to satisfy their basic needs and even come to employ others in small businesses.[87]

The technology divide threatens to further increase the gap between the rich and the poor. Nearly 80 percent of internet users are in the developed countries of the North, and English is the dominant language of the world-wide web. "Africa has less international bandwidth that Sao Paolo, Brazil. Latin America's bandwidth, in turn, is roughly equal to that of Seoul, Republic of Korea."[88] As Bill Gates, the CEO of Microsoft, Inc., discovered when he had the good and generous idea of distributing computers to developing countries, poor people first need a wall socket to put the plug into—a third of the world's people do not have electricity. Although developing the infrastructure to bridge the technology divide should be a priority of governments in developing countries, this is a task that demands wise and generous aid and investment and is ill-suited to the strengths of the market.

4. A focused investment in *women*'s capabilities through education, child care, credit, health care, and employment. Until recently most development projects tended to focus on men as the generators of capital. But it is actually women who are key to meeting the basic needs of their families and who often do the productive, but uncompensated, work in the village or household. Empowerment of women is also key to controlling population growth.[89]

5. A responsible *government* that gives high priority to the needs of all the people and controls corruption.[90] Such governments tend to be or to become participative or democratic, but authoritarian governments genuinely committed to national productivity and prosperity have also achieved economic growth and human development. Corrupt, self-serving governments have not.[91]

Inequity also affects social power.[92] Too often the very wealthy unduly influence politicians to enact policies that benefit them rather than the common good, and wealthy countries neglect or exploit their weaker neighbors. In the United States, for example, it seems that energy companies, including the corrupt leaders of Enron, basically wrote the energy policy of the George W. Bush administration that found conservation to be a nearly fanciful idea. When the Group of 8 (G8) of the world's most powerful countries met in Kananaskis, Canada, in June of 2002, African leaders lobbied them for a Marshall Plan for Africa, which has 32 of the world's least developed countries. The G8 countries responded with no trade concessions, about $1 billion in additional debt relief, and $6 billion in aid over four years—a response that will do little to improve the situation. At the same meeting the G8 countries approved a $20 billion aid package for its newest member, Russia, for decommissioning its nuclear weapons and handling its nuclear waste.[93]

Inequity also raises questions of social and moral responsibility. An annual contribution of 1 percent of the wealth of the 200 richest people (about $7 billion) could provide universal access to primary education for all the world's children.[94] How much is enough in a needy world? As Gandhi said, the earth has enough for everyone's need, but not for everyone's greed.[95]

For economic justice to be realized and human development to happen for the poor there have to be changes both in the global economic system and within the countries of the Two-Thirds World.

THE MILLENNIUM DEVELOPMENT GOALS

At the U.N.'s General Assembly meeting in 2000, heads of state, recognizing their collective responsibility for human development, set eight goals for poverty eradication and development, to be achieved by 2015. Many of the Millennium Development Goals have specific targets to monitor progress. These are the goals and their targets:

Goal 1. Eradicate extreme poverty and hunger.
   Target 1a. Halve the proportion of people living on less than a dollar a day.
   Target 1b. Halve the proportion of people suffering from hunger.
Goal 2. Achieve universal primary education.
Goal 3. Promote gender equality and the empowerment of women.
   Target. Eliminate gender disparities in primary and secondary education, preferably by 2005, and in all levels of education by 2015.
Goal 4. Reduce child mortality.
   Target. Reduce infant and under-five mortality rates by two-thirds.
Goal 5. Improve maternal health.
   Target. Reduce maternal mortality ratios by three-quarters.
Goal 6. Combat HIV/AIDS, malaria, and other diseases.
   Target 6a. Halt and begin to reverse the spread of HIV/AIDS.
   Target 6b. Halt and begin to reverse the incidence of malaria and other major diseases.
Goal 7. Ensure environmental sustainability.
   Target 7a. Integrate the principles of sustainable development into country policies and programs and reverse the loss of environmental resources.
   Target 7b. Halve the proportion of people without sustainable safe drinking water.
   Target 7c. Achieve, by 2020, a significant improvement in the lives of at least 100 million slum dwellers.
Goal 8. Develop a global partnership for development.

The Human Development Report 2002 attempts to assess, in some detail, the world's progress toward these goals. In general, the HDR concludes that, although many countries have made progress, much of the world, and especially the least developed countries, seems unlikely to achieve the targets. Sub-Saharan Africa, in particular, will need extraordinary efforts to make progress toward the goals. Even more disconcerting, a lack of data often makes it difficult to assess progress.[96]

Nevertheless, the Millennium Development Goals point to key objectives in the human struggle toward human dignity for every person. The developed countries should commit the resources necessary for making real progress toward these goals and targets.

POVERTY AND THE UNITED STATES ECONOMY

It is scandalous that significant poverty exists in the United States, one of the wealthiest countries in history. This section of the chapter examines income disparity in the United States and two issues that especially affect poor Americans—health care and welfare.

The United States is an extraordinarily wealthy and powerful country. It is the world's largest economy with a GDP twice that of Japan and equal to the combined GDP of all the countries of the European Union.[97] The standard of living in the United States is one of the highest in the world. Its technological sophistication, scientific research, and higher education are unparalleled. It has the world's mightiest military by far.

The gap between the rich and the poor within the United States, however, is the largest among the world's industrial nations. In 1998, the richest 5 percent of American families earned 20 percent of total U.S. income, compared to 15 percent in 1974.[98] This disparity is increasing and income is becoming more concentrated at the top of the scale. "That is, it's not simply that the top 20 percent of families have had bigger percentage gains than families near the middle: the top 5 percent have done better than the next 15, the top 1 percent better than the next 4, and so on up to Bill Gates. . . . [B]etween 1979 and 1997, the after-tax incomes of the top 1 percent of families rose 157 percent, compared with only a 10 percent gain for families near the middle of the income distribution. . . . [I]n 1970 the top 0.01 percent of taxpayers had 0.7 percent of total income—that is, they earned 'only' 70 times as much as the average, not enough to buy or maintain a mega-residence. But in 1998 the top 0.01 percent received more than 3 percent of all income. That meant that the 13,000 richest families in America had almost as much income as the 20 million poorest households; those 13,000 families had incomes 300 times that of average families."[99] The average annual salary in America, adjusted for inflation, increased about 10 percent over 29 years, from $32,522 in 1970 to $35,864 in 1999. During that same period the average real compensation of the top 100 CEO's rose from $1.3 million—39 times the pay of the average worker—to $37.5 million—over a thousand times the pay of workers.[100]

According to Nobel Prize-winning economist Paul Krugman, "The concentration of income at the top is a key reason that the United States, for all its economic achievements, has more poverty and lower life expectancy than any other major advanced nation. Above all, the growing concentration of wealth has reshaped our political system: it is at the root of a general shift to the right and of an extreme polarization of our politics."[101] Although the poverty rate is the lowest it has been since 1980, it rose significantly (to 11.7 percent from 11.3 percent) in 2001, and 32.9 million Americans live below the poverty line. One in six American children is poor, the highest child poverty rate among developed countries.[102] Such economic inequality and poverty in the world's wealthiest country is a moral outrage.

Also disturbing is the fact that the United States has gone from the world's leading lender to having the world's largest debt. The national debt was $1 trillion in 1980, grew to $3 trillion by the end of the decade, $5 trillion in 1996, and in 2002 is over $6 trillion, but growing more slowly. The reasons for this increasing indebtedness are large federal budget deficits and large trade deficits. The government is spending more than it takes in through taxes and the United States is importing more goods than it exports. The huge budget deficits during the Reagan years in the 1980s were due to tax cuts and increased military spending. The Clinton administration (1992–2000) gradually balanced the budget and even began to pay down the debt. The George W. Bush administration, however, enacted a tax cut that largely benefits the rich and is increasing military spending to fight the war on terrorism. Budget deficits have returned. Annually, about 18 percent of the federal budget ($300 billion) goes to pay interest on the debt. U.S. debt service is beginning to consume much of its annual economic growth, similar to the way population growth absorbs economic growth in developing countries. Even for an economy as large as that of the United States, deficits and debt are disturbing economic realities.[103]

The United States faces a number of social problems related to the political economy and to poverty: homelessness, crime,[104] urban violence, drugs,[105] racial tension, the feminization of poverty, the breakdown of the family, declining test scores and increasing school drop-out rates.[106] Since the Clinton administration, however, two domestic problems have dominated the national debate—health-care reform and welfare reform. Both are enormously complicated issues and although a thorough examination is beyond the scope of this chapter, they deserve at least some mention in that they demonstrate the direction of discussions about poverty in the United States.

Health-Care Reform

During the 1992 presidential campaign health-care reform re-emerged as a pressing national issue for two reasons: health-care costs were increasing and a significant and growing number of Americans were without health insurance. In 1992 the United States was spending about 12 percent of its GNP, or about $750 billion, on health care. This was about double the percentage of GNP spent for health care by other industrial countries, and the cost of health care in the United States was rising much faster than the rate of inflation. Nearly everyone agreed that strong measures to control the cost of health care were needed.

At the same time 37 million Americans did not have health insurance and therefore were without access to health care. Because the Medicaid program provides health care for the very poor and Medicare insures the elderly, the uninsured in the United States tended to be the working poor and the unemployed. Typically, Americans receive their health insurance through their employment. Many small businesses, however, cannot afford to offer health insurance to their employees, and the unemployed can seldom afford personal insurance policies. Thus, the United States was paying more for health care than any other Western nation, but it was the only Western nation without universal health care, and often ranked rather low in comparison with peer countries on health indices such as infant mortality.[107] U.S. medical technology was among the best in the world, but a significant number of Americans did not have access to even basic health care. Something needed to be done.

The difficulty here, of course, is that these two problems and two goals—cutting costs and universal access—appear directly opposed to one another. Insuring 37 million more people is likely to cost more, not less. Furthermore, the politics of health-care reform is complicated and conflictual. Some people consider health care a commodity and focus on cutting costs; others think health care is a right and stress universal access to quality care. Some think government intervention can respond to the problem; others wish to rely on the marketplace. The health-care system is complex, with many competing interest groups such as physicians, hospitals, insurance companies, drug companies and suppliers, and consumers.

In the end, by 1994, the Clinton administration's attempt to reform health care had failed. It was the victim of the administration's political mistakes (the overly complex plan was developed in secret), of interest group opposition (especially by the insurance industry), and of partisan politics.

Thus, in 2001, 41.2 million Americans (about 14.6 percent of the population) were without access to health care and the cost of health care was about 14 percent of the GNP, or nearly $1.2 trillion a year. The United States still pays the most for health care, but it may be of some consolation that other Western nations are also struggling to control costs.[108] Health-care spending, however, did grow more slowly in the years around the turn of the century. This is because of increases in managed care and managed competition and the rise of for-profit medicine in the United States—a genuine revolution in the way health care is delivered, which did cap costs at least for a while. Spending on health care, however, rose 6.9 percent in 2000, and health insurance premiums increased an average of 11 percent in 2001.[109] Managed care, moreover, has raised troubling questions regarding the doctor-patient relationship and the quality of care, and it has done nothing to directly increase access to care for the uninsured. Unfortunately, this glaring issue no longer seems to be on the national agenda.

Health care is not a commodity. Human beings have a right to basic health care that prevents disease and cures sickness. The United States remains the only industrial nation that does not have universal health care for all of its citizens. This is an injustice that still needs to be corrected.

Welfare Reform

Bill Clinton fulfilled his 1992 campaign pledge to "end welfare as we know it" with the enactment of the Personal Responsibility and Work Opportunity Act of 1996. It did indeed change the welfare program. This welfare reform legislation, which expired in October 2002, was debated by Congress at that time.

Prior to 1996 "welfare" generally referred to Aid to Families with Dependent Children (AFDC), but U.S. poverty programs also included food stamps, housing subsidies, Supplemental Security Income for the elderly poor and the disabled, and Medicaid. Federal and state governments share the cost of many of these programs and some states share the cost with local governments. Medicaid, the means-tested health-care program for the poor, is by far the most expensive of these programs, but it was not included in the welfare-reform debate. The reform focused on AFDC, a program aimed at poor children and their mothers. In 1995 AFDC cost about $30 billion (federal and state) and represented only about 1 percent of the federal budget. Its cost had remained steady, although the number of recipients rose 31 percent from 1989 through 1994.

Although nearly everyone agreed that the welfare system needed change, reformers had a variety of motives and objectives. Some contended that it cost too much and burdened taxpayers too heavily. Others thought that welfare was underwriting the breakdown of the family. Many agreed with President Clinton that "the current welfare system undermines the basic values of work, responsibility, and family, trapping generation after generation in dependency. [Welfare should be] a second chance, not a way of life."[110] Welfare recipients found the system bureaucratic, humiliating, and inadequate, and often agreed that its stipulations could result in dependency and a culture of poverty.

The primary goal of the Personal Responsibility and Work Opportunity Act of 1996 was to reduce the number of recipients of welfare and to reduce the cost of the program. Its provisions are complicated, but basically it eliminated AFDC and replaced it with federal block grants to the states, called Temporary Assistance to Needy Families (TANF), which each state can use for its own welfare and work programs. This eliminated a poor person's entitlement to federal aid. Federal spending on welfare and food stamps was cut by $60 billion over six years. Non-citizens, including legal immigrants, were no longer eligible for assistance. Every adult recipient of welfare had to have a job within two years or lose benefits, and a five-year lifetime cap on receiving benefits was instituted. States could provide assistance to a mother under 18 only if she resided at home and stayed in school. Funds for child care were slightly increased.

Assisted by the strongest economy in American history, welfare reform fulfilled its limited objective. Welfare rolls were reduced by nearly 60 percent, from about 13 million in 1996 to 5.8 million in June of 2000.[111] The poverty rate declined somewhat as well. One out of three children is born outside of marriage in the United States, and single-parent families are four times more likely to be poor. The proportion of births outside of marriage (the non-marital birth ratio), after climbing steadily by almost 1 percent per year for over twenty years, leveled off after 1994, and the birthrate of teenage mothers declined.[112] About 50 percent of the single mothers who left the welfare rolls found employment, and some of their lives and those of their children have significantly improved. For others, however, employment has been short-lived or it has not paid enough to better their situation.

Historically, most of the hodgepodge of welfare programs have done what they were meant to do.[113] They have reduced hunger and malnutrition, prevented illness and cured sickness, subsidized decent shelter, contributed to education and child development, supported the disabled and the elderly, and reduced the misery of children unlucky enough to be born into poverty. They have not, however, eliminated poverty in America—that has not been their objective. But isn't eliminating poverty a reasonable goal for the richest country on earth? Eradicating poverty would require bold new thinking aimed at full employment paying a living wage.

Instead of a bold new vision aimed at eliminating poverty in the richest country on earth, when the Temporary Assistance for Needy Families (TANF) legislation came up for renewal, Congress only tinkered with it. By contrast, progressive Christian groups, such as Bread for the World and Network, argued for the following sorts of changes in the TANF program:[114]

- Invest in people, by improving access to education and training. Women with a high school diploma earn one and a half times more than those without, and those with an associate's degree have twice the income of high school graduates.
- Ease the time limits for those receiving partial assistance while employed.
- Provide hardship exemptions to the time limits for those who cannot work consistently due to mental, emotional, or physical conditions.
- Federal TANF funding to the states remained at $16.5 billion per year from 1996 through 2002. It was not adjusted for inflation, nor for the possibility of economic recession. Given the demands for education, child care, and other pressing needs, and the strains on state budgets in a declining economy, the program needs increasing resources.

Unfortunately, Congress seems likely to increase requirements and decrease funding.

POVERTY AND CONFLICT

Finally, an observation that is perhaps obvious, but that needs to be stated: poverty is an important cause of revolutions, wars, and violence, and war results in poverty. There is an interrelationship between poverty and conflict.[115]

During the Cold War most conflicts and revolutions in the Two-Thirds World were viewed by the United States and the Soviet Union through the prism of the East-West conflict, as a struggle between communism and democratic capitalism. Very often, once the ideological shell was stripped away, these conflicts represented a struggle by a poor majority of people for justice and a better life. In many of the conflicts and revolutions in Latin America during the 1960s through the 1990s, a crucial element was the struggle of the poor for justice. This was true in Nicaragua, El Salvador, and Guatemala, in Haiti, Jamaica, and the Dominican Republic, in Chile, Brazil, and Colombia. Poverty was also an important ingredient in the struggle against apartheid in South Africa, the people power revolution in the Philippines, the troubles in Northern Ireland, the overthrow of the Shah of Iran, and the Palestinian conflict with Israel. Poverty is a seedbed for terrorism.

Poverty is in itself a violence against human dignity, and it sometimes leads the poor to violently respond to their desperate situations. A revolution by the poor generally begets a disproportionately violent response by the army or the government to protect the status quo. Poverty can result in a spiral of violence.[116]

The destructiveness of violence and war results in poverty. War creates refugees, people who leave their homes and often their homeland to escape the violence. Refugees leave behind their belongings and resources and become instantly impoverished. War destroys cities, homes, schools, hospitals, crops, offices, and factories. War perversely reverses the corporal works of mercy, creating conditions in which people's basic needs are not met. Crops are defoliated and people go hungry. Reservoirs are contaminated and people go thirsty. Homes are destroyed and people are without shelter or clothing. People are injured and sickness increases. Prisoners are taken. Sometimes the dead remain unburied.[117] Economic growth and human development are clearly impossible under conditions of war and violence.

The overwhelming majority of the people on earth live in poverty, unable to meet their basic needs and fulfill their God-given potential. This reality is a tremendous obstacle to the dream of creating a just and peaceful world order. It is even more of a scandal because it need not be. The poverty of the many exists in sharp contrast with the affluence of the few. The Parables of the Rich Fool (Lk 12:13–21), of the Rich Man and Lazarus (Lk 16:19–31), and of the Great Feast (Lk 14:15–24) stand as a warning to contemporary Christians who are comfortable with their riches in a hungry world. God invites humanity to a great banquet, but everyone must be included at the table.

STUDY QUESTIONS

1. Have you experienced or observed poverty? What does poverty do to the human spirit?
2. When Jesus says, "Blessed are the poor in spirit, for theirs is the kingdom of heaven" (Mt. 5:3), what does he mean?
3. Why are the countries of the North rich and the countries of the South poor?
4. Is globalization good news or bad news for the poor? What steps can be taken to make globalization work to benefit the poor?
5. When multi-national corporations move into developing countries, are they a blessing or a curse for the poor? What can be done to make their presence a blessing?
6. Are multi-national corporations a blessing or a curse for middle-class Americans? for poor Americans?

7. Is the United States generous with foreign aid? Should U.S. foreign aid be increased? What, if any, conditions should be placed on foreign aid?

8. From the perspective of the poor, is NAFTA a good idea or a bad idea? Should NAFTA be expanded into a Free Trade Agreement for the Americas?

9. Do you think the debt incurred by developing countries should be forgiven?

10. Is economic growth necessary for human development? Is economic growth the same as economic development? What can developing countries do to make sure that economic growth translates into human development? What can developed countries do to aid this process?

11. Do you think the Millennium Development Goals will be achieved?

12. Is health care a human right? Why did the attempt at health-care reform in the United States fail in 1994? How would you propose to reform the health care delivery system in the United States? How could global health care reform be accomplished?

13. What do you think are the benefits and liabilities of the welfare reform enacted by Congress in 1996? What further reforms do you think are needed? What can the United States do to eradicate poverty at home?

14. Do you think that peace on earth can coexist with global poverty? Are the rich in the North really threatened by the poor in the South?

CHAPTER THREE

Population Explosion, Resource Depletion, and Environmental Destruction

"Then God said to Noah and to his sons with him: 'As for me, I am establishing my covenant with you and your descendants after you, and with every living creature that is with you, the birds, the domestic animals, and every animal of the earth with you, as many as came out of the ark.'" (Genesis 9:8–10)

"Modern Society will find no solution to the ecological problem unless it takes a serious look at its lifestyle. In many parts of the world, society is given to instant gratification and consumerism while remaining indifferent to the damage which they cause. . . . Simplicity, moderation and discipline, as well as a spirit of sacrifice, must become part of everyday life, lest all suffer the negative consequences of the careless habits of a few."[1]

On a warm Saturday morning in the spring of 1974, shortly after the celebration of the fourth Earth Day, I was walking along 56th Street in New York City. A black Lincoln Town Car, with four big men in black suits and white shirts, windows rolled down, passed me going in the same direction. As the car slowed to stop at a red light, the man riding "shotgun" threw a big Styrofoam coffee cup out of the window. It fell at the feet of a young woman who was walking toward me. She picked up the cup, walked over to the stopped car, and threw it back in the window onto the lap of the astonished litterer, with the firm admonition, "New York is not your garbage can." Then she proceeded calmly down the sidewalk.

In some ways this story can function as a parable about environmental issues. I do not know what effect the woman's action had on the occupants of the car, but she certainly raised my consciousness and changed my behavior. I admired her conviction and her courage. Indeed the earth is not our garbage can, and we humans have got to take responsibility for our waste and encourage others to do so as well.

Yet environmental issues are complicated and ambiguous. If the man throws the cup into a garbage can, the city is cleaner and more pleasant. The cup, however, still has to be disposed of by being buried in a landfill or burned in an incinerator. It takes energy to produce the cup, and Styrofoam is potentially harmful to the earth and the atmosphere. Environmental responsibility may mean not buying or producing the cup in the first place.

But are there realistic alternatives for having our morning coffee on the run? Maybe it is our fast-food lifestyle that is the root problem. Yet the modern economy depends on that lifestyle. Even a brief reflection on a simple Styrofoam cup raises radical questions and seemingly intractable problems.

Here is the conundrum that humanity faces regarding environmental and economic justice. The earth's ecosystem is wondrously diverse and resilient, with a capacity to create and maintain life in countless forms. But the planet itself is finite and the balance of its resources is fragile. The human species has been so successful in reproducing of late that we are beginning to radically alter or destroy the ecosystem on which all life depends. The sheer number of humans is leaving a deep impression on planet earth. At the same time, as we have already noted, in order for humans to survive and flourish, in order to have economic and human development, economic growth seems necessary.[2] Indeed, as we shall see, economic development seems to be an essential ingredient in stopping the runaway growth of the human population. But economic growth, through increased industrial productivity, presently requires large quantities of nonrenewable energy and materials. This depletes the earth's resources and heats up the atmosphere, like an engine running faster and faster. "Since 1900, the number of people inhabiting the earth has multiplied more than three times. The world economy has expanded more than 20 times. The consumption of fossil fuels has grown by a factor of 30, and industrial production has increased by a factor of 50; four fifths of that increase has occurred since 1950."[3] How does society meet the needs of the 6 billion people now alive, the majority of whom are poor, without compromising the prospects of future generations by harming the ecosphere? Economic growth seems essential, but increased productivity may alter the biosphere in disastrous ways. This chapter will address the issues packed into this dilemma.

VALUES AND CONCEPTS

As mentioned in the Introduction, three interrelated levels of analysis (situation/information, interpretation/evaluation, and response) are involved in this examination of ecological problems. As we shall see, science yields tentative, ambiguous information, which further complicates the politics of environmental justice. Humanity's relationship with the earth, however, raises complex ethical and conceptual questions as well.

Christianity has been accused of being the culprit in the ecological crisis through its conception of human dominion over the earth and its creatures.[4] "God blessed them, saying: 'Be fertile and multiply; fill the earth and subdue it. Have dominion over the fish of the sea, the birds of the air, and all the living things that move on the earth.'"[5] This anthropocentric (human-centered) perspective encourages the exploitation of the earth, and Western cultures have done just that.

In response, many Christian theologians, while acknowledging a history of abuse, have interpreted the creation stories in terms of stewardship,[6] or more recently, companionship,[7] rather than dominion.[8] Other theologians, such as Thomas Berry, have moved toward an earth-centered perspective, drawing on sources outside the Christian tradition.[9] Philosophers have had their own version of this debate in the clash between "deep ecology,"[10] with its ecocentric approach, and the mainstream environmental movement, which calls for human responsibility toward the earth in the interests of humanity.[11]

It is not the purpose of this chapter to enter into this important discussion, but, of course, values and perspectives are the foundation of any analysis. Environmental issues are theological, philosophical, and ethical, as well as scientific, technological, economic, and political in nature. Neither a *biocentrism* that asserts the equal value of a person and a fly, nor an *anthropocentrism* that assigns only instrumental value to the natural world, make much sense. A *theocentric* vision that sees the universe and the earth as created by God who calls humanity into right relationship with God, one another, and all of creation seems at once more biblical and more realistic. Humanity is neither above, nor over against, nor below creation. We are earthlings, embedded in creation, and in relationship with the natural world. All of God's creation is good and valuable in itself; all of creation stands before God in profound poverty as creatures; and all of creation is a sacrament of God's goodness and creative power. Many Christian theologians feel that, in responding to the needs of the poor and in respecting the value of earth, humanity is seeking a right relationship with God, each other, and the natural world. "Right relationship" is what God has created us for and called us to.[12]

POPULATION EXPLOSION

Today global population reached a record high, and tomorrow it will break the record once again.[13] Most of the history of the human species has been a struggle to survive, to multiply and fill the earth. It took all of human history to reach a population of 1 billion (around 1825), but only 100 years to add a second billion people. Fifty years later, in 1975, global population had doubled again to 4 billion, and in 50 more years, in 2025, the population is expected to double again to at least 8 billion people.[14] (See Figure 3.1.) Only in the twentieth century did any human being witness the doubling of human population during his or her lifetime.[15] In 1999 the population reached 6 billion. About 80 million people (the equivalent of the population of Germany) are being added to the global population every year, more than 200,000 every day.[16] Humanity has been very successful at multiplying and filling the earth. Human flourishing now depends on stabilizing the human population.

To understand population growth and economic growth and their twin threat to the earth's ecosystem, it is important to grasp the concept of *exponential growth*. "Exponential growth occurs when some quantity continuously increases by a constant percentage over a given period of time—when, for example, a population grows by 2 percent every year."[17] This is the prin-

Figure 3.1
World Population Growth

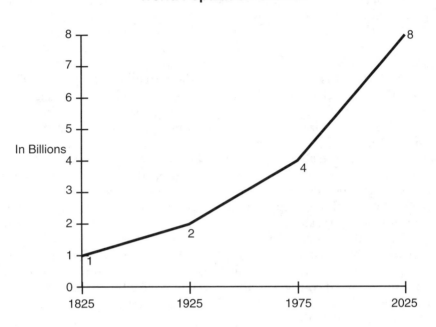

ciple behind compound interest on a savings account. At a growth rate of 1 percent a year, a quantity, such as population or savings, will double in 70 years. The doubling time at a 2 percent rate of growth is 35 years; 4 percent—18 years; 5 percent—14 years; 10 percent—7 years. The global population growth rate peaked sometime in the 1960s at 2.1 percent. Since then the rate of population growth has been steadily declining and was about 1.3 percent in 2002.[18] Even a low rate of exponential growth of a population within a finite ecosystem cannot continue indefinitely without negative consequences. Either the birth rate will have to decrease or the death rate will increase.[19]

Another way of viewing demographic trends is through the fertility rate. "The total fertility rate refers to the average number of children a woman would have in her lifetime on the basis of fertility rates in a given year."[20] A fertility rate of about 2 means that each couple is replacing itself, and population growth has stabilized. This does not mean, however, that population growth will level off immediately. There is a "demographic momentum" that increases population for some time before it finally levels off because the population has many couples in their reproductive years. In other words, although each woman is having fewer children, there are more women having children. Worldwide, the fertility rate is below 3, and steadily declining. In developed countries, the average is below 2. In developing countries as a whole, the fertility rate has dropped from 6.2 in 1960 to about 3 in 2002. In the least developed countries, however, it is still about 5.[21]

Obviously then, there are regional differences in the growth of population. Well over 90 percent of the growth is occurring in the Two-Thirds World. "The developing countries add a million people every five days to lands already overworked and depleted of water and cheap sources of energy."[22] Every other person on earth is an Asian, and Asia's population is expected to increase by 40 percent, from the current 3.46 billion to 4.9 billion, by 2025.[23] The largest absolute increases in numbers are taking place in Asia, but the fastest population growth rate (3.1 percent a year) is in Africa.[24] In 1950, Africa's population was half that of Europe; by 1985, their populations had drawn even at about 480 million each; and by 2025, Africa is expected to have about three times as many people as Europe (1.58 billion to 512 million).[25] In a historical perspective, however, this growth spurt in Africa and Asia simply balances that of Europe and North America during the Industrial Revolution. In 1650, Asia and Africa contained 78.4 percent of global population, and the U.N. predicts that 78.5 percent of the world's people will inhabit these two regions in 2050.[26] Unfortunately, however, about 70 percent of the world's HIV/AIDS infections are in Africa, and the epidemic is also catching hold in Asia. Nearly a million Africans are dying annually from AIDS. It is not known whether the AIDS crisis will significantly reduce population growth in developing countries, but no one wants disease to be part of the solution.

The populations of the countries of the former Soviet Union and of Central Europe are actually declining, and the population of most developed countries is stable or projected to decline. An exception is the United States, whose population continues to grow at a rate of about 1 percent, the same rate as China. This means that the number of Americans will increase from the current 280 million to about 325 million in 2025.[27] While the increase in the U.S. population is not especially significant in terms of the sheer numbers of global growth, an increase in the number of Americans is bad news for the planet's ecosystem. "According to one calculation, the average American baby represents twice the environmental damage of a Swedish child, three times that of an Italian, thirteen times that of a Brazilian, thirty-five times that of an Indian, and 280 (!) times that of a Chadian or Haitian because its level of consumption throughout its life will be so much greater."[28] While each American or Canadian consumes the equivalent of over 40 barrels of oil per year, a Chinese consumes less than 4 barrels, and an Indian or Nigerian, about 2 barrels.[29] What, then, is the significance of population growth for the ecosystem? Is the population explosion itself the problem?

Proliferating populations contribute heavily to stresses on both social systems and the ecosystem. Population growth can effectively cancel out the benefits of economic growth and of attempts to alleviate poverty. The economy has to create ever more jobs and wealth to meet the needs of ever more people. To do this, the economy must use more energy and more resources, which depletes the goods of the earth and produces more pollution.

Overcrowding can be another problem. The population density of Asia and Europe is ten times that of North America.[30] A friend who traveled to Calcutta, India, said that when she arrived, she thought that there must be some huge national festival going on to account for all the people who were there. Some days later, it finally dawned on her that shoulder-to-shoulder people was the ordinary state of Calcutta. Bangladesh, one of the most densely populated territories on earth with 810 people per square kilometer, will need to accommodate twice as many people by the middle of the twenty-first century, despite relatively successful efforts to curb population growth.[31] Already nearly half of the world's population lives in cities that occupy about only 4 percent of earth's land, and this concentration of people in urban areas is expected to increase in the near future.[32] North America has well over two acres of arable land to support each inhabitant, but Asia has little more than a third of an acre per person.[33]

The struggle for survival by rapidly growing populations in developing countries often results in damage to the environment. Trees, for example, are cut down for firewood, and this deforestation leads to soil erosion, which results in flooding and the washing away of valuable topsoil.[34] The result is a desert, incapable of supporting agriculture or grazing. This further impoverishes the people who depend on the land for their livelihood. The "slash and burn" farming methods of growing numbers of indigenous people in Brazil or the Philippines contribute to the destruction of tropical forests, although corporate logging and agribusiness are by far the greater culprits. In many places, land and water are becoming scarce resources.

As natural environments deteriorate from overuse, people *migrate* from rural areas to overcrowded cities and from the global South to the North.[35] While urbanization tends to lower fertility rates in the long run, the influx of people is overwhelming the capacity of cities to provide basic social services, such as housing, sanitation, water, education, health care, and work.[36] Mexico City, for instance, which could have a population of nearly 40 million by 2034, already faces air pollution that is a grave threat to human health.[37] Yet, while population pressure may play some part in the complex phenomenon of immigration, it is not the principal cause.[38]

Although it is true that the growing populations in the Two-Thirds World stress the ecosystem, most of the planet's problems are caused by the production and consumption patterns of the First World. "The industrialized countries of the Northern Hemisphere are home to one-fifth of the world's population, yet they consume two-thirds of the world's food, three-quarters of its energy and minerals and 85 percent of its wood."[39] The United States alone, with less than 5 percent of the world's population, consumes about 60 percent of the world's natural gas, 40 percent of coal and aluminum, and 30 percent of nickel, copper, and petroleum. The United States accounts for a quarter of global energy consumption and produces a quarter of the world's air pollution.[40] "Numbers per se are not the measure of overpopulation; instead it is the *impact* of people on ecosystems and nonrenewable resources. While developing countries severely tax their environments, clearly the populations of rich countries leave a vastly disproportionate mark on the planet."[41] Thus, it is the affluence and over-consumption of people in developed countries that is the major threat to the earth's ecosystem.

Population growth occurs when the birth rates exceed the death rates in a society. The process of economic development results in a fairly universal pattern known as the "demographic transition." First, death rates fall mostly due to public health measures, such as better sanitation and diet, and immunization against diseases. As a result, the population increases. Later, birth rates fall because people become more educated, more secure, more urbanized, and women's status in society rises. It then becomes reasonable to have fewer children, and population stabilizes. Great Britain went through this demographic transition with the Industrial Revolution. Other developed countries have followed the pattern.[42]

Agrarian people are acculturated to having large families because children are assets: their labor contributes to the family and they provide security in the parents' old age. An infant mortality rate of 50 percent, as is often the case in developing countries, means that half of all children die before age five. Having many children, then, makes sense for the rural poor. To make it more reasonable to have fewer children, economic development is necessary.[43] Thus, economic development seems to be the ordinary way to move through a demographic transition and stabilize population.

Thus we enter into an ecological and economic conundrum: economic growth is necessary (but not sufficient) for economic development, which is, in turn, necessary for stabilizing population growth. But economic growth, at least initially, tends to boost population growth. And, as we have seen, population growth can make economic growth very difficult to accomplish. Furthermore, industrialization (presently an important ingredient in economic growth) depletes resources and damages the environment. Yet economic development seems necessary to stabilize population growth, lest the human population exceed the carrying capacity of earth.

It should be noted that some developing countries have been successful in lowering the rate of population growth through aggressive government programs aimed at doing so.[44] Thailand's population growth was cut from 3.2 percent to 1.6 percent in only 15 years, in part through the efforts of Mechai Viravaidya, a dynamic and creative former government economist who has promoted various methods of contraception. Over 70 percent of couples in Thailand practice family planning.[45] Bangladesh has lowered the fertility rate from 7 to 4.5 through the efforts of family-planning workers. In 1993, 45 percent of couples practiced family planning, while only 6 percent did so in 1974.[46] Zimbabwe has used a similar program to slow the growth of its population "from catastrophic to merely dreadful."[47] China reduced its fertility rate from 6 to 2.5 in a single decade (the 1970s) through what many consider a Draconian policy of "one child per couple." India has had mixed success with a less coercive approach.[48]

Some government family-planning programs, like China's, seek to "override" the family's personal decision, and others try to "collaborate" with the family through education, access to birth control, and even incentives to limit family size. Public policies that expand education, health care, economic security, and access to contraceptives are surely necessary, but a central ethical concern is whether the programs increase or significantly reduce the choices open to parents and especially women.[49] Coercion is morally suspect, even in a legitimate cause.

Religion and culture interact with population policy in complex ways. Included in the mix are cultural understandings of gender roles and of the status of women. The Catholic Church's well-known opposition to artificial methods of birth control is based in a controversial interpretation of natural law philosophy, rather than in a directly pronatalist (supporting birth) position. In practice, however, it results in church opposition to most family-planning programs. Many Catholic theologians, however, have questioned the wisdom of the Catholic Church's position.[50] This critique is based on the desperate need to stabilize population growth and on an alternative interpretation of natural law.

Conservative Muslim clerics often oppose efforts at contraception as well, although the teaching of Mohammed on birth control is ambiguous at best. In Iran, for example, the politically influential Muslim religious leaders now officially approve of birth control. An educational session on birth control is required in Iran in order to get a marriage license, and condoms, pills, and sterilization are free.[51]

Most religious teachings were developed in a time and in a context in which procreation was essential for survival. Past cultural norms were logically pronatalist. Today the situation is quite different. Stabilizing population growth may be necessary for future human flourishing.

Economic development remains the primary way to accomplish the demographic transition, but it is also clear that aggressive government programs that make available a variety of contraceptive methods and provide education and incentives for family planning can lower the population growth rate. In particular, "If there is a single key to population control in developing countries, experts agree, it lies in improving the social status of women."[52] Population control is not a mystery; it is a difficult cultural, economic, and political task. In essence it requires alleviating poverty and raising the standard of living. A gradually declining population is a welcome side effect of efforts to directly improve people's (and especially women's) lives through greater access to health care and improved education.[53]

> **For Reflection**
> An Irish missionary was asked how long he had been in the Philippines. "Longer than most Filipinos," he said, "fifteen years." He was correct. More than 50 percent of the population of many developing countries, including the Philippines, is under the age of fifteen. Developed countries, which have already moved through the demographic transition, face the opposite problem of an aging society. Both situations are ripe for social conflict.

RESOURCE DEPLETION

Nearly everyone agrees that it is essential for humanity to control the growth of population, but Julian Simon, an economist at the University of Maryland, is an exception. Simon, an ecological optimist or "Cornucopian," argues that human ingenuity is the ultimate resource, the key to ecological stability and human well-being. Therefore, population growth is ultimately an asset because human ingenuity will develop the technology to respond to environmental problems, and to create the wealth necessary for economic development. The more humans, the better.[54]

Simon's nemesis has been Paul Erlich, an ecologist at Stanford University who is an eco-pessimist or Malthusian. Erlich argues that population growth is like a bomb that threatens the carrying capacity of spaceship earth by overextending its supplies of food, fresh water, and minerals.[55]

In 1980, Erlich and Simon chose a refreshingly nonacademic way to resolve their differences. They bet $1,000 on the future price of five metals—chrome, copper, nickel, tin, and tungsten. If in 1990 the price had gone up, Simon would pay Erlich the difference. If the price went down, Erlich would pay Simon. During the 1980s the population grew by more than 800 million, the greatest increase in history, and the earth's stock of metals stayed the same.

In the fall of 1990, however, Erlich sent Simon a check for $576.07. Each of the five metals had declined in price when adjusted for inflation. "Prices fell for the same Cornucopian reasons they had fallen in previous decades— entrepreneurship and continuing technological improvements."[56] New lodes were found, greater efficiency in mining and using the metals was implemented, and other materials, such as plastics, replaced metals in industries such as communications. As might be expected, Erlich was neither chastened nor silenced by losing the bet. "Julian Simon is like the guy who jumps off the Empire State Building and says how great things are going so far as he passes the 10th floor," said Erlich.[57] Simon proposed raising the wager on any other resource for any year in the future. Erlich passed.

The lesson of this story is not that ecological prophets such as the Erlichs and Lester Brown (the founder of the Worldwatch Institute and the Earth Policy Institute) can be safely ignored. The one point on which both Simon and Erlich could agree is the value of pointing out problems, of raising issues. Without an awareness of potential problems, human ingenuity cannot work to prevent or solve them. The subtlety of environmental changes and the complexity and uncertainty of scientific evidence can make it difficult to effect changes in people's behavior or to marshal the political will necessary to change social practices.

Energy: The Master Resource

Energy fuels industrialization and economic growth. Energy runs machines; it propels cars, trains, and airplanes; it heats and cools houses and offices, lights lamps, refrigerates and cooks food, and powers computers. Energy is consumed by industry, domestic use, and transportation. It has been called the master resource.[58]

"The commercial fuels that power the world's industrial economies are *oil* (39 percent of world energy consumption), *coal* (32 percent), *natural gas* (24 percent), and *hydroelectric and nuclear power* (5 percent). The fossil fuels (coal, oil, gas) thus account for 95 percent of world energy consumption."[59] As we shall see below, this reliance on fossil fuels is largely responsible for potentially catastrophic climate change. Overuse is also rapidly depleting these nonrenewable sources of energy. In one year humankind consumes an amount of fossil fuel that it took nature a million years to produce.[60] In 1993 global energy production was 40 percent higher than in 1973, but global energy consumption was 49 percent greater.[61] It has been projected that world energy consumption will rise over 50 percent within the next 20 years.[62] "If energy consumption were to remain constant at current levels, proved reserves would supply world petroleum needs for 40 years, natural gas needs for 60 years, and coal needs for well over 200 years."[63] Sometime in the future it seems quite probable that the generations of the twentieth and twenty-first centuries will be remembered as "the oil age," that time in human history when oil was discovered, developed, and depleted.[64]

The developed countries, with 15 percent of the global population, consume 50 percent of the energy.[65] On average North Americans consume the energy equivalent of 11 metric tons (24,200 pounds) of coal per person per year. In comparison, Western Europeans and Japanese consume 5 tons per capita, mostly because of greater efficiency. Latin Americans consume 1.4 tons per person, South Asians .4 of a ton, and Africans .3 of a ton because they are less industrialized.[66] (See Figure 3.2.) While the urban American is distinguished from the Asian peasant by vastly different levels of industrialization and domestic consumer goods, it is the amount and mode of movement—transportation—that make the most difference in energy consumption. The 500 million automobiles on the planet burn an average of 2 gallons of fuel a day. One-third of the world's oil consumption goes for this purpose. The United States also consumes twice as much oil per person as does Western Europe.[67] Much of the growth in energy consumption in the future, however, will take place in developing countries as they industrialize.

Although developed countries consume more than half of all commercial energy, they produce only slightly more than a third of it. Thus, most industrialized countries, including the United States, and especially Japan, depend on imported oil for the smooth functioning of their economies. The United States is dependent on imports for well over 40 percent of the oil it uses. Over 60 percent of the known reserves of petroleum are found in the politically volatile Middle East.[68]

Despite two oil crises in 1973 and 1979, the Gulf War in 1991, and increasing scientific evidence of global warming, the United States still has no coherent national energy policy.[69] On the contrary, there was a proposal in the summer of 1996 to reduce the national tax on gasoline by 4 cents. At that time, Americans were paying about $1.40 a gallon for gas, and national and state taxes accounted for only about 27 percent of the cost. European

Figure 3.2
Annual Energy Consumption per Capita

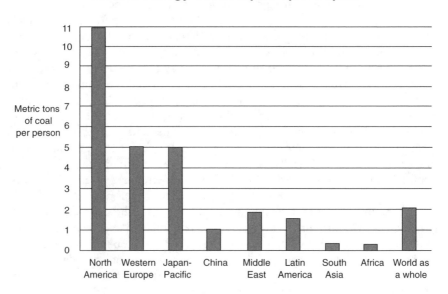

Figure 3.3
Price at the Pump

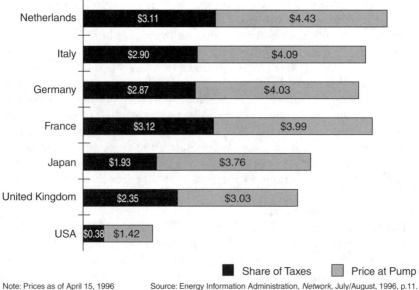

Note: Prices as of April 15, 1996   Source: Energy Information Administration, *Network,* July/August, 1996, p.11.

and Japanese drivers were paying about $4.00 a gallon, and in Europe taxes account for 74 percent of the price on average, and in Japan 51 percent.[70] (See Figure 3.3.) With gasoline in the United States cheaper than it was in the 1950s (after adjusting for inflation), Americans are embracing gas-guzzling vans, pickup trucks and sports utility vehicles (SUVs) with a vengeance. Nearly half of the vehicles sold in the United States are in the small truck/SUV category.[71] The Bush administration's National Energy Plan proposed in early September 2001 disparaged energy conservation and emphasized finding new supplies of fossil fuels. It suggested drilling for oil in Alaska's pristine Arctic National Wildlife Refuge.

Any rational energy policy in the United States would raise the tax on gas significantly, mandate higher fuel efficiency, and support the use of alternative sources of energy and alternative modes of transportation, such as mass transit and bicycles.[72] The goal would be to reduce dependence on oil imports, the consumption of a nonrenewable resource, and the pollution of earth's atmosphere.

Fossil fuels are not the only nonrenewable resources. The bet on planet earth between Simon and Erlich should caution against predicting the depletion of energy resources and other minerals. "Still, there are limits. A 1985 U.S. government study projected that with the 1985 rates of usage and even assuming *five times* the amount of known reserves, there were only 53 years of tin reserves, 72 years for lead, and 149 years for iron ore."[73] Technology and human ingenuity may well respond satisfactorily to the depletion of mineral resources, yet this generation should reflect on its moral responsibility for what may be a sin of gluttony.

Forests and Biodiversity

"An important paradox to bear in mind when examining natural resource trends is that so-called nonrenewable resources—such as coal, oil, and minerals—are in fact inexhaustible, while so-called renewable resources can be finite."[74] Scarcity of nonrenewable resources will generally increase prices and stimulate the development of alternative resources so that they will not be totally depleted. Trees, however, can sometimes be cut so quickly and extensively that a desert is formed, and the forest cannot be replenished. Forests, fresh water, and arable land are crucial resources at risk. What is happening all over the planet is the destruction of whole ecosystems.

The Amazon rainforest in Brazil has been called "the lungs of the earth." Since the 1970s, an estimated 20 percent of this tropical forest has been wiped out.[75] "Already the [tropical] forest has been reduced to approximately 55 percent of its original cover . . . , and it is being further reduced at a rate in excess of 100,000 square kilometers a year. This amount is 1 percent of the total cover, or more than the area of Switzerland and the Netherlands combined."[76] The tropical deforestation rates were highest in Asia. While forest area has increased slightly (less than 3 percent) in developed countries in the period from 1980 to 1995, it decreased by 10 percent in developing countries.[77]

The deforestation of tropical forests, that is, the attempted conversion of the forest to cropland or fields for grazing herds, makes no sense because it creates a desert. The emerald beauty of a rainforest is only skin deep. The luxuriant vegetation and canopy of 200-feet-tall trees is supported by the constant decay of its moist ground surface. When the vegetation and trees are cleared, the soil stops being replenished and quickly becomes barren. After only six or seven years it is worthless for agriculture or grazing.[78] Thus, such deforestation is the worst of both worlds: it is economically shortsighted and ecologically devastating. Clear-cut logging, while yielding a one-time profit, has a similar devastating environmental effect. The ancient temperate forest in the American northwest is being stripped and shipped to Japan.[79]

Forests are ecologically valuable as regulators of global climate, as conservators of soil and water resources, and as repositories of species and potentially valuable new products.[80] Trees and plants (and the oceans) absorb carbon (about 3 billion tons a year) and produce oxygen. Forests absorb fresh water and prevent soil erosion and flooding. But perhaps the greatest ecological tragedy of deforestation is the *loss of biodiversity* or the depletion of species of insects, plants, and animals.

Most people are now familiar with the notion of endangered species. The danger, of course, comes from humankind, sometimes through direct killing, as with buffalo and whales, but more often indirectly through the alteration or destruction of habitats, as with the spotted owl in the northwest or the timber rattlesnake in Connecticut. A few concerted efforts have managed to reverse the pattern of destruction, as in the case of the American eagle and some species of whale. When humans destroy huge swathes of tropical forest, we are terminating thousands of species whose existence will never be known to us.

"Tropical forests cover only 7% of the earth's surface, but they house between 50% and 80% of the planet's species."[81] There is a prodigious variety of species, and especially of insects. Harvard biologist E.O. Wilson tells of finding on one tree in Peru as many species of ants as exist in the whole of the British Isles.[82] No one knows how many species there are on earth. Estimates range from 4 million to 111 million, with 14 million an often cited number, of which only about 1.7 million species have been identified.[83] Species naturally evolve and sometimes disappear. Human activity, however, in polluting lakes and rivers, in consuming land through urban sprawl, and especially in cutting and clearing tropical forests, is extinguishing species at a rate thousands of times faster than the natural pace of evolution.[84] In doing this we are vastly diminishing the genetic heritage of earth, and we are hurting the interests of humanity itself. "Some 25% of the pharmaceuticals in use in the U.S. today contain ingredients originally derived from wild plants."[85] Who knows what miracle cures are going up in smoke today? Both economically and ecologically it would make much more sense to harvest carefully the genetic and biological fruits of the forest, rather than to cut it down.[86]

Fresh Water and Ocean Fisheries

Water, water, everywhere, and not a drop to drink![87] The lament of Coleridge's Ancient Mariner, stranded on a listless sea, is becoming a description of the human predicament today. Less than 1 percent of the water on earth is fresh water that is usable for consumption, agriculture, and industry.[88] "Worldwide, agriculture uses about 65 percent of all the water removed from rivers, lakes, and aquifers for human activities, compared with 25 percent for industries and 10 percent for households and municipalities. It takes about 1,000 tons of water to produce a ton of harvested grain."[89] To produce a pound of beef requires between 2,500 and 6,000 gallons of water. The manufacture of one automobile takes 100,000 gallons of water. "Water usage grows faster than population. It is estimated that water usage triples as population doubles."[90] The typical American consumes more than 70 times as much water every year as does the average Ghanaian.[91]

Water pollution (caused by domestic sewage, industrial waste, chemical run-off from agriculture and mining, and soil erosion), and increased use (due to irrigation, industrialization, and population growth) have resulted in a scarcity of fresh water in some regions. Aquifers in regions such as the Western United States, the Arabian Peninsula, Northern Africa, and Southeast Asia are being irreparably drained by the overuse of groundwater at rates faster than rains can replenish them. The Ganges River in India, the Colorado River in the United States, and the Jordan River in the Middle East often run dry before they reach the sea. The Aral Sea (between Kazakhstan and Uzbekistan), once the world's fourth largest lake, has lost half its area and three-fourths of its volume because of river diversions to grow cotton in the desert.[92]

Fresh water scarcity threatens three fundamental aspects of human and ecological security: food production, the health of the aquatic environment and those who consume the water, and social and political stability.[93]

Since agriculture uses two-thirds of fresh water supplies, it is not clear where more water will come from for irrigation in regions where aquifers have collapsed from overuse, or where rivers and lakes have been drained. And without water, crops will not grow. There are 80 countries that suffer water shortages.[94]

The health of river and lake ecosystems is a delicate balance. Human, industrial, and agricultural waste and pollution can damage these aquatic ecosystems and the life that teems within them. Ultimately, this reduces the recreational and utilitarian value of rivers and lakes for humans. Aquifers, which provide groundwater, can also be polluted, catching contaminants like a sink. Some of the water in today's aquifers dates back to the last ice age! Obviously the water in many aquifers is not flushed or changed very often, and thus pollution damage is often irreversible.[95] Fortunately, damaged aquatic ecosystems (lakes and rivers), unlike aquifers, can sometimes be restored to life.

In his ecological classic, *The Closing Circle,* Barry Commoner tells the story of the demise of Lake Erie, a 12,000-year-old natural wonder so polluted since the beginning of the twentieth century that it actually burst into flame at one point.[96] In 1971 when Commoner wrote, Lake Erie's beaches had been closed; each summer huge mounds of decaying fish and algae rotted on its shores; and the once sparkling water was dense with muck. The few fish to be caught were inedible. Happily, in the last 30 years, a concerted effort to clean up Lake Erie has been at least partially successful: beaches have been reopened, and healthy fish are returning.

The remarkable transformation of the Hudson River is a similar story. "Only 30 years ago, this magnificent river was little more than a 350-mile sewer stretching from the Adirondacks to Manhattan's Battery, choked with untreated human wastes, industrial chemicals, and agricultural runoff. Today the Hudson pulses with life."[97] The restoration of the Hudson is neither complete nor certain, but it is a resounding success story for energetic citizen action and careful government regulation.

Ecosystems can also be vulnerable to the introduction of foreign life forms or invasive species that then wreak havoc. Somehow, for example, the water hyacinth from the Amazon region in South America found its way to Lake Victoria in Africa. With no natural enemy around, the weed has thrived in the warm, nutrient-rich waters of the lake, blocking ports, clogging hydroelectric pipes, choking engines, jamming propellers, and sucking oxygen out of the water.[98] Similar stories could be told about kudzu in the American South or zebra mussels in Lake Michigan.[99]

Safe drinking water and adequate sanitation (in which water is too often key) are, of course, significant for human health. In 2000, even though more than 750 million people gained access to safer water and improved sanitation in the 1990s, nearly one in six (1.1 billion) lacked access to safe drinking water and over one in three (2.4 billion) had unsatisfactory sanitation. The devastating result is disease, which causes disability (such as blindness) or death—especially for children.[100]

Water is often under-priced or subsidized by the government, thus undermining the incentive to conserve it.[101] The concept of a "water stress index," measured as the annual renewable water resources per capita available to meet the needs of agriculture, industry, and domestic use, might be a way of highlighting vulnerable regions. A benchmark of 1,000 cubic meters per capita per year would seem to indicate places where chronic water shortage can be expected. Several countries, in the Middle East and North Africa in particular, fall well below this benchmark.[102] Since agriculture uses so much water, better irrigation efficiency can be a modest step in preserving the supply of fresh water, already a scarce resource in many regions on earth.[103]

Finally, the scarcity of fresh water can cause conflict within and between countries. States in the American West, for example, argue over who should have access to scarce water in aquifers and rivers and for what purpose. Egypt is utterly dependent on the Nile River, but the sources of the Nile are in Sudan and Ethiopia. Ethiopia now has the political stability to plan to use the water for irrigation and hydropower production. Egypt is clearly prepared to go to war if Ethiopia diverts Nile waters. Syria and Iraq are in a similar situation with regard to Turkey, which contains the source of both the Tigris and the Euphrates Rivers. Turkey is also planning a huge hydropower and irrigation scheme that will reduce the flow of the rivers and pollute them as well. Israel is angrily protesting an irrigation project in Lebanon that will divert water from a source of the Jordan River.[104]

There are clear signs that *ocean fisheries* are in trouble. Salt water oceans and seas cover 70 percent of the earth's surface and provide 8 out of every 10 fish caught. Fish provide 16 percent of the animal protein and 6 percent of all protein consumed by humans and are especially important in the diet of people in many developing countries. "Global marine fish and shellfish production has increased sixfold from 17 million tons in 1950 to 105 million metric tons in 1997. This rapid growth—particularly in the last 20 years—has come partly from growth in aquaculture, which now accounts for more than one-fifth of the total harvest (marine and inland)."[105] The marine fish harvest actually peaked in 1989, but the decline has been made up for by aquaculture. "In fish farming, it takes about 2 kilograms of grain to produce 1 kilogram of fish."[106] Such costly inefficiency means that it is unlikely that aquaculture will be able to replace significant declines in ocean fisheries.

Overfishing is a clear example of an unsustainable ecological practice. If year after year so many fish are taken that those remaining cannot replenish the stock, before long the fish will become depleted, or even extinct. In 1999, more than a quarter of all fish stocks were already depleted or in imminent danger of depletion. Almost half of all fish stocks were vulnerable to depletion.[107] In the North Sea, the stock of cod, a staple fish eaten in almost every country in the world, was half of that considered a minimum for assured propagation.[108] Worldwide, the fishing industry has at least 30 percent more harvesting capacity than fish stocks can support. Thus, it makes little sense for governments to continue to subsidize high-tech marine fishing fleets, which often displace local subsistence fishing boats and damage the marine environment with their trawling nets.[109] Politically, however, this pits ecology against economy, fish stocks against jobs and fishing villages. Of course once the fish are gone, there will be no more jobs and no more fish dinners.

Oceans are clearly part of the global commons, and thus there is the temptation for some to take more than is fair from the sea's bounty. One response is to enclose the commons by deciding who has jurisdiction. Negotiations sponsored by the United Nations Conference on the Law of the Sea (UNCLOS) from 1973 to 1982 resulted in a treaty that expanded the territorial waters of nations to 12 miles for shipping and 200 miles for economic activities such as fishing and mining. The treaty also affirmed the principle that the oceans are the common heritage of humankind by establishing international rules for the use of territorial waters and for sharing the wealth extracted from the ocean floor beyond 200 miles. The United States blocked the ratification of the treaty for over a decade, finally signing it in 1994.[110] It remains to be seen whether nations will practice the restraint necessary to allow fish and seafood stocks to renew themselves and to refrain from polluting or plundering the oceans.

Land and Food Security

The essence of the trap that Malthus predicted (see chapter 1) was that population would outstrip food production, resulting in massive famine. One out of every five people on earth is hungry and chronically malnourished, and another 20 percent is undernourished. Thus far, however, hunger seems to be caused by poverty and the maldistribution of resources, not by scarcity. Now, as in the time of Malthus, food production has increased even faster than population. There are some signs that this trend may be reversing, and we can only speculate as to the number of people that our finite planet can feed.[111]

Food production is another area where optimists and pessimists come to different conclusions. The Food and Agriculture Organization of the United Nations (FAO) and the World Bank predict that food production will be able to keep pace with population growth in the near future. Lester Brown, founder of the Worldwatch Institute and of the Earth Policy Institute, organizations that research and report on the ecological conditions of the earth, is critical of these projections and has called food scarcity the defining issue of the next decade.[112]

Everyone agrees that the rate of growth in annual food production is slowing. We have seen that growth in the world fish catch has apparently ended.[113] Growth in world agricultural production has slowed, dropping from 3 percent annually in the 1960s, to 2.3 percent per year in the 1970s, to 2 percent during the 1980s, and to 1.2 percent in the 1990s.[114] Thus global food production is now barely keeping pace with population growth. Whether this is the beginning of an ominous long-term trend in which population grows faster than food production is the question.[115]

The major reason for the growth in agricultural production is the "green revolution," that is, the development of high-yielding, high-input seeds. These modern varieties of rice, wheat, and corn yield many times the produce of traditional varieties, but they also require the intensive use of fertilizers, water, and pesticides.[116] High-input agriculture has both ecological and economic costs. Since fertilizers are often petroleum-based, developing countries using modern varieties of grains were hard hit by steep increases in oil prices of the 1970s. This sort of farming tends to wear out the soil, and we have already seen that water scarcity is an increasing problem in many regions of the world. Pesticide and fertilizer application and runoff have negative consequences for human health and aquatic ecosystems.

Raising the productivity of existing cropland is the key to having enough food for the 80 million people added to the human family each year and to feeding the 40 percent of the global population that is hungry.[117] Because humanity is facing limits with regard to land, water, and technology, increasing agricultural productivity is a serious challenge.

There is little arable land that can be added to productive use, and top-soil is being eroded and degraded in many places, making desertification a real problem.[118] Water scarcity has already been identified as a global problem, but greater efficiency in irrigation may be a partial solution. Since about 1985 grain yields have plateaued, raising the question of whether technology has reached its limits. After two decades of research, biotechnology has yet to produce a single variety of grain that dramatically increases yields.[119] Genetically modified food might offer the promise of drought-resistant crops, of greater pest resistance, and of added nutritional value, but GM crops also bring the risks of negative environmental or health effects.[120] Advances in biotechnology may also increase rural unemployment, inadvertently increasing the poverty that is the basic cause of hunger. Technology may not offer a panacea for food security.[121]

Food security demonstrates the interconnectedness of environmental issues. Pollution of water and erosion of the land diminish agricultural productivity. Climate change affects the weather, which has a direct effect on farming. And there is surely a limit on the number of people this finite planet can feed.[122] Thus far, hunger has been more an issue of access (poverty) than of scarcity itself. We may be approaching an age where hunger is a matter of both poverty and scarcity.

ATMOSPHERIC POLLUTION

Ozone Depletion

When chlorofluorocarbons (CFCs) were first synthesized in the 1920s, they seemed too good to be true. They were nontoxic and inert, cheap and simple to manufacture, and useful as coolants, propellant gases in spray cans, and in the production of plastic foam materials such as Styrofoam.[123] They were thoroughly tested and found to be benign, but their effect on the atmosphere and the remote stratosphere was never considered. In the atmosphere each CFC molecule is 20,000 times as efficient at trapping heat as is a molecule of carbon dioxide, thus contributing to the greenhouse effect and global warming. In the stratosphere the long-lived CFCs destroy ozone molecules. The ozone layer, between 10 and 30 miles up, prevents harmful solar ultraviolet radiation from reaching the earth. Ultraviolet radiation is very dangerous to life on earth. It causes skin cancer in humans and blindness in animals, kills vegetation, lowers agricultural yields, and disrupts ecosystems.[124]

Scientists in the 1970s discovered the potential for CFCs to destroy ozone and warned of the danger to the ozone layer. Then in 1985 researchers documented the existence of a huge hole in the ozone layer over Antarctica.[125] This set in motion a series of diplomatic conferences that resulted in the signing of the Montreal Protocol in 1987 to reduce the production of CFCs. In 1990, in London, 93 countries agreed to end production of ozone damaging chemicals by the year 2000. A follow-up meeting in 1992 in Copenhagen moved the date up to 1996. Thus, developed countries have now ceased production of CFCs and have set up a fund to enable developing countries to stop production within a decade.[126] This very constructive and cooperative response by the nations of the world is a model of environmental responsibility. The clarity of the danger and the development of effective and inexpensive substitutes for CFCs were important factors in accomplishing this remarkable ecological victory.[127] Scientists speculate that the stratosphere will repair the protective ozone layer gradually.

Global Warming

Air pollution has the quite apparent effect of creating smog, which burns the eyes, causes difficulty in breathing, harms health, sullies and erodes buildings and monuments, and damages trees and plants. But a less visible effect of air pollution is the concentration of certain gases in the atmosphere, creating one of the most serious issues facing humanity in the twenty-first century—a catastrophic change in the earth's climate.

Destruction of the stratospheric ozone layer lets harmful ultraviolet rays in; the buildup of specific gases in the atmosphere does not allow heat to get out; the atmosphere then functions like a greenhouse and warms the temperature of the earth. The primary greenhouse gases are CFCs, carbon dioxide, methane or natural gas, and nitrogen oxides. Since CFCs account for an estimated 15 percent of the greenhouse effect, it is good news that the world has stopped producing them. Methane is produced by a number of sources, including bacteria living in the stomachs of cattle and termites, the muck of rice paddies, and the rotting garbage of landfills. Although burning methane produces carbon dioxide, methane traps 20 times as much heat as carbon dioxide. Thus, burning methane produced by landfills would reduce the greenhouse effect.[128]

Carbon dioxide is released from the burning of wood and the fossil fuels—coal, oil, and natural gas.[129] "Fossil fuel burning is now releasing about 6 billion tons of carbon into the air each year, adding 3 billion tons annually to the 170 billion tons that have accumulated since the Industrial Revolution."[130] By the late 1800s atmospheric carbon dioxide had risen to about 285 parts per million volume (ppmv). Now it is over 350 ppmv, and it is projected to range from 540 to 970 ppmv by 2100.[131] Better exhaust technology has significantly reduced the amounts of lead, nitrous oxide, and carbon monoxide emitted by automobiles, but there is no filter that can reduce carbon dioxide emissions. A well-tuned car releases five-and-a-half pounds of carbon in the form of carbon dioxide for every gallon of gas it burns.[132]

Economic growth generally requires more energy, most of which at present comes from burning fossil fuels. "Global carbon emissions from fossil fuel combustion rose by 9.1 percent between 1990 and 2000. Cumulative global carbon emissions between 1990 and 2000, slightly over 68 billion tons, reflects a 15 percent increase over the 59 billion tons emitted worldwide between 1980 and 1990."[133] The United States accounted for 24 percent of total carbon emissions in 2000, up from 22 percent in 1990. Between 1990 and 2000, the United States increased its carbon output by 18.1 percent. In gross amounts the United States emits nearly twice as much carbon dioxide as China, the world's number two emitter. The United States also has the highest per capita emissions of carbon—about 5 tons per year—compared with the world average of 1.1, and with China's 0.68. While the United States continues to increase its emissions of carbon, China, Russia, and the countries of the European Union are all decreasing their emissions.[134] As developing countries industrialize, their share of air pollution is projected to increase from one-third in 1995 to one-half in 2010.[135] Imagine China or India with the same number of cars per capita as the United States!

The projected result of the accumulation of greenhouse gases in the atmosphere will be to raise the average world temperature by between 1.5 and 4.5 degrees Celsius (between 2.7 and 8.1 degrees Fahrenheit) over the next 50 years.[136] Any scientific ambiguity about global warming is being overcome by mounting evidence that it is taking place. The average annual temperature of the earth increased by 0.6 degree Celsius (about 1 degree Fahrenheit) in the twentieth century; the 1990s were the warmest decade and 1998 the hottest year since records began being kept in the 1860s.[137] Events such as the melting of a large chunk of Antarctica, the warming of Siberia, warmer winters in northern Europe, and heat waves in India are disconcerting signs. In August 2000, the North Pole melted, a phenomenon that probably has not occurred for 50 million years and thus has never been seen before by humans.[138] In 2002, Europe experienced devastating spring floods and killer windstorms in the fall, and in the United States a November storm system spawned 70 tornadoes from Tennessee to Pennsylvania. There is no doubt that greenhouse gases are accumulating in the atmosphere, and there is now little doubt that the earth is already experiencing the consequences.[139]

The effects of global warming include coastal inundation and flooding from rising sea levels, disruption of rainfall and therefore water use patterns, agricultural effects due to heat stress (drought), the spread of disease,[140] and ecosystem damage, such as the destruction of coral reefs by warmer water with the consequent loss of biodiversity.[141] There will probably be winners and losers from the disruption of weather patterns. Some deserts might bloom from greater rainfall, and in other places farmland might turn to desert. Nearly 50 percent of the world's population lives in coastal regions. Rising sea levels could have a catastrophic effect on the lives of these people and even eliminate some island nations, such as the Maldives (off the southern coast of India). Bangladesh and Egypt, for example, would be severely affected, as would the United States with its long, heavily populated coastlines. Developed countries could afford to adapt to changes more readily than poor countries.[142]

Carbon emissions are tied to energy use, and energy is necessary for economic growth. Thus, curbing air pollution will be neither simple nor cheap because of the conflict between the need for economic development and the need for environmental responsibility.[143] Pollution controls can make production more expensive. Developed countries, the major source of the problem today, often seem to hold developing countries to a higher standard when urging them not to harm the environment as they industrialize.

An important element in any strategy to reduce carbon emissions would be the efficient use of energy. One way to measure the energy efficiency of a nation is the amount of carbon emitted per million dollars of economic output. According to this standard some of the republics of the former Soviet Union have the worst records, including Kazakhstan, Ukraine, and Russia, although all of these countries report decreasing emissions because of slowing economies. Japan is nearly twice as efficient as the United States. Canada, the United States, and Australia—with their patterns of low energy prices, large houses, and heavy use of cars to travel greater distances—all show more rapid increase in emissions and lower energy efficiency than the countries of Western Europe or Japan.[144]

The Intergovernmental Panel on Climate Change (IPCC), a group of more than 1,500 scientists assembled from 60 nations by the United Nations, has recommended an immediate 60 percent reduction in fossil fuel use to prevent global warming. Achieving this goal would require more than energy efficiency; it would require a change in the lifestyle of those who live in the rich countries. It would mean fewer cars, more fuel-efficient cars, and more bicycles, smaller and better insulated houses and buildings, an intense effort (comparable to the one that put a human on the moon) to develop alternative energy sources such as solar and wind power, higher prices for energy and a tax on carbon emissions, and expanded research on and monitoring of the climate.[145] "Addicted to growth, busily spreading our vision of the good life around the globe, we are sprinting in the opposite direction."[146]

"The challenge of reducing carbon emissions is not so much technical or even economic as it is political, led by strong opposition of industries deeply vested in the fossil fuel economy."[147] The energy and automobile industries, for example, include many of the largest multi-national corporations in the world. Their tremendous wealth and profit are tied to fossil fuels. They tend to resist the development of renewable sources of energy such as the sun and wind, as well as the imposition of taxes on carbon emissions.

At international climate conferences, the United States, with its profligate use of energy, has resisted setting international limits on carbon emissions.[148] Although the United States was a party to the United Nations Framework Convention on Climate Change (UN FCCC) signed at the 1992 Earth Summit in Rio de Janeiro, it withdrew in March 2001 from the 1997 Kyoto Protocol, which was designed to strengthen global commitment to reduce carbon emissions.[149] President Bush decided not to attend the World Summit on Sustainable Development in Johannesburg in September 2002, instead sending Secretary of State Colin Powell to head the American delegation. The United States has argued that the carbon emission goals in the Kyoto Protocol would damage the American economy, and that it is unfair to exempt developing countries from binding limits on emissions. The Kyoto Protocol, which commits industrial nations to reduce their carbon emissions to 5.2 percent below 1990 levels during 2008–2012, is certainly not perfect.

Indeed, it may represent a halfhearted response to a cataclysmic problem, but it is a first step—one that the United States, the world's worst emitter, is unwilling to take. Thus, at the eighth conference of the parties to the UN FCCC, held in New Delhi in October 2002, the focus shifted to adapting to climate change rather than preventing it.[150]

While stopping the production of CFCs is a positive step, significantly reducing carbon emissions and other greenhouse gases is more complex and much more costly. Preventing global warming touches us where we live, work, and drive.[151] Nevertheless, it seems that industries, governments, and citizens need to confront "an inescapable fact: economies cannot remain forever healthy in an unhealthy environment."[152] Floods, fires, drought, and disease are also costly. Humanity will either pay the cost now of preventing climate change or pay the cost of the catastrophes that come.

Nuclear Power

Another controversial ethical issue related to global warming and energy development is nuclear power. Nuclear energy does not emit any greenhouse gases, and does not contribute to global warming. Thus, it could be an alternative energy source to fossil fuels. Nuclear energy, however, is saddled with another set of environmental and health problems. The two major concerns are safety and waste disposal.

The uncontained meltdown at Chernobyl in Ukraine in 1986 and the accident at Three Mile Island in Pennsylvania in 1979 demonstrate the safety issues from the operation of nuclear power plants. The release of radiation is very damaging to human health and to the environment. High doses of radiation can cause death, and lower doses can result in cancer and genetic defects.

One of the by-products of the nuclear fission of enriched uranium is plutonium, an extremely carcinogenic substance. Even a millionth of a gram of plutonium ingested into the lungs can cause lung cancer in 15 to 30 years. Nuclear power plants produce 400 to 500 pounds of plutonium and other highly radioactive wastes a year. Plutonium has a half-life of 24,400 years, which means it lasts virtually forever.[153] Although in 1982 Congress mandated the construction of a permanent storage site for high-level radioactive wastes by 1998, no state wants such a site in its backyard and in 2002 no facility had been approved to store the 30,000 tons of spent fuel already in existence in the United States alone.[154] The safe storage of such toxic and corrosive substances for tens of thousands of years may be an impossible assignment for fallible human beings in an ecosystem in flux. To make matters worse, plutonium can also be used in nuclear weapons. Storing plutonium clearly raises some serious issues of security and safety.

Since there is no place to store these highly radioactive wastes, they are being "temporarily" housed in cooling tanks adjacent to nuclear power plants. These spent fuel tanks, like the reactor core, pose a threat of a meltdown. A courageous engineer blew the whistle on both Northeast Utilities of Connecticut and on the Nuclear Regulatory Commission (NRC), which is mandated to protect public safety, because of unsafe practices in the storage of spent fuel rods. Northeast Utilities was forced to shut down its nuclear plants until essential repairs were made, costing the company hundreds of millions of dollars. This problem seems systemic to the industry, rather than specific to Connecticut.[155]

Although nuclear power accounts for 20 percent of the electricity consumed in the United States (and more in countries such as France and Japan), it costs twice as much as fossil fuel generated electricity. Recent experience suggests that decommissioning a nuclear power plant, which has a working life of perhaps 50 years, costs twice as much as it did to build the plant.[156] It is for economic reasons, then, that no new plants have been ordered in the United States since 1978.[157]

Waste Disposal

Highly radioactive wastes are so toxic and dangerous that they pose extremely difficult and thus far unresolved disposal problems. The disposal of other toxic chemicals is similarly costly and difficult, and the disposal of more ordinary refuse is complex and controversial.

In September of 1986 the freighter *Pelicano* was loaded with 14,000 tons of toxic ash from Philadelphia's trash incinerator. The intended recipient refused to take the toxic ash, and the ship spent over two years traveling the world seeking a country that would accept its cargo. Finally, with the ash mislabeled as fertilizer, 4,000 tons of it was dumped on a beach in Haiti. Eventually the rest was illegally spilled into the Indian Ocean. The long voyage of the *Pelicano* is a symbol of the difficulty of disposing of toxic wastes and of the potential environmental exploitation of poor countries by the rich.[158]

The 1980 Superfund Act authorized and funded the Environmental Protection Agency (EPA) to locate toxic waste sites and to force the responsible parties to clean them up. While over 27,000 sites have been identified, with 2,500 requiring immediate action, only a few hundred have received attention.[159]

There are several problems with cleaning up toxic waste, which is both expensive and dangerous. There are precious few effective methods of disposal and each has its own environmental and economic drawbacks.[160] Burning toxic waste, for example, can pollute the air and result in toxic ash that itself requires a dump site. Which chemicals are toxic and how dangerous they are (for example, how carcinogenic) is often not known. Clearly, it is a good idea to reduce the production of toxic chemicals, even if that might add to the cost of products. Industries should be required to properly dispose of toxic wastes and should surely contribute to cleaning up past messes. International agreements now prohibit dumping toxic and nuclear wastes at sea, and global norms now constrain the export of toxic wastes, a practice perceived as exploitative of developing countries.[161]

Garbage is another problem. The consumer society in the United States is a throw-away society. It is estimated that the average American produces over four pounds of garbage a day or 1,600 pounds a year. Each year Americans discard 16 billion disposable diapers and 220 million tires. All together, we produce 430 billion pounds of refuse a year.[162]

In the late 1980s, many regions of the United States faced a landfill crisis. In only a decade, 70 percent of the approximately 14,000 solid-waste landfills in the United States had closed, many others were nearing their capacity, and few were being opened. It was projected that a handful of states—Connecticut, Florida, Massachusetts, New Hampshire, and New Jersey—would close virtually all active landfills within a decade.[163]

Because landfill space became scarce, the price rose, which encouraged companies to construct more landfills. Today landfills are scarce in just a few places, notably in the Northeast and near some cities, where land is expensive. There still is ample opportunity for northern cities to ship their garbage to landfills in the South and Midwest. This arrangement, which might grate at first (take care of your own garbage!), can be beneficial to all concerned. Cities get rid of their refuse, and rural areas and distant regions benefit by the creation of jobs and the expansion of their tax base. Moreover, federal regulations require that new landfills be lined with clay and plastic, equipped with drainage and gas-collection pipes, covered daily, and regularly monitored. Modern landfills are much safer than their older, leaky, smelly predecessors.[164] Incinerators and hazardous-waste facilities, however, can be much more perilous for human health and the environment, and they are found too often in poor neighborhoods or areas.[165]

In the midst of the landfill crisis many places latched onto the idea of recycling as a response to the possibility of drowning in their own garbage. In 1988, the United States recycled about 10 percent of its waste. The Environmental Protection Agency (EPA) suggested that a five-year goal of 25 percent was reasonable, and some state and municipal legislatures enacted laws mandating recycling and setting even higher goals. Today the national rate is 25 percent, but it has been a costly achievement, since recycling programs routinely lose money.[166]

In the summer of 1996, New York City debated the benefits and costs of recycling. A 1989 municipal law mandated that the city recycle 25 percent of its garbage by 1994. Since the city was only recycling 14 percent of its 13,000 tons of daily residential refuse, environmentalists went to court to force the city to do better. Mayor Rudolph Giuliani argued that recycling may be more of an expensive nuisance than it is worth, and that the city budget could not afford the extra costs associated with increased recycling.[167]

Collecting recyclables in New York costs three times more per ton than collecting ordinary refuse. Because recyclable refuse cannot be compacted, collection takes more time and space. Because the processing costs of most recyclable material exceed the resale value, the city also has to pay between $10 and $40 a ton to vendors for recycling the refuse. This is, however, less than the $42 it costs to dump a ton of garbage in a landfill, and that cost is likely to go up considerably when the city has to transport its waste to more distant landfills. Thus, while recycling costs more at the moment, in the long term its costs are likely to compare favorably with dumping garbage in landfills. Recycling also employs people in productive work.[168]

Waste disposal may be one of those problems ripe for a market solution. Putting a price on garbage and making the consumer pay for it could go a long way toward resolving local problems of solid waste disposal. Some cities have tried this approach to good effect. When the cost of garbage disposal is clear rather than hidden in city taxes, people are less apt to take garbage removal for granted. They throw away less, remove their names from junk mail lists, shop differently, start a compost pile, and recycle.[169]

In the long run, however, nature itself, where there is no waste, should become the model for humanity. We must become conscious of producing less waste (in the way we package consumer goods, for example), of creating products that can be recycled (for example, sneakers with biodegradable soles), and of recycling the materials produced. For example, eco-industrial parks already exist where one company's waste becomes another's resource, where the sulfur dioxide scrubbed from a power plant's smokestacks becomes a raw material for a wallboard company.[170] This approach is not only good for the environment, but generally reduces costs and improves efficiency. It requires, however, not only technological innovation and creativity, but a new attitude, a new way of thinking.

ENVIRONMENT, CONFLICT, AND SECURITY

There is a complex connection between resources and environmental degradation on the one hand and conflict and war on the other. Competition over vital resources or scarce resources can cause or contribute to conflict. A wealth of resources, such as minerals, oil, or timber, can not only result in war, but also fuel a war. Environmental degradation often has dramatic social consequences, which can also contribute to conflict. And war is not green. War and preparations for war harm the environment.

Throughout history nations have gone to war over vital resources. The Gulf War (1991), for example, was fought, in large part, to insure the access of developed nations to Middle East oil. World security analyst Michael Klare suggests that the Cold War focus on containment momentarily suppressed this interest in resources, but it is now back and climbing the international security list of priorities. A strong and vibrant U.S. economy that is competitively engaged with the global economy is recognized as a top national security interest. Resources, especially oil, are key both to the global economy and to the U.S. economy. In this "econo-centric approach" to foreign policy, the U.S. military plays an important role by protecting supplies of vital resources. Thus the United States has engaged in joint military training exercises with Kazakhstan and Uzbekistan in the Caspian Sea region, which is now thought to have the second largest reserves of oil in the world after the Persian Gulf.[171] "Given the growing importance ascribed to economic vigor in the security policy of states, the rising worldwide demand for resources, the likelihood of significant shortages, and the existence of numerous ownership disputes, the incidence of conflict over vital materials is sure to grow."[172]

A second sort of conflict over resources, already mentioned above, might be called scarcity conflict. The scarcity of water, for example, can be a major factor in conflicts among nations and within countries. The Middle East and the North African region contain several examples of conflict over water: Turkey and Syria contest the Euphrates River; Egypt and Ethiopia, the Nile River; Israel, Lebanon, Syria, and Jordan draw on the Jordan River; and Israel and the Palestinians dispute the aquifer under the West Bank. Countries have found themselves nose to nose over fishing rights and other resource issues as well.[173]

A third sense of what might be called resource wars happens when resources not only contribute to the cause of the conflict, but also fuel the conflict. There are numerous examples of this phenomenon. In Sierra Leone, for example, diamonds not only triggered a brutal civil war, but produced the profits necessary to purchase the armaments to continue it. The same was true in the protracted civil war in Angola, and minerals are key to the conflict in the Congo. Precious stones and timber fueled the conflict in Cambodia, oil profits pay for the civil wars in Sudan and Colombia, and opium funded the civil war in Afghanistan.[174]

Finally, environmental change can result in social disruptions that contribute to conflicts:

- Expanding populations can cause deforestation, soil degradation, and water depletion, all of which can decrease agricultural production. Food scarcity can be a source of conflict, as can land and water scarcity.
- Poverty and environmental degradation can form a negative spiral, each creating more of the other. Economic decline and deprivation are major factors in the weakening of governments and in the strengthening of insurgencies.
- Environmental scarcity can be an important factor in population displacements and migration. Migrants and refugees often cause social tension and ethnic conflict.

And it should be noted that the rate and scope of environmental degradation as a source of conflict is likely to increase.[175]

One result of the growing awareness that environmental scarcity and social and economic deprivations are sources of conflict has been a "greening of U.S. diplomacy."[176] In trying to anticipate the global crises of tomorrow, American intelligence agencies are paying much closer attention to phenomena such as the water hyacinths choking Lake Victoria, droughts in Somalia or Senegal, overcrowding in Chinese cities, and the AIDS epidemic in East Africa.

Not only is environmental scarcity a source of international conflict, but war and preparation for war are also sources of environmental degradation. The environmental effect of war was highlighted during the Persian Gulf

War when Iraqi forces spilled large amounts of Kuwaiti oil into the Persian Gulf and blew up hundreds of Kuwaiti oil wells, leaving them burning as they retreated. Burning crops, defoliating fields, and poisoning water are common practices in warfare. Even in being prepared for war, military industries pollute the earth, use excessive amounts of energy, and deplete natural resources. The nuclear and chemical weapons programs have created a plethora of radioactive and toxic wastes, which are often stored in deteriorating facilities. A nuclear war would be the greatest potential environmental disaster imaginable.[177]

Another type of insecurity resulting from population growth and global warming is the spread of deadly viruses.[178] Overcrowding, poverty, disrupted ecosystems, and accelerated climate change are having profound and destabilizing impacts on the control of infectious disease. Illnesses thought to be under control, such as tuberculosis, dengue fever, and cholera, are making strong comebacks, and new viruses, such as HIV and ebola, are posing unforeseen threats to human health. Because of modern transportation, viruses can spread rapidly and widely. Infectious diseases are still the number one killer worldwide.[179]

SUSTAINABLE DEVELOPMENT?

The web of life in any ecosystem is interconnected and interdependent, and this is clearly true of the earth's ecosystem as a whole. The most serious ecological problems, such as atmospheric pollution, deforestation, and the depletion of ocean fisheries, are related to the global commons and require cooperative global responses. The interdependence of the whole earth community is an ecological truth.

Two of the laws of an interconnected, closed ecosystem are that "everything must go somewhere" and that "there is no such thing as a free lunch."[180] Unfortunately, the industrial and technological society, already achieved by the First World and being sought by the Two-Thirds World, has not paid attention to these laws of ecology. Exponential economic growth through increased industrialization, coupled with population growth, threatens to damage, or at least radically alter, the earth's ecosystem. Ecological theologian Thomas Berry proclaims that the human-induced changes inflicted on the planet over the last 150 years have been on a geological or biological order of magnitude. Humans are changing the chemistry of the planet, upsetting the entire earth system that has evolved over billions of years. The impact of humans on the earth since the industrial revolution is "paralleled only by the great geological and climatic upheavals that changed the earth in the distant past."[181]

Optimists may be correct in their belief that human ingenuity and technology will allow humanity to adapt to ecological transformations or even transcend the limits that seem to be set by a finite ecosystem. The pessimists, however, while sometimes excessively bleak in their predictions of doom, certainly raise ominous questions about environmental limits to economic growth.

If everyone's basic needs were being fulfilled and every human being had an opportunity to flourish, it might be reasonable and fair to stop economic growth. But that is not the case. A third of humanity lacks what is essential to meet basic needs and another third is unable to flourish. Economic growth, along with a more just distribution of goods, is thought to be essential for overcoming poverty.[182] Such economic development also seems essential to stabilize the worrisome growth of human population. But the resource depletion and pollution that attend economic growth might also irreparably alter the earth's ecosystem. And a radical change in the earth's ecosystem would damage not only the economy, but humanity itself. "Saving the earth" is really a misnomer; this is about saving the human species by maintaining a planet hospitable to human life and human flourishing.[183]

"Sustainable" development has been suggested as a way through the conundrum posed by the contradictory goals and consequences of economics and ecology. A Native American proverb expresses the vision and values necessary for sustainable development: We do not inherit the earth from our parents; we *borrow* it from our grandchildren. Thus, sustainable development means economic development that meets the needs of the present generation in a way that does not compromise the needs of future generations.[184]

A sustainable fishing policy, for example, would limit the catch to that amount that enables the remaining fish to replenish the stock for the following year. Overfishing can diminish the ecological capital of fish to the point of extinction. While ever increasing catches of fish might reap short-term profits, the practice becomes unsustainable. Similarly, if groundwater is used at a rate much faster than it can be replenished, the aquifer itself can compact, eliminating the pores and spaces that hold the water. The concept of sustainable development is easily understood, but it is not being practiced. Indeed, one wonders if this slogan is an oxymoron, a contradiction in itself.

Any serious resolution of the dilemma must address poverty. Not only is this a moral imperative, but economic development is fundamental to stabilizing population growth, which is a key ingredient in alleviating the plight both of the poor and of the earth.

Instead of concentrating on economic growth as a strategy for alleviating poverty, perhaps the focus should be on increasing economic equity. "Development strategies based on more equality within nations and across the entire globe could greatly improve living conditions of the world's poor. This improvement could be bought at a relatively modest cost."[185]

Life expectancy (expected life span at birth) is a key indicator of the quality of life and of human development in low-income countries. There is a correlation between life expectancy and income levels (Gross National Product per capita). Life expectancy goes up about a year for every $50 increase in income per capita, up to a GNP per capita of about $3,000. At that point, life expectancy usually rises to about 65, and it takes a $1,000 increment in income to add a year of life expectancy. Beyond a $6,000 GNP per capita there is almost no relationship between income and life expectancy.

"This pattern implies that major improvements in health and living conditions for the poor could be bought at a price not requiring major sacrifices by people in the rich countries. A transfer of income from rich countries to the poor need not hurt very much and could have an enormous impact."[186] Indeed, cuts in military budgets, in both the developed and developing countries, could underwrite this significant reduction in poverty. The cost would not exceed by much the doubling of current nonmilitary international development assistance. The aid would have to be carefully targeted to meet public health, education, and nutrition needs. Such a plan would be complicated and would require some sacrifice, but it could be done.[187] There is enough wealth in the world to alleviate poverty without huge strides in economic growth, but wealth needs to be creatively transferred to those who need it. A focus on economic equity and the fair distribution of goods, with less pressure for economic growth, may be the ticket to a healthy future, but this creative proposal does not appear to be politically realistic.

It would be ecologically disastrous for the Two-Thirds World to reach the standard of living of the developed North, a lifestyle that is already altering the earth's ecosystem on a magnitude similar to that of being struck by a devastating asteroid. Sustainable development, if taken seriously, means a new way of thinking and a different way of living for the North.[188]

Human flourishing includes the satisfaction of basic needs, intellectual challenge, creative expression, meaningful activity, healthy relationships, supportive community, and spiritual growth. Perhaps there are already more than enough goods for a meaningful and satisfying human life. Less might be better for the global North, and it would surely be beneficial for the earth.

Sustainable development is a radical idea that is more rhetoric than reality in today's public policy discussions.[189] There is a need for political, religious, and moral leaders who embody and proclaim these values and this vision. The words of Pope John Paul II, quoted at the beginning of this chapter, are challenging indeed. What if affluent Christians took seriously the call to simplicity, moderation, discipline, and a spirit of sacrifice? That would indeed be good news both for the poor and for the earth.

STUDY QUESTIONS

1. What are the practical implications of the different cosmologies (views of the universe): human-centered, biocentric, earth-centered, God-centered? What is your cosmology?
2. From an ecological perspective, has the Judeo-Christian tradition been a part of the problem? the basis of the problem? Can the Judeo-Christian tradition be part of the solution?
3. Do you think that the growth of the human population is approaching the carrying capacity of the earth? What proposals would you suggest to respond to population growth?
4. Discuss the bet on planet earth between Erlich and Simon. What are its implications regarding resource depletion and environmental issues?

5. What are the pros and cons of a significantly higher tax on gasoline in the United States? What would Jesus drive? (A question posed in advertisements sponsored by the National Religious Partnership for the Environment. See Danny Hakim, "A Group Links Fuel Economy to Religion," *New York Times* [November 19, 2002], pp. C1, C9.)

6. What is the evidence that global warming might already be upon us? What steps should be taken to address the issue?

7. Is it possible for humanity to emulate nature and eliminate waste? What can you do to reduce the more than four pounds of waste most Americans produce every day?

8. Can you name some places where you think resource competition and environmental issues will lead to violent conflict? How should U.S. foreign policy take "environmental security" into account?

9. Do you think there is a direct conflict between the need for economic development for the poor and the need to protect the environment? How can sustainable development be accomplished?

CHAPTER FOUR

Human Rights

"So God created humankind in his image, in the image of God he created them; male and female he created them." (Genesis 1:27)

"Any human society, if it is to be well-ordered and productive, must lay down as a foundation this principle, namely, that every human being is a person; that is, his nature is endowed with intelligence and free will. Indeed, precisely because he is a person he has rights and obligations flowing directly and simultaneously from his nature. And these rights and obligations are universal and inviolable, so they cannot in any way be surrendered."[1]

Throughout history humans have oppressed one another. On the basis of some accident, such as race, color, ethnicity, birth, nationality, gender, sexual orientation, age, class, caste, or religion, people's humanity has been violated. Oppression and discrimination can take many forms—slavery, imprisonment, torture, violence, impoverishment, exclusion, humiliation—but at its heart is dehumanization. The full humanity of the victim is denied, and, paradoxically, the oppressor becomes less human through the denial. Too often citizens have been persecuted by the state with the blessings of religion. Prejudice and discrimination are not new, but in the last 50 years the human community has begun to name this oppression as a violation of human rights and, at least in theory, to condemn these practices. Unfortunately, violations of human rights continue to plague our world, but there has been some progress, and there is the possibility of more.

Tyranny tolerates little dissent. During the Cold War, dissidents in Communist countries feared the midnight knock on the door by the secret police that would result in imprisonment in a work camp or "psychiatric hospital." China, North Korea, and Cuba continue to imprison people critical of Communist rule as does Saddam Hussein in Iraq. In El Salvador during the 1980s paramilitary death squads would snatch those who took the side of the poor, torture and kill them. When Archbishop Oscar Romero began to advocate for the poor and to criticize the military in El Salvador, he was assassinated while saying a public Mass. In the 1980s and 1990s four American churchwomen and six Jesuit priests added their blood to the tens of thousands of Salvadoran peasants slaughtered there. Similar events took place in other countries in Latin America, such as Argentina, Chile, and Guatemala, and elsewhere. In Sierra Leone, one of the "failed states" in West

Africa, sadistic rebels terrorized the population by randomly cutting off both hands of their victims or by burning people alive.[2]

Not all violations of human rights involve death squads, torture, maiming, or imprisonment. Some involve routine discrimination: being denied an education or job because of one's race or gender, or being refused housing because of one's sexual preference. In addition, poverty is an immense obstacle to the flourishing of the human spirit. The United States, with its tradition of racism, its record of support for military dictatorships, and as one of the few Western nations that practices capital punishment, is hardly immune to the charge of human rights violations. In some places throughout the world the repression has stopped or lessened, but in others it continues. This chapter will explore the struggle for human rights in all its complexity.

HISTORY AND CONTEXT

Before World War II, human rights were viewed as a purely domestic matter and not a topic for international relations. The horror of the Holocaust and the attempt at the Nuremberg trials to hold German army officers accountable gave international validity to human rights concerns.

The United Nations has played an important role in setting the standards for human rights. On December 10, 1948, the newly formed United Nations issued its Universal Declaration of Human Rights. No country voted against

---

The Nobel Prize for Peace has been awarded to several individuals who have been activists and advocates for human rights: Martin Luther King, Jr., the American civil rights leader (1964); Mairead Corrigan and Betty Williams, two women from Belfast, Northern Ireland, who sought a dialogue between Protestants and Catholics (1976); Mother Teresa of Calcutta, for her work among the poor (1979); Adolfo Perez Esquivel for resisting the repression of Argentina's military dictatorship (1980); Lech Walesa, the leader of the Polish trade union Solidarity (1983); Bishop Desmond Tutu, the South African anti-apartheid leader (1984); Holocaust survivor and witness Elie Wiesel (1986); the exiled Tibetan leader, the Dalai Lama (1989); Daw Aung San Suu Kyi, who is opposing the military rule of Myanmar (Burma) (1991); Rigoberta Menchu, who has campaigned courageously for the rights of indigenous people in Guatemala and against the repression of the rural poor by the military (1992); Nelson Mandela and F. W. de Klerk, for their leadership in ending apartheid in South Africa (1993); and Bishop Carlos Ximenes Belo and Mr. Jose Ramos-Horta, for their struggle for independence for East Timor (1996). Amnesty International, an organization that monitors human rights abuses throughout the world and advocates on behalf of political prisoners, received the Nobel Peace Prize in 1977, and Médecins Sans Frontières (Doctors Without Borders) was recognized in 1999 for its humanitarian work and human rights advocacy.

It would be interesting to choose one of these Nobel laureates and research his or her life.

the Declaration, although some abstained—the U.S.S.R. and its allies because there was not enough emphasis on social and economic rights, South Africa because of race, and Saudi Arabia because of gender issues.[3] Because the Declaration did not have the binding force of a treaty, the United Nations developed the International Covenant on Economic, Social, and Cultural Rights and the International Covenant on Civil and Political Rights.[4] Together these three documents are often referred to as the International Bill of Human Rights. They summarize the minimum social and political guarantees internationally recognized as necessary for a life of dignity in the contemporary world. Table 4.1 lists the human rights that have been recognized by the community of nations.[5]

The United Nations has also released several other conventions on particular aspects of human rights: on the Elimination of All Forms of Racial Discrimination (1965), on the Suppression and Punishment of the Crime of Apartheid (1973), on the Elimination of Discrimination against Women (1979), against Torture and Other Cruel, Inhuman, or Degrading Treatment or Punishment (1984), and on the Rights of the Child (1989). None of these conventions has enjoyed universal ratification, but together they have established clear norms regarding human rights. The United Nations has also issued a (non-binding) Declaration on the Right to Development (1986).

What a person or a nation has a right to will always be controversial. One such right, dear to the hearts of pacifists, is that of conscientious objection to war. While conscientious objection was not directly mentioned in the Universal Declaration on Human Rights, it is implied in Article 18—freedom of thought, conscience, and religion, and it has been recognized in a series of resolutions by the U.N. Commission on Human Rights in 1989, 1993, 1995, and 1998. The right to be recognized as a Conscientious Objector has also been affirmed by the Council of Europe, and it is increasingly being included in national constitutions.[6]

The doctrine of national sovereignty has made the United Nations less effective in redressing violations of human rights. The U.N. Commission on Human Rights, a permanent subsidiary body of the Economic and Social Council, is the world's most prominent forum for protesting infractions of human rights by states, but its hearings on individual countries are strictly confidential, and it has no enforcement authority. Many of the conventions regarding aspects of human rights also have implementation or monitoring committees, but they all depend on the cooperation of states. While these monitoring and enforcement mechanisms are admittedly weak and ineffective, the consciousness and behavior of some governments have been changed and victims have been aided.[7]

The creation of the International Criminal Court (ICC) on July 1, 2002, was a new attempt to put more bite into the protection of human rights. In the future the ICC will bring criminal cases against individuals accused of genocide, crimes against humanity, and war crimes. It will be housed at the Hague in the Netherlands where the International Court of Justice, which rules on civil disputes between nations, already resides. The impetus for the ICC was the atrocities committed in the Bosnian War and the genocide in

Table 4.1
Internationally Recognized Human Rights

The International Bill of Human Rights recognizes the rights to:

Equality of rights without discrimination (D1, D2, E2, E3, C2, C3; P30, 44, 48, 65, 86, 89)
Life (D3, C6; P11)
Liberty and security of person (D3, C9; P11)
Protection against slavery (D4, C8)
Protection against torture and cruel and inhuman punishment (D5, C7)
Recognition as a person before the law (D6, C16; P27 "juridical protection of [human] rights")
Equal protection of the law (D7, C14, C26; P69)
Access to legal remedies for rights violations (D8, C2)
Protection against arbitrary arrest or detention (D9, C9)
Hearing before an independent and impartial judiciary (D10, C14)
Presumption of innocence (D11, C14)
Protection against ex post facto laws (D11, C15)
Protection of privacy, family, and home (D12, C17)
Freedom of movement and residence (D13, C12; P25)
Seek asylum from persecution (D14; P103–08)
Nationality (D15)
Marry and found a family (D16, E10, C23; P15)
Own property (D17; P21)
Freedom of thought, conscience, and religion (D18, C18; P12,14)
Freedom of opinion, expression, and the press (D19, C19; P12)
Freedom of assembly and association (D20, C21, C22; P23)
Political participation (D21, C25; P26, 73, 146)
Social security (D22, E9; P11, 63–64)
Work, under favorable conditions (D23, E6, E7; P18, 19)
Free trade unions (D23, E8, C22)
Rest and leisure (D24, E7)
Food, clothing, and housing (D25, E11; P11)
Health care and social services (D25, E12; P11)
Special protections for children (D25, E10, C24)
Education (D26, E13, E14; P13)
Participation in cultural life (D27, E15; P12, 13, 64)
A social and international order needed to realize rights (D28; P60–63, 75–77, 139, 141)
Self-determination (E1, C1 [P42, 43, 94])
Humane treatment when detained or imprisoned (C10)
Protection against debtor's prison (C11)
Protection against arbitrary expulsion of aliens (C13; P103–08)
Protection of minority culture (C27; P56, 94–97)
[Assistance in development (P121–25)]

Note: This list includes all rights that are enumerated in two of the three documents of the International Bill of Human Rights or have a full article in one document. The source of each right is indicated in parentheses, by document and article number. D = Universal Declaration of Human Rights; E = International Covenant on Economic, Social, and Cultural Rights; C = International Covenant on Civil and Political Rights.

Source: Jack Donnelly, *International Human Rights* (Boulder, Col.: Westview Press, 1993), p. 9. The author has cross referenced Donnelly's list with Pope John XXIII's *Pacem in Terris* (Peace on Earth, abbreviated P in the list) in David J. O'Brien and Thomas A. Shannon, eds., *Catholic Social Thought: The Documentary Heritage* (Maryknoll, N.Y.: Orbis Books, 1992), pp. 131–62. Numbers refer to paragraphs in the document.

Rwanda in 1994. The first day of the court's existence coincided with the renewal of the U.N. peacekeeping mandate in Bosnia. The United States threatened to withdraw its troops from that peacekeeping mission unless given blanket immunity by the court. Although President Clinton signed the treaty establishing the ICC, Congress refused to ratify it, and the Bush administration is strongly opposed to the new court, fearing that U.S. troops could be vulnerable to politically motivated prosecutions. Neither Russia nor China has approved of the ICC, but European nations have adamantly advocated for it, and were vociferously critical of Washington's actions, which seemed to jeopardize U.N. peacekeeping operations all over the world.[8]

The Cold War twisted the principled concern for human rights into a weapon in the ideological battle between the East (the Soviet Union and the Warsaw Pact nations) and the West (the United States and NATO). The West focused its rhetoric on civil and political rights, such as freedom of the press and the right to peacefully assemble and protest, decrying the failure of Communist countries to honor these rights. The East emphasized social and economic rights, such as employment, housing, and health care, disparaging the condition of the underclass in the United States. Since both superpowers had logs in their own eyes, it was difficult to remove the log in the eye of the adversary. Peoples in the Two-Thirds World, meanwhile, were struggling toward self-determination in a global context that forced them to choose sides.

The Cold War period (1945–89) yields a paradox regarding human rights. It was an era when violations of human rights were routine and ubiquitous, and it was the time when the concept of human rights became established and accepted, and even extensively monitored.[9] The United Nations, as we have seen, was largely responsible for establishing human rights as an international norm. Non-governmental organizations (NGOs), such as Amnesty International and Human Rights Watch, built sterling reputations for impartially investigating human rights transgressions and accurately reporting their findings.

There was plenty of work for these NGOs to do. Communist countries were totalitarian societies. Two-thirds of the world was desperately poor, and those countries, with few exceptions, were ruled by brutal dictators or repressive militaries. Many of those countries were in a state of civil war characterized by guerrilla insurgencies and military counterinsurgencies. Innocent civilians were often caught in the middle, violated by both sides. While the world was coming to conceptual clarity that it is wrong to violate a person's human rights, such abuse was pervasive.

Happily, since about 1986, there has been a remarkable transformation regarding civil and political rights. In Asia the "People Power" revolution deposed the conjugal dictatorship of the Marcoses in the Philippines, while South Korea and then Taiwan moved toward representative government. Pakistan and Bangladesh held free elections with peaceful transfers of power, although Pakistan reverted to military rule. Except for Cuba, elected governments hold office in every country in the Western Hemisphere, although the democratic credentials of some, such as Paraguay, remain suspect. The political imprisonment, torture, and disappearances that were commonplace in Latin America in the early 1980s have abated.[10] Africa too has been touched by this wave of liberalization, although more lightly. The enfranchisement of the black majority in South Africa is the most startling success story, but other countries, such as Benin, Zambia, and Nigeria, have moved from one-man or one-party rule to genuine elections. Africa and the Middle East, however, remain civil-rights backwaters, as do such Asian countries as China, North Korea, Vietnam, Myanmar (Burma), and Singapore.

The "Velvet Revolution" (1989–91) converted Eastern Europe and the former Soviet Empire from police states into fledgling democracies. The human rights transition, however, has not been smooth. In the former Czechoslovakia, for example, a commission charged with investigating over 150,000 informants of the old secret police paid scant attention to due process. Merely turning the tables does not represent genuine progress toward respect for human rights. Indeed, *the treatment of the guilty and the despised is the litmus test of human rights in a society.*[11] The 1994 split of Czechoslovakia into the Czech Republic and Slovakia was due, in part, to concerns about the fair treatment of minorities. Old habits and ingrained prejudices are hard to change.

THE UNITED STATES

While there is no comparison between the human rights records of the United States and the former Soviet Union, Washington's actions during the Cold War were problematic regarding human rights. U.S. foreign policy during this period submerged human rights concerns in order to combat the threat of communism. Thus, the United States showered anti-Communist dictators with economic assistance and military aid throughout the Cold War, even those who were oppressive and corrupt. The United States supported, for example, the Shah in Iran, Marcos in the Philippines, Somoza in Nicaragua, Duvalier in Haiti, Stroessner in Paraguay, and Mobutu in Zaire. None of these men shied away from imprisoning opponents, torture, or murder. There are even disturbing examples of U.S. efforts to overthrow freely elected governments: in Guatemala in 1954, Chile in 1973, and Nicaragua after 1984, for example. The Soviet record was equally appalling, backing, for example, the Mengistu regime in Ethiopia, among the most barbaric on record.[12] The difference is that the United States is supposed to be committed to the principles of freedom and justice.

There were nuances of difference among the American administrations during the Cold War, but anti-communism was the cornerstone of U.S. foreign policy. President Jimmy Carter (1976–80) did give human rights an important role, but global realities often made it difficult for his administration to practice this principle. Ronald Reagan (1980–88) campaigned against the Carter human rights policy and on behalf of a single-minded focus on overcoming communism, and once elected he acted on these values.

Congress, however, gradually reasserted human rights as a foreign policy consideration during the 1980s.

The end of the Cold War could mean a more prominent place for human rights as an international interest and, as we have seen, there has been some decrease in political repression. National sovereignty, however, remains in tension with intervention on behalf of human rights. The benefits of trade also impinge on legitimate concerns about violations of human rights. China's repression of political protestors in Tiananmen Square in 1989 stands as a symbol of human rights abuse in the post-Cold War world, yet neither the Bush (1988–92) nor the Clinton (1992–2000) administrations took substantive action against China's human rights violations. While ideology no longer justifies allowing repression, sovereignty and economics continue to be obstacles to international advocacy for human rights.

The war on terrorism has tempted the United States to suspend civil liberties and renege on civil rights such as the protection against arbitrary arrest and detention and access to a fair trial. In the days following September 11, 2001, hundreds of aliens were rounded up and imprisoned without being charged with a crime or allowed legal representation. Under the aegis of preventing terrorism in the United States, passage of the Patriot Act in October 2001 lifted some restrictions on the "snooping" powers of U.S. intelligence agencies, possibly compromising the privacy of its citizens. Over 300 of the Taliban soldiers captured in Afghanistan were deported to the U.S. military base in Guantanamo Bay, Cuba. At first the Bush administration refused to grant them "prisoner of war" status, but Secretary of State Colin Powell argued that such a move could come back to haunt American troops in a future conflict. President Bush ultimately agreed to apply the protocols` of the Geneva Conventions to these prisoners but adamantly refused to call them prisoners of war.[13] During this debate it was never argued that these prisoners should be treated with respect and fairness simply because they were human beings. Again it needs to be said that it is the treatment of the guilty and despised, those who do evil, that is the litmus test of human rights in a society. In the aftermath of September 11, the United States is in danger of failing that test.

The Soviet Union's criticisms of the U.S. *domestic* record on social and economic rights during the Cold War were generally dismissed, but they contained more than a grain of truth. In the late 1980s, for example, the case could be made that Cuba's health-care system was better than America's in meeting the basic needs of their *entire* population. Homelessness in one of the richest nations on earth is a moral outrage. The United States seems to be afflicted with a certain blindness, perhaps born of self-righteousness, to its domestic failures in the area of human rights: "The United States, however, is said to suffer from, for example, police brutality, civil rights problems, or a health care crisis, which are spoken of as if they are qualitatively different from torture, racial discrimination, or denial of the right to health care."[14] The history of slavery and segregation and the near genocide of the indigenous peoples should certainly caution America about self-satisfaction regarding human rights; this history should also urge on us a genuine watch-fulness and a sense of the need for reform.

THE MEANING OF HUMAN RIGHTS

Human rights make strong claims. "Right" is not a word to be thrown around loosely. If a person has a right, then the community and other persons have a duty to respect and fulfill that right. Because a right confers an obligation on the community, it is not surprising that various societies have contested the foundation, meaning, and scope of human rights.

During the Cold War, each of the three "worlds" was said to emphasize a different aspect of human rights. The First World stressed civil and political rights and the right to private property. The Second World gave priority to social, economic, and cultural rights as prerequisites to civil and political rights. The Third World also emphasized social, economic, and cultural rights, as well as the right to self-determination and the right to development.[15] These, however, are self-serving, ideological distinctions that have little basis in any sound theory of rights. *All* of these rights are affirmed in the International Bill of Human Rights (Table 4.1) based on U.N. documents and all of them require respect and satisfaction if human beings are to flourish.

There is a remarkable parallel between the formulation of human rights by the United Nations and that found in contemporary Catholic social teaching. The clearest expression of the meaning and scope of human rights in Catholic thought is in the encyclical of Pope John XXIII titled *Peace on Earth*. It was written in 1963 while the Second Vatican Council was in progress. Pope John's list of human rights closely parallels that of the U.N. Universal Declaration of Human Rights (See Table 4.1). The convening of the United Nations (1948) and of the Second Vatican Council (1962–65) both produced transnational bodies with a focus on issues of justice and peace in a pluralistic world: "The need to find consensus on a normative basis for international justice and peace without suppressing the legitimate differences within regions and social systems led both bodies to a human rights focus."[16] Both Catholic social teaching and the standards set by the United Nations adopted human rights as a normative framework for a pluralistic world. Human rights have become the moral parameter within which a society must be ordered. There can be many legitimate ways of organizing a government and a society, but all of them have to recognize and respect human rights.[17]

Human rights are rights that a person has simply because one is human. Such rights are held equally by all human beings, and they are inalienable. Human rights are rooted, then, in a theory of human nature. Various philosophical systems provide stronger or weaker foundations for a concept of human rights.[18] The dignity of the human person, realized in community, is the foundation of Catholic social thought and its theory of human rights.[19] Thus, the Catholic conception of human rights is personalistic *and* communitarian, not individualistic as some Enlightenment philosophers would have it. The theological foundations of human dignity and human rights are based on the creation of all people in the image of God, the trinitarian concept of God,[20] redemption by Jesus Christ, and the call to a transcendent destiny. The Christian tradition provides a solid foundation for a theory of human rights. The concept of human rights, however, finds healthy roots in all of the major religious traditions.[21]

There are several ways of describing human rights. One is the Cold War division of rights into three "worlds." Perhaps a better way is to differentiate rights according to three sectors or spheres of the human person essential to the preservation of human dignity: basic needs, freedom, and relationships. Human beings, for example, need food and shelter for bodily existence. Similarly, the freedoms to associate with others, to participate in political decisions, and to express religious beliefs are fundamental to human dignity. Every person depends on community—the relationships into which we are born and the ones we form and choose—for his or her development and flourishing. To each of these essential areas of human existence—needs, freedom, and relationship—corresponds a set of human rights that defend human dignity within that sector.[22]

Rights can also be differentiated according to the way they are mediated by society and social institutions. Here, too, there are three dimensions:

First, there are *personal rights,* which protect fundamental characteristics of the person as such. Life, bodiliness, self-determination, sociability, work, sexuality, family, and core values are characteristics of every person that are shielded by personal rights. These personal attributes, however, can be actualized in different ways in different societies and cultures, and can be realized and safeguarded by a variety of institutional structures.

Second, there are *social rights,* which specify the positive obligations of society toward all its members for providing conditions that enable human beings to grow and thrive. These would include the rights to health care, political participation, adequate working conditions, education, and assembly.

Finally, there are *instrumental rights,* which promote participation in forming the institutions that shape and structure human life, such as the government, the economy, the health-care and educational systems, and the law. Instrumental rights require the structuring or institutionalization of human rights through, for example, court systems that protect one's personal and social rights or some system of social security. (See Figure 4.1.)

These two ways of elaborating human rights—1) according to sectors or spheres of the human person and 2) according to the kinds of personal, social, and institutional relationships involved—are helpful keys for unlocking the inner logic of the Catholic human rights tradition.[23] The result is a list of human rights like that found in *Peace on Earth* and in the International Bill of Human Rights.

These schema can also be helpful in identifying the sorts of policies that can best promote human rights. The framing of the discussion that arose during the Cold War set up a conflict between civil and political rights versus economic and social rights. The conflict, however, is not between polit-

Figure 4.1
Personal, Social and Instrumental Rights:
An Interpretation of *Pacem in Terris*

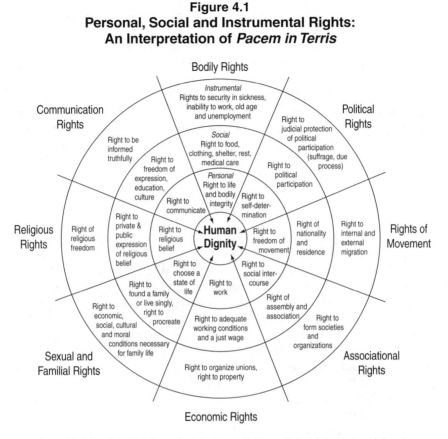

Source: Adapted from the Yale Task Force on Population Ethics (D. Christiansen, R. Garet, D. Hollenbach and C. Powers), "Moral Claims, Human Rights and Population Policies," *Theological Studies 35* (1974), p. 102 (with permission).

ical participation (voting) versus economic participation (jobs). The conflict in most societies is between the elite who are both politically and economically powerful versus the marginalized who are neither.

Constructive human rights policies, then, should focus on establishing the full set of social rights for the protection of human dignity. The full set of social rights would include the following: the rights to food, clothing, shelter, health care, and rest; the right to political participation; the rights to nationality and to migrate; the rights of assembly and association; the rights to work, to adequate working conditions, and to a just wage; the right to found a family or live singly; the rights to freedom of expression, to education, and to religious expression.[24] (See Figure 4.1.)

Three principles have been proposed that would guide the development of human rights policies designed to overcome the marginalization of the poor, minorities, and the oppressed:

1. The needs of the poor take priority over the wants of the rich.
2. The freedom of the dominated takes priority over the liberty of the powerful.
3. The participation of marginalized groups takes priority over the preservation of an order which excludes them.[25]

These principles are helpful yardsticks for measuring the impact of legislative or policy proposals on human rights and for assessing foreign policy. They also highlight the value of human rights as moral norms in a pluralistic world, and they expose the fundamental questions that human rights standards can raise in every sort of political and economic system.

CULTURAL RELATIVISM

The United Nations called its Declaration of Human Rights "Universal," that is, applicable to and binding on all nations and people. The claim of universal human rights, however, is controversial in a pluralistic world. Some nations have claimed that the International Bill of Human Rights, with its affirmation of equal rights for women, for example, is too Western in its conception and articulation. On the other hand, American conservatives have been reluctant to affirm some of the social, economic, and cultural rights, such as the right to work or the right to health care. Thoroughgoing relativists would deny the theoretical possibility of universal norms, noting the sometimes radical differences among cultures.

In arguing in favor of universal norms regarding human rights, it is not necessary to take an extreme or absolutist position. Not every value is absolute; indeed, there may be conflicts among and exceptions to universal norms. The fact of cultural relativism, however, does not mean that whatever a particular culture sanctions is right. There may well be universal norms that adhere to human beings as human and that transcend and critique culture.

In sorting out the tension between universal standards and the different practices of various cultures, it can be helpful to distinguish three levels of specification regarding human rights.[26] The first level is the *concept* of a human right, such as the right to work. This general statement of principle admits to little cultural variability. Second, there is the *interpretation* of the principle. A guaranteed job or unemployment insurance might be two legitimate interpretations of the right to work. Finally, there may be many different ways to *implement* an interpretation of a right. A government might employ a large percentage of the population in a wide network of civil service jobs, or it might stimulate the economy to provide ample employment opportunities for its people.

The right to political participation might be interpreted as the right to vote; voting itself can take place in a two-party system or a multi-party system, for individual candidates or for slates of candidates, or through direct referenda. But a one-party system that really admits of no choice may violate the right to political participation.

In Western societies, standards of modesty require women to cover their chest, while Muslim customs require women to wear a veil, often covering their entire bodies. It would seem, however, that the rights to equality of treatment without discrimination and to education would require every society to offer equal opportunities for education to women and men.

If the norms regarding human rights are not universal, then they offer little moral guidance for a pluralistic world.[27] While sensitivity is certainly called for in addressing clashes between cultural values, caution should not be equated with indifference or inaction. Even if we are not entitled to impose our values on others, we are responsible for owning our values, witnessing to them, and acting on them. Practices such as female infanticide, apartheid, anti-Semitism, slavery, sexual exploitation of children,[28] female genital mutilation, and torture deserve neither respect nor tolerance.[29]

DISCRIMINATION AGAINST WOMEN

Women are oppressed and subjugated throughout the entire world. Sexism is characteristic of every society and culture on earth. Indeed, only recently has feminism (a belief in the equality of the sexes) meaningfully challenged patriarchy (the institutionalized belief that men are superior to women and should dominate them). Although some nations have made significant progress toward the goal of gender equality, no society has reached that goal.

The *Human Development Report* devised its *gender-related development index* (GDI) in 1995. The GDI adjusted three factors in its human development index (HDI)—life expectancy, educational attainment, and income—for gender inequality. On a scale of 0 to 1, with 1 representing perfect equality, the highest score was .937 by Norway. (The United States ranked fourth with a GDI score of .932.) That no country scored 1 is remarkable because nearly everywhere in the world women's life expectancy is higher than that of men. Even given this edge, and, in most industrial countries an equal achievement in basic education, the disparity in income is enough to lower the GDI to below 1.[30]

The *Human Development Report 1996* drew several conclusions from the GDI rankings: 1) no society treats its women as well as its men; 2) the pursuit of gender equality is not necessarily associated with high growth in income, and it can be pursued at all levels of income; and 3) progress in gender equality can be attained by nations characterized by different political ideologies, economic conditions, cultures, and stages of development.[31] The key to progress toward gender equality seems simply to be the will to succeed, that is, an awareness that discrimination exists, that it is wrong and needs to change, followed by the removal of restrictions on women and targeted social programs on women's behalf.

In 1995 the *Human Development Report* also introduced the *gender empowerment measure* (GEM), which focused on women's participation in economic and political decision-making by noting the percentage of women who hold seats in congresses or parliaments, administrative or managerial positions, professional or technical jobs, and women's share of earned income. The highest score, with 1 representing perfect equality between men and women, was Norway's .836. The U.S. ranked tenth in the world with a score of .738. In 2001, only 14 percent of the seats in the U.S. Congress were held by women, and U.S. women's average income was only 61 percent of that of men.[32] Only 12 countries had a GEM rating higher than .700, and 25 countries had a GEM lower than .500. Surprisingly, some industrial countries, such as Japan and Italy, were actually behind some developing countries such as Barbados, Costa Rica, and Trinidad and Tobago.[33] Female government leaders are still rare in the modern world—in only eight countries do women comprise 30 percent or more of parliament. While women have led Israel, the Philippines, Pakistan, Bangladesh, Sri Lanka, and Great Britain, for example, they have not occupied the highest office in the United States, Japan, France, Russia, or China.

Throughout the world equal rights for women are denied in nearly every aspect of life. Wherever people are oppressed, women suffer more, first as members of the oppressed group and then as women. When people are hungry, it is often the custom for the men and boys to eat first, and for the women and girls to eat what is left over. Thus in India, where this practice is common, the rate of female mortality is higher.[34] The "feminization of poverty," that is, the much higher incidence of poverty among households headed by women, is a reality in both industrial and developing countries.[35] This is due in part to economic exploitation and wage discrimination. Women suffer discrimination in salaries and in opportunities for employment and promotion. It is no accident that sweatshops in Latin America and Asia employ mostly women: they can be paid less and are more vulnerable to exploitation. In the United States, women doing work comparable to men are paid on average about three-fourths of what men are paid. In addition, throughout the world women are often excluded from educational opportunities.[36] In Saudi Arabia women are even prohibited from driving a car.

It was only in 1920 that women in the United States received the right to vote. Political participation is still restricted for women, either through law or common practice, in countries such as Kuwait, Iran, South Korea, Turkey, Egypt, Brazil, Pakistan, Nigeria, Togo, and Russia.[37] In 1997, women held only 11.7 percent of all the seats in the world's 179 parliaments, even though females comprised 49.6 percent of the world's population.[38] In many countries women do not enjoy the full protection of the law. Wives and daughters are not allowed to inherit the property or wealth of their husbands or fathers, for example, or women do not have the standing to be granted credit in their own name.

In many countries of the world, women do not fare any better at home than in public life. In less developed countries, the life of a poor peasant woman is one of unending menial labor: gathering wood for cooking, hauling water, washing clothes by hand, preparing food from scratch, and working the fields, while perhaps caring for a half-dozen children. In industrial countries, some of the drudgery has been eliminated from household duties by washing machines and vacuum cleaners, but most women have jobs and then go home to their "second shift" of cooking, cleaning, and child care. In many cultures, women remain subject to the rule of their father or husband and can be forced to marry the man chosen by their father. Throughout much of the world, the dependency of women on men and the inferiority of women to men is socially constructed and institutionalized, so much so that it seems natural to women and men. Such attitudes and practices, deeply embedded in culture, are very difficult to change.

Perhaps the most shocking problem of women is their everyday experience of violence and brutality as well as the threat of violence. In nearly every country, across all classes, women are beaten by their husbands and fathers, assaulted and raped by relatives, acquaintances, and strangers, and harassed and intimidated on the street, in school, and at work. Muslim women were systematically raped by Serbian soldiers in Bosnia, as were Tutsi women during the slaughter by the Hutu in Rwanda. This sexual violence is not random; it is aimed at women as women, and meant to frighten and control them. It amounts to "sexual terrorism," a system perpetuated by men for the domination of women.[39]

The most abhorrent custom related to gender violence and men's inordinate desire to control female sexuality is the practice of female genital mutilation. Female genital cutting is practiced by a wide variety of ethnic groups, whether their religion is Christian, Muslim, or Traditional, in a band of 28 countries in north-central Africa, from Egypt and Somalia to Senegal and the Ivory Coast.[40] In 1998, the World Health Organization estimated that 137 million women have undergone this centuries-old practice, and each year about 2 million more girls endure the procedure.[41] One form of the procedure involves a clitoridectomy, the removal of the clitoris and sometimes some of the labial tissue. In some countries, such as Mali, Ethiopia, and Sudan, infibulation, a more severe form of genital mutilation, is practiced. The clitoris and all of the woman's external genitalia are removed and the wound is sewn shut until she is married, leaving a small hole for urination and menstruation.[42] In some places genital cutting is done on girls aged 4 to 10; among other peoples it is a ritual of adolescence. It is done, usually without anesthesia, by local excisers, midwives, barbers, or relatives using a razor blade or crude knife. Female genital mutilation diminishes or eliminates a woman's ability to experience sexual pleasure. Besides the physical and psychological trauma of the procedure itself and its primary consequence, the cutting can result in difficult childbirth, serious infections, and even death.[43]

The purpose of the cutting, according to a local exciser in the Ivory Coast, is to insure a woman's fidelity to her husband and her family. A woman's role in life is to care for her children, keep house, and cook. If she has not been cut she might be distracted by her own sexual pleasure.[44] Many people who practice genital cutting believe that a woman will be sexually aggressive, even promiscuous, without the procedure. As an Egyptian farmer

One Woman's Story

In the spring of 1996, the story of Fauziya Kassindja, a 19-year-old woman who had fled from Togo in West Africa to the United States in order to avoid genital mutilation, became public. Ms. Kassindja arrived in the United States in December of 1994 and requested asylum. She was immediately imprisoned where she remained for sixteen months. Finally, public pressure led to her release, and her request for asylum was eventually granted.

Fauziya is the youngest of a family of seven children—two sons and five daughters—born to Muhammad and Hajia Kassindja. Among the Muslim Tchamba people in her city in rural Togo, polygamy is common and female genital cutting is nearly universal. Her mother's older sister died as a result of the practice, so Hajia was spared the procedure. Muhammad Kassindja started a trucking business that made his family rich by local standards and allowed him to thwart some of his people's traditions. He took only one wife; he made sure all of his children were educated; and, one by one, his daughters married men of their own choosing without being cut, until Fauziya was the only one remaining at home.

The situation changed drastically when Muhammad Kassindja died in 1993. Fauziya was then 16. According to Tchamba custom, Mrs. Kassindja was required to hand over her home and to cede the responsibility for Fauziya to her husband's widowed sister, Hadja Mamoude. The Kassindja family gave the widow an inheritance of about $3,500. Mouhamadou Kassindja, the family patriarch and a cousin of Muhammad, and Mrs. Mamoude promptly took Fauziya out of school and began negotiating with Issakah Ibrahim for her to become his fourth wife. Mr. Ibrahim insisted that Fauziya be cut, and the family readily agreed. Fauziya resisted both the marriage and the cutting. Her mother and an older sister helped Fauziya to run away on the eve of her wedding, literally minutes before her genital mutilation. Haija's inheritance was given to Fauziya so she could flee the country.

After Haija Kassindja was sure that her daughter was safe, she went before the family patriarch to beg for his forgiveness and ask to be allowed to live in his plain cement compound. Some male members of her family accompanied her to the formal apology. As a woman, she did not speak; a male cousin apologized on her behalf. She sat mute and motionless, head hung low, while Mouhamadou Kassindja upbraided her before finally accepting her apology. That afternoon she moved into his compound with two of the patriarch's four wives (the other two wives live in two different cities). The compound with its dingy courtyard will define her existence from now on, because the patriarch does not allow his wives to leave it.

explained, "If a woman is more passive it is in her interest, it is in her father's interest and in her husband's interest."[45]

The story of Fauziya Kassindja[46] (see sidebar above) illustrates many of the aspects of the oppression of women in the Two-Thirds World: the narrow definition of their domestic role, their subjection to patriarchal rule, their vulnerability to violence, and their lack of protection under the law.[47] While a government official in Togo admitted that excision is a problem, he insisted that poverty is the primary problem. Human rights and economic development, however, are not mutually exclusive goals, nor is development a prerequisite for respecting the human rights of women. Female genital cutting is mutilation. Education campaigns can be developed aimed at changing attitudes, and policies and laws can be enacted and enforced to prohibit female genital mutilation.

This is true not only in Togo or Egypt, but also in the United States. The custom of female genital mutilation has been imported to the United States by immigrants from Africa and the Middle East.[48] This practice has been illegal in most of Europe for over a decade. In the fall of 1996, the United States Congress also outlawed female genital mutilation. The new law requires federal authorities to inform immigrants that parents who arrange for their children to be cut here, and those who perform the cutting, face up to five years in prison. The law also requires U.S. representatives to international financial institutions to oppose loans to countries where the practice is common and whose governments have not carried out educational programs to prevent it.[49]

Violence and discrimination against women are among the most pervasive problems facing the global community, yet in many parts of the world women's rights are not commonly classified as human rights.[50] Although sexism is often fostered by religious practices, it is seldom intrinsic to such religious beliefs or tenets.[51] The dignity and equality of women need to be tenaciously fostered through education, public policy, and law.

RACE, RELIGION, CASTE

Discrimination also can be based on race, caste, or ethnicity. Ethnic conflict has become such a problem in the post-Cold War world that it will be the subject of the following chapter. This section will focus on the denial of human rights based on race or caste.

Race is difficult to define. Biologically and psychologically the human species is more alike than different, and the differences among individuals of a given race are far greater than the differences among races.[52] Theologically there is one human family with God as our common parent; we are all brothers and sisters to one another. But this theological affirmation of solidarity and community could just as well be based in biology. There are different blood types, but they are found throughout the human species. Any female human being can theoretically procreate with any other male human being. Tissue type and size, not race, are the obstacles to organ transplantation. Genetically human beings are one people. Nevertheless, race refers to the physical characteristics, primarily skin color, that distinguish one group of human beings from another. While race may be a social fabrication rooted in skin color, it is a differentiation that has led to much conflict, injustice, and suffering.

Race, then, is not the problem; *racism* is. Racism consists in a *belief* that one racial group is inherently superior to another racial group. In the twentieth century much attention has been paid to white racism—the attitude of superiority and supremacy of whites toward peoples of other colors—and justly so, since the European colonizers brought an insufferable belief in their innate superiority to their conquest of the world.[53] Racism is not the sole preserve of whites, but white racism has a particularly sordid modern history.

The Europeans who settled the United States developed a belief in "manifest destiny"—that they were a people chosen by God to rule this land, which had been given to them by God—to justify taking the land inhabited by the indigenous people and slaughtering the Native Americans. Dee Brown tells this story from the Indian perspective in his bestselling book, *Bury My Heart at Wounded Knee*.[54] It is a story of broken promises and savage massacres.

One example of the violence wrought is the massacre at Sand Creek in Colorado in November of 1864. Cheyenne and Arapaho Indians had camped at Sand Creek, about 40 miles from Fort Lyon, with the assurance that they were safe from attack. Major Anthony, the commander of Fort Lyon, had even encouraged the warriors to hunt buffalo to feed the tribe. Most of the men were away from the camp, when 700 U.S. cavalrymen under the command of Colonel Chivington and Major Anthony descended on the camp at sunrise, firing randomly at the Indians. Chief Black Kettle came out of his lodge and raised an American flag and a white flag of surrender on a long lodgepole. He called to his people not to be afraid, that the soldiers wouldn't hurt them. As hundreds of women and children gathered under Black Kettle's American flag, the soldiers opened fire from two sides of the camp. The cavalry indiscriminately slaughtered men, women, and children. Most of the dead Indians were scalped by the soldiers and many were mutilated. Although lack of discipline, drunkenness, cowardice, and poor marksmanship allowed many Indians to escape, when the shooting ended 105 Indian women and children and 28 men were dead. Most had been unarmed and had offered no resistance. Of the 47 casualties among the soldiers, most were the result of their careless firing on each other.[55] This is sadly characteristic of the way the West was won.

Those Native Americans who still live on reservations experience the highest rate of poverty and the shortest life span of any group of Americans. A few tribes, such as the Mashantucket Pequot and the Mohegan in Connecticut, have exploited loopholes in the law to open casinos that have been financially successful. Native peoples have been victims of white racism in the United States and, as we saw in the section on colonialism in the first chapter, throughout the world.

One of the most repulsive examples of racism was the trade in African slaves. As many as nine million Africans were captured and shipped to the New World prior to 1863, nearly half of them to the southern United States.[56] Many died from the horrid conditions on slave ships. When they arrived, they were bought and sold like cattle. Their labor was key to the plantation system in the southern United States, the Caribbean, and South America. African slaves were beaten, tortured, and raped by their white masters. Families were broken apart and living conditions were abominable. In the movie *Roots,* a captured runaway slave is given the choice between castration and having his foot cut off. Slaves were totally stripped of their dignity as human beings.

In the United States, when the system of slavery was abolished after the Civil War (1861–65), it was replaced with a system of segregation that lasted for over a hundred years. Blacks in the South were kept separate from whites. Blacks received an inadequate education, were excluded from better-paying jobs, denied the vote, and confined to substandard housing with few public services. "Whites Only" signs forced blacks to use different rest rooms, public parks, drinking fountains, and restaurants.[57] The Civil Rights Act of 1964, enacted after years of non-violent protests led by the Reverend Dr. Martin Luther King, Jr. and others, prohibited segregated public facilities in the United States, and the Voting Rights Act of the following year enfranchised blacks in America.[58]

Slavery and the system of segregation have been abolished in the United States, but racism and its effects persist. Progress has been made, but intermarriage and genuinely integrated neighborhoods, schools, and churches remain rare, while discrimination, direct or systematic, is still too common.[59] At present, the United States is a multi-racial society rather than a truly integrated community. America's history of white racism will not be easy to transform.

Racism is a belief in racial superiority. Once it has been taught and ingrained in a person's consciousness and a culture's structure, it is very difficult to change. Since racial superiority is *believed* rather than factual, it tends to be immune to evidence to the contrary and selective in reflecting on experience. Thus, for instance, if a white person believes that blacks are stupid, the white person will tend not to notice a brilliant black physicist or a competent black businessperson. Because racism is a belief, not a logical conclusion, it is difficult to correct. This is even more true when racism is imbedded in and reinforced by culture.

South Africa's recently ended system of apartheid (separateness in the Afrikaner language) provides another particularly appalling example of white racism. This system of state-enforced segregation, which was the last bastion of white supremacy in Africa, allowed a white minority—only 18 percent of a population of over 40 million—to keep strict control of the black majority. Apartheid guaranteed 87 percent of the land and 75 percent of the income to the white minority. Blacks were legally allowed to live only in one of twelve *bantustans* (so-called homelands), and were required to have a special permit to live and work in the other 87 percent of the country. Blacks were required to carry a valid passbook with them at all times or be imprisoned. Public facilities, schools, and residences were strictly segregated. Blacks had no civil or political standing in the Republic of South Africa. Resisting the system of apartheid could result in arrest, detention, torture, and death. Nelson Mandela, the first black president of a reformed South Africa, spent nearly forty years of his life in prison for resisting apartheid.[60]

The formal system of apartheid in South Africa collapsed in 1994 because of courageous resistance from blacks and because of economic, social, and political sanctions imposed by the world community. As in the United States, the system has been abolished, but racism and its effects persist.

While Europe has long been split by ethnic conflict, racial tensions were less noticeable until recently. Now racism is rearing its ugly head in response to the immigration of people of color. Asians, Africans, and Caribbean blacks from the Commonwealth countries of the former British Empire are flowing into Great Britain, changing the complexion of British society and causing a conflict of cultures. Prejudice is sometimes expressed violently toward immigrants, who often respond with more violence. France continues to experience an influx of immigrants and refugees from former colonies in Africa, especially Algeria, and is having similar problems in integrating them into French society. Neo-Nazis and skinheads in Germany have attacked "guestworkers" from Turkey and immigrants and refugees from developing countries.[61]

Because of the slave trade, Brazil has the largest African population outside of Africa. Blacks comprise one-third to one-half of Brazil's 160 million people. Because there has been considerable intermarriage among Brazilians, Brazilians use more than twenty terms to describe their various hues. Such color consciousness has been developed by a social preference for light-skinned persons and a subtle pattern of discrimination that has relegated blacks to the bottom of the economic order. The percentage of blacks in college or public employment, for example, is minuscule.[62]

Only 1 percent of Peru's population is black, but these people are employed almost exclusively in menial jobs, such as pallbearers and doormen, where their skin color is thought to add prestige. The country's Indian majority suffers much of the same racism at the hands of the Hispanic elite, but hostilities born of colonial history keep Indians and blacks from uniting against discrimination. In fact they often discriminate against each other.[63]

Racism, unfortunately, is hardly a white prerogative. Reverse racism in response to racial oppression, while perhaps understandable, is still racism and is unjust. At least some elements of the Black Muslim movement in the United States have engaged in reverse racism. Asian shopkeepers in black communities in the United States have sometimes experienced discrimination, and there is documented tension between black and Hispanic communities.

In Central and East Africa, black Africans treated Asian immigrants with harsh discrimination in the years after independence. The Asians were descendants of Indian immigrants who had arrived in Kenya, Malawi, Tanzania, Zambia, and Uganda as part of the free immigration policy of the British Empire in the late nineteenth century. Many became shopkeepers and traders. When these countries gained their independence, the Asians found themselves excluded in the effort to Africanize the management of the government and local companies. The discrimination was clearest in Uganda, where the dictator Idi Amin expelled all Asians from the country and confiscated their property.[64]

There is resentment in the Philippines and Malaysia toward families of Chinese origin who have often enjoyed business success. In recent history, the Japanese have exhibited xenophobic tendencies, especially in their conquest of Korea and China during the period during World War II. Racism, prejudice, and discrimination are universal temptations.

Anti-Semitism is widespread in Europe and in much of the world. It found its most horrific expression in the Holocaust during World War II,[65] and unfortunately it continues to the present. Since September 11, 2001, Islamaphobia, the fear of and consequent discrimination against Muslims, has increased in the West. The Ku Klux Klan in the United States persecuted blacks, Jews, and Catholics. Surely Muslims would have been on the list had there been more of them around during the heyday of the Klan. Christians have been persecuted by radical Hindus in India, and Muslims and Hindus engage in sporadic bloodbaths against one another there. Religion exacerbates the conflicts in the Middle East and in Northern Ireland.

Caste refers to prejudice and discrimination based on one's birth family. It means that one's position in life is determined by one's birth family. It is similar to class, which is an economic distinction between groups of people, but it is even more insidious in that caste implies little possibility of improving one's lot in life. It is a kind of predestination. In India's Hindu culture, people are born into one of four castes. But about 15 percent of India's population are born outside of a caste, into a fifth caste called the "Untouchables." These people were considered unclean, and they were relegated into the lowest occupations—waste removal, disposing of dead animals, or working with leather. In the past they were made to live on the margins of the village or city and were excluded from temples and public facilities. Mahatma Gandhi called the Untouchables *Harijans,* the children of God, and he vigorously campaigned for their inclusion into society. India's present constitution completely outlaws the exclusion of Untouchables, making the observance of this practice a crime. Specific laws forbid discrimination and set up affirmative action programs for the *Harijans.* But the laws are hard to enforce and implementation has been slow.[66]

While the plight of the Untouchables in India (also known as the *Dalits*) is perhaps the clearest example of discrimination based on caste, it is practiced in more subtle forms in many other societies. Caste and class can often largely determine one's fate in life.

DISCRIMINATION AGAINST HOMOSEXUALS

Gay bashing, verbal and physical, is so widespread and so controversial as to deserve special mention. Homosexuality has been condemned by many religions and cultures in the past. As a result, homosexuals have been marginalized and persecuted. Many perished in the concentration camps of the Holocaust, for example. There is good reason today to confess this past as sordid and sinful, to repent, and to recognize the full humanity of homosexuals. Because this is "a Christian primer," the focus here will be on the church and its teaching on and treatment of homosexuals.

Until the emergence of psychology in the twentieth century, sex acts between people of the same sex were thought to be unnatural. But now we know that a certain percentage of the population is sexually attracted to persons of the same sex rather than of the opposite sex. This idea of sexual orientation or sexual preference, like the term "homosexual" itself, is relatively new. One's sexual orientation, whether heterosexual, homosexual, or bisexual, is experienced as a given, not a choice. This new understanding necessitates a re-thinking of the traditional condemnation of homosexuals.

The Catholic Church and many Protestant denominations have responded by distinguishing between homosexuals, that is, *persons* who prefer the same sex and homosexual *acts* of genital expression. Homosexuals are not condemned, but homosexual acts are still considered sinful. While many theologians and some denominations would go further and accept both homosexuals and homosexual acts in a committed relationship, even this official distinction between person and act calls into question any discrimination or persecution against homosexuals. Even if one considers a person's lifestyle immoral (e.g., too materialistic or sexually unfaithful), that does not justify violence against that person or discrimination in employment, housing, education, or other opportunities enjoyed by every citizen. Disrespect for and discrimination against homosexuals is wrong, and it should be made illegal in order to offer protection for rights long denied.

CONCLUSION

Human rights, as articulated in the International Bill of Rights, are rooted in the dignity of persons created in the image of God, a dignity realized in community. A guarantee of human rights is the minimal obligation of any state worthy of allegiance, and human rights are important standards for guiding the international obligations of states and foreign policy. The ultimate litmus test of human rights in any society is how the guilty and despised are treated.

STUDY QUESTIONS

1. How do you explain the paradox that while human rights are increasingly recognized in theory, they continue to be abused in practice?
2. Should human rights be a cornerstone of U.S. foreign policy? What would be the implications of a principled human rights foreign policy for trade policy with countries such as China, Saudi Arabia, Pakistan, Myanmar (Burma), Congo, and Syria, for example?
3. Is the idea of "rights" being taken too far in U.S. society today? What *are* the rights of human beings?
4. Discuss the cultural practice of female genital mutilation. Is this a legitimate cultural practice or a violation of human rights? When are practices relative to a particular culture? Are there universal human rights whose violation can never be justified?

5. Discuss the inequality between men and women, in the world and in U.S. society. Is religion a cause of the inequality?
6. Many contend that the United States continues to be a society deeply divided along racial lines. What do you think? How can racism be addressed in the United States?
7. Discuss homophobia.

CHAPTER FIVE

Conflict and War

"You have heard that it was said, 'an eye for an eye, and a tooth for a tooth.' But now I tell you: do not take revenge on one who does you wrong. If anyone slaps you on your right cheek, let him slap your left cheek too. . . . You have heard that it was said, 'Love your friends, hate your enemies.' But now I tell you: love your enemies and pray for those who persecute you, . . ." (Matthew 5:38–39, 43–44, Good News Version)

"One of the most disturbing threats to peace in the post-Cold War world has been the spread of conflicts rooted in national, ethnic, racial, and religious differences. . . . Precisely because of their intractable and explosive nature, ethnic conflicts can be resolved only through political dialogue and negotiation. War and violence are unacceptable means for resolving ethnic conflicts; they serve only to exacerbate them. Nor are political solutions alone sufficient. Also needed is the commitment to reconciliation that is at the heart of the Christian and other religious traditions. For religious believers can imagine what some would dismiss as unrealistic: that even the most intense hatreds can be overcome by love, that free human beings can break historic cycles of violence and injustice, and that deeply divided people can learn to live together in peace."[1]

"No peace without justice, no justice without forgiveness."[2]

The twentieth century was surely among the bloodiest in a bloody history, with two world wars, wars of independence, wars to contain or spread communism under the umbrella of the Cold War, and a goodly number of revolutions and civil wars. The last decade of the century was characterized by an eruption of ethno-nationalist conflict in places such as Bosnia and Rwanda. In the early years of the twenty-first century, ethno-nationalist conflict has subsided somewhat, only to be supplanted by the re-emergence of "nearly resolved" conflicts and by terrorism. The multiple causes of conflict make the resolution of conflict and the prevention of war especially complicated at this moment in history.

Conflict is inevitable. Nearly everyone agrees that war is the worst way to respond to conflict, but many will also argue that it is sometimes necessary. Conflict results from a clash of interests and/or ideas. Fortunately, most of the time conflict between states or within a state can be resolved without violence.

The pacifist or nonviolent strand within the Christian tradition contends that war can never be morally justified, that war is always wrong. In the fifth century, when the Holy Roman Empire was faced with a Barbarian invasion, St. Augustine baptized the Greek and Roman concept of a "just" war into the Christian tradition. Augustine taught that war could be a rule-governed exception in which the state could depart from Jesus' command to love our enemies. If fought for a just cause, under legitimate authority, and with the right attitude, war could be morally justified.

The idea of just war has developed through Christian history, becoming what might be called a "justified war tradition." Woven through the tapestry of Christian tradition has been a minor thread of Christian nonviolence.[3] Today some theologians are developing a third paradigm for the moral analysis of conflict called "just peacemaking," which aims to emphasize God's call to be peacemakers in a realistic and practical way.[4] War itself has mutated dramatically in contemporary times. Can modern war still be morally justified? To respond to that question we need to examine modern warfare as well as the resources for analyzing war and peace within the Christian tradition.

This chapter will explore the new landscape of global conflict[5] at the beginning of the twenty-first century. In light of the just-war and just-peacemaking paradigms for the moral analysis of conflict within the Christian tradition, it will examine the potential causes of conflict and highlight some areas where war or peace is breaking out. The major themes of the chapter will be ethno-nationalist conflict, humanitarian intervention, and a moral response to terrorism.

ETHNO-NATIONALIST CONFLICT AND HUMANITARIAN INTERVENTION

The decade of the 1990s may well be remembered as ushering in an era of ethno-nationalist conflict. When the Cold War ended, many people expected a period of peace and prosperity to follow. One analyst even proclaimed "the end of history."[6] History, however, did not move into a peaceful reign of democratic capitalism, but degenerated into a morass of ethnic conflict. The international community found itself torn between the principles of national sovereignty, territorial integrity, and nonintervention on the one hand, and the principles of self-determination and human rights on the other hand, and did not know how to respond. Ethnic conflict, in its many apparitions, which resulted in gross violations of human rights, remains a serious barrier to peace in the contemporary world.

Although, in a sense, ethnic conflict is as old as human history, nationalism gives it a new color. Clans and tribes have always fought one another over territory or resources, or sometimes simply because of fear of people outside of their own group. Peoples have united to form empires by conquering other peoples. The idea of a sovereign state, however, is relatively new in history and the principle of self-determination that decrees that nations should be states is even newer.

Americans tend to have difficulty understanding ethno-nationalist conflict. Because the European colonizers nearly annihilated the indigenous people in North America and because the United States has been settled by wave after wave of immigrants, the United States has always been a multi-ethnic society. Most large American cities have their "little Italy," "Germantown," or "Chinatown" sections, but today that often designates a cluster of good ethnic restaurants rather than a genuinely ethnic enclave. There is much debate about whether America is truly a melting pot, but while there are surely ethnic and especially racial tensions and conflicts, the American reality is quite different from that of most countries in the world. Since every ethnic group has come here at some point to establish a new home, no ethnic group in the United States (except the remaining indigenous people) can claim that this is *its* ancestral home. In most other countries several competing ethnic groups do make that claim. Thus, to understand the power of ethno-nationalism in other countries, Americans often have to disregard their own experience.

When Nations Want to Become States

Ethnicity is difficult to define, with no strictly objective criteria essential for its existence. Rather, ethnicity is subjective, a conviction of commonality. Groups of people can distinguish themselves from other groups by characteristics such as language, religion, social customs, physical appearance, region of residence, or by a combination of these features.[7] In a way, ethnic groups are "psychological communities" whose members share a persisting sense of common interest and identity that is based on some combination of shared historical experience and valued cultural traits.[8] When an ethnic group becomes politicized and begins to claim a certain territory as its homeland, it becomes a "nation."[9]

Technically, there is a difference between a nation and a state and between nationalism and patriotism, although the terms are often used interchangeably. Properly speaking, "nation" refers to a group of people who believe they share a common ancestry, or to the largest human grouping predicated on a myth of common ancestry. It is close to the notion of a fully extended family.[10] There is no need for the belief in a common ancestry to be factual or historical. Indeed, as Walker Connor, an expert on ethnicity and nationalism, says, "the myth of common and exclusive descent can overcome a battery of contrary fact."[11] In another place, Connor puts it this way, "It is not chronological or factual history that is the key to the nation, but sentient or felt history. All that is required for the existence of a nation is that the members share an intuitive conviction of the group's separate origin and evolution."[12] Thus, the existence of a nation—a people—is subjective, subconscious, and sometimes even sentimental in nature. It is based on blood and belonging. It is a phenomenon of the masses, not a proclamation of an elite.[13] Nationalism, then, is the love and loyalty one feels for one's nation or people.

An important aspect of nationalism is the sense of a homeland. There are a few immigrant societies, such as the United States, Argentina, and Australia, but most of the land masses of the world are divided into ethnic homelands: a Scotland (land of the Scots), Poland, Finland, Zululand, Kazakhstan (*stan* means "land of"), Afghanistan, and the like. Nations have a strong attachment to a place—where they feel they originated, where their ancestors are buried, where their blood has been spilled. Again, this perception need not, and often will not, accord with historical fact, but that in no way diminishes a people's attachment to the "land of their forebears." Since a nation feels a sense of primal ownership for a place, its people view others, even those who may have lived there for centuries, as aliens or outsiders in their homeland.[14] Nationalism, then, when stirred by some change or current event, comes to mean the reclamation of a people's homeland by ejecting aliens who have taken up residence there. In the period from 1991 to 1995, in the villages of the Krajina section of Croatia and in much of Bosnia, this meant literally the elimination and expulsion of one's neighbors.[15]

A "state," on the other hand, is a legal and political entity, a government that exercises control over a defined territory.[16] Contemporary states are recognized as sovereign, both internally and externally. States exercise control over the people within their territory, and they interact autonomously with one another, signing treaties, joining organizations, setting trade policies, and the like. The love and loyalty one feels for one's country or state is properly called patriotism.

Thus, one may correctly refer to British patriotism, but to Scottish, Welsh, or English nationalism; to Canadian patriotism, but to Quebecois nationalism; to Belgian patriotism, but Flemish nationalism, and so on. The difficulty is that in a world of perhaps 5,000 nations, there are only around 195 states. Of those states, only about 15, such as Japan, Iceland, and Portugal, are ethnically homogeneous, or genuine nation-states. Thus, more than 90 percent of all states are ethnically heterogeneous, that is, they are comprised of more than one significant ethnic group. In 40 percent of these states, there are five or more significant ethnic groups, and in nearly one-third the largest ethnic group is not even a majority (e.g., Kazakhstan). The state of Nigeria contains more than 100 different ethnic groups (as did the former Soviet Union).[17]

Many ethnic groups coexist amicably within a single state, as do Swedes who live in Finland, for example. Others become assimilated into multi-ethnic societies, such as the Irish in the United States. But when an ethnic group begins to coalesce to take political action because of its swelling sense of identity or because of its victimization through discrimination, the resulting conflict can threaten to rip apart a state. The principle of national self-determination, which says that nations or peoples should be autonomous and free to control their own destiny, can wreak havoc in multi-national states.[18]

Ethno-national conflict does not always lead to violence or civil war. Since the end of the Cold War, for example, Czechoslovakia has amicably split into the Czech Republic and Slovakia. The breakup of the Soviet Union into its fifteen constituent republics created fifteen new states by political fiat rather than by war. Most of these new states, however, face their own internal ethnic conflicts and these have not always been peacefully resolved, as the war in Chechnya illustrates.

When ethno-national conflict does become violent, the struggle is often protracted and brutal. States do not readily cede territory or authority, and ethnic groups who have power do not easily accede to the demands of the minority or the oppressed. Thus, fighting can linger for decades as it has in Northern Ireland, Israel, and Sri Lanka. Ethnic conflict is often motivated by hatred of the other group. This polarizes the conflict and the out-group is often dehumanized and stripped of all human rights. Atrocities by one group provoke atrocities by the other group, resulting in a destructive spiral of violence. Any restraints called for by the rules and conventions of war fall by the wayside. Genocide—killing members of a group because of their ethnicity with the intent to destroy in whole or in part the ethnic group itself[19]—becomes the logic of much inter-ethnic warfare. Because such conflicts are not only about politics or economics but are filled with personal and cultural animosity, they tend to be extremely difficult to resolve.[20] The trust necessary for negotiation and conflict resolution is often absent.

Although there may be as many as 5,000 "nations" in the contemporary world (since there are at least that many linguistic groups),[21] Ted Robert Gurr, director of the Minorities at Risk project, counted 275 communal groups in 1999 (down from 292 in 1994) that were taking political action to assert their collective interests against the states that claim to govern them. This number includes both national peoples asserting their need for autonomy or independence and minority groups trying to protect or improve their status within a state. These 275 politically active ethnic groups comprise over a billion people, or about 17 percent of the world's population. While no region of the world is immune from serious ethnic conflict, sub-Saharan Africa has the greatest concentration of minorities at risk—67 groups incorporating over a third of the regional population. At the turn of the century 59 armed, ethnically based rebellions were under way in the world.[22]

Contemporary ethnic conflict is often part of the heritage of history. Israel, for example, was at the crossroad of empires and civilizations dating back to the Egyptians, Assyrians, and Babylonians, and later the Greeks and Romans. Jerusalem has changed hands dozens of times. Similarly, the Balkans marked the dividing line between the Ottoman Empire in the East and the Roman Empire in the West. Thus, division and conflict in Bosnia go back nearly a millennium.

Not surprisingly, colonialism is key to many of the ethnic conflicts in the Two-Thirds World. In the first chapter we noted that the European powers arbitrarily divided up Africa among themselves at the Congress of Berlin in 1884, drawing boundaries on a map with little regard for ethno-national territories.

The legacy of colonialism has also left its mark on South Asia. India, a patchwork of principalities and a tapestry of tribes tied to villages, was united only by British rule (1757–1947). Religious conflict between Hindus and Muslims led to the creation of Pakistan in 1947, and then to the war that resulted in Bangladesh in 1971. Religious tension continues to cause conflicts as Sikh and Kashmir rebels seek independence from India. The potential for other ethnic rebellions in the region is great.

Colonialism has also had lasting effects on the world's indigenous peoples. The 36 million indigenous peoples of the Americas comprise only 5 percent of the total population, but they are half the population in Bolivia, Peru, and Guatemala. As a consequence of colonialism, Africans were transported as slaves to the new world, and immigrant workers were moved from colony to colony (from India to Africa, for example) for their managerial or commercial skills or for their labor. Thus did colonialism plant the seeds of ethnic conflict: "Conquered peoples seek to regain their lost autonomy; indigenous peoples ask for restoration of their traditional lands; immigrant workers and the descendants of slaves demand full equality."[23]

Contemporary ethnic conflict, however, is not inevitable. Although imperial conquest and colonial rule provide a historical backdrop, past divisions or discrimination do not necessarily lead to present conflict. Nor can ethnic conflict simply be ascribed to human nature. Human beings are capable of transcending the social psychology of in-group/out-group violence. While belonging to a community of like-minded persons is important for healthy human development (both identity and relationships), it does not follow that other communities must be hated and fought. Ethnic conflict, although all too common, is neither historically inevitable nor biologically determined.

Christian Ethics and the Idolatry of Nationalism

Christian theology and ethics can provide a critical perspective for evaluating ethnic conflict and nationalism. In the Christian framework the particular and the universal are not in opposition to one another; the Christian tradition affirms both.[24] An ethic faithful to the Gospel must be universal in scope, extending love to each and every person. Since all of humanity shares a common Creator, Redeemer, and Sanctifier, we are one human family, brothers and sisters all. Christian love cannot discriminate; it must embrace every person, near and far.

The teachings of Christian tradition are also incarnational and sacramental, particular and practical.[25] Christian love is concrete and real, and Christian living is essentially relational and communal. The church is catholic (universal) and apostolic (a tradition inherited from our ancestors in the faith), but it is also local—incarnated in the lives of those who gather together to hear the story, share a meal, and become the body of Christ in the world.

Contemporary Catholic social thought has used the virtue and principle of "solidarity" to try to capture the concrete, communal, and universal nature of the Christian faith. "[Solidarity] is not a feeling of vague compassion or shallow distress at the misfortunes of so many people, both near and far. On the contrary, it is a firm and persevering determination to commit oneself to the common good; that is to say to the good of all and of each individual, because we are all really responsible for all."[26]

In light of this framework, patriotism and nationalism can be good, but neither is an absolute good. When loyalty and love for country or nation become absolute and fanatical, they become idolatrous and can be harmful. Love of country or nation is good and valuable. It is a source of identity and of relationships and community that create special duties and obligations, just as the special relationships of marriage, parenthood, and friendship create special responsibilities. But neither patriotism or nationalism should be an ultimate or primary loyalty, exercising unquestioned authority in our lives. State or nation can become an idol, and that sort of allegiance should be guarded against, resisted, and rejected.

Our devotion to state or nation should be characterized by a certain emotional detachment that tempers its passion. Loyalty to one's country or people must be balanced by other commitments, both more intimate and more universal.[27]

A distinction between civic nationalism and ethnic nationalism, made by Michael Ignatieff, can be helpful. Civic nationalism is capable of uniting diverse people around a political creed and a civic ethos. It is based on a constitutional rule of law that facilitates the participation of every citizen and of every community in the public life of the state. One chooses to be loyal to the state because of one's experience of justice and order in the society. Ethnic nationalism, in contrast, claims that an individual's deepest attachments are inherited, not chosen. Such allegiance tends to be uncritical, even idolatrous.[28]

A commitment to human rights can reconcile loyalty to a particular state or nation with a global ethic that encourages a universal love. Patriotism or nationalism must be embraced only as part of a larger morality of solidarity and human rights. Love of country or nation can no more justify hatred of foreigners than friendship can legitimize despising those with whom one is not acquainted. National sovereignty is, then, a real but relative value: patriotism and nationalism are real values, but they are relative to respecting the human rights of every person in the human family.[29] In given circumstances, human rights claims can override the principle of territorial sovereignty and nonintervention. Belief in the theory of human rights points to minimal requirements for right relationships with one another in a just society. Protecting human rights is a helpful way to articulate what it means to reverence the dignity of the human person and to embrace all of humanity as family.

In more practical terms, ethical analysis suggests that communal or group rights should be recognized in international law. Thus far, the declarations and covenants promulgated by the United Nations focus on individual rights and the rights of states. Formal international recognition of the rights and responsibilities of ethnic groups or communities within states, the rights of "nations,"[30] would help to balance the needs of individuals versus those of the common good.

Religion seems to be an important factor in many ethnic conflicts: between Catholics and Protestants in Northern Ireland, Jewish Israelis and Muslim Palestinians, Buddhist Sinhala and Hindu Tamils in Sri Lanka, and among Catholic Croats, Orthodox Serbs, and Bosnian Muslims. Religion is one of the features that can distinguish one ethnic group from another. Since religion pertains to core values, it can inflate the intensity and intractability of ethnic conflict.[31]Religious belief can even be used to legitimate or authorize intolerance toward another ethnic group.[32] Most analysts, however, have concluded that while religious divisions can be a contributing factor, religion itself is seldom the root cause, main motivation, or principal reason for ethnic conflict.[33]

While it may be true that religion is more peripheral than central to ethnic conflict, the use of religion to inflame nationalism remains troubling. Religious traditions profess universal love, forgiveness, and reconciliation. Ethno-nationalism preaches hatred, revenge, and division. How is it that religion can be co-opted to espouse hatred and violence? Why isn't religion a powerful force for forgiveness, reconciliation, and peace in Bosnia, the Middle East, or Sri Lanka? The American Catholic bishops deserve to be heard and heeded when they proclaim:

> Every child murdered, every woman raped, every town "cleansed," every hatred uttered in the name of religion is a crime against God and a scandal for religious believers. Religious violence and nationalism deny what we profess in faith: We are all created in the image of the same God and destined for the same eternal salvation. "[N]o Christian can knowingly foster or support structures and attitudes that unjustly divide individuals or groups."[34]

Religion can be and has been a source of courage, forgiveness, and reconciliation in places of ethnic conflict, yet the shadow side of religion remains troubling.[35]

THE GLOBAL LANDSCAPE OF CONFLICT AND WAR

At the end of the twentieth century Ted Robert Gurr, the director of the Minorities at Risk project, wrote, "Comparative evidence shows that the intensity of ethnopolitical conflict subsided in most world regions from the mid- through late 1990s and that relatively few new contenders have emerged since the early 1990s."[36] Since then, however, the peace process involving Israel and the Palestinians has broken down and Russia has renewed hostilities in Chechnya. It seems that when one fire in Africa is brought under control, such as the civil war in Sierra Leone, another fire breaks out somewhere else, such as the Ivory Coast. And now the United States is waging war on terrorism. Thus, Gurr's optimistic assessment at the end of the twentieth century may already require re-assessment in the early years of the twenty-first century.

It is impossible to predict when conflict will erupt into war.[37] It is clear, however, that our world continues to be a violent and dangerous place. This section will attempt to sketch the global landscape of ethno-nationalist conflict at the beginning of the twentieth century.

The Middle East

Israel/Palestine

In the Middle East, the Israeli Jews and the Palestinians, who are Arab and mostly Muslim, both claim the small territory on the eastern edge of the Mediterranean Sea as their homeland. The roots of both claims go back centuries—to the Hebrew Scriptures in the case of the Jews and to the first and seventh centuries of the Common Era for the Palestinians.

The more immediate claims go back to the first and second world wars. During World War I the desperate (and duplicitous) British promised the Palestinians their independence in the Hussein-McMahon Correspondence (1915–16), while promising Jews a homeland in Palestine in the Balfour Declaration (1917), in exchange for support for the British cause against Germany.[38] After World War II displaced Jews who had survived the Holocaust poured into Palestine fired by the Zionist dream of a homeland; then in late 1947, the newly formed United Nations voted to partition

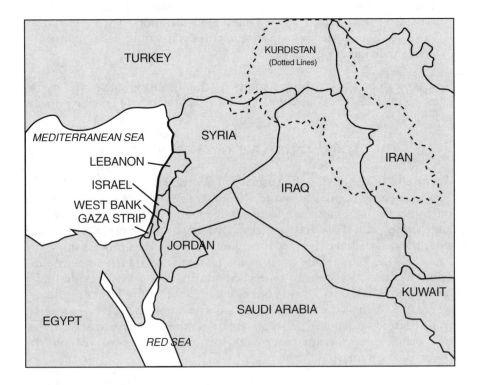

Palestine. By spring 1948, Israel declared itself a state.[39] The five surrounding Arab states—Lebanon, Syria, Jordan, Iraq, and Egypt—vehemently refused to recognize Israel and immediately mounted a half-hearted attack that failed.[40]

The creation of Israel in 1948 provided a homeland and place of refuge for Jews who had been victims of anti-Semitism, which had manifested itself in the horror of the Holocaust. At the same time it displaced the Arab people who had been living in Palestine for well over a millennium. As a result of the partition and the 1948 war, many Palestinians fled the region or were settled in refugee camps on the West Bank of the Jordan River or in the Gaza Strip. The surrounding Arab countries attacked Israel in 1967 and again in 1973 and were soundly defeated both times. In 1967 Israel took control of the whole of Palestine, occupying both the West Bank and Gaza. U.N. Resolution 242 called on Israel to withdraw to its pre-1967 borders, but Israel has refused to do so in the name of its own security.

The pendulum has swung between peace and war and hope and despair several times since 1973, but the conflict has thus far proven impossible to resolve. In 1979, U.S. President Jimmy Carter brokered a peace agreement between Egypt's Anwar Sadat and Israel's Menachem Begin at Camp David. In 1982, however, the Israeli army crossed into southern Lebanon and took control of Palestinian refugee camps that had been sources of intermittent attacks on Israel. In late 1987 the first *intifada,* a Palestinian uprising characterized by strikes, protests, riots, and Palestinian teenagers throwing stones at Israeli tanks and soldiers, began and persisted for three years. Israel responded with increasing violence and repression. In 1993 negotiations took place in Oslo, Norway, resulting in a resolution for increasing Palestinian autonomy that was signed at the White House by Israeli Prime Minister Yitzhak Rabin and Palestinian Liberation Organization (PLO) Chairman Yasser Arafat.[41] In the summer of 2000, President Clinton called Yasser Arafat and Israeli prime minister Ehud Barak to another meeting, this time at Camp David, to try to complete the Oslo process, but an agreement could not be reached. A month later, a visit by Israeli politician and former defense minister Ariel Sharon to the Muslim holy site, the Al-Aqsa Mosque on Temple Mount in Jerusalem, sparked a second Palestinian *intifada* and some of the worst violence in the conflict.[42] Since then Palestinian suicide bombers have been blowing up buses, restaurants, and shopping centers in Israel, and in response to each attack the Israeli security forces have escalated the level of violence and repression in the West Bank and the Gaza Strip.

Although some, including President Clinton, blamed Arafat's intransigence for the failure of the second Camp David summit,[43] from the Palestinian perspective the Oslo accords only institutionalized Israeli control in the West Bank and the Gaza Strip.[44] In a broader sense, efforts to resolve this conflict have failed because the interests and goals of the two sides are diametrically opposed. Israel wants a Jewish state that is a safe homeland for oppressed Jews and that is secure from attacks by its Arab neighbors. Palestinians do not recognize Israel's right to exist on land confiscated from them. They want their land back, and they want an independent Palestine with contiguous borders and free access so that some five million Palestinian refugees can return. Both sides claim Jerusalem as their capital. Most outside analysts point to the creation of two independent states—Israel and Palestine—as the solution, but this obvious step fails to satisfy the interests of either side.

Iraq

There are other conflicts in the Middle East. In August 1990, Iraq invaded and occupied its tiny, oil-rich neighbor, Kuwait. Saddam Hussein, Iraq's tyrannical leader, had economic and historical reasons for invading Kuwait. Iraq had borrowed money from Kuwait to wage a war against Iran in the 1980s, and Saddam thought this debt should be forgiven in light of Iraqi suffering for the Sunni Muslim cause in that war. There was also a dispute about oil wells on the Iraq-Kuwait border. Kuwait had been split off from Iraq at the end of the colonial period in an attempt to limit Iraq's power in the region. Thus Iraq was reclaiming territory it considered its own and asserting its hegemony in the region. The Iraqi occupation of Kuwait was violent and brutal.

None of these reasons justified the Iraqi invasion in the eyes of the rest of the world, which became gravely concerned at the prospect of Saddam Hussein gaining increasing control of the world's oil supply. The first President Bush was able to assemble a U.S.-led coalition, under the auspices of the United Nations and with the approval of the U.S. Congress, to reverse the first cross-border aggression of the post-Cold War world. The coalition that fought the Persian Gulf War in early 1991 was supported by all the major powers and by nearly every country in the Middle East. After several weeks of intense bombing of Iraq, allied ground troops liberated Kuwait from a devastated and terrified Iraqi army. Having accomplished the objective, the Bush administration stopped short of marching into Baghdad and overthrowing Saddam Hussein.

The cease-fire agreement required Iraq to destroy its chemical and biological weapons and its nuclear weapons program; it also imposed economic sanctions on Iraq until U.N. weapons inspectors certified that these weapons had been eliminated. The weapons inspectors found that Iraq's nuclear weapons program was more advanced than most experts thought, and they supervised the destruction of much of Iraq's cache of weapons of mass destruction. Iraq, however, never fully cooperated with this process, and Saddam Hussein became increasingly resistant to weapons inspections. In 1998 he finally barred the U.N. inspection teams from Iraq, claiming that the inspectors were spies and that their invasive inspections were disrespectful of Iraqi sovereignty. Meanwhile, the economic sanctions, coupled with the callous irresponsibility of Saddam's regime, were creating a human tragedy in Iraq. In the period from 1990 to 1997 it is likely that the economic sanctions contributed to the deaths of about 500,000 Iraqis, with nearly two-thirds of them children.[45] As of this writing the sanctions and the deaths of vulnerable Iraqis due to malnutrition and lack of medicines and medical technology continue.

After the Persian Gulf War, the United States also created two "no-fly zones" in northern and southern Iraq to protect the Kurdish minority in the north and the Shiite majority in the south. American (and some British) warplanes patrolling these no-fly zones regularly return fire when threatened by Iraqi air defenses.[46] Thus, there has been continuous low-intensity conflict in Iraqi airspace for over a decade.

In the summer of 2002, the second President Bush declared that Saddam Hussein was developing nuclear weapons and possessed chemical and biological weapons that threatened the security and interests of the United States and that the Iraqi regime supported terrorists, including Al Qaeda. President Bush called for "regime change" in Iraq and asserted that the United States could mount a pre-emptive attack on Iraq to prevent an Iraqi-sponsored terrorist attack on the United States or its security interests. The Bush administration seemed committed to invading Iraq, deposing Saddam Hussein, and establishing an Arab democracy in Iraq—unilaterally if necessary. (It should be noted that Iraq has the second largest proven reserves of oil in the world after Saudi Arabia.[47])

Most of America's allies from the Persian Gulf War, with the exception of Prime Minister Tony Blair of Great Britain, opposed the idea of a pre-emptive strike on Iraq. There was scant evidence that Iraq supported Al Qaeda, in part because the radical Muslim political philosophy of Al Qaeda views Saddam Hussein's secular state as an enemy.[48] Although most analysts thought that Iraq continued to possess chemical and biological weapons and wanted to develop a nuclear bomb, there was no evidence that Iraq had a nuclear weapon or missiles capable of striking the United States. Saddam Hussein was a bad man, but why wouldn't he be deterred from using weapons of mass destruction by the threat of his own destruction? Indeed wouldn't an attack aimed at his demise encourage him to use his chemical and biological weapons? While a modern democracy in Iraq might be a good idea, bringing it about would be a difficult task probably requiring a long occupation. France, Russia, Germany, and others thought it best to work through the United Nations Security Council to disarm Iraq through renewed weapons inspections. The Bush administration, however, in the prelude to the November 2002 elections, did procure permission from Congress to attack Iraq if the president decided it was necessary.

The Kurds

One of the problems of a post-Saddam Iraq would be the situation of the Kurds, an ethnic group that forms a majority in the north of Iraq, an area with significant oil deposits. Kurdish clans have lived in the Caucasus Mountains for some four thousand years. The Kurds are clearly a nation without a state: "The Kurd's identity is based on a number of shared traits: a common homeland and culture, a myth of common origin, a shared faith in Islam, similar languages, and a history of bitter conflict with outsiders."[49]

Kurdistan, their homeland, is divided among five states: Turkey, Syria, Iraq, Iran, and Armenia. The Kurds have had the misfortune of living at a major intersection or crossroads: of two empires—the Ottoman and the Persian; of three significant peoples—Turks to the northwest, Persians (Iranians) to the east, and Arabs to the south; and of four aggressive nationalisms—Turkish, Syrian, Iraqi, and Iranian.[50] The riptides of these rivalries have resulted in the violent repression of the Kurds, and have thwarted their desire for recognition as a nation-state.

The Shiite Muslims who took over Iran in 1979 slaughtered about 50,000 of the Sunni Muslim Kurds.[51] In 1988 Saddam Hussein slaughtered about 200,000 Kurds because they had supported Iran in the Iraq-Iran war. The Iraqi army killed every man, woman, and child (5,000 people) in the town of Halabja by dropping poison gas on them.[52] Yet perhaps the worst oppression of the Kurds occurred in Turkey, where Kurds comprise 23 percent of the population and are a majority in the eastern section. Kurds in Turkey have been forcibly dispersed and brutally repressed, their language has been banned, and they have been slaughtered by the tens of thousands. A 1991 anti-terrorism law allowed the imprisonment of anyone speaking on behalf of Kurdish rights.[53] Both Turkey and Iran would vehemently object (albeit unjustly) to any autonomy granted to Kurds in a post-Saddam Iraq.

At the beginning of the twenty-first century, the Middle East remains a caldron of ethnic, religious, and territorial conflict.

Europe

Northern Ireland

Great Britain ruled Ireland harshly for about eight hundred years (1169–1921). When the Irish Free State (which later evolved into the Republic of Ireland) was established in 1921, six of the nine counties of Ulster, those counties where there was a Protestant majority, were partitioned off into Northern Ireland, and remained part of the United Kingdom.[54]

The basic division in Northern Ireland is the native people versus the colonial settlers. "Politically, the natives were nationalists and the settlers unionists; socially, the nationalists were deprived and the unionists privileged; and religiously, the deprived were Catholic and the privileged Protestant."[55] This has always been a conflict about power and privilege, participation and justice. The antagonists happen to be Protestant and Catholic.

The Protestants in Northern Ireland are descendants of the seventeenth-century colonial settlers. They are loyal (Loyalist) to the union (Unionist) between Northern Ireland and Great Britain. They identify themselves as citizens of Ulster (Ulstermen), the northern region of Ireland. On July 12 the Orange Order (Orangemen) celebrates the victory of William of Orange at the Battle of the Boyne (1690) with marches and bonfires in its neighborhoods and in those of Catholics as well.[56] They fly the Union Jack flag of Great Britain and the Red Hand flag of Ulster. Most Christians attend the Church of Ireland (Anglican), although some are Presbyterian. About 60 percent (950,000) of Northern Ireland's 1.6 million people are Protestant. Over the years, the Unionist majority developed a system of governance that kept it in a politically and economically superior position.

The Catholic minority (650,000) in Northern Ireland identifies with the Republic of Ireland and with the Roman Catholic Church. These Catholics consider themselves Irish and think that Northern Ireland should be reunited with the Republic of Ireland. The majority of them are Nationalist, that is, they favor a legal and constitutional approach to unification. Republicans share the same goal, but think that force is necessary to accomplish unification.[57]

The violence of the current "troubles" was precipitated by a nonviolent civil rights movement in 1969. In the mid-1960s, Catholics, inspired by the wave of civil rights agitation in the United States and elsewhere, decided to temporarily table the goal of unification with Ireland in favor of a civil rights movement. Catholics contended that if Northern Ireland was to belong to the United Kingdom, they were entitled to their rights as British citizens. These rights included a right to vote for all adults, fair representation in government, legislation barring discrimination in jobs and housing, and freedom from harassment by the police and militia. Catholic demonstrations for civil rights were met by violent resistance on the part of the Royal Ulster Constabulary (RUC—the police force) and the Unionists, forcing Britain to send in troops to maintain order.[58] The situation quickly degenerated into a cycle of violence that persisted until a cease-fire was declared in September of 1994.

The toll has been staggering. By the time of the cease-fire in 1994, 3,173 people had been killed in sectarian warfare, about half of them Protestant and half Catholic, with roughly two-thirds of them civilians and one-third members of the security forces.[59] Over 35,500 people had been wounded in over 33,350 shootings and 9,760 bombings.[60]

This terrible cycle of violence and terrorism was interrupted in the fall of 1994 when the Irish Republican Army (IRA) unilaterally declared a cease-fire, and the Protestant paramilitary groups (such as the Ulster Defense Association and the Ulster Volunteer Force) followed suit a month later. The intent of the IRA cease-fire was to get its political arm, Sinn Fein ("We Ourselves"), led by Gerry Adams, invited to the negotiating table about the future of Northern Ireland. In 1993, Great Britain had promised that if the violence ceased, Sinn Fein could join the dialogue between the governments and the political parties.

The Conservative government of Prime Minister John Major in Great Britain, however, reneged on its promise by throwing up obstacles to and conditions for Sinn Fein participation. Then the IRA broke its cease-fire with a February 9, 1996, bomb blast in the eastern dock area of London followed by other bombs in London and Manchester. When a Liberal government headed by Tony Blair was elected in 1997, the IRA renewed its cease-fire.

By Easter 1998, all-party talks resulted in a Northern Ireland peace agreement that was accepted by a referendum. The agreement established a Northern Ireland Assembly that shared power among the Unionist and

Nationalist parties. In October 2002, however, Britain suspended the Assembly for the fourth time in as many years rather than have it disintegrate. The Unionists are continually disgruntled by the slow pace of IRA disarmament, and the Nationalists by the slow pace of police reform and genuine power-sharing. While the leaders bicker and bluster, fueled by the diametrically conflicting interests of union with the United Kingdom and reunion with the Republic of Ireland and by the hate and distrust born of years of mutual violence and terror, the people of Northern Ireland have flourished in the years of peace brought about by the 1998 agreement. Peace in Northern Ireland is precarious, but surely no one wants to return to the violence of the past.

The Balkan Peninsula

Former U.S. Senator Daniel Patrick Moynihan once said, "Ethnic conflict does not require great differences, small will do."[61] That certainly applies to the brutal ethnic conflict among the nations in what was the state of Yugoslavia. There is no apparent difference among the peoples who have at times lived together in harmony. They are all southern Slav (Yugoslav) people. They speak basically the same language, Serbo-Croatian, but the Serbs use a Cyrillic alphabet and the Croats use a Roman alphabet. Most Serbs are Orthodox Christians, most Croats are Roman Catholics, and the majority of Bosnians (45 percent) are Muslim. But there are significant Serbian (33 percent) and Croatian (18 percent) minorities in Bosnia and a significant Serbian minority (15 percent) in Croatia. These peoples, who have so much

in common, once again began massacring each other shortly after the end of the Cold War, primarily because of their ethnic differences and their fear and hatred of each other, which had been enflamed by self-serving nationalist leaders.

The Balkan Peninsula is the section of southeastern Europe bordered by the Adriatic, Mediterranean, Aegean, and the Black Seas. In the fourth century, the Balkans became the dividing line between the Roman and the Byzantine Empires, and since then the area has been a battleground between the forces of empire rising in the West and in the East. The Croats identified with the West (Austria and Germany) and the Serbs with the East (Russia).[62]

In 1389 the Turks conquered Serbia at the Battle of Kosovo and established five centuries of rule under the Ottoman Empire. It was during this period that some of the Slavs in Bosnia converted to Islam. By the twentieth century, Serbia was free from the crumbling Ottoman Empire and in conflict with Croatia, which had allied itself with the rising powers in Western Europe. This conflict became the match that sparked World War I. World War II provided a backdrop for a Balkan civil war between Serbian "Chetnik" forces allied with Russia and Croatian "Ustashe" forces allied with Nazi Germany; the two sides engaged in mutual slaughter from 1941 to 1945. In some sense, the current conflict is a continuation of that long-unresolved civil war.[63]

Yugoslavia, which had been created after World War I, was re-established under Tito (Josip Broz), a Communist partisan who emerged victorious from the fractious fighting following World War II. Although Communist and totalitarian, Tito declared his independence from the Soviet Union and found himself courted and aided by both the West and the East during the Cold War.[64] Under the rule of Tito, Yugoslavia consisted of eight republics: Slovenia, Croatia, Bosnia-Herzegovina, Serbia, Macedonia, Montenegro, Vojvodina, and Kosovo. Tito died in 1980, and with the collapse of communism in 1990, the republics began to break away from the Serb-dominated Yugoslav federation. When Slovenia and Croatia declared their independence in June 1991 and were recognized by the West, multi-ethnic Bosnia was left with little choice but to declare its independence under the Muslim leadership of Alija Izetbegovic, which it did in February of 1992.

The Bosnian Serbs, led by Radovan Karadzic and supported by Serbian President Slobodan Milosevic, immediately declared a separate state, promptly took over military control of about 70 percent of Bosnia, and began their siege of Sarajevo. Atrocities, mostly committed by the more militarily powerful Serbs against the relatively defenseless Muslims, followed in rapid succession.

The pre-war (1991) population of Bosnia was 4.3 million people. During the war (1991–1995), 3.4 million people (or three out of every four people) became internal or external refugees.[65] Ethnic cleansing, which was used as a weapon of war, meant that Serbs (Orthodox Christians), Croats (Roman Catholics), and Bosnian Muslims killed or drove out their neighbors (literally the family living next door) and blew up their houses. Serbian soldiers systematically raped an estimated 20,000 Muslim women,[66] snipers intentionally shot children in Sarajevo, and Serbs put Muslims into concentration camps.

The response of the international community was weak and ineffectual. United Nations troops entered the scene to offer humanitarian relief and to secure so-called safe areas, but found themselves on a peacekeeping mission where there was no peace to keep.

The tide of the war changed in August 1995 when the Croat-Muslim alliance rolled back Serbian gains in the northwest of Bosnia and in Croatia (engaging in their own ethnic cleansing against the Serbs) and NATO mounted air attacks on Serbian positions around Sarajevo. By this time the economic sanctions imposed on Serbia at the beginning of the war were crippling Belgrade's economy. Suddenly Milosevic was ready to negotiate.

At the invitation of United States diplomat Richard Holbrooke, the three leaders—Croatia's Franjo Tudjman, Serbia's Slobodan Milosevic, and Bosnian Muslim Alija Izetbegovic—met for three weeks in Dayton, Ohio, and reached a complex agreement. Sixty thousand NATO troops, including a U.S. contingent of twenty thousand, were sent into Bosnia to monitor the cease-fire and to ensure compliance with the Dayton Agreement. As of this writing, NATO troops are still stationed in Bosnia to keep the peace, but the dream of a multi-ethnic Bosnia enshrined in the 1995 Dayton agreement has been fragmented. Ethnic distrust and hatred, legitimated by a religious veneer and stirred up by nationalist leaders, continue to divide Bosnia into three separate parts.[67]

Kosovo

Slobodan Milosevic and the Serbs, however, were not finished wreaking havoc in the Balkans. In the Serbian-controlled province of Kosovo, 90 percent of the population of two million was comprised of Albanian Muslims—Kosovars. The 1974 Yugoslavian constitution had granted Kosovo autonomy, but in 1989 Milosevic, resurrecting the nationalist Serbian myth of the 1389 Battle of Kosovo as hallowed ground, rescinded this gesture and instituted a repressive Serbian control. Albanians in all positions of power were replaced by Serbs and Serbo-Croatian replaced the Albanian language in schools and official business. The torture and disappearance of political detainees became commonplace.[68]

The Kosovo Albanians, under the leadership of Ibrahim Rugova, responded nonviolently, establishing parallel schools and institutions, and their culture flourished.[69] The rest of the world, however, paid little attention to the Serbian repression of the Albanians in Kosovo or to their creative and courageous nonviolent resistance.

This international indifference resulted in the formation of the Kosovo Liberation Army (KLA), which used guerrilla warfare to kill a few Serbian police in early 1998. This provoked a massive Serbian counter-attack from Milosevic—a devastating assault on dozens of villages, killing nearly a thousand and displacing 300,000 Kosovars who became refugees. When the Serbian Army renewed its attack in the spring of 1999, NATO responded by bombing Serbia from the air. Instead of withdrawing, Milosevic doubled the attack on the Kosovo Albanians, resulting in massacres and a massive flow of refugees. Serbia absorbed 78 days of bombing before capitulating and then the returning Albanians took revenge on the fleeing Serbs.

At the beginning of the twenty-first century, NATO troops are keeping the peace in Kosovo and protecting its autonomy, although Kosovo remains under Serbian control. To grant independence to the Kosovo Albanians would set a dangerous precedent for neighboring Macedonia, which has a small Albanian minority, and Montenegro, the only republic remaining with Serbia in the Yugoslav Federation. It would also disconcert Turkey with its Kurdish minority, Russia where the Chechens seek their independence, and other countries with restless ethnic groups.[70]

The Balkans continue to be a very troubled spot in the new landscape of global conflict. Besides the uneasy peace in Bosnia and Kosovo, Macedonia faces ethnic conflict, Montenegro seeks more independence from Serbia, and Albania is nearly a failed state. Nevertheless the situation has been quieter there since the turn of the century, in part because Serbia managed to depose its ultra-nationalist ruler, Slobodan Milosevic, in October 2000. Milosevic lost the election to the leader of the Democratic Opposition of Serbia, Vojislav Kostunica, and the people filled the streets and stood up to the military to protect their choice and to oust Milosevic, who has been tried at the World Court in the Hague for war crimes. With a democratic and more moderate leadership in Serbia, the future of the Balkans looks brighter.

Chechnya

One of the reasons that Ted Robert Gurr was conditionally more optimistic regarding ethno-nationalist conflict at the beginning of the twenty-first century was that the shocks of state reformation in Eastern Europe and the former Soviet sphere seemed to have subsided.[71] Chechnya, however, is an enduring and disturbing exception to this trend.

The Chechens are a Muslim, clan-based, ethnic group with a long history of resistance to Russian control of the northern Caucasus Mountains. When the Soviet Union disintegrated in 1991, Chechnya declared its independence. Chechnyan independence raises two issues: first, Chechnya holds some economic importance for Moscow, and second, the precedent of Chechen independence could snowball throughout Russia. Thus in December 1994 Russia invaded Chechnya to put down the rebellion. The Chechens have a reputation as fierce fighters, and a peace settlement in August 1996 recognized a stalemate rather than a Russian victory.[72]

In autumn 1999 Vladimir Putin, a former KGB chief and a man with his eye on the Russian presidency, ordered Russian troops back into Chechnya. Three years later the war for control of Chechnya continued. More than 4,500 Russian forces have been killed, and as many as 100,000 Chechens have died and more than 300,000 are refugees from their battered, nearly leveled country. Both sides have been guilty of human rights abuses, but the Russian army has massacred, tortured, raped and pillaged.[73]

Since September 11, 2001, President Putin has portrayed the Chechen rebels as Muslim terrorists and has even threatened to carry out a pre-emptive strike against neighboring Georgia, which he accuses of aiding the terrorists with surface-to-air missiles. This rhetoric, coupled with Russia's support for the Bush administration's war on terrorism, has silenced any U.S. criticism of the human rights abuses in Chechnya.[74]

Asia

Sri Lanka

One of the longest and most brutal ethnic conflicts in the modern world has taken place in Sri Lanka, a teardrop-shaped island off the southern coast of India with a population of about 18 million. The conflict between the Sinhala majority (75 percent) who are predominantly Buddhist, and the Tamil minority (18 percent) who are mainly Hindu, emerged only in the twentieth century. For centuries the Sinhala (or Sinhalese) and Tamils had lived together in respectful peace. But an enmity between the two peoples, kindled by the last decades of British colonial rule, was stoked by political leaders after independence in 1948. It exploded into a civil war in 1983, which has resulted in the deaths of approximately 60,000 people and nearly a half million refugees.[75] Both sides in the conflict have been guilty of human rights violations.

Terrorist acts, such as suicide bombings aimed at Sinhala political leaders or government targets and often killing dozens of bystanders, have been a specialty of the Liberation Tigers of Tamil Eelam (LTTE, Eelam means state). In 1988 an LTTE suicide bomber assassinated Rajiv Gandhi, the Indian leader, after India tried to intervene in the conflict. Disappearances and torture have been common practices of the Sri Lankan army and of the death squads they sponsor. Civilians on both sides, but especially the Tamil, who have been victimized by both the Sri Lankan army and the extremist LTTE, have suffered the most.[76]

A cease-fire and peace talks failed to end the conflict in 1995, and in early 1996, in response to a bloody government campaign to retake Jaffna, the Tamil center in the north of the country, the LTTE bombed the Central Bank building in Colombo, killing 80 and wounding 1,400.

In February 2002, however, Norway brokered a cease-fire, and the LTTE and the government entered peace talks with an apparent sincerity unseen before.[77] That Buddhism and Hinduism have been twisted to condone political violence and ethnic hatred is perverse indeed. There is new hope that these two ancient communities, the Sinhala and the Tamil, who lived together in peace for centuries, will do so once again.

Kashmir

One of the most dangerous places in the landscape of global conflict is the Indian state commonly called Kashmir (technically Jammu and Kashmir). When India and Pakistan were partitioned in 1947 at the end of British colo-

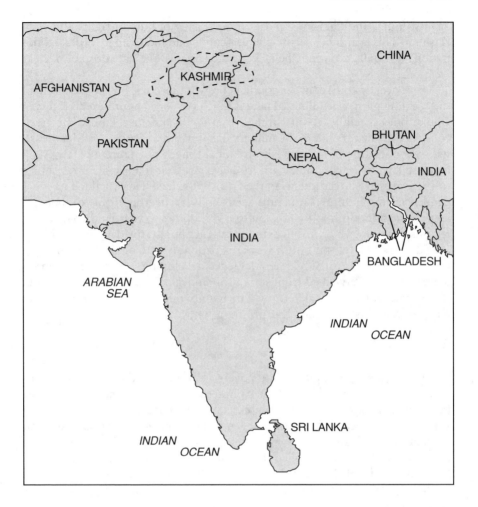

nial rule, the Hindu ruler of Muslim-majority Kashmir chose to join India. India and Pakistan immediately went to war over Kashmir, and Pakistan gained control of part of the territory. This ethnic and territorial dispute has continued ever since and has intensified through the 1990s into the beginning of the twenty-first century. At the end of 2002, India had more than 250,000 troops in the region, and at least 30,000 people had been killed in the conflict.[78] It is especially dangerous because both India and Pakistan have nuclear weapons and the missiles to deliver them, and both have threatened to do so if attacked.

Kashmir is a difficult conflict to resolve, in part because for both India and Pakistan it represents a founding principle of the nation. Pakistan considers itself a homeland for Muslims in Southeast Asia, and the Muslims who are the majority in Kashmir resent being ruled by "infidels." On the other hand, India proclaims itself a secular, multicultural state and fears the precedent that ceding Kashmir would set for other ethnic minorities within its borders.[79] India accuses Pakistan of supporting Islamic terrorists in attacks against India, and Pakistan accuses India's army of human-rights abuses in Kashmir. This is another seemingly intractable and increasingly brutal ethno-nationalist conflict, but one being contested against the backdrop of nuclear weapons.

There are, of course, other conflicts brewing in Asia, but at the moment they seldom garner headlines. There is much concern about human rights in China, but especially about China's occupation of Tibet. China has given considerable military aid to the military dictatorship in Burma (or Myanmar), which counts among the opposition Nobel Peace Prize laureate Daw Aung San Suu Kyi, who won the award for her courageous, nonviolent resistance to the repressive government. In the late 1990s, East Timor gained its independence from Indonesia and now seems to be recovering from years of violent oppression. Both Indonesia and the Philippines have been the victims of terrorist bombings by Muslim extremists. And, finally, the demilitarized zone that divides North and South Korea is probably one of the most heavily armed areas on earth. While democracy is developing in prosperous South Korea, millions have died from starvation under the Communist tyranny in the North, which seems determined to acquire nuclear weapons. (See chapter 6 for a discussion of nuclear proliferation.)

Africa

On April 6, 1994, *Rwanda*'s Hutu government unleashed the bloodiest hundred days in the second half of the twentieth century. At least 500,000 Tutsi (and their sympathizers) were slaughtered, mostly with machetes.[80] This massacre is rightly regarded as an act of genocide.[81] The world was aghast when a river of their bloated bodies emptied into Lake Kivu. Nearly 100,000 Hutu and Tutsi have also been killed in neighboring Burundi. This complex conflict between the Hutu and Tutsi peoples in Rwanda and Burundi was rooted in the colonial history of the region and was motivated by politics, the scarcity of resources, and ethnic enmity.

Once the massacre began in Rwanda, the Rwandan Patriotic Front (RPF), comprised of well-trained Tutsi exiles in the region, invaded Rwanda and rapidly advanced across the country. By July 1994, the RPF had soundly defeated the Hutu military and militia, gained control of Rwanda, and stopped the genocide. As the RPF advanced, millions of Hutu, either fearing reprisals and/or coerced by armed Hutu extremists, fled from Rwanda into Burundi and Zaire (now the Democratic Republic of Congo). Although there were some reprisals, the RPF showed restraint and discipline and set up an inclusive government in Rwanda.

The international community, and especially the West with its colonial stakes in Central Africa, failed miserably in responding to the crisis in Rwanda. Although the United Nations worked for a peace agreement prior to April 1994, it abandoned hundreds of thousands of Rwandans to genocidal slaughter when that process broke down. The international community, often willing to provide humanitarian aid to refugees, still seems stubbornly unwilling to aid the fledgling Rwandan government in economic development and nation building. This is admittedly a more complex, costly, and controversial assignment than providing emergency relief to refugees, but it seems essential to prevent the next violent outburst.

Soon the conflict in Rwanda spilled over into *Zaire*. In May of 1997 the central government of Zaire, under longtime dictator Mobutu Sese Seko, was overthrown without much of a fight by a revolutionary army under Laurent Kabila, who re-named the country the Democratic Republic of Congo.[82] Although rich in resources, especially minerals, Congo is among the world's poorest countries. It is the third largest country in Africa, has a population of diverse and divided ethnic groups, and contains no infrastructure for transportation or communication and no system of education or government services worth noting. When Laurent Kabila was assassinated in the capital of Kinshasa in January 2001, armies supported by six of Congo's neighbors—Angola, Namibia, Zimbabwe, Uganda, Rwanda, and Burundi—as well as various independent militias were active in the country.[83] Mr. Kabila's inexperienced son, Joseph, succeeded him. By the summer of 2002 there was even talk of a peace agreement brokered by South Africa's former president Nelson Mandela—not that it would matter much to the people caught in the crossfire of uncontrolled militias and plagued by poverty and disease.[84]

The continent of Africa is filled with ethnic conflict, wars over resources, and failed states. From south to north, west to east, fighting burns or simmers in Africa.[85] Besides the conflicts in central Africa, a civil war rages in *Sudan* between the Islamic government in the Muslim north and rebel groups in the Christian and animist south; fighting and famine in Sudan have claimed two million lives since 1983.

Somalia, although ethnically homogenous, remains embroiled in the chaos of clan conflict since the U.S.-led United Nations intervention to alleviate a famine in 1993.[86] There are also two rebel groups active in *Kenya,* although the government there seems relatively stable.

From 1998 to 2000, *Eritrea* and *Ethiopia* fought a senseless war over a border dispute in the desert. Eritrea won its independence from the much larger Ethiopia by referendum in 1993.[87] The war devastated the promising economy of Eritrea and increased the poverty of Ethiopia.

A civil war has raged in *Angola* for well over 25 years, killing nearly a million and maiming tens of thousands with land mines. The death of Jonas Savimbi, the leader of the rebel Unita group, in 2002 might ease the tension. And Angola's conflict spilled across the borders into Namibia and Zambia.

Oil-rich *Nigeria*, where one in six Africans lives, returned to democracy in May of 1999 with the election of Olusegun Obasanjo to the presidency, but it still faces continuing outbursts of religious and ethnic violence and crushing poverty. Corruption seems deeply rooted in the Nigerian society and government.

In West Africa, *Liberia,* founded by freed American slaves in 1847, has been plundered by a civil war started in 1989 by American-educated warlord

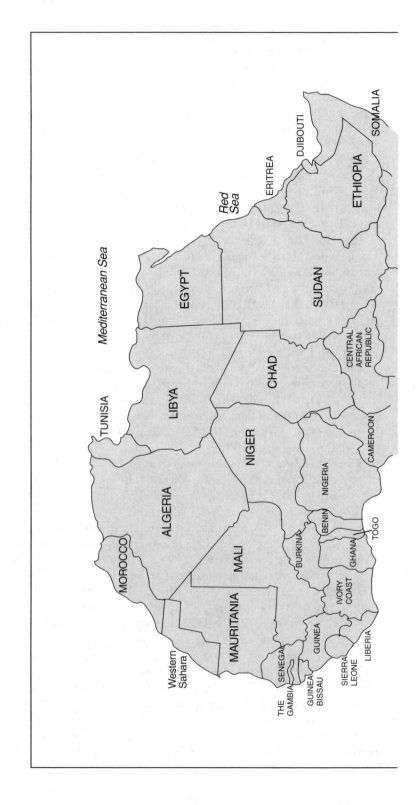

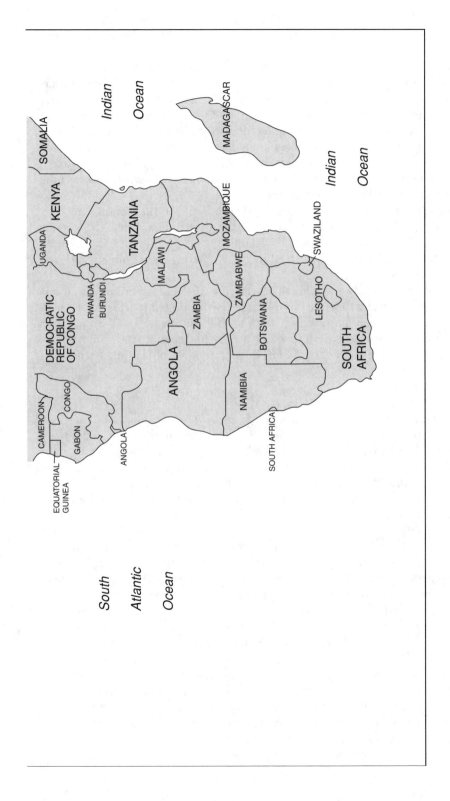

Charles Taylor, who was "elected" president in 1997. Previously one of the continent's better-off nations, its capital, Monrovia, has neither electricity nor running water.

In 1991, Taylor helped his friend, Foday Sankoh, begin a rebellion in *Sierra Leone,* a diamond-rich neighbor. Sankoh copied Taylor's brutal guerrilla tactics, coercing child soldiers to commit atrocities on civilians after being forced to watch their parents murdered.[88] The trademark of the Sierra Leone rebels was randomly chopping off arms or legs of villagers to frighten the village into submission. Fortunately Sierra Leone entered the new century under a U.N.-protected peace. Liberia's other neighbor, *Ivory Coast,* once a model of stability, suffered a military coup and militia unrest in the first years of the twenty-first century.

In 1992 a savage war erupted in *Algeria* between the nation's military rulers and Islamic guerrilla groups when the government cancelled elections because it appeared that a militant Islamic group would win. After at least 80,000 deaths the situation eased in 1999 when the government allowed new elections.[89]

While the conflicts and wars that permeate Africa are about power or territory or resources, they are complicated by the almost total lack of correspondence between nations and states on the continent. The colonial map of Africa paid little attention to ethnic groups and their historic animosities. Ethno-nationalist conflict continues to be a major problem in Africa.

Latin America

As we enter the twenty-first century, *Latin America,* while not exactly an oasis of peace in a world of conflict, is calmer than in the thirty years from around 1960 to 1990. The government of Colombia continues to fight against revolutionary guerrillas in the context of drug wars, and there is still tension in the Chiapas region of Mexico between the Zapatista rebels and the government's forces; this struggle began in early 1994 when the North American Free Trade Agreement (NAFTA) went into effect.[90]

Yet the incessant coups, the military governments, and the revolutions that characterized Latin America in the twentieth century have been almost universally replaced by democratic governments, which are struggling to be responsive to the needs of their people who are oppressed by poverty. There is no guarantee that this experiment in peaceful democracy will last, but it is a welcome development.

IS HUMANITARIAN INTERVENTION JUSTIFIED?

Ethno-nationalist conflict raises one of the most vexing questions for foreign policy in the new century—whether and when military intervention on behalf of human rights might be justified. Humanitarian intervention can be defined as "the forceful, direct intervention by one or more states or international organizations in the internal affairs of other states for essentially humanitarian purposes."[91]

There is nothing new about intervention, but the post-Cold War context poses the question in a fresh way. Both superpowers indulged in interventions during the Cold War—in Korea, Vietnam, Afghanistan, Central America, and the Caribbean, for example—but for reasons of power politics and national self-interest. In terms of justice, democracy, and peacemaking, most of the Cold War interventions, in hindsight, turned out badly.

Today, tensions such as ethnic conflict, chaos, and anarchy in states where the government appears to have failed, the proliferation of weapons of mass destruction, and gross violations of human rights raise the issue of intervention on behalf of human life and human rights, rather than for purposes of national self-interest.

The principles of the *sovereignty* of states and, therefore, of *nonintervention* in the internal affairs of a sovereign state stand against the right or the duty to intervene on behalf of human rights. These two principles—sovereignty and nonintervention—have imposed some semblance of order upon an international system with no central government.[92] Sovereign states resent interference in their internal affairs. (How would Americans have reacted if China or France had sent troops to protect civil rights protesters on their march from Selma to Montgomery in 1965?) Such intervention could easily result in escalating regional wars.

A second reason against intervention is the tendency of states to rationalize national self-interest under the cloak of humanitarian rhetoric.[93] Colonial powers always thought of themselves as benevolent, bringing a "higher civilization" to primitive peoples, while taking or exploiting their land, wealth, and resources. Although the United Nations authorized the U.S.-led intervention in Haiti in 1994, the Organization of American States did not support it because of well-founded suspicions of previous U.S. interventions in Latin America.[94]

A third set of concerns about intervention arises from the difficulty of developing a policy for intervention that is clear and consistent, rather than arbitrary and selective. What violations of human rights would justify intervention? Who would authorize it? What would be the feasible goals of humanitarian intervention? Would short-term actions create more severe long-term problems?[95]

Arrayed against these reasons for nonintervention are the very real horrors of genocide in Rwanda, ethnic cleansing in Bosnia, famine caused by the collapse of the state in Somalia, repression by military rulers in Haiti,[96] and pogroms against the Kurds in Iraq and Turkey. Such human suffering cries out to the conscience of the international community.

Christian ethics can be helpful in working through this foreign policy dilemma. First of all, as discussed above, Christian ethics contends that the sovereignty of the state is a real, but relative, value. State sovereignty is conditioned from below by human rights and from above by the international common good. Thus, when states grievously abuse the human rights of their citizens, they cannot use sovereignty to silence the concern of others.[97] Neither sovereignty nor nonintervention are absolute principles, although both carry real moral weight. The challenge, then, is to develop clear criteria for justified military intervention into the internal affairs of states.

The Christian tradition offers two perspectives on war and military intervention—nonviolence (or pacifism), and just-war theory—although it has long been dominated by the just-war position.[98]

Christians and others who adhere to nonviolence have been perplexed by the question of military intervention for humanitarian purposes. Pacifists oppose warfare in principle. During the Cold War, with every conflict potentially a spark for a nuclear holocaust and with power politics the primary purpose of military interventions, Christian pacifists passionately resisted America's military excursions abroad. But humanitarian interventions in the post-Cold War world have often been motivated by efforts to remedy injustice and alleviate human suffering. When these cherished values are genuinely the purpose of intervention, and when the violence of the armed intervention is expected to be minimal, can a pacifist condone it?

Many pacifists have been able to justify humanitarian interventions, such as those in Somalia, Haiti, and Bosnia, under the rubric of police actions rather than warfare. Most pacifists are not opposed to all uses of force (although some are), and see the threat of force, or the limited use of force, to be justified by the greater human good that can be accomplished. It is analogous to the force used by the police to protect the community from violent criminals.[99] Although it is true that there can be a real difference between humanitarian armed intervention and aggressive warfare, the willingness to use violence will continue to trouble pacifists. Once violence is justified, one has inevitably crossed the line into just-war thinking.

The criteria developed by the just-war tradition can also offer a framework for justifying humanitarian intervention. The transition from nonviolence to justified force yields the first point in a revised ethic of intervention: military intervention should be a *last resort*. The just-war tradition has always maintained that war is evil, a rule-governed exception to the presumption in favor of peace. Preventative efforts and nonviolent remedies should be applied before force is justified.[100] Economic sanctions can be effective and should be considered, although these too are fraught with ethical problems. When economic sanctions were applied against Haiti in the early 1990s, for example, they seemed to cause the most suffering among poor children, while the wealthy ruling elite escaped their sting. The last-resort criterion also gives the necessary weight to the principles of sovereignty and nonintervention. "Because of the diversity of states and the dangers of rationalization, the wisdom of Westphalia [regarding respect for the sovereignty of states] should be heeded. Intervention may be necessary, but it should not be made easy."[101] The burden of proof should always rest on those who are in favor of military intervention.

It is the *just-cause* criterion that makes humanitarian intervention tempting. Everyone agrees that genocide demands an exception to the nonintervention principle, but how serious and egregious must a violation against human rights be in order to justify intervention? This judgment, no doubt, looks different from the perspective of the victims than from that of the offenders, or of the potential interveners. The genocide in Rwanda, famine in Somalia, ethnic cleansing in Bosnia, the slaughter of Kurds in Iraq, the military repression in Haiti, and the development of weapons of mass destruction in Iraq or North Korea all appear to be just causes for intervention. Just cause, however, is a necessary, but not a sufficient, criterion for intervention.[102]

The just-war tradition insists that war must be declared by a *legitimate authority* based on the idea that only the state can be allowed to authorize the taking of life. Because of the danger of rationalization on the part of individual states, the decision to intervene should ordinarily be authorized by an international organization such as the United Nations and/or a regional security organization. The decision should be multilateral, not unilateral. Given the power differential among states, this does not guarantee probity in judgment, but it does enhance it through procedural restrictions.[103]

The just-war criteria of *right intention* and *the probability of success* are also important as parts of a framework of ethical analysis regarding humanitarian intervention. These criteria focus attention on clearly defining the political goals of the intervention and on the feasibility of effective intervention.

There is no such thing as apolitical military intervention, and it is a dangerous delusion to pretend that political goals can be avoided while offering humanitarian aid. It is also cruel to bring a people back from the brink of death, through famine aid, for example, only to have them continue to suffer from government oppression or social chaos. Thus, it may be that for intervention to be truly humanitarian and just, in many cases it will need to go beyond mere aid or even peacekeeping. It may have to engage in constructive nation-building, that is, in reforming or creating the social and political structures necessary for honoring human rights.[104] This means some sort of ongoing assistance in reorganizing government, disarming military or paramilitary forces, establishing safe enclaves, re-establishing civic peace, supporting negotiated settlements of grievances, punishing the perpetrators of genocide or ethnic cleansing, instituting a judicial system, training and equipping an impartial police force, and so on.[105]

Such goals may require a lengthy commitment of personnel and resources, as in Bosnia and Kosovo and now Afghanistan. Such an expanded agenda opens the interveners to the charge of a sort of colonial control over other nations or even of naked imperialism. Yet, to exclude such political goals from intervention is to risk doing more harm than good, or not enough good to bring about permanent change.

This, of course, raises the question of feasibility. If armed interveners must have clearly defined political goals and must be prepared to see the process through to completion, then humanitarian intervention is likely to be rare indeed. By its very nature, humanitarian intervention does not directly serve the national interests of the interveners. Thus, the interveners are placing their soldiers in harm's way, and expending talent and treasure for no real direct national benefit. Nor will criminals quickly come to heel, nor chaos be easily corrected where havoc is being wreaked. Humanitarian intervention will not always be possible or morally justified, and it will nearly always be difficult to gain popular support for it. Indeed, popular support for the U.S. interventions in Somalia, Haiti, Bosnia, and Kosovo has been lukewarm or non-existent. Perhaps, however, this is partly due to the lack of a clearly argued foreign policy on behalf of intervention.[106]

Finally, the just-war tradition requires that the *means* used be proportionate, and that the conduct of the intervention should also be just. The principles of noncombatant immunity and of proportionality have traditionally governed the conduct of warfare. Since the Vietnam debacle, U.S. military strategy has maintained that, in an intervention, massive military power should be brought to bear on an enemy for a short, defined period of time in the pursuit of a clearly defined and limited objective. This strategy seemed to work in the Persian Gulf War (1991), but even there questions of proportionality persist. This hit-and-run strategy poses both moral and political concerns for humanitarian intervention. Massive firepower suggests problems of indiscriminate and/or disproportionate attacks, and quickly withdrawing from the scene precludes the commitment necessary for nation-building activities.[107]

A third paradigm for analyzing the morality of conflict from a Christian perspective has recently been proposed by American Baptist theologian Glen Stassen and others as a way to break the inertia of the debate between nonviolence and just war and to take seriously the Gospel call to peacemaking.[108] The steps or strategies in just peacemaking include: confession and repentance, affirmation of common security, transforming initiatives, serious diplomacy aimed at conflict resolution, seeking justice and human rights, and citizen advocacy.[109]

Just peacemaking would emphasize *prevention* of conflict, first of all, by creating a just community and by recognizing and abiding by human rights. Just peacemaking would also urge the use of diplomacy and conflict-resolution strategies and of the techniques of nonviolent direct action before pursuing military intervention as a last resort. Although the just-peacemaking paradigm argues that there is nearly always a realistic and effective *alternative* to war, it is open to humanitarian intervention. Just peacemaking would encourage nation-building, either through diplomacy or in the aftermath of humanitarian intervention. It believes Christians have a responsibility to *create just community*, which is the only realistic foundation for peace.[110]

Humanitarian intervention can be ethically justified, although the need for it must be decided case-by-case. The just-war tradition provides a framework for the ethical analysis of situations where military intervention is being considered, and just peacemaking proposes practical strategies for preventing and resolving conflict without resort to violence. A public articulation of this framework, these strategies for peacemaking, and the reasons that might justify intervention can be used to build public support for a foreign policy willing to take risks and pay the costs of a just world order.

A MORAL RESPONSE TO TERRORISM

Prior to September 11, 2001, humanitarian intervention was the focus of American analysts in the area of ethics and international relations. The attack by suicidal Islamic terrorists that destroyed the twin towers of the World Trade Center and damaged the Pentagon, killing about 3,000 civilians, refocused U.S. foreign policy on global terrorism.

The response of U.S. President George W. Bush was to declare a global war on terrorism. In his address on September 20, 2001, to a joint session of Congress and to the nation, President Bush said, "We will direct every resource at our command . . . to the destruction and to the defeat of the global terror network. . . . And we will pursue nations that provide aid or safe haven to terrorism. Every nation in every region now has a decision to make: Either you are with us or you are with the terrorists."[111]

The United States demanded that the Taliban, an extremist Muslim group that controlled the government of Afghanistan, apprehend and extradite Osama Bin Laden and other members of Al Qaeda, the terrorist group thought responsible for the attack. When the Taliban did not comply, the United States gave extensive military support to the Northern Alliance in overthrowing the Taliban in Afghanistan. The United States has also sent a limited number of troops to advise and train the Philippine army in defeating Muslim guerrillas on the southern island of Mindanao.

Terrorism is hardly a new phenomenon. It is probably as old as warfare itself, and it was often used in the twentieth century. The German blitz on London during World War II and the allied firebombing of Dresden and Tokyo could be considered acts of state-sponsored terrorism. Tyrants (whether Communist or anti-Communist during the Cold War) tend to use the military or police to terrorize their subjects through arrest, torture, and disappearances. Often both sides in a conflict accuse the other of terrorism, as has been true in Northern Ireland, Israel versus the Palestinians, and in Sri Lanka. Thus, while terrorism is far too common an experience of many people worldwide, until September 11 it was foreign to Americans. The incredible horror of the September 11 attack naturally turned terrorism and the response to terrorism into an American preoccupation. What, then, is terrorism, and what is a moral response to terrorism?

President Bush has made terrorism synonymous with evil, reinforcing the use of "terrorist" as an epithet. Although terrorism is always wrong, it is a complex phenomenon that is difficult to define. Pope John Paul II called terrorism a "true crime against humanity."[112] Terrorism is a crime (such as the Oklahoma City bombing for which Timothy McVeigh was executed) or a war crime (Palestinian suicide bombers or the allied firebombing of Dresden) because it consciously targets civilians or non-combatants. This makes terrorism always and everywhere wrong, even though the innocence of civilians can be debated (for example, are all Israelis somehow responsible for the occupation of Palestine? Or did all Germans share the responsibility for World War II?). If the moral responsibility to discriminate between civilians and combatants and to direct the violence of warfare only at combatants is lost, then any notion of a morally justified war collapses into a crusade. Terrorism can be perpetrated by a state, by a nation or ethnic group, by a group of dissidents or criminals, even by an individual. Under certain circumstances, state terrorism can be legal.[113]

Terrorism is always immoral, and can rightly be condemned. But a moral response to this crime against humanity may depend on who commits it and why. Although I would like to avoid the cliché that one person's terrorist is another person's freedom fighter, there is unfortunately some truth to it.[114] No cause, however just or noble, can justify the use of terrorism, but redressing the just grievances of an oppressed group or nation may be a better and more effective response than quick reprisals. Not all terrorists, however, are freedom fighters or have just grievances or a just cause.[115] A careful analysis would distinguish, for example, between the Palestinian suicide bombers and those associated with Al Qaeda.

The incessant killing of Israeli civilians by Palestinian suicide bombers that began in the fall of 2000 during the second *intifada* is a repugnant series of war crimes. It is not surprising that Israel's consistent response has been immediate, overwhelming reprisals against the Palestinian groups and areas held responsible. Israel has sent its army to occupy and shut down Palestinian towns, sometimes imposing a total curfew and always restricting the movement of Palestinians. The bomber's family home is often bulldozed to the ground. If found, Palestinians associated with the group responsible, such as Hamas, will be arrested or simply killed. The Israeli security forces make an effort to be discriminate, but civilians, including children, are too often killed by mistake. All Palestinians suffer. Israel's harsh reprisals only fuel more Palestinian hatred and violence, perpetuating a cycle of increasing violence.[116] Perhaps the only way out of this spiral of violence is for Israel to acknowledge the repressive nature of its occupation in the West Bank and the Gaza Strip and to redress the just grievances of the Palestinian people.[117] Nonetheless, terrorism is the wrong way to resist Israeli oppression. It is possible that if the Palestinian *intifada* had picked up the tools of courageous, mass, nonviolent direct action, instead of stones and bombs, Palestinians might be living in their own state today.

In the case of Al Qaeda terrorists, it is unclear what grievances they want redressed and whether their cause is just. Osama Bin Laden and other militant Muslim leaders accuse the United States and its allies of engaging in a vast conspiracy "to negate the influence of Islam, undercut the Muslim community, and control the resources of Islamic communities."[118] These extremist Muslims are particularly concerned about the U.S. military presence in Saudi Arabia, where the holy city of Mecca is located, and about the plight of the Palestinians and of Iraq. They are more generally concerned about globalization, secularization, and Western decadence, which they perceive as a threat to the values and success of Islam, and they hold the United States symbolically and practically responsible. Thus the "World Islamic Front" issued the following *fatwa* (opinion based on the Qur'an) to all Muslims, "The ruling to kill the Americans and their allies—civilians and military— is an individual duty for every Muslim who can do it in any country in which it is possible to do it, in order to liberate the al-Aqsa Mosque [Jerusalem] and the Holy Mosque [Mecca] from their grip, and in order for their armies to move out of all the lands of Islam, defeated and unable to threaten any Muslim."[119]

The Al Qaeda terrorists, who seem more mass murderers than freedom fighters, are attempting to manipulate a larger people. Their radical interpretation of Islam, however, seems to have struck a chord in the Muslim world. Although the United States would do well to critically examine its foreign policy toward the Arab and Islamic world, there is no real hope that withdrawing troops from Saudi Arabia or lifting the economic sanctions on Iraq would placate the World Islamic Front. When terrorists act as criminals, a moral response includes measured retaliation to capture and destroy them.[120]

The Bush administration's "war on terrorism," based on an absolutist good (the United States) versus evil (the terrorists and their supporters) perspective, is inadequate and unhelpful for a number of reasons.[121]

- It does not allow for any distinction between mass murderers and freedom fighters. While all terrorists are criminals and should be punished, there are situations where reprisals and retaliation will only make things worse. Sometimes legitimate grievances should be redressed.
- Once a nation brands its enemy as terrorists there is no incentive for critically examining its policies, which may have led to the desperation that terrorism often represents.
- The idea that a nation is at war stifles national debate about government policies and tends to lead to the suspension of civil liberties and human rights.

A moral response to terrorism must be more nuanced than is allowed by the metaphors of a "war" or a "crusade against evil."

JUST PEACEMAKING AND TERRORISM

Use of the just-peacemaking paradigm could lead to a more holistic approach to preventing and responding to terrorism. Just peacemaking suggests national self-criticism, acknowledgment of wrongdoing (confession), and repairing wrongs (repentance). Al Qaeda has much to confess and repent: it has distorted the teachings of Islam, especially in its indiscriminant attacks on civilians, and its absolutist world analysis is fraught with errors. Although the United States has hardly been anti-Islam (see Bosnia and Kosovo), perhaps it has been too uncritically pro-Israel. In addition, the United States has often pushed or forced its interests on other states. The phrase "No peace without justice, no justice without forgiveness" summarizes Pope John Paul II's 2002 World Peace Day Message. One wonders if this message of forgiveness, proclaimed in the Gospel and repeated by the pope, is being heeded by American Christians.

Just peacemaking recognizes that justice is the only sound foundation for peace and that it is essential in preventing terrorism. If the United States wants to make the world safer, it must make it healthier, more equitable, and more environmentally sound.[122] Policies such as a new Marshall Plan for the Arab and Muslim world, free trade accords with Muslim countries, and U.S. fiscal responsibility (rather than miserliness, protectionism, and budget deficits) might be more effective in preventing terrorism than military action. Respect for human rights is a key ingredient in addressing the unjust conditions that usually tend to breed terrorism.

Transforming initiatives are key to a just-peacemaking strategy. They must be creative policies, even if they carry a reasonable risk, designed to reverse a spiral of violence by enhancing trust between adversaries. For example, given that U.S. support for Israel is a significant irritant to Arab countries and Islamic groups, the United States could pressure Israel to stop its settlements in the West Bank and the Gaza Strip and even channel U.S. economic aid toward buying back Israeli settlements for Palestinians.[123] The United States could develop a serious energy policy to promote conservation and environmental responsibility and thus diminish the U.S. addiction to oil from the authoritarian regime in Saudi Arabia. The United States could also support treaties aimed at diminishing and controlling weapons of mass destruction, such as the Comprehensive Test Ban, and the treaty on Biological and Chemical Weapons. Instead of increasing defense spending, the United States, whose military superiority is unrivaled and perhaps unparalleled in history, could channel funds into a Marshall Plan for developing countries, including Muslim countries.[124]

CONCLUSION

Ethnic conflict is primarily about power and oppression. Although antagonisms between ethnic groups or nations may have a long history, such enmity is neither natural nor inevitable. Ethnic enmity is invented. National leaders have fanned the flames of ethnic hatred with little regard for the common good or for finding constructive solutions to complex conflicts. Self-serving leadership is often responsible for ethnic conflagrations and the brutal violence that too often characterizes them, and for terrorism. In order to prevent and to resolve ethnic conflict, there is no substitute for leaders who have the genuine interests of their people at heart and who are able to recognize that other people also have genuine interests at stake as well. The world needs fewer demagogues like Slobodan Milosevic (Serbia), Franjo Tudjman (Croatia), Rev. Ian Paisley (Ulster), and Saddam Hussein (Iraq), and more statesmen and stateswomen like Nelson Mandela (South Africa), Vaclav Havel (Czech Republic), Anwar Sadat (Egypt), and Yitzhak Rabin (Israel).

Unfortunately, religion has been used to add fuel to the fires of nationalism and extremism, provoking ethnic conflict and terrorism. Since both religion and nationalism relate to core values, it is understandable that they become intertwined, but when religion legitimizes ethnic nationalism, religion becomes bastardized. Authentic religion should critique any ideology that inculcates hatred and division or that absolutizes any value other than God.

Religious communities should advocate for conversion, forgiveness, and reconciliation; they should be forces for justice, solidarity, nonviolence, and peace. Religious communities should produce leaders who serve their communities and work for the common good—such as Gandhi (India), Martin Luther King, Jr. (United States), Bishop Desmond Tutu (South Africa), Dag Hammarskjöld (U.N.), Cory Aquino (Philippines), and Jimmy Carter (United States). And when those in power spew hatred and do violence, religious communities must produce prophets and martyrs, such as Bishop Oscar Romero in El Salvador and Franz Jaegerstaetter and Dietrich Bonhoeffer in Nazi Germany. Religion can and should always be a constructive force for justice, equality, reconciliation, and peace in situations of ethnic conflict.

Finally, in order to establish a lasting peace, the international community may have to evolve new conceptions of state, nation, and sovereignty, and different institutional arrangements for civil societies.[125] The reality of sovereign states is itself only centuries old. Different conceptions and arrangements are surely possible and may even be better. Key to any peaceful arrangement of civil society are the twin values of 1) the *participation* of citizens in decisions that affect their well-being and 2) respect for *human rights*. When people have a real share in the exercise of power by the government, change can usually be accomplished without demagoguery, polarization, or resort to violence. When human rights are honored, especially the rights of minorities and the marginalized, violent conflict is rare. Any scheme that attempts to reorganize states and nations will need to pay particular attention to participation and human rights.

STUDY QUESTIONS

1. Distinguish between a nation and a state. Do you think every nation should be a state?
2. Is nationalism a danger in the contemporary world? How can nationalism be harnessed as a positive force and be reined in as a negative force?
3. What is the basis of the conflict between Israel and the Palestinians? What do you think would be a just resolution of the conflict? What role should the United States play?
4. Was the 1991 Persian Gulf War morally justified? Was it morally justified to wage war on Iraq in 2002–03?
5. Why isn't there a Kurdistan?
6. Can there be peace in Northern Ireland? Is this a religious conflict?
7. Explain the situation in Bosnia and Kosovo. What do you think that

NATO and/or the United Nations should do in response to the situation? How can religion be a constructive force in the former Yugoslavia?

8. Is Russia correct when it justifies its war in Chechnya as part of the worldwide war on terrorism?

9. Why care about the ethnic conflict in Sri Lanka? What moved the two sides into peace negotiations?

10. What makes the conflict between India and Pakistan over Kashmir so dangerous? Do you see a way out of this conflict?

11. Was the slaughter of the Tutsi by the Hutu in 1994 in Rwanda an act of genocide? Should other nations have intervened to stop the slaughter? How?

12. Many of the countries in Africa are faced with destitution, disease, and violence. If you were to design a "Marshall Plan" for Africa, what would it look like?

13. Do you think armed intervention on behalf of human rights is morally justified? wise? sound foreign policy? Should nation building be an objective of such interventions?

14. Discuss a moral response to terrorism.

CHAPTER SIX

Weapons and Disarmament

"Finally, be strong in the Lord and in the strength of his power. Put on the whole armor of God, so that you may be able to stand against the wiles of the devil. . . . Stand therefore and fasten the belt of truth around your waist, and put on the breastplate of righteousness. As shoes for your feet put on whatever will make you ready to proclaim the gospel of peace. With all of these, take the shield of faith, with which you will be able to quench all the flaming arrows of the evil one. Take the helmet of salvation, and the sword of the spirit, which is the word of God." (Ephesians 6: 10–11, 14–17)

"We must re-emphasize with all our being, nonetheless, that it is not only nuclear war that must be prevented, but war itself. Therefore with Pope John Paul II we declare:

> *Today, the scale and the horror of modern warfare—whether nuclear or not—makes it totally unacceptable as a means of settling differences between nations. War should belong to the tragic past, to history; it should find no place on humanity's agenda for the future.*

> *Reason and experience tell us that a continuing upward spiral, even in conventional arms, coupled with an unbridled increase in armed forces, instead of securing true peace will almost certainly be provocative of war."*[1]

World security analyst Michael Klare says there is a "deadly convergence" of three trends in the post-Cold War world.[2] One trend is the emergence of ethno-nationalist conflict. The other two trends are the proliferation of weapons of mass destruction (nuclear, chemical, and biological weapons), and the spread through the arms trade of ever more sophisticated conventional weapons and delivery systems. These three trends are likely to increase the number and severity of regional conflicts unless the global community takes decisive steps to defuse them. Previous chapters have looked at some of the motives for war in the twenty-first century: empire building and exploitation, poverty and the gap between the rich and the poor, environmental scarcity, violations of human rights, ethno-nationalism, religious extremism, greed, and conflict over land and power. This chapter will explore the issues of nuclear weapons and other weapons of mass destruc-

149

tion, and then the traffic in conventional arms and military spending. Weapons are not only the means to conduct war, but are often a contributing cause to war itself.

NUCLEAR MATTERS

The forty-five years of the Cold War (1945–1990) were characterized by a nuclear stalemate between the Union of Soviet Socialist Republics (U.S.S.R.) and the United States, between the East and the West. The watchword for U.S. foreign policy was "containment." Communism was to be contained and resisted wherever possible. This led the United States into wars in Korea in the 1950s and in Vietnam in the 1960s to keep the nations of Southeast Asia from falling, like dominoes, into Communist hands; it also led the United States into interventions in Latin America (Cuba, Chile, El Salvador, Nicaragua, and so on) during the 1970s and 1980s.

The two superpowers divided the world into "spheres of influence" and competed with one another for the allegiance of unaligned states. Foreign aid, especially in the form of weapons and military assistance, was a major tactic in this strategy. For example:

- When Anwar Sadat decided to expel the Soviets in 1972 and switch allegiance to the United States, Egypt quickly became the second largest beneficiary, after Israel, of U.S. foreign aid.
- Cuba was heavily subsidized by the Soviet Union in recognition of Castro's allegiance to communism. Cuba then became a conduit for Soviet aid to rebel armies in Central America and Africa.
- In the 1970s Ethiopia and Somalia, neighbors and combatants over disputed territory, each switched allegiances between the two superpowers. When Marxist guerrillas took control of Ethiopia, that country dropped its close relationship with Washington and turned to Moscow. Somalia, which had forged close links with the Soviet Union, then allied itself with the United States in 1978. The United States showered Somalia's dictatorship with the weapons used in the early 1990s in civil unrest and against U.N. and American troops.[3]
- In the 1980s the United States backed rebel armies in the Soviet-allied states of Angola and Nicaragua.

Thus, during the Cold War, the world map was like a chessboard for the superpowers.

The arms race, however, was the major field of competition between the superpowers. Each tried to build bigger, better, and more nuclear weapons than the other. The paradoxical strategic doctrine that made this insane arms race marginally rational was deterrence through "mutually assured destruction" (MAD). MAD meant that both sides would be deterred from using nuclear weapons by the assurance that the victim of a nuclear attack could literally destroy the aggressor in retaliation. The populations of the United

States and the Soviet Union were both, in effect, hostages in a situation of nuclear terrorism.

The word terrorism is not used lightly here. It is important to remember and appreciate the fear that characterized the Cold War in order to understand the feelings of relief when it ended and the task that still remains. While the fall of communism in Eastern Europe and the former Soviet Union dispelled the political tensions that produced this terror, most of the weapons themselves still exist. While we no longer live in daily fear that we will suddenly be engulfed in a nuclear firestorm, as long as nuclear weapons exist, the unimaginable can still happen.[4]

Lest We Forget: Uuimaginable Destruction

The power of nuclear weapons is truly awesome. The *blast effect* from a one megaton (a million tons of TNT) warhead exploded over a major city would crush and vaporize everything within a one-and-a-half mile radius. The temperature at the center of the fireball would be eight times hotter than the sun. All human beings within this zone would immediately die.

A shock front with winds exceeding 600 miles per hour would create a vacuum that would be filled with in-rushing winds of greater than hurricane force. Nearly everything would be destroyed in a three-mile radius from ground zero. Asphalt paving would melt; wood and clothes would ignite. Trucks would be thrown about like giant Molotov cocktails. Over eight miles from ground zero, winds would reach hurricane force, and most people would suffer second- or third-degree burns from this firestorm. People and animals dozens of miles away who saw the flash from the explosion would be blinded or suffer eye damage. Much of the rubble near the blast would be highly radioactive.

Survivors would envy the dead. Many would die slowly from radiation sickness, severe burns, broken bones, and lacerations. Hospitals and health-care personnel would

> **For Reflection**
> During the 1950s, Senator Joseph McCarthy stirred anti-Communist sentiment in the United States to the point of blacklisting writers, actors, and other celebrities. At the same time, Americans were building bomb shelters and conducting air-raid drills in schools. Those who have no experience of this fear of communism and of nuclear weapons might want to interview someone about the climate in the United States during the Cold War or see films such as *The Front* (1976) or *Testament* (1983).

be destroyed, disabled, or overwhelmed, as would fire departments, water treatment plants, and food stores. Many of the uninjured would die from epidemics or hunger. Some, no doubt, would commit suicide out of grief or shock. Radioactive particles, pulled into the upper atmosphere by the mushroom cloud, would fall hundreds or thousands of miles away, contaminating milk or food and causing cancer decades later. Survivors of the atomic bomb dropped on Hiroshima in 1945 lived in fear of falling victim to cancer because of their exposure to radiation. The *radiation effect* of a nuclear bomb is utterly indiscriminate. In a nuclear war, of course, a city could be hit with several warheads. The cumulative effect of a full-scale nuclear war would most likely produce a *nuclear winter*, lowering the temperature of earth so that little food could be produced.[5]

At the height of the arms race the two superpowers possessed over 50,000 nuclear bombs. Humanity still has the power to undo creation as the twenty-first century opens. Jonathan Schell hauntingly reflected on the meaning of this in *The Fate of the Earth*.

> Four and a half billion years ago, the earth was formed. Perhaps a half billion years after that life arose on the planet. For the next four billion years life became more complex, more varied, and more ingenious, until, around a million years ago, it produced mankind [sic]—the most complex and ingenious species of all. Only six or seven thousand years ago— a period that is to the history of the earth as less than a minute is to a year—civilization emerged, enabling us to build up a human world, and to add to the marvels of evolution marvels of our own: marvels of art, of science, of social organization, of spiritual attainment. . . . [A]nd now, . . . we hold this entire terrestrial creation hostage to nuclear destruction, threatening to hurl it back into the inanimate darkness from which it came. And this threat of self-destruction and planetary destruction is . . . here now, hanging over the heads of all of us at every moment. The machinery of destruction is complete, poised on a hair trigger, waiting for the "button" to be "pushed" by some misguided or deranged human being or for some faulty computer chip to send out the instruction to fire. That so much should be balanced on so fine a point—that the fruit of four and a half billion years can be undone in a careless moment—is a fact against which belief rebels. And there is another even vaster measure of the loss, for stretching ahead from our present are billions of years of life on earth, all of which can be filled not only with human life but with human civilization. . . . And yet we threaten, in the name of our transient aims and fallible convictions, to foreclose it all. If our species does destroy itself, it will be a death in the cradle—a case of infant mortality. The disparity between the cause and the effect of our peril is so great that our minds seem all but powerless to encompass it. . . . It is almost an illusion. Now we are sitting at the breakfast table drinking our coffee and reading our newspaper, but in a moment we may be inside a fireball whose temperature is tens of thousands of degrees. Now we are on our way to work, walking through the city streets, but in a moment we may be standing on an empty plain under a darkened sky looking for the charred remnants of our children. Now we are alive, but in a moment we may be dead. Now there is human life on earth, but in a moment it may be gone.[6]

But horrific weapons and the policy of deterrence are still with us. It is still possible for "some misguided or deranged human being or faulty computer chip" to launch nuclear warheads. It is still possible for the comman-der of a Trident submarine, with its capacity to deliver over 190 warheads on as many targets, to blackmail the world or to effectively destroy a conti-nent. And as quickly as the political rationale for nuclear terrorism dissolved, it could return, if, for example, the precarious Russian experiment with democracy were to fail.[7] After September 11, there is increasing concern that terrorists might procure a nuclear weapon or create a crude atomic bomb.[8] The weapons themselves, quite apart from the threat or the will to use them, are terrifying.

The end of the Cold War, which has given the world a window of oppor-tunity for nuclear disarmament, ironically saps the motivation to do so. The citizen anti-nuclear movement that ebbed and flowed in intensity from the 1960s through the 1980s seems to have lost much of its momentum in the 1990s. Since it seems less likely today that nuclear weapons will be used, it is difficult to generate much concern about the existence of such destructive power or much debate about the meaning or wisdom of deterrence in such a changed political context. We need to remember the power of these weapons and take advantage of this opportunity to move toward a policy of minimal deterrence as a first step toward living in a nuclear-free world.

Nuclear Proliferation

The nuclear age dawned because of a race, in the midst of World War II, to create an atomic bomb. The United States tested the bomb on July 16, 1945, and used it a few weeks later, on August 6 at Hiroshima and August 9 at Nagasaki, Japan. Shortly thereafter, Japan surrendered.[9]

The Soviet Union soon developed its own bomb in 1949, and the numer-ical and technological arms race was off and running. In the arms race, the United States always maintained a creative and technological lead and the Soviet Union effectively played catch-up, mimicking each American advance and even building more and bigger warheads and inter-continental ballistic missiles (ICBM). After the early 1960s, when both superpowers could totally obliterate the other, it became ludicrous to speak of winning the arms race.

For Reflection

The controversy over whether the use of the atomic bomb was morally right or historically necessary still rages. Opponents contend that Japan was on the verge of surrendering anyway and that the bomb was used to prevent the Soviet Union from sharing in the victory in the Pacific. They also question the morality of using an indiscriminate weapon with the intention of killing civilians. Proponents con-tend that a bloody invasion would have been necessary before Japan would have surrendered, and that the use of the atomic bombs saved tens of thousands of American lives. This controversy was publicly re-kindled when the Smithsonian Institution developed a display to commemorate the fiftieth anniversary of the Hiroshima and Nagasaki attacks in 1995.

From that point on, each superpower was simply adding to its overkill capacity and making sure that its nuclear weapons (not its people) could survive a first strike by the other side.

Great Britain and France developed their own nuclear weapons and delivery systems in order to help deter the Soviet Union from attacking Western Europe, to enhance their prestige as major players in the world, and to maintain their independence. China, feeling threatened by its Soviet neighbor and desiring global prestige, developed nuclear weapons. These three nations together have about 1,200 nuclear warheads. For many years, the United States, the Soviet Union (Russia), Great Britain, France, and China constituted the nuclear club of acknowledged nuclear powers. These countries also happen to be the five permanent members of the United Nations Security Council. This limited increase of nuclear weapons' states left the doctrine of deterrence intact, but proliferation became a concern.

The spread of nuclear weapons has been curbed primarily by the Nuclear Non-Proliferation Treaty (NPT). This 1968 accord took effect in 1970. The NPT binds together the acknowledged nuclear powers with non-nuclear nations. Those without nuclear weapons pledge not to acquire them and to submit to the purview of the International Atomic Energy Agency (IAEA), which monitors their compliance. Nuclear powers agree to share nuclear energy technology with other nations, under the watchful eye of the IAEA, and to take steps toward reversing the arms race, nuclear disarmament, and a treaty on "general and complete disarmament" (Article VI).

When the Soviet Union splintered into fifteen independent republics in 1991, Ukraine, Kazakhstan, and Belarus became nuclear powers by virtue of having Soviet missiles based in their territory. All three agreed to have these weapons dismantled and removed to Russia, with the aid of Russia and the United States, and this has now been accomplished.[10] Thus, all three countries have disarmed and joined the Non-Proliferation Treaty (NPT) protocol. This is good news given the historical and current tensions between these countries and Russia, as well as the continuing ethnic and political turmoil within these states.

Three other countries are now recognized as nuclear weapons states. Israel, although it does not officially admit it, has built and stockpiled nuclear weapons. India twisted the Atoms for Peace program, which assisted countries in the development of nuclear energy, into a nuclear bomb, which it first tested in 1974. Pakistan, India's neighbor and nemesis, produced and tested a nuclear weapon in 1998. This development led India to conduct further tests to establish its nuclear capability as a deterrent to Pakistan. None of these three had signed the Non-Proliferation Treaty.

This means that nuclear weapons have been introduced into two of the most volatile regions in the world. Israel's nuclear capability has been a major spur for its non-democratic Arab neighbors to buy or build one of their own. India and Pakistan have fought two wars against each other since their independence in 1947 and are locked in a territorial dispute over Kashmir. In 1999 and in 2002 the conflict over Kashmir led India and Pakistan to mass troops along their border in preparation for war. And both times India and Pakistan threatened to use nuclear weapons.

Today's nuclear "wannabes" present a definite cause for alarm. The aftermath of the Persian Gulf War made it clear that Iraq, despite signing the NPT, was closer to developing a nuclear bomb than most experts thought. It also appears that Iraq has stockpiles of chemical and biological weapons, and it has used chemical weapons in its conflict with Iran and on its own Kurdish minority. Iran has made little secret of its desire to develop a nuclear weapon. Syria, Libya, and Algeria are also known to be envious of nuclear capability. All of these five Middle Eastern or North African states could be considered "loose cannons." The thought of Iraq's Saddam Hussein, or Syria's Bashar al-Asad, or Libya's Muammar al-Qaddafi with a finger on the nuclear button is terrifying indeed. The Middle East is a volatile area that contains multiple fault lines for war: Israel vs. the Palestinians and the Arab countries, Iraq vs. Iran or Kuwait or Saudi Arabia, the Kurdish struggle for independence, tensions between the Sunni and Shiite branches of Islam and with Muslim fundamentalists, various other ethnic and religious tensions, and a gap between the oil-rich minority and the poor majority. Introducing weapons of mass destruction and sophisticated delivery systems such as ballistic missiles and high-tech fighter-bombers into this region is an invitation for trouble and tribulation.

An equally troubling situation is North Korea's attempt to acquire nuclear weapons. North Korea is a deeply impoverished, heavily armed, and totally repressive Communist dictatorship that in the years surrounding the turn of the century endured a terrible famine. Since 1953, a precarious standoff has existed between North Korea and South Korea, its increasingly democratic and economically prosperous better half. Enmity also exists between North Korea and Japan. These relationships are further complicated by the proximity of China. North Korea's development of nuclear weapons could trigger an Asian nuclear arms race, and radically change the politics of the Far East for the worse. Certainly Japan, South Korea, and Taiwan have the technological capability of rapidly becoming nuclear powers if they so desire. In 1994, the United States declared that it would not allow North Korea to make a nuclear bomb. After strained negotiations, North Korea agreed to dismantle its nuclear program in exchange for assistance in developing alternative energy sources less amenable to bomb making.[11] Late in 2002, the United States accused North Korea of breaking this agreement and North Korea admitted that it was indeed making nuclear weapons. Early in 2003, North Korea withdrew fron the NPT and banished the IAEA inspectors from the country.

It is important to note that there have been some successes in regard to nuclear non-proliferation. South Africa developed, tested, and stockpiled a small number of bombs, then decided to destroy them and is now nuclear-free. At one time, Argentina and Brazil seemed poised to embark on a nuclear arms race like that between India and Pakistan, but the replacement of their military governments with democracies has eased the tension between the two countries and resulted in the termination of their nuclear weapons programs. Most nations seem comfortable without nuclear weapons, but all are wary of those that do exist and of the countries that possess them.

At the meeting to renew the NPT on its twenty-fifth anniversary in 1995, the nuclear powers pushed for its indefinite extension. Some of the non-nuclear nations—notably Mexico, Venezuela, Nigeria, and Indonesia—argued for extending the treaty for fixed periods of time, as in the past. These countries argued that the nuclear powers had not lived up to the nuclear disarmament provisions of the treaty and were unlikely to do so unless they were subjected to continued pressure. The treaty was indefinitely and unconditionally renewed in 1995, but the arguments of the non-nuclear nations retain considerable merit. The NPT regime will work only if there is a genuine consensus of opinion and effective implementation of its provisions. The nuclear-weapons states, in particular, must make good-faith efforts toward the abolition of nuclear weapons.[12]

Arms Control

As the arms race developed so did efforts at arms control, and these efforts bore fruit in various treaties and agreements. We have already seen that the 1968 Non-Proliferation Treaty has been effective in keeping the nuclear club rather exclusive. The 1963 Limited Test Ban Treaty prohibited above-ground testing of nuclear weapons. It was signed in the aftermath of the Cuban missile crisis, one of the tensest moments in the Cold War. The Anti-Ballistic Missile treaty (ABM) of 1972, which severely curtailed the development of defensive systems to counter a nuclear attack, effectively closed off a whole new direction (i.e., defense) for the arms race. The Strategic Arms Limitation Talks (SALT), which resulted in the 1972 SALT I and 1979 SALT II agreements, slowed the arms race, but did not result in the destruction of any nuclear warheads, missiles, or bombers.[13]

The Reagan years (the early and middle 1980s) brought a lull in arms-control agreements, a leap in the arms race, and a corresponding surge in nuclear anxiety. This impasse ended when Mikhail Gorbachev, the Soviet premier, accepted the U.S. position regarding intermediate-range ballistic missiles in Europe. These were missiles on both sides of the Iron Curtain that could reach targets in Western Europe or in the Soviet Union. Although the Soviet Union had a substantial lead in the number of missiles and warheads, Gorbachev agreed that both sides would destroy *all* of their intermediate nuclear forces (INF). The INF treaty (1987) was the first treaty that actually reduced the number of missiles and warheads.[14]

After that historic agreement, the two superpowers began Strategic Arms Reduction Talks (START), which resulted in two agreements—START I (1991) and START II (1993). START I led to mutual reductions in strategic weapons to about 6,000 each, and START II called for the United States and Russia to dramatically reduce their stockpiles of strategic nuclear warheads (to about 3,500 each) and of tactical nuclear weapons.[15] The U.S. Senate, however, did not ratify START II until January 1996. The treaty could be interpreted as favoring the United States in that it gave the United States a numerical advantage and it required Russia to dismantle all of its big land-based missiles, while the United States kept many of its advantageous submarine-based missiles. The Russian Duma (parliament) hesitated to ratify the treaty, giving it only partial assent in 2000. Thus START II was never implemented, and the Clinton administration began a START III process as a way to overcome Russia's concerns.[16]

In 2001 President George W. Bush came into office having stated two clear goals regarding strategic nuclear weapons: to reduce America's nuclear arsenal to about 2,000 strategic warheads and to build a missile defense system. In May 2002, he signed a simple three-page treaty (START I is over 700 pages long) with Russian President Vladimir Putin that commits both sides to reduce their operationally deployed strategic nuclear warheads to no more than 2,200 by 2012. Bush had wanted an informal gentlemen's agreement to this effect, but both the Russians and the U.S. Senate insisted on a formal treaty. When ratified and implemented, this agreement will significantly reduce the number of strategic warheads deployed by each side (from about 6,000 to 2,200), while giving both countries maximum flexibility in how those warheads are deployed.

There are, however, some lingering concerns related to this positive process:

- The Bush-Putin treaty does not require that any warheads or delivery system be destroyed, only that it not be operational. Thus warheads and missiles could be stored for deployment at a later time. Some critics have suggested that Russian nuclear warheads in particular may be safer atop a missile than in *storage* at a poorly guarded facility. This also seems to allow Russia to keep its big land-based, multi-warhead missiles that Bush Sr. worked so hard to eliminate in START II.
- There is *no timeline* in the treaty other than the ten-year deadline. The treaty expires in 2012 and can be renewed at that time. Either side can leave the treaty on three months notice.
- The agreement completely ignores tactical or battlefield nuclear weapons.
- The treaty keeps the elaborate procedures for *verification* built into the SALT and START agreements, but this process is hampered by a legacy of suspicion from the secrecy of the Cold War. Moreover, the maximum flexibility built into the agreement does not leave much to be verified.
- The process of breaking down the warheads and the missiles, storing or recycling the fissionable material, and verifying that this is being done is very *expensive*. This is a particularly difficult problem for Russia. Its struggling economy cannot bear the cost of this process.
- Atomic know-how and nuclear material are scarce assets that can earn Russia hard currency. Official export (for example, to Iran[17]) or black-market profit are constant temptations. There have already been cases of *fissionable material being sold or stolen*.[18] The dispersion of fissionable material or nuclear weapons can, of course, result in either "rogue" states or terrorist groups acquiring nuclear capability.[19]
- It is difficult to dismantle nuclear weapons in a *safe and environmentally responsible way*. In the United States this is being done at the

Pantex plant in Amarillo, Texas. Workers who once built bombs are now carefully taking them apart. This is hazardous work and questions have been raised about adherence to safety procedures at the plant.[20] If the United States is struggling with safety issues, there is little doubt that Russia, with a weaker economy and lax government controls, is having an even harder time.

- Storing or *disposing* of fissionable uranium and plutonium in bomb-grade form is even more difficult than disposing of highly radioactive waste from nuclear power plants. (See chapter 3.) As long as it remains in bomb-grade form, a warhead can be quickly re-assembled. The United States has agreed to purchase much of the former Soviet Union's fissionable material for use in nuclear power plants, but that arrangement seems to be in jeopardy.[21] The United States already has a surplus of uranium and plutonium for its stalled nuclear-energy program and has yet to solve the problem of how to safely store or dispose of this highly radioactive and virtually everlasting material.[22]

Although dismantling nuclear weapons is an expensive and hazardous process, keeping them is also costly. This is one reason that Bush and Putin can so readily agree to reduce them—the overkill capacity of both nations is unnecessary and is expensive to maintain. Although the atomic arms program was touted by the Pentagon as being cheaper than spending on conventional weapons, a 1995 study showed that the United States spent about $4 trillion (in 1995 dollars) over a fifty-year period on its nuclear arsenal. This amounts to more than a fourth of all United States military spending since World War II.[23] As the Second Vatican Council pointed out as early as 1965, "the arms race is an utterly treacherous trap for humanity, and one which injures the poor to an intolerable degree."[24] Even without being used, nuclear weapons represent a theft from the poor and create a threat to the earth.[25]

Missile Defense

President Bush's other goal was to build a National Missile Defense (NMD) system to defend the United States (and perhaps its NATO allies) against an attack from a rogue nation using a nuclear-armed ballistic missile. The Bush administration has steadfastly pursued this controversial plan.

A defensive missile shield is meant to destroy a nuclear missile or its nuclear warhead before it hits its target. The administration has been vague about the details of a NMD system. Components could be sea-based (missiles shot from ships), air-based (planes with lasers or missiles), land-based, or, perhaps, space-based (satellites with lasers). The latter is especially controversial in that thus far space has been considered off-limits for weapons. The missile defense system would try to hit an offensive missile in its boost phase (2 to 5 minutes) or hit the warhead as it re-enters the atmosphere—comparable to hitting a bullet with a bullet in a sea of decoys.

This idea, which first arose in the Eisenhower administration, was pursued by President Johnson. The Nixon administration realized that an effective missile defense system would be technologically difficult, could be continually overcome by better offensive strategies, and would make the arms race even more costly. Thus the United States and the Soviet Union wisely stopped the defensive side of the arms race by signing the ABM (Anti-Ballistic Missile) treaty in 1972. The idea of a missile shield was revived by President Reagan's "Star Wars" proposal in 1983 and again by a Republican Congress in 1996. The Clinton administration was less enthusiastic about the idea, but also did not want to be painted as weak on defense issues by a more hawkish Republican Congress. President Clinton ordered three tests of an anti-missile system, beginning in October 1999 and concluding in July 2000. The second and third tests clearly failed and the success of the first was questionable. The Clinton administration became increasingly reluctant to spend billions of dollars on an unproven technology. Thus President Clinton deferred the decision to the next administration. George W. Bush committed himself to building a National Missile Defense Shield during his campaign and chose Donald Rumsfeld, a leading proponent of the idea, as his secretary of defense.

President Bush and his supporters argue that the post-Cold War world presents a new threat—rogue nations, such as North Korea, Iraq, Iran, and Libya, armed with nuclear weapons and ballistic missiles capable of reaching the United States. While a missile defense system would be overwhelmed by the thousands of warheads that Russia has (and thus made little sense during the Cold War), it could handle the handful of missiles and warheads possessed by a rogue state. Without NMD, a rogue state could blackmail or terrorize the United States. The Bush administration contends that the United States should no longer remain defenseless against this threat. Thus, after announcing its intentions in December 2001, the United States officially terminated its participation in the Anti-Ballistic Missile Treaty on June 13, 2002, and broke ground at an NMD construction site in Fort Greeley, Alaska, two days later.

The Clinton administration established four reasonable criteria for evaluating a National Missile Defense system: the missile threat, the system's technological feasibility, its impact on national security and particularly on arms control, and its cost. Critics contend that NMD flunks all four criteria:

- The basic rationale for the NMD is the missile threat from "rogue" states. No rogue state, however, currently threatens the United States, in that none of them has nuclear weapons, nor do any have ballistic missiles capable of reaching the United States. Furthermore, the NMD would be useless against the more realistic, but still fanciful, threat of a nuclear bomb delivered by land (truck or suitcase) or sea (speedboat or freighter).[26] The NMD would be a very costly, probably unworkable system designed to protect the United States from a hypothetical threat that good diplomacy should guarantee would never materialize.
- The NMD clearly failed two of the three tests by the Pentagon and it may have failed all three. President Bush admits that effective missile defense technology does not yet exist, but he is confident that America's

best minds can rise to the challenge. Even if this defensive technology could be developed, most analysts think that better offensive technology would quickly be developed to defeat it. The Bush administration claims that even an imperfect system would deter nuclear blackmail. This raises the question of whether these so-called rogue tyrants are rational or suicidal. They cannot be both. If they are rational enough to be deterred by an ineffective missile shield, then couldn't they be reasoned with through diplomacy or deterred by the sure threat of their annihilation should they attack the United States?

- None of America's allies in Europe was in favor of the U.S. renunciation of the ABM treaty in order to build a National Missile Defense system, especially one that is unlikely to protect Europe. Russia refused to amend the ABM treaty, a cornerstone of Cold War arms control, to allow the construction of the U.S. missile shield. China, noting that the threat from rogue nations is only hypothetical, not unreasonably interprets the missile shield as protecting the United States from its two dozen ballistic missiles. With the missile shield, China fears that the United States will not be deterred from terrorizing or blackmailing or threatening China. The NMD, which seems much more likely to trigger an arms race than to abet arms control, has strained relations with both friends and foes.

- Sixty billion dollars has already been spent on the Star Wars fantasy. The projected cost of the limited missile shield contemplated by the Clinton administration was another $60 billion. Although vague on the details and the cost, the Bush administration is clearly planning a more extensive shield. Given that the NMD will protect the United States from a hypothetical threat, while alienating us from allies and adversaries, and that it is unlikely to work, this seems to be basically a cornucopia for the defense industry. Such wasteful spending is a theft from the poor, and it is a poor use of our tax dollars.

Although it would seem that the September 11, 2001, terrorist attack demonstrated that ballistic missiles are hardly the primary threat to America, the Bush administration has unilaterally withdrawn the United States from the ABM treaty and is constructing a National Missile Defense system.

Deterence or Disarmament?

There is, however, a more fundamental question facing policy makers and citizens. Should the goal be a world disarmed of nuclear weapons or should the doctrine of deterrence, based on a limited stockpile of nuclear weapons, continue to guide U.S. foreign policy?

If it is decided that deterrence is the more secure policy (and it appears to have worked thus far), a few hundred or a thousand nuclear warheads probably would be sufficient. Thus, deterrence could be achieved at the level agreed by the Bush-Putin treaty (2,200) or even lower. Since the credibility of deterrence depends on a country's ability to strike back after an attack, mobile submarines and bombers as delivery vehicles would be superior to missiles in fixed silos, which are more vulnerable to a first-strike attack.

But if nuclear weapons are unusable in any moral or rational approach to warfare, and if they are dangerous and terrifying in themselves, then why have them at all? Would not the United States and the world be more secure if nuclear weapons were abolished? The difficulty, of course, is that the nuclear genie cannot be put back in the bottle. Humankind will always have the capability to make a nuclear bomb.

While the design of a bomb is not overly daunting, producing bomb-grade fissionable material is a complex process requiring sophisticated and scarce equipment.[27] Thus a non-nuclear world could be maintained through strict controls on producing weapons-grade material. Indeed, although it has not been foolproof, the International Atomic Energy Agency (IAEA) does keep track of fissionable material throughout the world. Protocols for managing this doubly dangerous material are already in place, although they undoubtedly should be strengthened.

Catholic social teaching certainly leans in the direction of nuclear disarmament. In their 1983 pastoral letter on *The Challenge of Peace*, the American Catholic bishops, following statements by Pope John Paul II, arrived at a "strictly conditioned moral acceptance of nuclear deterrence . . . as a step on the way toward progressive disarmament (#186–187)." Ten years later in their anniversary statement titled *The Harvest of Justice Is Sown in Peace*, the bishops continued to accept deterrence, but only as a step toward a post-nuclear form of security that lies in the abolition of nuclear weapons and the strengthening of international law. Five years later (1998) a group of 73 "Pax Christi USA Bishops" issued a statement on "The Morality of Nuclear Deterrence" that concluded, "Nuclear deterrence as a national policy must be condemned as morally abhorrent because it is the excuse and justification for the continued possession of these horrendous weapons. We urge all to join in taking up the challenge to begin the effort to eliminate nuclear weapons now, rather than relying on them indefinitely." Pope John XXIII seemed to be well ahead of his successors when he wrote in his 1963 encyclical *Peace on Earth:*

> Justice, then, right reason and consideration for human dignity and life urgently demand that the arms race should cease, that the stockpiles which exist in various countries should be reduced equally and simultaneously by the parties concerned, that nuclear weapons should be banned, and finally that all come to an agreement on a fitting program of disarmament, employing mutual and effective controls. (#112)

The Catholic Church, then, calls for nuclear disarmament, but allows deterrence to stand as a step along the way.[28]

Remarkably, a growing number of diplomats, military leaders, and defense experts in the United States, (such as General Andrew Goodpaster, former

Commander of the North Atlantic Treaty Organization [NATO], General George Lee Butler, former Commander-in-Chief of the U.S. Strategic Command, Paul Nitze, former arms negotiator, and Robert McNamara, former Secretary of Defense), have urged "a fundamental re-evaluation of long-standing assumptions regarding the benefits of nuclear weapons," and total nuclear disarmament as realistic goals.[29] One of the most outspoken proponents of this view is General Charles A. Horner, head of the United States Space Command, leader of the North American Aerospace Defense Command (which is responsible for defending the United States and Canada from nuclear attack), and commander of the coalition air forces during the Persian Gulf War. General Horner says nuclear weapons are "obsolete and unusable," and the United States should take "the high moral ground" and "get rid of them all." "It's kind of hard for us to say to North Korea, 'You are a terrible people, you're developing a nuclear weapon,' when we have, oh, 8000."[30] Didn't Jesus suggest that we get the log out of our own eye before we try to remove the speck from our neighbor's eye (Mt 7:1–5)?

It seems that the Bush-Putin agreement is moving the United States and Russia toward a policy of minimal deterrence, although one might wish for a clearer statement of this objective, a more definite timeline, and the destruction (not storage) of warheads and specific delivery systems. Perhaps, however, it is time for Nuclear Weapons Elimination Talks (NWET), which would need to move beyond the bilateral approach of SALT and START and include all the members, official and de facto, of the nuclear club.

A first step toward nuclear disarmament would be a comprehensive ban on testing nuclear weapons. In order to win the vote for an indefinite extension of the Non-Proliferation Treaty, the nuclear powers agreed early in 1996 to reach an accord banning nuclear testing. The road leading to a Comprehensive Test Ban (CTB) treaty was full of twists and turns. The United States began quibbling about the definition of a nuclear test, and then France decided to hold its first tests in three years in the fall of 1995.[31] China set off a nuclear test in July 1996, but then agreed to join a test-ban accord. This meant that the five official members of the nuclear club had all declared moratoriums on testing and were ready to support a CTB treaty. In September 1996, the United Nations overwhelmingly endorsed the CTB treaty as a vehicle to halt all nuclear testing. In order for the treaty to become universal law, however, all forty-four nations possessing nuclear reactors must sign and ratify the treaty. Incredibly, in October 1999, the Republican majority in the U.S. Senate decisively refused to ratify the Comprehensive Test Ban treaty. President Bush opposes the treaty, but thus far has continued to abide by it. India and Pakistan refused to sign the treaty and both have now tested nuclear weapons. Despite the failure to have a universally ratified CTB treaty, the twenty-first century opened with a de facto moratorium on nuclear testing.

Other steps toward nuclear disarmament would include a global ban on the production of fissionable materials for use in nuclear weapons and strengthening the International Atomic Energy Agency, whose role is expanding beyond the constraints of its limited budget. The United States and Russia should quickly implement the Bush-Putin treaty and also begin discussion of further reductions of their nuclear stockpiles or, even better, enter into multilateral discussions aimed at the elimination of nuclear weapons.

The United States foreign-policy establishment seems to vacillate on the issue of nuclear weapons, decrying the efforts of others to acquire them, but clinging to our own like a security blanket. Unfortunately, nuclear weapons are more like a grenade than a security blanket. The nuclear Non-Proliferation Treaty clearly commits the nuclear powers to disarm. If the United States is a country of integrity that honors the treaties it signs, then the United States has chosen the path of nuclear disarmament. The American Catholic bishops point this out in their 1983 pastoral letter, *The Challenge of Peace* (#208). If this were acknowledged with conviction by the President and the State Department, the United States would be moving steadfastly down the path toward a safer world order, one without the fear of a nuclear holocaust shadowing the future. The contours of that path are clear: adherence to the Comprehensive Test Ban Treaty, a global freeze on the production of weapons-grade fissionable material, strengthening the IAEA, and dismantling all nuclear weapons and their delivery systems.

CHEMICAL AND BIOLOGICAL WEAPONS

Although nuclear weapons are the most destructive, chemical and biological weapons share many of the same characteristics:

- They are indiscriminate.
- They can cause the horror of mass death.
- They are difficult to control.
- They are prone to proliferation.
- They are problematic to destroy.

Chemical Weapons

Chemical weapons release chemicals, such as nerve gas or tear gas, which kill or disable people. They have been called the "poor country's atom bomb" because they represent an inexpensive way for a country to acquire weapons of mass destruction for potential leverage in international conflicts. Protective clothing and gas masks can often defend against a chemical threat. Chemical weapons are intrinsically indiscriminate and have sometimes been intentionally used to massacre civilians—in the gas chambers of the concentration camps during the Holocaust and against Iraqi Kurds in 1988. Chemical weapons have only rarely been used in warfare. The results of their use during World War I were so horrible that the *use* of chemical (and biological) weapons was banned by the 1925 Geneva Convention, and it seems that only Iraq has clearly violated this prohibition and that was during its war with Iran in the 1980s.

Because many chemicals have both a peaceful use and can also be used in weapons (the bomb set off in Oklahoma City in 1995 was made from chemicals used in the manufacture of fertilizer), it is very difficult to control the proliferation of chemical weapons. For example, U.S. intelligence sources say that Libya is building the world's largest underground chemical weapons plant in a hollowed-out mountain forty miles from Tripoli. Colonel Qaddafi, Libya's tyrannical leader, says this is an irrigation project. In another instance, he claimed a suspected chemical weapons plant was a pharmaceutical installation company.[32] Without on-site inspection, such claims are difficult to refute.

In 1992, a new Chemical Weapons Convention (CWC) was introduced through the United Nations to ban the *production and possession* of chemical weapons.[33] This convention went into effect in April of 1997. By 2001, 143 states were party to the CWC, including the United States, Russia, China, India, Iran, and South Korea. Several states thought to possess chemical weapons, however, including Iraq, Libya, Syria, Egypt, Israel, and North Korea, have not signed on to the convention.[34]

Opponents of the Chemical Weapons Convention have argued that, given the dual use of many chemicals, the treaty is impossible to verify, and that it may even contribute to the proliferation of chemical weapons by allowing freer exports to countries that have ratified it.[35] The CWC, however, seems to strike a reasonable balance between the transparency and on-site verification needed to build confidence in compliance and protecting trade secrets and confidential national security information. Unfortunately, during its first four years of operation, the actions of states, and especially the United States, have tilted this delicate balance away from verification and toward protecting confidentiality.[36]

In its domestic legislation that ratified and implemented the CWC, the United States unilaterally provided itself with three exemptions. This has undermined the treaty by setting a bad example for other countries to follow. Moreover, the majority of the parties to the treaty have not paid their regular assessments or have failed to reimburse the Organization for the Prohibition of Chemical Weapons for the cost of inspections, resulting in a financial crisis. The United States is one of the countries at greatest risk from the spread of chemical weapons, yet the treaty has failed to live up to its promise, in part because of a lack of U.S. leadership.[37]

As with nuclear weapons, the dismantling and disposal of chemical weapons has proved to be costly and hazardous. During the first Bush administration Congress committed the United States to destroying its chemical weapons stockpile by 2004. By 2001 it became clear that the United States was going to miss the CWC 2007 deadline for destroying all of its chemical weapons and that the United States might even have difficulty meeting an extended deadline of 2012. The estimated cost of destroying the 30,000-metric-ton U.S. chemical arsenal had risen to $20 billion.[38] These weapons are stored at eight sites in the United States; since transporting them is particularly dangerous, it has been decided that they will be incinerated on site. The safety of the first incinerator made operational, at Tooele, Utah, where about 40 percent of the United States' chemical arsenal is stored in underground igloos, has been criticized by its dismissed manager and others. The plant experienced three emergency shutdowns in its first hundred days of operation. Meanwhile, thirty-year-old M-55 rockets containing the deadly poison sarin are corroding and beginning to leak. At this point, it is probably less risky to continue with the incineration than to continue to store the leaky chemical warheads.[39] Paralleling the problems associated with nuclear weapons are concerns that Russia's weak economy cannot afford to safely dispose of Moscow's 40,000 ton stockpile of chemical weapons, nor to maintain adequate security around the storage sites.[40] Other countries, especially in the Two-Thirds World, face similar problems.

Biological Weapons

Biological weapons use micro-organisms or biologically derived toxins instead of chemicals. Some organisms, such as the ebola virus, anthrax bacterial spores, or smallpox, can cause fatal diseases; others, can be incapacitating. Deadly viruses could cause an epidemic that would be impossible to control and that might rebound to destroy the nation that used the weapon. To date, biological weapons have not yet been used in warfare.

The development, production, and possession of biological weapons are prohibited by the 1972 Biological Weapons Convention (BWC), which has been ratified by 144 states or about 75 percent.[41] The treaty makes no provision for inspection or verification. This lack of teeth reduces the BWC to little more than a gentlemen's agreement. Consequently the BWC member states established an Ad Hoc Group in 1994 to develop a system of on-site inspections to monitor compliance with the treaty. As with chemical weapons, the dual use of biological agents makes inspection and verification delicate and difficult. In July of 2001, the U.S. delegation of the new Bush administration not only rejected the verification protocol that was on the table, but withdrew from the Ad Hoc Group, effectively ending the process.[42] Since the United States is under threat from bio-terrorism, one wonders about the wisdom of unilaterally withdrawing from the process to verify compliance with the BWC. The United States and perhaps a dozen other countries all engage in biological weapons research, which is not banned by the treaty, ostensibly to deter each other from developing such weapons.[43]

LAND MINES

Although land mines do not threaten mass destruction, they have actually claimed more victims than nuclear, chemical, and biological weapons together, and they kill and maim civilians long after the conflict in which they were sown has ended.[44]

There are perhaps 100 million mines buried in 64 countries around the world, and they kill or maim about 20,000 people, mostly civilians, each year. A new mine costs as little as $3, but uprooting a mine can cost between

$200 and $1,000, and an arm, a leg, or a life. Only about 100,000 mines are removed each year and mines are still being sown in about 20 ongoing conflicts.[45] The most mine-afflicted countries in the world are probably Afghanistan, Cambodia, and Angola, in that order, and other poor countries with significant concentrations include the former Yugoslavia, Mozambique, Somalia, and Sudan.[46] In Cambodia, a country of 8 million people, there are an estimated 10 million mines, rendering about 20 percent of fertile land uncultivated. Cambodia has the highest rate of amputees in the world, with approximately one out of every 200 Cambodians an amputee.[47]

The civilian casualties caused by mines are a strong argument for their condemnation, but mines can serve a defensive military purpose. Bernard E. Trainor, a retired Marine lieutenant general and director of the national security program at Harvard's Kennedy School of Government, conveys the ambiguity of land mines in recounting his experience in the Korean War. As his platoon was taking Hill 59 from Chinese Communist forces, Trainor tripped on a wire. "I heard a 'thip' as it activated a mine, and I steeled myself for the explosion that would rip off my legs. Nothing happened. The mine had failed to function." Two nights later, when the enemy forces tried to recapture the hill, the mines his platoon had planted to protect their position saved them from being overrun. Trainor thinks that trying to outlaw mines would be futile and unverifiable and, since mines can protect American troops in certain circumstances, perhaps immoral.[48] He and others favor the use of sophisticated, so-called "smart" mines that automatically deactivate after a few months, along with restrictions on the sale of mines. Other American military officers, however, including General Norman Schwarzkopf, the commander of the war against Iraq, and General David Jones, a former chair of the Joint Chiefs of Staff, argue that antipersonnel land mines are not essential in modern warfare and ought to be banned.[49]

Two international treaties pertain to land mines—the Convention on Certain Conventional Weapons (CWC) and the Ottawa Convention. The United States is a party to the CWC, which restricts but permits certain antipersonnel land mines (APL), but did not sign the Ottawa Convention, which proscribes the use, stockpiling, production, and transfer of APLs.[50] The 1997 Ottawa Convention resulted from the grassroots, internet-based movement of the International Campaign to Ban Landmines (ICBL), which was championed by the likes of Princess Diana of Great Britain and Queen Noor of Jordan. The ICBL received the Nobel Peace Prize in 1997. By 2001, 141 states had signed the Ottawa Convention, and 28 countries had completed destruction of their stockpiles of APLs, while another 19 were in the process of doing so. The annual casualty rate due to APLs dropped from about 26,000 to less than 20,000. Major powers, such as the United States, Russia, and China, are not party to the Ottawa Convention, nor are most of the countries in the Near East and many in the Asia-Pacific region.[51] The United States argues that it needs APLs to protect its anti-tank mines in the demilitarized zone in Korea and wants to keep the APL military option open in other situations. Critics contend that concern for discriminate warfare and civilian casualties should motivate the United States (and all countries) to stop using or producing antipersonnel mines and to destroy its stockpile of these weapons.

FUEL TO THE FIRE: THE TRADE IN CONVENTIONAL ARMS

Few would argue that weapons in themselves start wars. While the arms trade is not the match that ignites conflict, the proliferation of weapons adds fuel to the fire.[52] The availability of armaments can encourage potential belligerents to rely on a military rather than a political solution to their dispute. And once combat begins, the influx of weapons tends to prolong and magnify the dispute. One thinks of the almost total destruction of Grozny, the capital of Chechnya, in the early months of 1995 or the damage inflicted on Palestine in 2002. Similarly, one of the lessons of Rwanda (1994) is that, while artillery may be necessary to destroy buildings, simple machetes and small arms are sufficient for slaughtering hundreds of thousands of human beings.

Arms transfers have also contributed to escalating a war. The acquisition of missiles, for example, enabled both Iran and Iraq to engage in a variety of escalatory moves during their conflict (1980–1988), such as bombing each other's ports and cities. Both sides used chemical weapons. But what would have happened if one or both had had nuclear weapons?

The proliferation of conventional arms, therefore, leads to more, longer, and more destructive wars.[53] Adding fuel to the fire of international conflict is hardly conducive to a more peaceful world order. The arms trade, however, is very profitable, and thus the weapons industries and their governments have a vested interest in its continuation. A rudimentary understanding of the mechanics and motivation for the arms trade is essential for deciding whether and how to curtail it.

The Arms Trade

Global arms sales average over $50 billion a year. For decades the Soviet Union exported the most weapons (usually accounting for about 40 percent of the world market), while the United States was second, with about a 20 percent share of the sales.[54] In 1991, however, with the decline of the Russian economy and with the United States' display of the technological superiority of its weapons in the Gulf War, the United States raced past Russia to become the world's premier arms exporter, controlling over 60 percent of the global market in arms exports by 1994.[55] At the turn of the century the United States was regularly accounting for nearly 50 percent of world arms sales. The five permanent members of the U.N. Security Council supply 75 percent of all arms sold, with the United States and the countries of the European Union now providing the lion's share.[56]

These first-tier merchants are full-service suppliers. A second-tier of sellers tend to specialize in certain types of weapons and carve out a market niche for themselves. They include smaller countries in Europe, such as the

Netherlands, and some of the newly industrialized nations, including Singapore, South Korea, Israel, Brazil, and China, which has a reputation for a willingness to sell anything to anyone.[57]

The motives for arms transfer involve a push (supply) and a pull (purchase). *Suppliers* push weapons for political and economic reasons. Suppliers want to arm their allies or to reward friends through the transfer of weapons. Thus the Center for Defense Information reports that there has been a dramatic increase in U.S. arms sales and military assistance to countries that have aided the post-September 11 war on terrorism, such as Pakistan, Azerbaijan, Tajikistan, and the Philippines. But it is largely the profit motive that removes restraints. The United States suffers from a serious trade deficit that would be worse without its arms sales. Thus the U.S. government has vigorously supported the arms industry through easing restrictions and fees on foreign weapons purchases, financially assisting friendly nations in buying American armaments, and aiding the U.S. defense industry in research and development.[58] For Russia, the sale of weapons is one of its few sources of hard currency and indeed one of its few exports.

In the post-Cold War environment, when the military-industrial complex in both superpowers faced declining government purchases of their wares, they turned their attention to increasing their share of the global market. The arms industry in the United States has elicited government support for selling its weapons in the world market by arguing that American jobs depend on its success. Ironically, the global success of the American arms industry has been accompanied by deep cuts in its workforce due to government-subsidized mergers within the industry and for arms agreements abroad (known as "offsets"), which transfer production and jobs, along with weapons, to buying countries. According to Department of Defense statistics, the defense industry lost more than 1,700,000 jobs in the decade of the 1990s.[59] At the same time, the highest paid CEO in the defense industry, James Mellor of General Dynamics, which cut over 35,000 jobs from 1990 to 1995, made $11.3 million in 1994.[60] Nonetheless, arms manufacturers contend that even more jobs would have been lost if they were not exporting arms to the world.

Buyers purchase armaments for security and also for symbolic reasons. Some nations have neighbors or other enemies against which they need to defend themselves. Repressive governments in other countries need to defend themselves against their own people. And, unfortunately, high-tech weapons can function as symbols of power, pride, and modernity for developing countries.

There can be irony in the convergence of these two purposes for procuring weapons. The Shah of Iran, for example, developed a very sophisticated air force by purchasing top-grade American planes in the early 1970s. But these were of little use when his own people rebelled against him. He could not bomb his own capital. The fighter-bombers were put to use, however, by the Islamic fundamentalists, who ousted the Shah, in defending Iran against an opportunistic attack from Saddam Hussein's Iraq.[61]

The largest market for weapons is the Middle East. With about 3.5 percent of the world's population, this area purchases about a third of the arms traded in a given year. For consumers of weapons, a combination of means and motive is key and the oil-rich countries of the Middle East have both.[62] In the years before the turn of the century a new arms race seemed to emerge in East Asia, with Taiwan, China, South Korea, and Japan all modernizing their armed forces with the acquisition of hi-tech weapons.[63] Pakistan and India also seemed to be engaged in a disturbing arms competition.

Traffic in conventional weapons steals from the poor even more directly than the nuclear arms race. Although the market for arms in the developing world shrank from $61 billion in 1988 (about three-fourths of the world total) to about $20 billion in 1999 (or about two-thirds of the world total), it remains true that those countries that can least afford it are buying bombs; instead, their people need food.

The 1990s were characterized by intra-state ethnic and sectarian conflicts rather than wars between states. The widespread death and suffering, mostly to civilians, that resulted from these intra-state conflicts were caused by small arms and light weapons. This reality drew attention to the global diffusion of assault rifles, machine guns, mortars and rocket-propelled grenades, and other weapons easily carried or transported by an ordinary vehicle. Such "light" weapons were not even included in the statistics for trade in conventional arms and little attention had been paid to this particular market. Beginning around 1997 there was an explosion of interest by researchers and activists in a movement to curtail the diffusion of small arms and light weapons in the hope of replicating the success of the International Campaign to Ban Landmines. While the trade in light weapons is now better understood, its complexity makes it much more difficult to control and resist.[64]

Given the U.S. dominance of the free market and the reality of the black market in arms, it is not unusual to find American weapons on both sides of a particular war. In the decade 1985–1995, the United States supplied more than $42 billion worth of weapons to parties involved in 45 of the 50 global conflicts. Among the recipients were Turkey, Somalia, Liberia, Zaire/Congo, Pakistan, Indonesia, Haiti, Guatemala, Colombia, Mexico, and the Philippines. Often American-made weapons have been used to slaughter poor peasants who have rebelled against repressive regimes. U.S.-made helicopters, financed with U.S. assistance, were used to kill and control Palestinians in response to the *intifada* that began in 2000. Ironically, United States fighter planes, stationed in Turkey, protect Kurds in northern Iraq, while American-financed fighter planes sold to Turkey are used to bomb Kurdish villages in Turkey.[65]

The threat of American-made weapons being turned against U.S. troops is known as the "boomerang effect" or "blow-back" in military jargon. "In virtually every conflict into which the United States has sent troops since the 1989 collapse of the Soviet Union—Panama, Haiti, Somalia, Iraq, [Afghanistan], and, to a limited extent, Bosnia—American forces have faced American-made weapons."[66]

Curtailing the Arms Trade

Both profits and politics make the arms trade very difficult to control. Since the United States is now the world's top arms exporter, it is logical to expect American leadership in developing a policy to control the arms trade.

The first Bush administration tried to lobby the five permanent members of the U.N. Security Council to join a system of multilateral controls on the arms market after the Persian Gulf War (1991). The system broke down after the United States announced billions of dollars of sales to Israel, Kuwait, Saudi Arabia, Turkey, and Taiwan—contrary to the agreed-upon regime.[67] This took place in spite of the reality that the arming of Iraq, mostly by Russia and Western Europe, had been an important ingredient in Iraq's invasion of Kuwait, which led to the Gulf War. Arms sales are often a clear case of profit eclipsing prudence.

The four components of an arms control regime are relatively clear:

- The first is *transparency*. The nations of the world need to declare and account for both imports and exports of arms, probably through the United Nations. Records need to be kept in order to understand the dynamics of the arms trade, to defuse arms races based on worst-case conjecture, and to curtail the black market in weapons.
- Second, there need to be *supply-side restraints*. Although high-minded and principled, it is bad business for a country to refuse to sell arms when other nations are eagerly in line to do so. Rather than try to cut off sales "cold turkey," it is probably more realistic to set incremental goals toward the objective of disarmament. For example, a ceiling on volume could be set based on a current percentage of the market. Certain types of high-tech weapons could be banned from trade.
- Third, *economic conversion* is essential. Unless the military-industrial complex is converted to serve civilian markets, suppliers will not be restrained, and when efforts are made to reduce the arms trade, politicians will continually be faced with the unhappy prospect of the loss of domestic jobs.
- Finally, *regional arms control agreements* can begin to restrain recipients from filling their perceived need for more arms.[68]

Obviously such an arms control regime will need to be connected to a broader effort toward building common security, preventing and resolving conflict, recognizing human rights, diminishing poverty, and promoting democracy. Putting out fires and preventing them are at least as important as cutting off the fuel.

U.S. MILITARY SPENDING

The Reagan administration (1980–88) dramatically increased U.S. military spending in order to counter the perceived threat of the Soviet "evil empire." Some analysts argue that the Soviet Union was not able to match the

American spending spree and that Reagan's strategy was in part responsible for ending the Cold War. Whether or not that is true, the deficit spending required by huge military budgets and simultaneous tax cuts were responsible for turning U.S. debt (over $4 trillion in 1997) into the world's largest and for the economic recession at the beginning of the 1990s. Thus, many people expected that the demise of the Soviet empire would yield a large "peace dividend"—a dramatic reduction in military spending that would free funds for social spending, debt reduction, and the like.

Early in his presidency, Bill Clinton managed to get Congress to balance the federal budget and, by the end of his presidency, aided by the most expansive American economy in history, the United States began to reduce its debt. After the Persian Gulf War, the United States did decrease its military spending, but not dramatically. In inflation-adjusted dollars, defense spending during the 1990s held steady at about the same amount as the average peacetime budgets during the Cold War.[69] In other words, there was no noticeable peace dividend.

In his first year in office (2001), the administration of President George W. Bush surprised the Pentagon by holding to its campaign pledge to review defense spending thoroughly and to reduce it by eliminating outdated military programs designed for the Cold War. But September 11, 2001, and the war on terrorism changed all that. Encouraged by the patriotic mood of the country, the Bush administration asked a compliant Congress for a

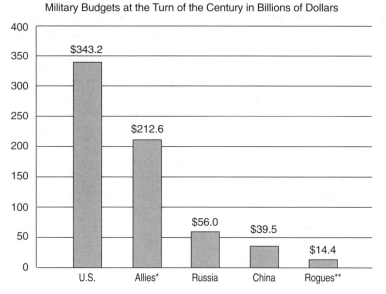

Figure 6.1
Comparisons of Global Military Budgets
Military Budgets at the Turn of the Century in Billions of Dollars

* "Allies" include NATO countries, Australia, Japan, and South Korea

** The "Rogue" states are Cuba, Iraq, Iran, Libya, North Korea, Sudan, and Syria

Source: Center for Defense Information

significant increase in military spending in fiscal years (October to October) 2002 and 2003. The resistant-to-change Pentagon was able to keep producing the tanks, jet fighters, and aircraft carriers it wanted and to develop the mobile Special Forces units and hi-tech, laser-guided munitions it seeks for the future. The Bush administration's strategy now seems to be permanent military superiority.[70]

When United States military spending is compared to that of competing nations, U.S. superiority becomes clear. The $45 billion increase in American military spending since fiscal year 2001 is greater than any other nation's annual defense budget, with the exception of Russia.[71] According to the Center for Defense Information, in 2003 the United States will spend more on its military than the next 25 nations combined, and the United States and its close allies (NATO countries, Australia, Japan, and South Korea) will spend more than the rest of the world combined. In 2000, the United States spent well over $300 billion on defense. Rogue states that might oppose the United States, such as Iran, Iraq, Libya, Syria, North Korea, and Cuba, spent a combined total of about $15 billion. The Bush administration projects a stunning $470 billion defense budget for 2007.

As with the arms trade, the military-industrial complex justifies defense spending in part by arguing that cuts will jeopardize jobs. We have already seen that the arms industry is radically downsizing despite high defense spending and healthy arms sales. Furthermore, while it is true that decreases in defense spending would cost jobs in the short run, it would have a long-term economic benefit. This is so because military spending produces goods that have little economic benefit. (Tanks and submarines drain the economy rather than contribute to it, as trucks and fishing boats do.) In addition, military spending creates fewer jobs per dollar than does civilian spending, either public or private. (Teachers, social workers, nurses, and construction workers make less on average than do defense workers who weld submarines or program guided missile systems; defense work also tends to be less labor intensive than most civilian employment.)[72]

The United States is the world's only remaining superpower. The U.S. military is already far superior to that of any other nation, and no nation is a credible threat to the United States. Given the comparatively disproportionate U.S. military spending, it would not be surprising if the rest of the world becomes uncomfortable about the possibility of American imperialism. The United States is building a military that can do anything, anywhere, anytime.[73] This raises several questions about American foreign policy and military strategy:

- Has the United States moved from a defensive stance to an aggressive posture?
- Will the present combination of tax cuts and increased military spending throw the U.S. economy into a recession (as happened under the Reagan administration)?
- Will this unduly expand the influence of the military-industrial complex in American life?

Table 6.1
America's Political/Economic Choices

$114 billion =	650 new F-22 fighters the Air Force is asking for	or	modernization and expansion of all U.S. mass-transit systems
$100 billion =	Trident II submarine and F-18 jet fighter programs	or	cleaning up the 3,000 worst hazardous U.S. waste dumps
$25 billion =	a fleet of C-17 jet cargo planes	or	rehabilitation for more than 1 million public housing units
$4.9 billion =	the ATACM and Hellfire Missile programs	or	funding to allow all eligible children to enter the Head Start program
$3.7 billion =	the Tow-2 missile program	or	funding to extend Medicare to an additional 4 million adults and 2 million children
$2.9 billion =	extra funding recommended by the Senate Appropriations Subcommittee on Defense for two Seawolf submarines	or	subway lines for three U.S. cities
$2 billion =	a single B-2 bomber	or	400 new elementary schools
$2 billion =	annual operating cost of one of the army's heavy-tank divisions	or	textbooks for 16 million students
$1.66 billion =	39 F-15E fighter bomber aircraft	or	funding to extend the WIC program to cover all eligible women, infants, and children
$1.4 billion =	1 Trident submarine	or	global 5-year child immunization programs against six diseases, preventing 1 million deaths a year
$942 million =	973 Patriot missiles	or	cost of providing medical/social services to AIDS patients to reduce hospital stays and increase life expectancy
$940 million =	80 Apache Attack helicopters	or	Pell grants to all eligible college students
$479 million =	28 F-16 fighter aircraft	or	40,000 new teachers for U.S. schools
$263 million =	14 AV-8B Harriers Ground Attack aircraft	or	amount needed by states to meet the EPA's Safe Drinking Water Act standards
$224 million =	136 Tomahawk cruise missiles	or	a domestic program to encourage solar energy development and home energy conservation
$12 million =	1 nuclear weapon test	or	80,000 hand pumps to give Third-World villages safe water

Sources: Department of Defense, *Selected Acquisitions Report*, 1990; and *Program Acquisition Cost by Weapon System, FY 1990–91*; Congressional Budget Office, *Selected Weapons Cost*, 1989; Employment Research Association, *Converting the American Economy*, 1991; S. Kufson and J. Yang, "Congress Set to Tackle Issue of War's Cost," *Washington Post*, January 24, 1991; D. Evans, "How the 'Pentagon Tax' Is Bleeding America's Cities," *Chicago Tribune*, May 8, 1992; R. Sivard, *World Military and Social Expenditures* (World Priorities, 1988); Fund for Renewable Energy and the Environment, *State of the States*, 1987 (from Seymour Melman, "Book Review of *World Military and Social Expenditures, Annual, 1974–1991* by Ruth L. Sivard," in *Peace & Change* 18 [January, 1993]: 86–87).

- Will military spending make Americans more secure than spending on education and health care?
- Will U.S. military superiority become a self-fulfilling prophecy by creating enemies and fostering anti-Americanism?
- Is the United States becoming imperialist?

It seems that the American response to terrorism might be sweeping the United States in a direction contrary to its highest ideals.

If the United States is the world's lone remaining military superpower, and if military spending actually hurts the economy in the long run, and if the government is struggling to balance the budget, why is defense spending regarded as sacrosanct and untouchable? It seems that a serious national effort focused on economic conversion and drastic reductions in defense spending to reasonable and strategically justifiable levels would immensely strengthen the American economy. And it may be that a healthy economy will be the real measure of a superpower in the twenty-first century. (See Table 6.1.)

The Gospel calls Christians to be peacemakers. Weapons of mass destruction appear to be intrinsically evil, and the trade in armaments prepares the world for war, rather than creating the conditions for peace. In the face of human misery, the amount spent on the military is sinful. If Christians are to be peacemakers we will need to "beat our swords into plowshares," our tanks into buses; we will need to close the book on war and become skilled in conflict resolution (Is 2:4).

STUDY QUESTIONS

1. Describe the effects of a nuclear blast. Should you be anxious that nuclear weapons might be used in the contemporary world?
2. If it became clear that a country, for example, North Korea or Iraq, was building a nuclear bomb, would the world community be justified in undertaking a military intervention to prevent this? Would unilateral U.S. intervention be justified?
3. The United States has unilaterally withdrawn from the Anti-Ballistic Missile Treaty in order to build a Missile Defense System. Is this a good idea?
4. Should the international community be working toward the goal of minimal deterrence or total nuclear disarmament?
5. Some pundits (conservative columnist George Will, for example) think the Chemical and Biological Convention ratified by the U.S. Senate in 1997 is a bad idea. What are the arguments pro and con? What do you think?
6. Should land mines be banned?
7. Whom does the trade in conventional weapons benefit? Whom does it harm? What should be done about it?
8. Does the United States spend too much on defense? How would you prioritize the needs and budget allocations if you were the U.S. president?

CHAPTER SEVEN

Peace and Security in the Twenty-First Century

In days to come
  the mountain of the Lord's house
shall be established as the highest of the mountains,
  and shall be raised above the hills;
all the nations shall stream to it.
  Many peoples shall come and say,
"Come, let us go up to the mountain of the Lord,
  to the house of the God of Jacob;
that he may teach us his ways
  and that we may walk in his paths."
For out of Zion shall go forth instruction,
  and the word of the Lord from Jerusalem.
He shall judge between the nations,
  and shall arbitrate for many peoples;
they shall beat their swords into plowshares,
  and their spears into pruning hooks;
nation shall not lift up sword against nation,
  neither shall they learn war anymore. (Isaiah 2:2–4)

*Building peace, combating poverty and despair, and protecting free-
dom and human rights are not only moral imperatives, but also wise
national priorities. They can shape a world that will be a safer, more
secure, and more just home for all of us. Responsible international
engagement is based on the conviction that our national interests and
the interests of the international community, our common good, and
the global common good are intertwined.[1]*

Early in the twenty-first century, the United States seems to lack a vision
or a set of organizing principles for its foreign policy. Since September 11,
2001 the war on terrorism has been America's overriding concern, but does
this add up to a full-fledged foreign policy?

During the Cold War (1945–1989) the foreign policy of the United States
had a clear focus. It was the doctrine of containment that directed U.S. foreign
policy: the goal was to contain the spread of communism. U.S. anti-communism
was rooted in the political philosophy called *realpolitik* or realism.

With the collapse of communism in Eastern Europe in 1989 and the disintegration of the Soviet Union in 1991, the policy of containment became irrelevant and useless. The United States had defined itself in opposition to communism—the antithesis of the Soviet Union—and now there was nothing to oppose, no enemy to stand against. The foreign policy establishment, the State Department, and military planners—men and a few women who had built their careers around anti-communism—suddenly faced a new world that required fresh ideas.[2]

This chapter describes the search for a new vision or a new template that can give direction to foreign policy in the twenty-first century.[3] It suggests that a "principled foreign policy" that focuses on peacemaking rather than "realism" is more adequate in responding to and managing the complexity and chaos of the interdependent, yet divided, contemporary world.

FROM REALISM TO COMPREHENSIVE SECURITY

The theory of international relations called realism has deep roots in thinkers such as the ancient Chinese strategist Sun Tzu, the ancient Greek historian Thucydides, the Renaissance adviser of Italian princes Niccolo Machiavelli, the seventeenth-century English philosopher Thomas Hobbes, and the nineteenth-century German military strategist Karl von Clausewitz. Realism rose to dominate political and strategic thinking during the Cold War period in reaction to the idealism or liberalism of the period between the world wars. The policies of appeasement that led to the sobering experience of World War II signaled the failure of liberalism. Twentieth-century exponents of realism have included the scholar Hans Morgenthau, the scholar-statesmen George Kennan and Henry Kissinger, and the Protestant theologian Reinhold Niebuhr. The foreign policy establishment—those who developed international political theory, those who translated theory into policy, and those who implemented policy through strategic decisions and tactical deployments—were predominantly practitioners of *realpolitik* during the Cold War period.[4]

Political realists tend to be pessimistic about human nature and even more suspicious of the behavior of groups. Four propositions can summarize the realist framework:

1. The sovereign state is the most important actor in world affairs.
2. States rationally pursue their own national self-interest, defined as power, in competition with other states.
3. In an international system with no central government (anarchy), a balance of power is a realistic way to ensure precarious order and stability and a situation of relative peace.
4. Conflict and war are always possibilities and a credible military defense is essential for the security of the state.

Realists, thus, hold to a Darwinian view of the law of the jungle (rather than the rule of law) where only the strongest survive and win. National security, in the realist perspective, is the province of each individual state pursuing its own self-interest and power in competition with other states.[5]

There were many thoughtful critiques of realism during the Cold War, but *realpolitik* dominated American foreign policy and global statecraft. Now, however, critiques of realism, old and new, are gaining currency and influencing policy, as well they should. A consistent criticism of realism is that it tries to exclude or minimize the role of ethics in decisions about foreign policy and national security. In a realist framework, power eclipses all other considerations, including morality, ideology, culture, and economics. This amounts to an ethics of consequentialist self-interest; in other words, national self-interest is the overriding value by which the consequences or results of a policy or choice are evaluated. This is not so much amoral as it is a sort of national egoism. Obviously, a Christian ethic rooted in human dignity and human rights, solidarity and community, justice and equality might not have much in common with a realist foreign policy.[6]

While the ethical shortcomings of realism have long troubled its critics, in the twenty-first century realism seems politically inadequate to address the spectrum of issues posed by the contemporary world. Realism is narrowly focused on issues of security and power, the military, and war. Of the issues covered thus far in this book, weapons and security (chapter 6) would dominate the interest of a realist. "A conceptual framework for the study of international relations that has nothing to say about the challenges of development, of the environment, of refugees, of population growth, or about the new religious and cultural antagonisms, or that reduces these phenomena to traditional interstate confrontations is necessarily incomplete, and therefore inadequate."[7] Realism is too reductionist and too constricted to handle the complexity, chaos, interdependence, and divisions of the contemporary world. Human security depends on factors that go well beyond military strength and political power.[8]

Clearly a new paradigm is needed. Political scientists Michael Klare and Daniel Thomas reject the "national security" model of realism with its focus on competition for power among the individual nation-states. They propose instead a "world security" framework that recognizes the global interdependence of nation-states and seeks to develop structures and institutions that support cooperation in the interest of human security.[9] Several scholars of international relations have fleshed out this world security paradigm by articulating it in terms of "three Cs": collective security, common security, and comprehensive security.[10]

The concept of *collective security* is most clearly visible in the contemporary world at the United Nations. The idea is to bind together all or most of the major actors in an international system for the purpose of jointly opposing aggression by any of them. Collective security goes beyond the solitary security of each state, which is the reasoning behind realism. Collective security depends on members of the alliance keeping their commitments to the group and on agreement among the members as to what constitutes aggression. The U.N.-sponsored rebuff of Iraq's invasion of Kuwait in 1990–1991 is a successful example of collective security in action. The case of Bosnia, however, turned out to be too complex and too costly for collective security to be immediately effective, although NATO eventually responded to stop the killing there and later in Kosovo.[11]

Common security lies a conceptual step beyond collective security. Common security is the notion that no country can be secure unless every country, especially one's enemies, is secure. The security of nations is interdependent: actions by one state that threaten the security of another state diminish the security of all, including that of the aggressor. If this concept were to gain more currency, its effect would be to move the world community beyond war and toward structures and institutions designed to facilitate international conflict resolution.

Comprehensive security means that *all* of the perils and problems of our world need to be addressed if humanity is truly to be secure. Comprehensive security enlarges the scope of security concerns to include issues such as the gap between rich and poor, ecological concerns, human rights, ethno-nationalism and minority rights, as well as arms races and power politics. America, for example, clearly has the military strength to defend itself against any foreseeable threat to its borders or its interests, but is vulnerable nonetheless to global warming and ozone depletion, to resource scarcity, to economic collapse, to terrorism, and to internal class divisions. Indeed, all humankind, inhabiting what is really a global village, is vulnerable to a variety of threats to its security and well-being. "Rather than fortifying or defending borders, a successful quest for peace must entail strategies for easing and erasing the rifts in society, by eliminating the causes of dissension or finding ways to peacefully bridge the gap between mutually antagonistic groups."[12] A muscular military will hardly be enough to insure human security in the twenty-first century.

A PRINCIPLED FOREIGN POLICY FOR A JUST WORLD ORDER

The United States Institute of Peace has published two thick volumes on managing international conflict. The titles of these volumes provide us with two metaphors for understanding our world. The period immediately after the end of the Cold War was characterized by "global chaos,"[13] a metaphor that continues to be illuminating. The ingredients of global chaos include the proliferation of "failed states," ethno-nationalist conflict, religious and cultural militancy, increasing migration due to environmental degradation, resource wars, globalization, and destabilizing new military technology.[14] Viewed together and alongside traditional causes of conflict, these factors point to a world that is increasingly fragmented and disordered, a world approaching global chaos.

By the beginning of the twenty-first century, the world had entered a period of "turbulent peace," in which the frequency and intensity of ethnic conflict was declining, and some conflicts had been settled through negotiation, but where new conflicts are brewing and negotiated peace is fragile. State sovereignty is being eroded by the diffusion of power throughout the international system, which adds new layers of complexity to efforts to manage global conflict.[15] Regional tension between states is rising, as is international criminality and global terrorism. It is a turbulent and chaotic world indeed.

Yet political scientists Klare and Thomas are confident that this chaos and complexity can be managed. With imaginative leadership and concentrated effort, the global community can move closer to a just world order, which is the foundation for peace. Being a peacemaker and working for justice, however, are particularly challenging in the face of the global chaos and turbulence that characterize the world at the beginning of the twenty-first century.

Some specialists in international affairs who are in tune with this vision suggest the construction of a *principled* world policy to guide the Christian vocation for global responsibility, to manage global conflict, and to create a more just world order.

There are at least three reasons to base foreign policy on stated principles. First, a conscious declaration of the principles underlying foreign policy can solidify any commitment to act on those principles and can bring consistency and constancy to national policy. This would be preferable to the apparently spontaneous crisis-management style that seems to have characterized U.S. foreign policy since the Cold War. Second, principles can focus foreign policy on its proper constituency—humanity in its entirety rather than narrow national interests. Third, a principled world policy can yield clear common standards of conduct to which every nation is held accountable. This can enhance a sense of fair play for all in world affairs.[16]

The principles that might direct world policy can be articulated in four "Ds": diplomacy, sustainable development, democratization, and demilitarization.[17]

Diplomacy

The principle of diplomacy means a commitment to *conflict resolution and peacemaking* and to the structures, institutions, and regimes that will promote a peaceful resolution of conflict. The spirit of diplomacy places war in the position of an absolute last resort, and commits the world's nations to negotiate in good faith toward a constructive resolution of disputes and conflicts.

The skills and techniques of conflict resolution, which are well known, are the subject of much academic reflection.[18] The difficult part is approaching conflict constructively—by letting go of the need to win and by honestly acknowledging our own faults and selfishness. Then it is possible to move forward to seek a creative solution that incorporates the legitimate interests of all parties involved. This requires a sensitivity to the other, rather than anger, hatred, and self-righteousness. It demands a sense of the common good and a willingness to dialogue, adhering to the justice of one's own cause, but attending to the justice in one's adversary's position as well.

The principle of *reciprocity* is a good foundation for diplomacy. Basically reciprocity refers to the Golden Rule—do unto others as you would have them do unto you (Lk 6:31).[19] Each state should evaluate its own actions by the same standards it holds for the behavior of other nations.[20] Reciprocity can foster the sort of self-critical reflection necessary for constructive conflict resolution. For example, if the United States does not want North Korea or Iraq to possess nuclear weapons, then the United States must be willing to dismantle its own nuclear weapons. Otherwise the United States is holding North Korea and Iraq to a standard it is not willing to heed itself. The nuclear Non-Proliferation Treaty (NPT) realistically requires the members of the nuclear club to disarm, while it prohibits other states from procuring nuclear weapons. The NPT incorporates the principle of reciprocity.

An interdependent world requires *international institutions* and agencies to enhance the world's capacity for multilateral peacemaking.

> This means, first of all, improving the United Nations' ability to conduct the many critical tasks it has been saddled with over the past fifty years, including its peacekeeping functions, international mediation services, nonproliferation and disarmament activities, refugee assistance, health protection services, and its work for the advancement of human rights.[21]

To be more effective in peacemaking the United Nations will need more financial resources and administrative and organizational reform. Under the leadership of Secretary General Boutros Boutros-Ghali (Egypt, 1991–1996), the United Nations became less bureaucratic and more efficient, and his successor, Kofi Annan (Ghana, 1996–), has moved further toward this objective.

Changes that could make the United Nations more representative and democratic, such as restructuring the membership of the Security Council and rethinking the veto power of its permanent members, might also improve the effectiveness and consistency of the United Nations.[22] At the heart of any organizational reform is the willingness of all nations to accept the legitimate authority of the United Nations and to bolster its capacity to enforce international law. The proposal of Secretary General Boutros-Ghali of a standby peacekeeping force for rapid deployment to areas of incipient violence deserves serious consideration.[23]

The virtual deadlock on the Security Council during the Cold War, with the two superpowers routinely vetoing each other's proposals, prevented the United Nations from fulfilling its founding promise of making and keeping peace. Since the end of the Cold War, the United Nations has been utilized much more often, but with mixed success. The key to future success of the United Nations seems to be greater clarity about its goals and functions, increased support for its authority by member states, and the consent of the parties involved in peace making.[24]

The principle of *subsidiarity* (rooted in Catholic social thought) suggests the resolution of problems and conflicts at the lowest or most local level possible. Global issues require the attention of a global institution such as the United Nations, but regional disputes and difficulties might best be addressed by *regional organizations*. Therefore, world policy should support regional organizations, such as the Conference on Security and Cooperation in Europe (CSCE), the Organization of American States (OAS), and the Organization of African Unity (OAU), and their peacemaking and development efforts. The United States and others should assist in establishing such bodies where they do not now exist, such as in Asia. *Nongovernmental organizations* (NGOs), such as human rights groups, humanitarian organizations, and religious bodies should also be encouraged in appropriate efforts to resolve conflict, aid victims, and alleviate poverty.[25]

Sustainable Development

Throughout history injustice and inequity have been the two fundamental causes of conflict and violence. Chapter 2 documented the disparity between the rich and the poor, between the North and the South. "Today, less than one-fifth of the world's people have more than four-fifths of global wealth, but the poorest billion have less than one-fiftieth." More than half of the earth's food is consumed by rich nations, while every day a half billion people go hungry, and a billion and a half are chronically ill.[26] Poverty stimulates population growth, and pressures people into environmentally destructive behavior, resulting in deforestation, desertification, and resource depletion. These ecological calamities, in turn, force people to migrate in search of food, water, and land (see chapter 3). These social, economic, and environmental burdens contribute to conflict and violence in a descending spiral of suffering.

The principle of sustainable development aims to expand economic opportunity, to achieve a fairer distribution of wealth and power, and to satisfy basic needs without jeopardizing the prospects of future generations.[27] One-third of the global population cannot hope to live in peace and security when two-thirds of the world's people suffer in poverty. No one can be secure unless humanity takes the necessary steps to protect the earth, the home of us all.

This principle reinforces the idea that justice is the foundation for peace. Moreover, there is increasing empirical evidence for this principle, which has led journalist Thomas Friedman to propose "The Golden Arches Theory of Conflict Prevention." Friedman observed that no two countries that both had McDonald's restaurants have had a war with each other. This does not indicate support of McDonald's, or of transnationals, but rather stipulates that when a country reaches a level of economic development where it has a middle class large enough to support a McDonald's franchise, its people will not want to fight wars anymore.[28] Friedman does not naively think that globalization can end geopolitics, but development does change the calculation of conflict.

As with diplomacy, sustainable development needs to be implemented through structures and institutions developed to abolish poverty and to protect the environment. International institutions such as the World Bank, the International Monetary Fund (IMF), and the World Trade Organization

(WTO) need to be reformed to focus more on promoting equitable development. Robert Johansen suggests a development fund, supported by a progressive tax on the nations of the world, with the goal of abolishing extreme poverty within twenty-five years. Johansen also proposes an environmental council within the United Nations to better coordinate global and national efforts aimed at managing climate change, ozone depletion, and other global environmental issues.[29] Nongovernmental organizations will continue to play a key role in sustainable development and will need the support of states and their citizens.

Democratization

Participation in the state (civic) and in society (economic and cultural) is key to human dignity and human rights. The principle of democratization, which aims at increasing every government's and every society's accountability to its people, enhances civic and social participation.

This principle embraces a strong commitment to securing and defending a holistic conception of *human rights*. If minority peoples and oppressed people can truly participate in government and society, their grievances are much more likely to be addressed without violence and strife. World policy aimed at implementing human rights treaties and strengthening human rights institutions will contribute to global peace and security.[30]

It has been observed that established democracies have fought no wars against each other in the twentieth century.[31] Democratization, then, would seem to enhance security and peace. Today 140 of the world's nearly 200 countries hold multiparty elections, but only 80 of them, with 55 percent of the world's people, can be considered fully democratic, while some 35 others are in some stage of transition toward democracy.[32] World policy should support and promote progress toward democracy wherever it can, without the contradiction of imposing or forcing democracy on a nation. This is especially crucial in the formerly Communist countries of Eastern Europe and the former Soviet Union, in the Arab countries of the Middle East, and in China. In general, it seems that economic development is a key factor in the stabilization of blossoming democracies.[33] Thus development and democracy are mutually reinforcing, and both enhance security and reduce conflict. The United Nations and regional organizations can also offer support such as election monitoring and technical assistance.[34]

Demilitarization

The principle of demilitarization includes, but also transcends, the idea of disarmament. It means reducing the role of military power in international relations. "Demilitarization aims at dismantling national and international military cultures and replacing them with a culture of legal obligation and non-lethal forms of dispute settlement."[35] In a sense, weapons are the tip of the iceberg in the militarization of global culture.

Demilitarization includes many of the topics addressed in the previous chapter. Nuclear disarmament is essential if the world is to be weaned from its reliance on "gods of metal." Controls on other weapons of mass destruction, such as chemical and biological weapons, and on weapons that destroy people one at a time, such as land mines, are also urgent.

Demilitarization requires the global community to curb drastically international traffic in conventional armaments. While weapons seldom cause war, they contribute to the initiation and escalation of wars. Despite the dangers of a proliferating traffic in weapons, the United States and the other permanent members of the United Nations Security Council continue to sell arms and to reap scandalous profits from their sale. "However expedient in the short term, American arms sales are contributing to a global glut in military hardware and facilitating the efforts of future belligerents to gear up for war. It is essential, therefore, that the United States work with other arms suppliers to establish new multilateral restraints on the weapons trade."[36] The world community is in need of weapons control if it is to have security and peace.

Demilitarization implies a dramatic reduction in military spending. Clearly the United States spends a disproportionate amount of its GNP on defense. Catholic social teaching has consistently proclaimed that, in a world where two-thirds of humanity is deprived, military spending steals from the poor.

There should be a relationship between the size, configuration, and cost of the U.S. military and the goals and strategies of U.S. foreign policy. The huge sums spent on defense suggest that war and aggression, rather than peace and conflict resolution, are the objectives of U.S. foreign policy. The military-industrial complex constantly concocts justifications for high defense spending and high profits for weapons producers. During the Cold War, the doctrine of containment and an anti-Communist foreign policy were used to justify spending huge amounts on defense. Political scientist Michael Klare argues that after the Cold War the Pentagon substituted a "rogue" doctrine for the doctrine of containment in order to keep United States military spending and military preparation at Cold War levels.[37] In the aftermath of September 11, 2001, the rogue doctrine was quickly transformed into the war on terrorism against an "axis of evil."

The rogue doctrine justified U.S. defense spending for a military force capable of fighting two major regional wars simultaneously to contain so-called rogue states, such as Iran, Iraq, Syria, and Libya, thought to be yearning to become regional powers. This resulted in defense spending at levels similar to peacetime years during the Cold War, a strong military establishment, and a powerful military presence in American life. The war on terrorism has justified even greater defense spending to root out terrorists in states that support them, such as the so-called axis of evil—Iraq, Iran, and North Korea. Indeed, the war on terrorism seems to have resulted in a blank check for the Pentagon.

Because the demands for military power have changed, the military itself needs to change to function effectively. Anti-terrorism and humanitarian intervention require a leaner and more mobile military force. Humanitarian intervention and peacekeeping entail military skills that are more like those of police or even social workers. This requires different education, training, and equipment. Perhaps this function could even be separated from the traditional defense role with more clearly defined types of forces.[38] Reduced and re-directed defense spending could free funds for the construction of educational and industrial infrastructures, and for sustainable development and peacemaking efforts, which could remove the seed beds and roots of terrorism and conflict. A sensible and realistic military strategy can produce a peace dividend instead of profligate defense spending.

The United States Army School of the Americas (SOA) at Fort Benning, Georgia, renamed the Western Hemisphere Institute for Security Cooperation (WHISC) by Congress in 2000, stands as a symbol of the ill effects of militarization. It was established in 1946 at a U.S. base in Panama and moved to Fort Benning in 1984. The SOA's ostensible purpose was to develop ties with Latin American militaries to educate them in the virtues of democracy and civilian control over the military. Instead, it trained them in counter-insurgency warfare, recommending torture, extortion, censorship, false arrest, execution, and "neutralizing" of enemies. Among its nearly 60,000 graduates were some of Latin America's most notorious strongmen, including Panama's drug-dealing dictator, Manuel Noriega, and Roberto D'Aubuisson, a leader of El Salvador's death squads. Other alumni included the military officers who did the bidding of such leaders—the Salvadoran officers linked to the rape and murder of four United States missionaries and to the slaughter of six Jesuit priests, six Peruvian officers involved in killing nine students and a college professor, and the Guatemalan colonel who covered up the murder of an American innkeeper and condoned the killing of a captive revolutionary married to an American lawyer.[39] The values being taught to Latin American military personnel at the School of the Americas are hardly "liberty and justice for all." Many people, including Representative Joseph P. Kennedy II, actress Susan Sarandon, and actor Martin Sheen, feel the school, which they see as anachronistic and injurious, should be closed, and that the values and techniques it teaches should be expunged from the American military.

> **For Reflection**
>
> During the Cold War, U.S. foreign policy was clear. The Soviet Union was the enemy and the policy was to contain the spread of communism. Since the end of the Cold War, the United States has been searching for a new foreign policy and an appropriate defense strategy. If you were the Secretary of State, what would you propose as the key themes for a renewed U.S. foreign policy? Which states, if any, do you think are potential foes: rogue states? Russia? China? a re-united Germany? Japan? State-sponsored terrorist groups?
>
> What is the relative importance of military and economic strength in the twenty-first century? How much should the United States spend on defense? What sort of military does the United States need?

Disarmament and economic conversion are essential aspects of demilitarization, but they are not sufficient. Because war and the military pervade so much of our contemporary thinking and culture, this influence needs to be critically examined and changed. During the Cold War, for example, colleges and universities became sites for military research and for training military officers through the Reserve Officers' Training Corp (ROTC) program. Whether military training and research should continue to be an integral part of higher education in this country is an important question. Violent metaphors or sayings, such as "killing two birds with one stone" or being "blown away," permeate our language and influence our thinking. Violence is pervasive in the media, numbing its viewers to human suffering and death. Military training is steeped in extreme *machismo,* which, in turn, has reinforced sexism in society, thereby making the integration of women into the armed forces more difficult. The demilitarization of American and world culture will require a deep transformation. However, such a conversion will be an important step toward a more secure and peaceful world.

These four principles—diplomacy, sustainable development, democratization, and demilitarization—could be the cornerstones of U.S. foreign policy and of a world policy that could move the global community toward a more just world order. A just world order, based on a principled international policy, seems a more solid foundation for security and peace.

STUDY QUESTIONS

1. Discuss realism or *realpolitik*. What are its strengths and weaknesses? Is it an adequate theory of international relations in the post-Cold War world?
2. How would comprehensive security (the three Cs) differ from realism? Which do you think would be better?
3. Explain the meaning of a principled foreign policy. Is such a foreign policy realistic in a world of competing states? Aren't principles a luxury that the United States cannot afford in foreign policy?

CHAPTER EIGHT

Christian Faith, Jesus, and Catholic Social Teaching

"You are the light of the world. A city built on a hill cannot be hid. No one after lighting a lamp puts it under the bushel basket, but on the lampstand, and it gives light to all in the house. In the same way, let your light shine before others, so that they may see your good works and give glory to your Father in heaven." (Matthew 5:14–16)

"To set out on the road to discipleship is to dispose oneself for a share in the cross (cf. Jn. 16:20). To be a Christian, according to the New Testament, is not simply to believe with one's mind, but also to become a doer of the word, a wayfarer with and a witness to Jesus. This means, of course, that we never expect complete success within history and that we must regard as normal even the path of persecution and the possibility of martyrdom."[1]

This book explores issues of justice and peace that face humanity in the twenty-first century because Christians need to understand these issues in order to create a global community that is more just and at peace. This chapter will try to make explicit *why* Christians should work for justice and make peace.

CHRISTIAN FAITH

Faith is a *relationship* with God; Christian faith is a relationship with God who is revealed by Jesus, the Christ. It is important to understand faith as a relationship and not primarily as a set of beliefs or a checklist of moral requirements. Creeds and commandments are important for persons of faith because they begin to name the God who loves us and they guide us in our response to God. But the relationship of each person with God is primary and central.

As with any relationship, faith is rooted in experience. Since God is spirit, it is sometimes difficult for modern people, convinced of the efficacy of the scientific method and closed to mystery and transcendence, to open themselves to experience the Spirit. There are human experiences that tend to pull us beyond ourselves, such as falling in love or the birth of a child or the death of someone we love or a breathtaking sunrise, but faith always requires the leap that acknowledges the presence of God's Spirit.

Like lovers bursting to recount the experience of being in love,[2] an encounter with transcendent mystery begs to be shared, reflected upon, and responded to. Religious believers gather with other people of faith in community to tell stories of God, to seek to understand their relationship with God (doing theology), to celebrate their faith (worshiping God), and to respond to it (right living). This is how "church" is formed and tradition passed on. Eventually the narratives about God and faith are written down in scripture. Creeds are formulated, liturgy is designed, and principles are put into practice. All of this happens in response to the human relationship with God that rightfully becomes the core and compass of human life.

JESUS AND THE SPIRIT

Jesus was a person of faith. "The most crucial fact about Jesus was that he was a "spirit person," a "mediator of the sacred," one of those persons in human history for whom the Spirit was an experiential reality."[3] At the center of Jesus' life was an intimate and continuous relationship with the divine Spirit. Jesus was the culmination of a stream of Spirit persons in the Jewish tradition—Abraham, Moses, and the prophets—and others following in Jesus' wake—Peter and Paul, Benedict and Ignatius, Francis of Assisi, Teresa of Avila, and Mother Teresa of Calcutta.

Jesus knew God. He had visions of God at his baptism by John (Mt 3:13–17), in the desert (Mt 4:1–11), and on the mountaintop (Mt 17:1–13).[4] Jesus sought out isolated places where he prayed to God throughout the night (Mt 14:23, Mk 1:35). In a culture afraid to utter the Almighty's name, Jesus called God *Abba* (Mk 14:35), Aramaic for "Papa." As the Spirit's healing and liberating power flowed through Jesus, he taught about God and faith "with authority," that is, on the basis of his own profound experience of the divine mystery at the heart of reality. At the beginning of his public ministry Jesus applied the words of Isaiah the prophet to himself:

> The Spirit of the Lord is upon me,
>> because he has anointed me
>>> to bring good news to the poor.
> He has sent me to proclaim release to the captives
>> and recovery of sight to the blind,
>>> to let the oppressed go free,
>>> to proclaim the year of the Lord's favor. (Lk 4:18–19)

Jesus invited everyone he met to faith, to encounter the same Spirit he knew and to live in relationship with God.

THE POLITICS OF COMPASSION

Who is the God whom Jesus knew and obeyed and revealed? "For Jesus, compassion was the central quality of God and the central moral quality of a life centered on God."[5] "Be compassionate as your Father is compassionate"

(Lk 6:36).[6] Moreover, Jesus, "God-with-a-face,"[7] is the embodiment of the divine compassion in the world.[8]

The Hebrew word translated as "compassion" is the plural of the word for womb. It connotes giving life, nourishing, caring, and tenderness, a warm and gentle embrace. It is often used in referring to God in the Hebrew Scriptures. For Jesus, then, God is like a mother who feels for and loves the children of her womb; as followers of Jesus, Christians are to imitate God, being compassionate toward each other. Compassion is both a feeling—being moved by the suffering of others—and a way of being, a willingness to share that suffering and do something about it.[9] In and through Jesus, God shares the suffering of humanity and transforms it into new life.

For Jesus, compassion was neither sentimental nor an individual virtue; rather, compassion was political. When compassion led Jesus to touch a leper, heal a woman with constant menstruation, feed the hungry, forgive sinners, or share a meal with tax collectors and prostitutes, it was moving him to challenge the dominant sociopolitical paradigm of his social world. Thus, Jesus was engaged in what might be called the "politics of compassion," in contrast to the "politics of purity" that dominated his social world.[10]

In the first century, Jewish society was structured around avoiding anything that would make one religiously unclean. The biblical roots of this purity system were found in the Book of Leviticus, especially in the verse, "You shall be holy, for I the Lord your God am holy" (Lev 19:2). Set in the context of laws about ritual and religious purity, the holiness of the Jewish community was defined in terms of purity.

This purity system tended to be hierarchical and exclusionary. It divided those who were born into the tribe of priests and Levites from those who were not, the righteous who observed the purity laws from sinners who were unclean and impure, the whole and the well from the handicapped and the ill, the rich (blessed by God) from the poor, males from females, and Jews from Gentiles. In effect, the purity system created a world with sharp social boundaries, a world where many were treated as outcasts.[11]

In opposition to the teaching of the Pharisees and of Jewish leaders to "Be holy [pure] as God is holy," Jesus proclaimed, "Be compassionate as God is compassionate." Jesus' call to compassion can be seen as a radical challenge to the theology and the politics of the dominant social system of the time, a social structure that placed an oppressive burden on the poor and the marginalized.

Jesus' parables and sayings often indicted the purity system and those who used it for power and privilege. In the parable of the Good Samaritan (Lk 10:29–37), for example, it is probable that the priest and the Levite passed by the man beaten by robbers because they were afraid of becoming ritually unclean by drawing too close to him. The Samaritan, who was by definition impure, acted compassionately toward the wounded man and became the model for loving one's neighbor. Speaking in the style of the prophets of Israel, Jesus denounced the Pharisees and other religious leaders for their rigorous following of the religious codes to the neglect of practicing "justice and mercy and faith."[12] Indeed, the string of Jesus' denunciations of the Pharisees and leaders collected in Luke 11 and Matthew 23 are dense with allusions to the purity system and the Pharisaic preoccupation with the outside and external, the law and duty, to the neglect of the spirit and the heart, of justice and compassion.

Here, Jesus stands in the tradition of the Hebrew prophets who reminded the people of Israel that God was more concerned with justice and mercy and righteousness than with ritual or periodic fasting.

> I hate, I despise your festivals,
> > and I take no delight in your solemn assemblies. . . .
> But let justice roll down like waters
> > and righteousness like an ever-flowing stream.
> > (Am 5:21, 24)

> Is not this the fast that I choose:
> > to loose the bonds of injustice,
> > to undo the thongs of the yoke,
> > to let the oppressed go free,
> > and to break every yoke?
> Is it not to share your bread with the hungry,
> > and to bring the homeless poor into your house.
> > (Is 58:6–7)[13]

Sincere worship and humble fasting are good and important, of course, but the Hebrew prophets and Jesus pointed out that such rituals became outrageous hypocrisy if not accompanied by justice and mercy for the oppressed and the poor.

Jesus' healings and exorcisms and practices of table fellowship shattered the purity boundaries of his social world. Jesus touched lepers who were so unclean that they were literally cast out of the city, and he was touched by a hemorrhaging woman (Mk 5:25–34) and had his feet washed by an unclean woman when he was at dinner at Simon's house (Lk 7:36–50). Jesus entered a graveyard to free a man of a "legion" of unclean spirits who entered a herd of unclean pigs (Mk 5:1–20). Jesus frequently "reclined at table" with impure social outcasts such as tax collectors and sinners.[14]

AN INCLUSIVE EARLY CHURCH

The Christian movement in the early church was characterized by the inclusiveness of compassion rather than the exclusiveness of the purity system. Even an Ethiopian eunuch, a man at the bottom of the purity system, was baptized into the church without hesitation (Acts 8:26–40). And in his letter to the Galatians, Paul resoundingly declared the unity of all in the Spirit of Christ: "There is no longer Jew or Greek, there is no longer slave or free, there is no longer male and female; for all of you are one in Christ Jesus" (Gal 3:28).

The apostles, filled with the spirit of Christ, founded communities that were inclusive and egalitarian, generous and loving. The Acts of the Apostles describes the Christian community at Jerusalem in this way:

> All who believed were together and had all things in common; they would sell their possessions and goods and distribute the proceeds to all, as any had need. Day by day, as they spent much time together in the temple, they broke bread at home and ate their food with glad and generous hearts, praising God and having the goodwill of all the people. And day by day the Lord added to their number those who were being saved. (Acts 2:44–47)[15]

Evangelical theologian Ronald Sider characterizes the practice of the Jerusalem community as "unlimited liability" for each other and "total availability" to each other.[16]

When, through a unique set of historical circumstances, the Jerusalem community became impoverished, Paul took up a great collection from the Gentile churches to bring to the church in Jerusalem. Thus Paul logically enlarged the scope of Christian unity and generosity to the universal church, giving us a model of interchurch sharing. And when Paul heard about class divisions in eucharistic celebrations at Corinth, he angrily declared that if wealthy Christians were feasting while poor believers went hungry, then they were not eating the Lord's Supper at all, but profaning the Body of Christ (1 Cor 11:17–34). On the basis of the practice of the early church and the meaning of the Eucharist, Sider concludes, "As long as any Christian anywhere in the world is hungry, the eucharistic celebration of all Christians everywhere in the world is imperfect."[17] Along the same lines, we might legitimately wonder if Christ is really present at a racially segregated Eucharist, noting that ten o'clock Sunday morning probably remains the most segregated hour in the week in the United States.

JESUS' THIRD WAY

Jesus' politics of compassion addressed not only the Jewish purity system, but also the oppression of the Roman Empire.[18] In the first century, Israel was occupied by the Romans, who ruled somewhat indirectly through Jewish leaders. Roman rule was still domineering and exploitative and the Jews understandably resented it. Thus, revolutionary sentiment and messianic expectations were high in Jesus' social world.

The Jewish people were expecting God to send them a messiah, someone like David, who would throw out the Romans and re-establish the kingdom of Israel. And there were Jewish groups, some called Zealots, who were ready to engage in violent resistance to Roman rule. The politics of Jesus' world were highly charged. Indeed, the Pharisees and the Essenes hoped that their faithful following of the purity laws and the holiness code would persuade God to send the messiah.[19]

Ordinary people—the peasants, shepherds, housekeepers, fisherfolk, shop-keepers, and merchants—experienced a double oppression by both Jewish and Roman leaders. The taxes paid to the Romans, which amounted to as much as 40 percent of their income, drove many people into debt. These taxes were collected by fellow Jews who not only collaborated with the hated Romans but enriched themselves in the process. And the religious leaders burdened the people with the onus of the purity system, adding religious guilt to their economic woes.[20]

In this oppressive context Jesus proclaimed the good news that the reign of God was at hand, offering liberation, justice, and compassion. It was a welcome message. Understanding this social context, doubly oppressive and tense with revolutionary fervor, helps to make sense of some of Jesus' sayings and of events that at first seem strange to contemporary Christians.

Jesus' Sermon on the Mount as reported in Matthew 5–8 and Luke 6:20–49 is a challenging statement of his alternative way and of the politics of compassion. This teaching of Jesus has been a stumbling block for his followers throughout Christian history. Eileen Egan, a longtime advocate of peace and justice in the Catholic Worker tradition, once said that she thought all of theology might be understood as a way to get around the Sermon on the Mount. She thought Christians should walk through it instead.[21] Is it possible to practice this ethic outlined by Jesus?

The first step in a realistic interpretation of the Sermon on the Mount is to see it in the context of Jesus' social world. Biblical scholar Walter Wink provides surprising insight by applying this method to one of the most perplexing passages in Jesus' discourse.[22]

> "You have heard that it was said, 'An eye for an eye and a tooth for a tooth.' But I say to you, Do not resist an evildoer. But if anyone strikes you on the right cheek, turn the other also; and if anyone wants to sue you and take your coat, give your cloak as well; and if anyone forces you to go one mile, go also the second mile." (Mt 5:38–41; see also Lk 6:29–31)

Is Jesus asking his followers to be human doormats, cowardly and complicit in the face of injustice?

First, Wink argues persuasively that the Greek word *antistenai*, translated as "resist not evil" in the King James version of the Bible, should be more accurately rendered "Do not take revenge on someone who does you wrong," as is found in the Good News version. The sense is to not retaliate against violence with violence. But if Jesus counsels his followers not to *fight* back, neither does he allow *flight* in response to injustice. Rather, he calls for courageous and *creative resistance* and he gives his audience—people who know about injustice first-hand—three examples of his alternative or "third way" to respond.

In the first example, the reference to the right cheek is key. The ancient world was a right-handed world where even to gesture with the left hand was offensive and insulting. The only way to hit the right cheek with the right hand is with the back of the hand. (Try acting out the scene.) So Jesus is saying: when someone gives you the back of their hand, turn your other cheek to them. A backhand slap was the normal way of reprimanding inferiors, and it still carries the connotation of putting someone down. ("Masters backhanded slaves; husbands, wives; parents, children; men, women; Romans, Jews."[23]) The expected response is cowering submission. Jesus counsels neither hitting back nor turning tail, but rather turning the other cheek, which is an act of remarkably creative resistance. It allows the inferior in the relationship to assert her or his equal humanity with the oppressor, and it forces the oppressor to take stock of the relationship and perhaps of the social system that supports such inequality. It is risky, to be sure, and demands courage, but it is a creative way to challenge an unhealthy relationship and an unjust system. Both Gandhi and Martin Luther King, Jr., grasped this well and molded this idea into a tool for resisting social injustice and creating a more just community.[24]

In Jesus' second example someone is being sued for his coat or outer garment by a creditor. Indebtedness was the most difficult social problem in first-century Palestine and only the poorest person would have nothing but his coat to serve as collateral.[25] Now he is being hauled into court to have even that stripped away.

Jesus recommends clowning and nudity as a creative response. The people of the time wore only an outer garment and an inner garment. In effect, Jesus would have the debtor say, "Here, take not only my coat, but my underwear as well. Then, you'll have everything!" and walk out of the court naked, leaving the red-faced creditor with a coat in one hand and underwear in the other. The creditor would be embarrassed and shamed—and unmasked. This is not a respectable moneylender, but a loan shark who perpetuates a system that has reduced an entire social class of his own people to landlessness and destitution. This burlesque offers the creditor the chance to see the human consequences of these practices and to repent, and it empowers the oppressed to take the initiative and burst the delusion that this is a just system. It is a brave and ingenious form of resistance.

Jesus' third example refers to a practice of the Roman occupation troops. When Roman troops were moving about, a soldier could force a civilian to carry his sixty-five pound pack for him, but only for one mile. To force a civilian to go further risked severe penalties under military law. This sort of practice was a bitter reminder to the Jews that they were a subject people even in the Promised Land. Imagine, then, the soldier's surprise when, upon arrival at the next mile marker, he absent-mindedly reaches for his pack, looking for his next human pack-mule, and the Jew says with a smile, "That's all right, I'll carry it for another mile," and strides off down the road. Going the second mile knocks the oppressor off balance and reveals the injustice of the situation. It also affirms the dignity of the oppressed by allowing the victim to seize the initiative. Without shedding blood or even raising one's voice in anger, the oppressed person has started down the road to liberation.

Given such an interpretation, this passage becomes a different sort of stumbling block to Christian discipleship. Rather than being dismayed by complacency or submissiveness in the face of evil and injustice, which at first glance seems implied by Jesus' sayings, one can be put off by the courage and creativity called for by Jesus. But if the Christian disciple is to stumble over this teaching, it should be by the challenge of creative resistance, Jesus' third way between the ordinary options of fight or flight in response to injustice.

In Matthew's Gospel Jesus goes on to say,

> "You have heard that it was said, 'You shall love your neighbor and hate your enemy.' But I say to you, Love your enemies and pray for those who persecute you, so that you may be children of your Father in heaven; for he makes his sun rise on the evil and on the good, and sends rain on the righteous and the unrighteous. For if you love those who love you, what reward do you have? Do not even the tax collectors do the same? And if you greet only your brothers and sisters, what more are you doing than others? Do not even the Gentiles do the same? Be perfect [compassionate], therefore, as your heavenly Father is perfect [compassionate]. (Mt 5: 43–48)[26]

Love of enemies is challenging indeed, but love expressed in creative resistance has the power to free the oppressed from docility and the oppressor from sin, affirming the image of God in both. This is the way, says Jesus, that is consistent with the nature of God, who is compassion, and with our relationship with God, who calls us to create a just community through love.

Jesus lived what he taught, as the events of his life attest. He rode into Jerusalem on a donkey rather than a white horse and was crucified at the hands of the Romans at the insistence of the Jewish leaders. The inscription that Pilate put on his cross read, "The King of the Jews." Jesus' suffering in love redeemed humanity from personal and social sin and established the kingdom of God. Jesus rejected dominating power and insisted instead on the power of love.[27]

At the beginning of his public ministry, Jesus is presented as traveling through Galilee, proclaiming a message of *metanoia* or conversion in response to the coming of the reign of God.[28] This notion of conversion is central to understanding the message of Jesus and the meaning of Christian discipleship. Basically this means turning from selfishness toward love by placing God and the teachings of Jesus at the center of life. Conversion, then, is a call to "Be compassionate as your Father is compassionate." St. Paul puts it this way: "Let each of you look not to your own interests, but to the interests of others. Let the same mind be in you that was in Christ Jesus, who, . . . emptied himself, . . . and became obedient to the point of death—even death on a cross" (Phil 2:4–5, 7, 8).

Conversion of the heart, then, means that Christians are to be socially subversive, that disciples of Christ must work to transform the world.[29] Conversion means to turn around; subversion means to turn over. The implication is that the Christian, like a plow moving through a field, will turn society over, from oppression to justice, from violence to peace. "The Christian is called not only to change his [or her] own heart but also to change the social, political, economic, and cultural structures of human existence. Conversion is not addressed to the heart alone."[30]

It is interesting to note that the Christian community eschewed violence and warfare and embraced nonviolence and peace, even in the face of persecution, during the first three centuries of its existence. There are multiple and complex reasons why Christians refused military participation during this period, but the basic reason was its incompatibility with Christian love. This practice of pacifism changed rather dramatically in 313 when the Roman Empire became the Holy Roman Empire after the conversion of the Emperor Constantine.[31]

CATHOLIC SOCIAL TEACHING

The social teaching of the churches, Protestant and Catholic, attempts to interpret the social dimension of Christian discipleship in the context of the contemporary world. The World Council of Churches (WCC), which includes nearly all Orthodox and Protestant churches, has held international assemblies every seven years since its founding in 1948, most recently in Harare, Zimbabwe, in 1998 (see its web site at www.wcc-coe.org). The documents produced by these world assemblies have emphasized the theme of a "responsible society" and have clearly expressed the notion that justice demands the transformation of social structures.[32] In recent years there has also been a particular focus on justice, peace, and the integrity of creation. The National Council of Churches (NCC), the comparable body in the United States (see its web site at www.ncccusa.org), has likewise given consistent and concerted attention to issues of justice and peace, as have the national assemblies of the various Protestant denominations.

"Catholic social teaching" refers to the body of work produced by the popes, the Second Vatican Council, the Vatican synods, and the national conferences of bishops, beginning with the encyclical *Rerum Novarum* (*The Condition of Labor*) issued by Pope Leo XIII in 1891 and continued in the writings of Pope John Paul II and the various bishops' conferences.[33] The documents produced by the Vatican address global concerns of the universal Church (see the web site for the Vatican at www.vatican.va), and those of the bishops' conferences tend to take more national or regional perspectives on justice and peace issues (see, for example the web site for the United States Catholic Conference of Bishops at www.nccbuscc.org).

Catholic social thought has not always developed in a systematic manner. Sometimes popes and bishops' conferences have decided to address specific issues that seemed pressing at a particular moment in history. Thus Pope Leo XIII addressed labor conditions in 1891; Pope John XXIII wrote on human rights and the arms race in 1963; Pope Paul VI took on poverty and development in 1967; the Latin American bishops, poverty and liberation in 1968 (at Medellín) and in 1979 (at Puebla); and the American Catholic bishops prepared statements on the arms race and deterrence in 1983 and the U.S. economy in 1986. Other social encyclicals have been produced to mark the anniversary of a previous encyclical, such as *Quadragesimo Anno* by Pope Pius XI, *Octogesima Adveniens* by Pope Paul VI, and *Centesimus Annus* by Pope John Paul II, to mark the fortieth, eightieth, and hundredth anniversaries of *Rerum Novarum* (1891). These documents tend to have a broader, more general scope, while also engaging issues of the day. Although there is much cross-referencing among these documents and a certain consistency both in theory and in positions taken, there is no conscious philosophical or theological foundation adopted and developed, nor do they expound a clear economic, social, or political theory. Although Catholic social thought has paid much more attention to its biblical basis since the Second Vatican Council (1962–65), its use of scripture has remained uneven. Nevertheless, the Magisterium (the pope and the bishops) of the Catholic Church has managed to produce a substantial and credible body of social teaching, one that, unfortunately, has been accurately referred to as "our best kept secret."[34]

The documents comprising Catholic social teaching over the past hundred years fill several volumes and theological reflection on this body of thought fills yet more volumes.[35] While it is not possible here to give a thorough overview of Catholic social thought, it is important to note several key themes related to the issues addressed in this book.

First, Catholic social teaching unambiguously affirms that the church and individual Christians are to be *engaged in the work of transforming the world*. This is clearly expressed in a famous sentence from the document produced by an international Synod of Bishops in 1971, *Justice in the World:* "Action on behalf of justice and participation in the transformation of the world fully appear to us as a constitutive dimension of the preaching of the Gospel, or, in other words, of the church's mission for the redemption of the human race and its liberation from every oppressive situation."[36] Working for justice is not peripheral or optional, but rather central and essential for a life lived in relationship with God. Faith affects every aspect of the believer's life, including the social, cultural, economic, and political dimensions. "Our faith is not just a weekend obligation, a mystery to be celebrated around the altar on Sunday. It is a pervasive reality to be practiced in homes, offices, factories, schools, and businesses across our land."[37]

Second, the two values that form the foundation of Catholic social thought are *human dignity*, realized in *community*. The human person is both sacred and social. The church's profound commitment to the values of human dignity and community is based on the biblical stories of *creation* and of God's *covenant* with the people of Israel.

Human beings are created in the image and likeness of God (Gen 1:27) and gifted with an unearned and inestimable value and dignity. Each person is obligated to respect this human dignity and to treat one another as sacraments of God and as sisters and brothers. Through the call of Abraham and his descendants and through God's revelation to Moses at Sinai, God established a covenant with the Hebrew people.

> Then Moses went up to God; the LORD called to him from the mountain, saying, "Thus you shall say to the house of Jacob, and tell the Israelites: You have seen what I did to the Egyptians, and how I bore you on eagles' wings and brought you to myself. Now therefore, if you obey my voice and keep my covenant, you shall be my treasured possession out of all the peoples. Indeed the whole earth is mine, but you shall be for me a priestly kingdom and a holy nation. These are the words that you shall speak to the Israelites." (Ex 19:3–6)

God acted in the history of the people of Israel, liberating them from bondage in Egypt and thus demonstrating compassion, faithfulness, and concern for justice and freedom. At Sinai God promised to take care of the people if they would keep the covenant with God. The following chapters in the book of Exodus (chapters 20–23) detail the code that is to characterize their lives: faithful worship of God alone, care for one another, creation of a just community, and a special concern for the vulnerable members of the community—widows and orphans, the poor and strangers. Thus the people of Israel are called into community, a just community that becomes the norm of their faithful response to God's love for them.[38]

The principles of the community of Israel include the *Sabbatical Year* (the seventh year) and the Year of *Jubilee* (the fiftieth year or the Grand Sabbatical) when Israelites recognize that the land is to be cared for as God's gift and that a people liberated from bondage should take care of the poor and oppressed in their midst. During the Sabbatical Year (Ex 23:11; Lev 25:1–7) land was to remain uncultivated, slaves were to be freed, and debts forgiven. During the Year of Jubilee (Lev 25:8–41) all members of the community were to be returned to their rightful place in the community and property was to be restored to its original owners. Thus, in principle, the tribes of Israel were to be kept in a sort of egalitarian equilibrium.[39]

In the eighth century, B.C.E., when idolatry and social injustice had come to characterize the people of Israel, *prophets* called Israel back to the demands of the covenant. The prophets spoke in God's name, and functioned as the conscience of the nation. They identified Israel's sin: the people's infidelity to the covenant with God. Israel had turned to other gods and had put its trust in alliances rather than in Yahweh. In Israel, the rich oppressed the poor, and the rulers were corrupt, violent, and exploitative.

> Alas for those who devise wickedness
> and evil deeds on their beds!

When morning dawns, they perform it,
　　because it is in their power.
They covet fields and seize them;
　　houses, and take them away;
they oppress the householder and house,
　　people and their inheritance. (Mic 2:1–2)

Hear this you rulers of the house of Jacob
　　and chiefs of the house of Israel,
who abhor justice
　　and pervert all equity,
who build Zion with blood
　　and Jerusalem with wrong!
Its rulers give judgment for a bribe,
　　its priests teach for a price,
　　its prophets give oracles for money;
Yet they lean upon the LORD and say,
　　"Surely the LORD is with us!
　　No harm shall come upon us."
Therefore because of you
　　Zion shall be plowed as a field;
Jerusalem shall become a heap of ruins,
　　and the mountain of the house a wooded height.
　　　　(Mic 3:9–12)

Thus, the prophets announced the judgment of God, a punishment meant to correct the people's evil ways and to bring them back to the covenant with God.

God's requirements for right living in accord with the covenant were clear.

He has told you, O mortal, what is good;
　　and what does the LORD require of you
but to do justice, and to love kindness,
　　and to walk humbly with your God. (Mic 6:8)

The prophets reveal a God who requires fidelity, justice, and righteousness, but who, in the end, is compassionate and merciful, forgiving and faithful.[40] God's steadfast love gives the prophets and Israel reason to hope.

Who is a God like you, pardoning iniquity
　　and passing over the transgression
　　of the remnant of your possession?
He does not retain his anger forever,
　　because he delights in showing clemency.
He will again have compassion upon us;
　　he will tread our iniquities under foot.

You will cast all our sins
    into the depths of the sea.
You will show faithfulness to Jacob
    and unswerving loyalty to Abraham,
as you have sworn to our ancestors
    from the days of old. (Mic 7:18–20)[41]

Jesus stands in the tradition of the Hebrew prophets. Like the prophets of Israel, Jesus calls his followers to fidelity, justice, righteousness, and community, and he proclaims the presence of a God who is faithful, compassionate, and gracious. (See, for example, the parable of the prodigal son and his brother in Lk 15:11–32, or the story of the sinful woman who is forgiven at the house of a Pharisee in Lk 7:36–50.) Through his death and resurrection Jesus renews the covenant and expands its scope to include all of humanity. Through Jesus, God establishes a *new covenant* with all people and calls on humankind to become a just community throughout the earth. In the new covenant, as in the original one, the way the community responds to the needs of the poor is the "litmus test" of its justice or injustice, of its fidelity to the covenant with God.[42]

These two values, then, human dignity and just community, rooted in the stories of creation and covenant, are the foundation for the major principles developed in Catholic social teaching. Although listings of the principles may differ somewhat, those most relevant to the themes developed in this book are human rights, social sin, solidarity, participation, the preferential option for the poor, and peacemaking. Although some of these have been touched on in previous chapters, each will receive at least a brief reflection here.

The meaning of *human rights* and the development of this principle in Catholic social thought was explored earlier (see chapter 4). Clearly the concept of human rights is rooted in the creation of humanity in the image of God and in the obligations of life in community. Pope John XXIII provides the fullest exposition of human rights from the church's perspective in his encyclical *Peace on Earth* (1963).[43]

Whenever the church talks about human rights, it is always careful to give equal attention to human responsibility. Catholic social thought has used human rights as a normative framework for addressing the minimal obligations of any society or polity in a pluralistic world.[44] In other words, the least that can be expected of any government is to create a society where basic human needs (for food, water, health care, shelter, safety) are met and where there is the opportunity to develop one's potential and to participate in society through work and through the political process. Each person, then, has the responsibility to use his or her gifts for the betterment of society and to participate in creating a more just community.

There is an abiding awareness in Catholic social thought that evil and sin tend to become embedded in the structures and institutions of society, that is, there is a consciousness of *social sin* or the "structures of sin." This concept is deeply rooted in the theology of the Hebrew prophets who accused

Israel of infidelity and who functioned as the conscience of the nation.

The social sciences, which have convincingly argued that all knowledge is socially constructed—that is, that each person is so immersed in culture and society that it is virtually impossible to understand or know anything outside of our social framework—add an empirical dimension to the concept of social sin. Thus, for example, racism transcends the sum total of individual acts of discrimination and can become institutionalized and self-perpetuating in a society. The same claim can be made for other social sins, such as sexism, violence, ethnic hatred, and materialism or consumerism.

In his encyclical *On Social Concern,* Pope John Paul II speaks of "'structures of sin,' which . . . are rooted in personal sin, and thus always linked to the concrete acts of individuals who introduce these structures, consolidate them and make them difficult to remove. And thus they grow stronger, spread, and become the source of other sins, and so influence people's behavior."[45] Pope John Paul II then points to two interrelated actions and attitudes that seem to him to be at the root of structures of sin in the contemporary world—"the all-consuming desire for profit" and "the thirst for power." They give rise to "certain forms of modern imperialism" and to "real forms of idolatry: of money, ideology, class and technology."[46] Certainly race, ethnicity, and gender could be added to the idolatries mentioned by the pope.

> **For Reflection**
>
> It is generally easier to see the social sin of other nations than it is to see the sinful structures of one's own nation. The anti-Semitism of Nazi Germany clearly transcended the acts of individuals and became the sin of the nation. The same was true of apartheid in South Africa. What are the social sins of contemporary America? How can social redemption be accomplished?

If evil is structured into a society, its remedy must include social transformation, that is, changing the structures and institutions of society. Christian responsibility, then, must include both *charity,* personal acts of compassion in response to individual suffering, and *justice,* social and political action aimed at transforming the root causes of evil and suffering. Christians should be found in soup kitchens, tutoring programs, and inner-city clinics, and on picket lines, in political campaigns and congressional lobbies.[47]

Pope John Paul II recommends the virtue of *solidarity* as the antidote to structures of sin. He sees solidarity as the moral virtue and social attitude that correspond to the reality of global interdependence. "[Solidarity] then is not a feeling of vague compassion or shallow distress at the misfortunes of so many people, both near and far. On the contrary, it is a firm and persevering determination to commit oneself to the common good; that is to say to the good of all and of each individual, because we are all really responsible for all."[48] Solidarity is diametrically opposed to the desire for profit or a thirst for power. It calls for a readiness to sacrifice oneself for the sake of the other and to serve the neighbor, as opposed to a willingness to exploit or oppress the other for one's own advantage. Because of the unity and interdependence of humanity, the virtue of solidarity is a commitment to recognize the equality of persons and peoples, to share the goods of creation with all, and to work with others as partners on behalf of development, justice, and peace.[49]

Increasingly Catholic social thought has understood social justice in terms of *participation*.[50] "Social justice implies that persons have an obligation to be active and productive participants in the life of society and that society has a duty to enable them to participate in this way."[51] The principle of participation is rooted in the created dignity of the human person, who is endowed with freedom and charged with self-determination, and in the obligations of a just community.

The church's understanding of participation is broad and inclusive and it involves reciprocal obligations on the part of individuals and society. Pope John Paul II and the American and Canadian bishops have stressed both the right to civil or *political* participation and the right to meaningful work, or *economic* participation.[52] As citizens and workers, persons should have the opportunity and the obligation to participate in a whole range of voluntary organizations and associations, including political parties and unions, and in the full spectrum of political and economic decisions. Nations, as well, large and small, rich and poor, should have the opportunity and the obligation to participate in international organizations such as regional associations, the World Trade Organization (WTO), and the United Nations.[53] It is the principle of participation that empowers persons and nations to have a voice in decisions that affect them.

There is a balanced appreciation of the role of the government in Catholic social thought. On the one hand, the principle of subsidiarity, which insists that larger communities should not usurp the proper role and authority of smaller communities, tends to decentralize power and to limit the authority of central governments.[54] On the other hand, the principle often called "socialization" insists on the proper role of central government, especially in the increasingly complex contemporary world, to help promote the common good and to advocate for the poor.[55] Government should not render citizens and local communities powerless by throwing its weight around where inappropriate, but government should not fail to exercise power where it is needed. Both individual initiative and government intervention can be proper forms of participation.

In their pastoral letter on the American economy, the U.S. Catholic bishops highlight "*the preferential option for the poor*."[56] The bishops stated that Christians must judge the morality and the justice of public policies from the perspective of the poor:

Decisions must be judged in light of what they do *for* the poor, what they do *to* the poor, and what they enable the poor to do *for themselves*. The fundamental moral criterion for all economic decisions, policies, and institutions is this: They must be at the service of *all people, especially the poor*.[57]

This option for the poor and the powerless is a remarkably challenging way to invite contemporary Christians to "Be compassionate as your Father is compassionate."

The U.S. bishops adapted this principle from their brother bishops in Latin America. In 1968, the Latin American Bishops' Conference met at Medellín, Colombia, to reflect on the implications of the Second Vatican Council and especially its *Pastoral Constitution on the Church in the Modern World.* That document said that ". . . the Church has always had the duty of scrutinizing the signs of the times and of interpreting them in the light of the gospel."[58] The most significant "sign of the time" in Latin America was the crushing poverty of the overwhelming majority of people and the glaring gap between the rich and the poor. At Medellín the church began to move decisively from the side of the rich to stand with the poor. When the Latin American bishops met again in 1979 in Puebla, Mexico, they articulated this move as the preferential option for the poor.[59] This Latin American theology was consistent with Pope Paul VI's encyclical *On the Development of Peoples* (1971) and, after being picked up by the U.S. bishops, was also employed by Pope John Paul II in his *On Social Concern* (1987, #42–45).[60] It presents a key principle of Catholic social teaching.

The preferential option for the poor has deep biblical roots. God's compassionate and caring concern for the poor is a dominant theme in the Hebrew Scriptures and in the message and ministry of Jesus and the early Christian community. The commitment of God's people to the covenant was manifested in their treatment of the widow, the orphan, and the stranger. Jesus identified himself with the hungry, the thirsty, the stranger, the naked, the sick, and the imprisoned—with "the least of these" (Mt 25:31–46).

Who are the poor? "[T]he poor are the economically disadvantaged, the materially deprived, who as a consequence suffer powerlessness, exploitation and oppression."[61] Poverty, then, is primarily an economic and material reality in this usage. The U.S. bishops acknowledge the many spiritual and physical diminishments affecting people, but add that material poverty compounds these problems.[62] The option for the poor calls Christians and the church to stand with the hungry, the homeless, the unemployed, those without access to adequate education or basic health care, those on the margins of society.

The "option" for the poor is not optional. "Rather it is a decisive action and a deliberate choice, reflecting values as well as desires, flowing from the core of . . . faith."[63] Standing with the poor,[64] being present to the poor, seeing the world from the perspective of the poor, working with the poor, advocating for the poor, this is *essential* to being a follower of Christ. Christians stand with the poor because God stands with the poor. Given the scandalous extent and depth of poverty in the United States and in the world (see chapter 2), the preferential option for the poor is a radical challenge. How is it possible that there can be rich Christians in a hungry world?[65]

Peacemaking (a central issue in chapter 7) has been another prominent and consistent theme in Catholic social thought. The Catholic tradition, at least from the fourth century on, has not taken a pacifist position. Rather, it has justified war as a rule-governed exception to the moral presumption in favor of peace. Indeed, when the U.S. bishops, in their pastoral letter *The Challenge of Peace*, affirmed nonviolence as a legitimate position for Christians to hold, many hailed this as significant progress.[66] Yet, despite its refusal to say a definitive no to war or military intervention as a last resort, the church has been a vocal advocate for peace in four specific ways:

1. By promoting and working for justice—through development, human rights, and participation—the church has sought to overcome the causes of war. Pope John XXIII's advocacy of human rights in his encyclical *Peace on Earth* was an important step in this direction. Following John XXIII, Pope Paul VI said that "the new name for peace is development," a sentiment reiterated by Pope John Paul II again and again.[67] The church has clearly identified the connection between working for justice and making peace and has not been fooled into thinking that calm in the midst of injustice, oppression, hostility, or hatred is genuine peace.[68] Justice and forgiveness are the only sure foundations for peace.[69]

2. By developing the just-war tradition and applying it to policies and situations, the church has insisted that military intervention and warfare are *moral* questions, not merely tools of the state or techniques of *realpolitik*. And the church's moral analysis has yielded important conclusions, such as the condemnation of "any act of war aimed indiscriminately at the destruction of entire cities or of extensive areas along with their population. . . ,"[70] its prohibition on the use of nuclear weapons,[71] and the "strictly conditioned moral acceptance of nuclear deterrence . . . as a step on the way toward progressive disarmament."[72]

By persuasively articulating the criteria of the just-war tradition, the Roman Catholic Magisterium has provided a moral framework that has significantly influenced public policy discussions and the policies themselves. The decision about military intervention in the Persian Gulf, for example, was debated largely in terms of the just-war tradition, and the Pentagon took pains to persuade the public that it was fighting the war within the bounds of the principle of discrimination.[73] Recently the church has increasingly fostered nonviolence, with its insistence on conflict resolution, diplomacy, and alternatives to violence. Indeed, Pope John Paul II sometimes comes across as at least a practical pacifist in his continual calls for peace and his criticisms of war and violence.[74]

3. By decrying the arms race and the misplaced priorities evident in military spending, the church has functioned as a moral check on an irrational situation. In the words of the Second Vatican Council, "the arms race is an utterly treacherous trap for humanity, and one which injures the poor to an intolerable degree."[75] Again, the church is making the connection between justice and peace, pointing out not only the danger of accumulating weapons of mass destruction, but also the theft from the poor represented by military spending.

4. By supporting institutions designed to promote peace, the church has played a constructive role in creating the conditions for peace. By reminding

the world of the fact of interdependence and by calling for the virtue of solidarity that is necessary for creating a just global community, the church has advocated a world order that is essential for justice and peace.[76] The church continually supports and suggests strengthening the United Nations and other regimes that foster cooperation and conflict resolution. And the church has been willing, sometimes behind the scenes as in Poland and sometimes more publicly as in El Salvador, to participate directly in conflict resolution.

Finally, it is important to note something of an oversight in official Catholic social teaching—a major statement on the environment. Although John Paul II included passing mention of ecological concerns in two of his social encyclicals and also addressed the issue in his World Day of Peace Message in 1990 and the U.S. bishops have produced some statements on the issue, the Magisterium has yet to give this subject sufficient attention.[77] The theological literature on theology and ecology is blossoming.[78] Although principles such as "stewardship," "just and sustainable development," and "humanity as co-creators with God" can be found in Catholic social thought, neither the Vatican nor the U.S. bishops have produced a significant statement on this crucial issue.

Given that contemporary Catholic social teaching was developed in a Cold War world characterized by a deep polarization of competing ideologies, there is a remarkable *balance* in Catholic social thought. To the polarizations of "either/or," Catholic social thought responds with "both/and." Catholic social teaching affirms both the value and dignity of each human person and the value of the community, both individual freedom and the common good, both human rights and human responsibility, both personal sin and structures of sin and the redemption of persons and nations and all of creation, both the obligation of society to enable persons to participate in political and economic life and the responsibility of the person to participate in society, both the principle of subsidiarity or decentralization of decision-making and the principle of socialization or the proper role of the central government, both nonviolence and the justified use of force.

There is much to be said for this balance in Catholic social teaching. It focuses on seeking the truth rather than getting trapped in a one-sided ideology that is popular at the moment. It allows the church to criticize both capitalism and socialism and to call for the integral or wholistic development of the human person. It also allows the church to be critical and constructive without being politically partisan.

The danger of such balance, however, is the tendency to be dispassionate or lukewarm when a situation calls for the passionate defense of justice or a burning condemnation of oppression. There are times when the church and Christians should be prophetic, should take sides. Indeed, the preferential option for the poor and the church's clear stand on behalf of human dignity, human rights, just community, and peacemaking call for precisely such committed advocacy and action. Reason and truth are not obstacles to a passion for justice and peace; selfishness and apathy are the problems.

No doubt that there are many who would urge the church to take even stronger stands for justice and peace, but the record of the christian community as a justice seeker and peacemaker is, on the whole, positive and constructive. Included in that record is the witness and service of individual Christians whose lives have introduced neighbors and friends to Catholic social thought and the social teaching of the churches. Some of these Christian witnesses have become well known, including Dorothy Day, Helder Camara, Oscar Romero, Jean Donovan, Martin Luther King, Jr., Desmond Tutu, Mother Teresa, Cesar Chavez, Helen Prejean, and Philip and Daniel Berrigan.[79] Those who practice justice and peace are eloquent witnesses to the healing presence and reconciling power of God in our world.

STUDY QUESTIONS

1. Is the idea that faith is a relationship with God meaningful for you?
2. What is the message of Jesus? What makes you think Jesus was or was not interested in justice and peace issues? Is the Gospel message relevant to social and political issues?
3. Is it possible to validly celebrate the Eucharist in a church that is divided along lines of race, gender, sexual orientation, or class?
4. Can you think of a personal experience where Jesus' Third Way could have offered you an alternative between fighting or fleeing?
5. Should converted Christians be socially subversive?
6. Catholic social teaching has been called the church's "best kept secret." What strategies would you propose for getting this message out to the people in the church and into society? What is the message? What are the central themes in Catholic social teaching?
7. What is the difference between charity and justice? How can Christians be both charitable and just?
8. How can Christians follow Christ in a consumer society? How should rich Christians respond to a hungry world? What would it mean to take seriously the "preferential option for the poor?"
9. In what ways do you think the church has been successful in being a peacemaker and an advocate for justice? In what ways has the church fallen short in these roles?

CHAPTER NINE

Christian Citizenship and Resources for Involvement

"What good is it, my brothers and sisters, if you say you have faith but do not have works? Can faith save you? If a brother or sister is naked and lacks daily food, and one of you says to them, "Go in peace; keep warm and eat your fill," and yet do not supply their daily needs, what is the good in that? So faith by itself, if it has no works, is dead." (James 2: 14–17)

"Let love be genuine; hate what is evil, hold fast to what is good; love one another with mutual affection; out do one another in showing honor. Do not lag in zeal, be ardent in spirit, serve the Lord. Rejoice in hope, be patient in suffering, persevere in prayer. Contribute to the needs of the saints; extend hospitality to strangers." (Romans 12: 9–13)

Christian discipleship requires that one work for justice and make peace. This is the social and global dimension of striving to be compassionate. Christians must be *hearers* of the Word, that is, attentive to the presence and call of God in their lives, and *doers* of the Word, actively responding to God's call in the world. This chapter discusses *how* Christians can become constructively involved in working for justice and making peace.

Discipleship requires both an inner journey and an outer journey, both contemplation and resistance.[1] There are at least four dimensions to this journey: growing in knowledge and wisdom, personal conversion and changes in lifestyle, working within a faith community, and public policy advocacy or exercising one's citizenship. Growth in each of these areas contributes to living a life of compassion and justice.

In Luke's Gospel the transition between the infancy narrative and Jesus' public ministry is accomplished with the statement: "And Jesus increased in wisdom and in years, and in divine and human favor" (Lk 2:52). "To grow in knowledge and wisdom" requires information and education, and it requires the development of a heart and conscience able to discern right from wrong.[2] If knowledge is the queen of virtues, wisdom is the grandmother of virtues—earthy, practical, sensitive, caring, and authentic. Knowledge can be gained from books, but wisdom is born of experience. Wisdom comes from making love, tending to sick children, weathering conflict patiently, and growing older gracefully.

Researching an Issue

Once one chooses an issue where one wants to make a difference, then specialized knowledge can be sought. A file for articles and news clippings can be begun, and a library of books started. One could take a college course on the subject, or integrate the topic into a college major or minor or as the focus of a graduate degree. One could attend lectures, seminars, or workshops and films related to a particular justice and peace interest. Eventually the learner will want to make the transition to teacher (since teaching is a wonderful way to keep learning), sharing information informally with friends and family, leading a study group or joining a speakers' bureau, and writing letters-to-the-editor, op-ed pieces, or articles on the topic. And of course one will want to work for constructive change through direct service and public policy advocacy. Reflection, in the context of a community of people with similar interests and commitments, on the information one is gathering and on one's experiences of trying to change society for the better, generates wisdom.

This book has provided a considerable amount of information on global issues. Justice seekers and peacemakers should crave information, constantly searching for truth. In the movie *Gandhi* there is a scene in which hungry peasants oppressed by the landowners ask Gandhi to help them. The first thing Gandhi does upon arrival (after persuading the local magistrate that there is no reason to arrest him) is to carefully document the abuses. Gathering information is a critical first step in working for justice.

Karl Barth, one of the twentieth century's great Protestant theologians, said that the Christian should face the world with the Bible in one hand and a newspaper in the other. An educated person should read a daily paper or make it a habit to watch the news or subscribe to a weekly news magazine to keep up with what is going on in the world. (See the Resources section of this chapter for a list of helpful periodicals.)

Those who are working for justice because of their faith often include "contemplation" in their process of reflection, that is, a conscious listening for God's voice by paying attention to the presence and movement of God's Spirit in our lives and our world. Conversion calls for continual growth.[3]

This growth in the Spirit will inevitably affect our lifestyle, the way we live life. An awareness of the simplicity of Jesus' life, of the gap between the rich and the poor, and of the way patterns of human consumption injure the earth and its ecosystems will push the Christian to "live simply so that others can simply live."

Materialism or consumerism is one of the most insidious ideologies of the last part of the twentieth century.[4] Its victims are not only the poor and the planet, but also its practitioners. It has often been said that consumerism is a form of idolatry that promises personal fulfillment but yields only frustration and alienation—from God, from each other, and from nature. Thus a simpler lifestyle is good, first of all, for the one who lives it.

Asceticism and voluntary poverty have deep roots in the Christian tradition. A simple lifestyle is not the pursuit of suffering or hardship for its own sake, but rather a conscious effort to live in harmony with God, the community, and nature. The "Shakertown Pledge," first taken by a group of justice- and peace-minded Christians on a retreat at Shakertown, Kentucky, in 1973, raises the right questions for intentionally moving toward a life of creative simplicity:

Recognizing that the earth and the fullness thereof is a gift from our gracious God, and that we are called to cherish, nurture, and provide loving stewardship for the earth's resources, and recognizing that life itself is a gift, and a call to responsibility, joy, and celebration, I make the following declarations:

1. I declare myself to be a world citizen.
2. I commit myself to lead an ecologically sound life.
3. I commit myself to lead a life of creative simplicity and to share my personal wealth with the world's poor.
4. I commit myself to join with others in the reshaping of institutions in order to bring about a more just global society in which all people have full access to the needed resources for their physical, emotional, intellectual, and spiritual growth.
5. I commit myself to occupational accountability, and so doing I will seek to avoid the creation of products which cause harm to others.
6. I affirm the gift of my body and commit myself to its proper nourishment and physical well-being.
7. I commit myself to examine continually my relations with others, and to attempt to relate honestly, morally, and lovingly to those around me.
8. I commit myself to personal renewal through prayer, meditation, and study.
9. I commit myself to responsible participation in a community of faith.[5]

There are many ways for different persons to apply these commitments to their own lives, but a few examples might stimulate further reflection.

Most people are familiar with steps that they can take to lead a more ecologically sound life—buying a fuel-efficient car, using the car less and walking or bicycling more, turning off lights and turning the thermostat down in the winter and up in the summer, and recycling or not buying products that are packaged in ways harmful to the atmosphere. Many states require deposits on cans and bottles to reduce litter and encourage recycling and that residents separate waste from recyclable materials for garbage pickup. It is surprising that these practices are not universal.

Tithing—giving away one-tenth of one's income to either religious institutions or to other charities—has biblical roots and represents a practical way to share wealth.[6] Average Americans give only between 1 or 2 percent of their income to charity. Some parishes and churches tithe their collections for the poor and the cause of justice and peace.

Another example is that of a man who discovered that the Gospel calls disciples toward nonviolence. His first step, he concluded, would be to disarm himself and his household. He had been in the army and owned three rifles, worth several hundred dollars. He decided that to sell the rifles would have no impact on disarming the world, so he and his wife took the rifles into the backyard and ceremoniously broke them into a pile of scrap metal and wood and threw it away. For him, this was a powerful symbol of personal transformation and of a commitment to work to disarm the world.

A third example is provided by a white couple, deeply committed to racial equality, who deliberately moved into an integrated neighborhood. They felt that they could not raise their children in the segregated environment of most suburbs.

Occupation or employment can also be signs of Christian vocation. According to Catholic social thought, ideally work should be a meaningful way for us to use talents and gifts to contribute to the community, and it should pay a wage that allows people to meet their needs.[7] "The investment of wealth, talent, and human energy should be specially directed to benefit those who are poor or economically insecure."[8]

Nearly any profession or job can be directed toward justice for the poor. A physician can work in an urban clinic or a remote rural area. A lawyer can work for legal aid or promote civil rights or defend the environment.[9] A business person can make responsibility for customers and employees the number-one priority. A salesclerk can treat customers with respect.

Financial investments can also be evaluated with a social conscience. Saving for the future can be reasonable and responsible, but, for example, banks that engage in "redlining" should not receive support. Christians can seek out money market funds or investment portfolios with a social conscience.

Christians usually seek justice and peace through *working within a faith community*. A faith community can support the individual Christian in the sometimes risky and often painful struggle to overcome injustice and it can challenge its members to continue to strive to transform society into a just community. The institutional church can often add clout to efforts to reform society or change social structures or institutions.

The themes of justice and peace should be integrated into the worship and prayer of faith communities. The connections between, for example, the Eucharist—the Lord's Supper—and world hunger and the oppression of the poor should always be apparent.[10] The inclusive table fellowship of the Lord demands that Christians oppose segregation and discrimination and the violation of human rights and that they work continuously to feed the hungry and give drink to the thirsty. The memory of Jesus' crucifixion demands Christians stand in solidarity with those who suffer imprisonment, torture, or are killed because they oppose tyranny and want a better life for their communities. Weaving concerns about justice and peace into the worship and the life of a faith community is the responsibility of every member.

The church should be a model or a sign of a just community in the world,[11] but inevitably this community of sinners falls short in this regard. Thus, working for justice includes efforts to transform the institutional church and local congregations as well as efforts to transform the larger society. Are fair wages paid to church employees? Are there equal opportunities for women? Does the church have an "edifice complex" that distracts from a commitment to the poor? Is wealth wasted or hoarded or spent on the needs of the community and especially the least of these? Are the church's investments made with a social conscience? Is authority exercised in terms of service? Is the faith community engaged in direct service to the poor and courageous advocacy for justice? Are luxury cars in the church parking lot consistent with a preferential option for the poor? Does self-righteousness creep into attitudes and service?

Finally, it must be emphasized that *public policy advocacy* or *the exercise of one's citizenship* is an essential dimension of Christian discipleship. Christian and church involvement in politics is not only appropriate, it is necessary. Social structures are set up through public policy decisions, and they are changed and reformed through public policy decisions. Working for a society that is more just necessarily involves critical participation in these decisions.

It is important for churches to set up shelters for the homeless and soup kitchens for the hungry and for Christians to work at shelters and soup kitchens. But it is just as important for churches to lobby for affordable housing and for welfare policies that ensure that no one is hungry. Indeed fundamental social changes regarding housing and feeding the hungry would make shelters and soup kitchens unnecessary. The more just a society is, the less need there is for charity.

The United States has an important constitutional principle that separates the church from the state, but it is often misunderstood. The Constitution takes pains to keep the *institutions* of church and state separate. History has taught us that when the church becomes a secular power, the church is usually corrupted and harms society. Likewise the state has no business either establishing a particular religion or forbidding the free exercise of any religion, which is a fundamental human right.

The separation of religion from life, however, or of faith from politics is "pure heresy."[12] A Christian's relationship with God should affect every dimension of life, from what we eat to how we vote. Christian faith *should* influence the exercise of citizenship. The Christian community, the church, has as much right to lobby for its perspective and policy choices as does the National Rifle Association, the American Medical Association, or a coalition of insurance companies. Nor does the Constitution prohibit Christians from exercising their citizenship rights or the church from *proper* involvement in public policy discussions and decisions.

It is important, however, that the church influence public policy in a theologically and politically appropriate manner. The following five guidelines can assist the church in properly participating in politics:[13]

1. The role of the church is to lift up for discussion the *moral* dimensions of public policy issues. Morality should be the consistent focus of the church's social pronouncements.

2. The church should endeavor to be *persuasive* when it enters public policy debate. The church's social analysis must be competent and informed, clear and reasonable. The church cannot rely exclusively on authority, or revelation, in public debate in a pluralistic society.

3. One of the most persuasive and effective ways for the church to influence public policy is through *example,* by modeling its moral teachings. The church must practice what it preaches. It must incarnate its moral vision through programs and structures that stand as beacons to society.

4. Because of the nature of the church's social mission and the nature of politics, it is almost always prudent for the church to *avoid single-issue politics and to remain clearly non-partisan.* The church's mission is broad and encompassing, and political issues are complex and interconnected. The pursuit of single-issue politics, on the other hand, is narrow and reductionist, and partisan positions often exclude people of good will and tend to be short-sighted. Thus, ordinarily, the church should avoid endorsing candidates or political parties and avoid evaluating candidates or political platforms on the basis of any single issue.

5. In a pluralistic society public policy and legislation should be able to satisfy the criteria of *feasibility* and *enforceability.* Politics involves building a consensus around a reasonable and viable position. An unenforceable law is a bad law because it lessens respect for the law. A public policy that is forced on an unwilling public is divisive and alienating.

These five guidelines pertain to the church's official involvement in public policy discussions and decisions. The individual Christian's participation in politics is, of course, less constrained and might be more partisan, since individuals speak and act for themselves and not the community.

The primary act of political involvement is to register and to cast an informed and conscientious ballot for candidates who represent values and

---

Return Address
Date

Dear Senator X,

The Women, Infants and Children (WIC) program is in danger of being cut back. I urge you to vote to restore the President's funding request, rather than cut the program by 25 percent.

Every dollar spent on prenatal care under the WIC program saves $3.50 in later Medicaid costs, according to the General Accounting Office. Not only does WIC save money, it is also a wise investment in human resources. A 25 percent cut in funding would reduce the number of recipients by nearly 100,000. Given that WIC is one of the nation's most successful and cost-effective nutrition intervention programs, this simply does not make sense.

I hope you will vote for women, infants, and children, and that you will encourage your colleagues to do so as well. Please inform me of your position.

Sincerely,
Your name

positions consistent with Christian faith. Financial support and active campaigning for candidates are important ways to participate in the political process. Committed Christians can also choose to run for local, state, or federal offices. Every country certainly needs politicians of integrity who are willing to serve the public and to work for the common good.

Voting and campaigning are only the first steps in shaping public policy. Just as organizations, corporations, and interest groups *lobby* elected officials in an effort to get their perspectives enacted into legislation and policy, so all citizens should lobby their representatives on behalf of their point of view, and Christian citizens should advocate for the poor and oppressed, the powerless and voiceless. Communication with elected representatives through letters, telegrams, e-mail, phone calls, and visits can influence government policy.[14]

Some people are intimidated by the prospect of writing government officials, but there is no reason for this. Representatives to the House and Senate are, after all, *representatives*. Their job is to represent citizens' views in the government, and if they do not, they are held accountable at election time. They *should* be interested in knowing what people think. Sometimes a dozen or so well-timed letters can have a dramatic impact in focusing a representative's attention on a piece of legislation and in shaping his or her views.

An effective letter is courteous, brief, and clear. It is usually best to focus on one issue at a time and to be specific about the legislation under discussion. Most legislators will respond. It is a good idea to write a follow-up letter thanking the representative for making such a wise choice or continuing the dialogue on the issue. An example of a lobby letter is on page 210.[15]

Important addresses:

The White House	The U.S. Senate	The U.S. House of
Washington, D.C.	Washington, D.C.	Representatives
20500	20510	Washington, D.C.
		20515

White House phone: (202) 456-1414
Capitol phone: (202) 224-3121

Most senators and congresspersons now have e-mail addresses that are available through internet servers. The web site for "Contacting the Congress" at www.visi.com/juan/congress makes e-mailing your representative convenient. The president's e-mail address is president@whitehouse.gov. Network, a Catholic social justice lobby, now has a system that allows you to send a pre-formulated e-mail on timely issues to your representative through its web site: www.networklobby.org.

Writing a letter to the editor of a local newspaper or writing an informative op-ed piece can also be effective ways to engage in public policy discussion. Such efforts allow citizens to take a public stand and to educate and encourage others as well.

Direct communication with elected officials can be accomplished by arranging a visit with them, either on a trip to Washington, D.C., or in their home district. Government representatives are busy people, but most realize that they must be accessible to the citizens they represent. Their office is more likely to schedule a personal visit with a small group that represents an organization such as Bread for the World or Network (see resources section in this chapter). Even if the representative is not available, it is worthwhile to meet with a member of his or her staff.

There are times, of course, when public policy advocacy and social change require steps beyond dialogue. Nonviolent direct confrontation through protest marches, demonstrations, strikes, boycotts, street theater, or civil disobedience can be important steps in transforming society into a just community.[16] Such actions were instrumental in the civil rights and the labor movements, for example. In the United States rights to free speech and to assemble and protest are recognized and generally protected. Still, it often requires personal courage to take a public stand or to court arrest on behalf of the poor and for the cause of justice and peace in the midst of controversy. Resistance against tyranny and oppression and standing for liberty and justice for all are the founding principles of the American nation. Christian citizens should not find it extraordinary to engage in public protest in the name of justice and peace. After all, the church has produced a wealth of prisoners and martyrs, beginning with its founder and his apostles.

In sum, Christian discipleship requires the maturation of compassion, wisdom, and courage. "Go therefore and make disciples of all nations, baptizing them in the name of the Father and of the Son and of the Holy Spirit, and teaching them to obey everything that I have commanded you. And remember, I am with you always, to the end of the age"(Mt 28:19–20).

RESOURCES FOR INVOLVEMENT AND INFORMATION

This section of the chapter aims to steer the reader toward further resources for action and information. The first part focuses on organizations that feed the hungry, enhance self-reliance, work for structural change, preserve the environment, advocate for human rights, and promote peace and disarmament. The second part offers some suggestions for research projects on justice and peace issues and lists resources for further information and study.

Organizations

There are many organizations working for justice and peace. Some are like comets streaking across the sky, burning brightly, but soon fading from view. Some have a very specific focus. Nearly all have a particular perspective or ideology that motivates their activities and colors their approach. Unfortunately internecine conflict characterizes even the struggle for justice and peace.

The following list is highly subjective and selective, even idiosyncratic. It makes no claim to being thorough or complete. Rather than list hundreds of organizations, I have chosen to list only a few. An exhaustive list of organizations working for justice and peace can be found in the *Encyclopedia of*

Associations, published annually by the Gale Group, Detroit. It provides an annotated guide to more than 23,000 national and international organizations, and can be found in many libraries.

Many of the following are Catholic or Christian in their perspective, and most have been in existence long enough to have both a solid track record and a probable future. They can provide motivation, information, and guidance in attempting to change things for the better. Many of these organizations have local branches on campuses, in places of worship, or in communities or congressional districts.

Economic Justice

The first two organizations, Bread for the World and NETWORK, engage in public policy advocacy on behalf of the poor. The next two organizations, Oxfam America and Catholic Relief Services, engage in relief work and development efforts.

Bread for the World, 50 F Street, Suite 500, Washington, D.C. 20001. 800-82-BREAD or (202) 639-9400; www.bread.org

Bread for the World is a Christian citizens' lobby on behalf of the poor at home and abroad. Its goal is to influence public policy in a way that benefits the poor, but it does no direct relief work. It is organized by congressional districts and through Christian congregations, with many local groups throughout the United States. It publishes a very informative monthly newsletter. Bread for the World sponsors an annual "offering of letters" in churches focused on a particular hunger issue. Its board of directors includes activists, academics, farmers, religious leaders, and politicians.

NETWORK: A National Catholic Social Justice Lobby, 801 Pennsylvania Ave., S.E., Suite 460, Washington, D.C. 20003-2167; (202) 547-5556; www. networklobby.org

Founded by Catholic sisters in 1971, NETWORK is the only Catholic registered lobby in Washington, D.C. Although still staffed mostly by sisters of various religious orders, its membership is open to anyone. Rooted in the vision articulated in Catholic social teaching, NETWORK organizes, educates, and lobbies for socially just legislation. Its bimonthly magazine, information packets, and weekly e-mail alerts on timely issues before Congress keep its members up-to-date on public policy issues.

Oxfam America, 26 West Street, Boston, Mass. 02111-1206; (617) 482-1211; (800) 77-Oxfamusa; or 1112 16th Street, N.W., Suite 600, Washington, D.C. 20036; www.oxfamamerica.org

Oxfam America is a member of Oxfam International (www.oxfam.org), begun in Oxford, England, and now comprising twelve autonomous Oxfams working in eighty countries. Oxfam America fights global poverty and hunger by working with grassroots organizations promoting sustainable development in Africa, Asia, the Americas, and the Caribbean. Besides emergency relief, Oxfam supports development projects to enable the poor to become self-sufficient. Although Oxfam also engages in advocacy and education, its primary focus is on development projects. Oxfam America works with colleges, schools, communities, and places of worship in promoting an annual "Fast for a World Harvest" every November close to Thanksgiving.

Catholic Relief Services (CRS), 209 West Fayette Street, Baltimore, Md. 21201-3443; (800) 235-2772; (410) 625-2220; www.catholicrelief.org

Catholic Relief Services is the global assistance arm of the United States Catholic Bishops' Conference. CRS responds to victims of natural and human-caused disasters, provides assistance to meet the basic needs of the poor, and supports self-help programs to lift people out of poverty and restore their dignity. Its reach is global. Recently, for example, CRS has been assisting refugees and helping to rebuild in Afghanistan, and supporting development projects all over the world and especially in Africa. CRS is engaged in direct assistance to the victims of disasters and in self-help programs.

Catholic Campaign for Human Development, 3211 Fourth St., N.E., Washington, D.C. 20017-1194; (202) 541-3000; www.nccbuscc.org/cchd/

The domestic development arm of the U.S. Catholic Bishops' Conference, the Campaign for Human Development fosters local and national self-help projects for the poor in the United States.

The Interfaith Center on Corporate Responsibility (ICCR), 475 Riverside Drive, Rm. 566, New York, N.Y. 10115; (212) 870–2295.

ICCR is a coalition of church-based investors from Protestant denominations and Catholic religious communities who are concerned about corporate responsibility. ICCR researches the practices of corporations in light of justice and peace concerns and seeks to influence corporate policy through investment and proxy votes at annual corporate meetings. ICCR offers a variety of educational materials on corporate social responsibility, including *The Corporate Examiner,* which it publishes ten times a year.

Environment/Ecology

Greenpeace (USA), 702 H Street, N.W., Suite 300, Washington, D.C. 20001; (202) 462-1177; www.greenpeace.org

Greenpeace educates, organizes, lobbies, and engages in nonviolent direct action on behalf of environmental issues throughout the world. Greenpeace activists are renowned for trying to impose themselves between whaling ships and whales and for sailing the *Rainbow Warrior* into the danger zone in order to stop the atmospheric testing of nuclear weapons in the Pacific. Greenpeace publishes a magazine and provides a variety of educational materials.

The National Audubon Society, 700 Broadway, New York, N.Y. 10003; (212) 979-3000; www.audubon.org

The Audubon Society maintains seventy wildlife preserves in the United States. It has recently expanded its focus from wildlife to a host of environmental concerns. With local clubs acting as watchdogs and advocates, this organization can be a powerful force for conservation. The Society produces excellent wildlife films and other educational materials, including the *Audubon Magazine*, a bimonthly that keeps members informed on public policy developments regarding environmental issues.

Friends of the Earth, 1025 Vermont Ave., N.W., Suite 300, Washington, D.C. 20005; (877) 843-8687; (202) 783-7400; www.foe.org

This multinational environmental organization, founded in 1969, focuses on public policy advocacy on behalf of the environment and sustainable development. It publishes books, reports, and a bimonthly newsletter on environmental issues.

EarthAction, 30 Cottage Street, Amherst, Mass. 01002; (413) 549-8118; www.oneworld.org/earthaction/ E-mail: amherst@earthaction.org

EarthAction consists of a global network of 1,900 citizen groups in 160 countries. It has international offices in London, Santiago, Chile, and Amherst, Massachusetts. Its purpose is to enable thousands of organizations, journalists, citizens, and parliamentarians to act together around the world on global issues affecting the environment, social justice and peace. Eight or more times a year EarthAction sends an Action Kit to its members focusing on a particular global issue. The kit provides background information and suggestions for action. A recent Action Kit, for example, titled "The Heat Is On" focused on climate change, featuring a message from actor Leonardo DiCaprio.

Human Rights

There are any number of organizations that work for the rights of various ethnic groups or minorities and for civil rights and the rights of women. This section will simply mention two organizations that defend human rights globally.

Amnesty International (AI), 322 Eighth Ave., New York, N.Y. 10001; (212) 807-8400; (800) AMNESTY; www.amnesty.org and www.amnestyusa.org

Amnesty International began in 1961 with a determination to work on behalf of "prisoners of conscience" throughout the world. Amnesty asks its members and affiliate groups to "adopt" a prisoner, to write to those prisoners letting them know that they are not forgotten, and to work for their release. AI investigates allegations of human rights abuses and of torture, and surveys the human rights situation in various countries. Amnesty International Reports are known for their accuracy and fairness. Amnesty was awarded the Nobel Peace Prize in 1977. AI focuses on specific human rights violations and on patterns of abuse, but does not get directly involved in politics.

Human Rights Watch, 350 Fifth Ave., 34th floor, New York, N.Y. 10118-3299; (212) 290-4700; www.hrw.org.

Human Rights Watch is a nongovernmental organization that monitors human rights abuses internationally and publishes an excellent quarterly newsletter, as well as annual reports and country reports. Like Amnesty International, Human Rights Watch is known for accurate and unbiased reporting.

Peace and Disarmament

Pax Christi USA, 532 W. Eighth St., Erie, Penn. 16502; (814) 453-4955; www. paxchristiusa.org

This Catholic peace organization, affiliated with Pax Christi International (www.paxchristi.net), has been working for disarmament and human rights and against violence in the United States since 1972. Through publications, a newsletter, an annual conference, lobbying, and nonviolent direct action, Pax Christi (Peace of Christ) promotes nonviolence and opposes violence in all forms. There are regional, campus, parish, and community Pax Christi groups throughout the country.

Fellowship of Reconciliation (FOR), 521 N. Broadway (or P.O. Box 271), Nyack, N.Y. 10960; (845) 358-4601; www.forusa.org

FOR is an international (www.ifor.org) and interfaith pacifist group begun in Europe during World War I. FOR has been working courageously and creatively against war and for justice and human rights ever since. The nonviolent spirit of the civil rights movement in the United States in the 1960s was fostered by FOR, which was, of course, simultaneously working against the Vietnam War. FOR publishes a magazine, *Fellowship*, eight times a year, and holds a biannual conference. It is also organized into local groups who educate and agitate for peace in their regions.

American Friends Service Committee, 1501 Cherry Street, Philadelphia, Penn. 19102; (215) 241-7000; (800) 226-9816; www.afsc.org

This Quaker-inspired pacifist organization has been in business about as long as FOR. AFSC covers the gamut of peace and justice work, from education, to lobbying, to relief assistance, to nonviolent direct action. Its regional offices throughout the country and the world give AFSC national and global reach. AFSC was the co-recipient of the Nobel Peace Prize in 1947.

Center for Defense Information, 1779 Massachusetts Ave. N.W., Washington, D.C. 20026; (202) 332-0600; www.cdi.org

This is primarily a research and educational center dedicated to keeping the public informed about weapons spending and disarmament. Its newsletter, *The Defense Monitor*, is an excellent resource on weapons and defense spending and on foreign policy analysis.

Catholic Social Teaching

Center of Concern, 1225 Otis St., N.E., Washington, D.C. 20017; (202) 635-2757; www.coc.org

Founded in 1971, the Center of Concern functions as a think tank providing resources that analyze global social problems and offer constructive responses from the perspective of Catholic social teaching. The Center publishes a bimonthly newsletter and educational materials, and its staff lectures and offers workshops on global justice and peace. The Center is an important educational resource that complements the *United States Conference of Catholic Bishops* (USCCB), 3211 Fourth St., N.E., Washington, D.C. 20017; (202) 541-3000; www.nccbuscc.org, the official educational arm of the Catholic Church in the United States.

PROJECTS

There are many interesting research projects that can be undertaken in connection with this material. For example:

- A film festival related to a global issue. On colonialism, for example, one could see *Black Robe, Mister Johnson, The Mission,* and *Gandhi.* On Central America, *Romero, Under Fire, El Norte,* and *Choices of the Heart.*
- Research a commodity, such as coffee or sugar, uncovering the justice questions involved in its production and marketing.
- Research a country, paying attention to questions of justice and peace.
- Follow an issue in the news related to justice and peace, keeping a file of clippings from newspapers and news magazines, and summarizing your thoughts on the issue.
- Offer your time and energy to a soup kitchen, shelter, prison, or community agency, and keep a journal of reflections on your experience.
- Identify an issue related to justice or conflict resolution at your school, workplace, community, or household, and try to accomplish some constructive change.
- Do an internship with the legislature, or identify a piece of legislation related to justice and lobby for its passage.
- Start a justice and peace committee at your place of worship, in your local community or at your school.
- Organize a lecture series on justice and peace issues at your school or for your community.
- Start or join a discussion group on justice and peace issues. If you do, you might use this book as a discussion starter.

FOR FURTHER INFORMATION AND STUDY

The notes to the chapters can steer the reader toward books and articles related to the particular issues addressed in this book. The purpose of this section is to highlight journals, books, and web sites that are dedicated in a general way to the themes of justice and peace.

Periodicals and Journals

It was noted above that many organizations publish a periodical or newsletter to keep their members informed about issues, such as *Bread* (BFW), *Connection* (Network), *Fellowship* (FOR), *Greenpeace Quarterly, Human Rights Quarterly,* and *The Defense Monitor.* There are other periodicals, such as *Sojourners, Maryknoll, The National Catholic Reporter, The Catholic Worker, The Journal for Peace & Justice Studies, Cross Currents, America,* and *Commonweal* that regularly address social issues from a Christian perspective. There are also journals, such as *Current History, The Nation, Foreign Affairs, Foreign Policy,* and *Ethics and International Affairs,* that can provide background information and analysis on global issues. Most libraries carry these sources of information or can get articles for patrons through inter-library loan. A daily newspaper that has good international coverage, such as *The New York Times* or *The Washington Post,* can provide a wealth of information, as can weekly news magazines such as *Time, Newsweek,* and *U.S. News and World Report.*

Books

The following is an annotated list of books that are good general reference books on issues related to justice and peace:

Brown, Lester R. et al., *State of the World.* New York: W.W. Norton, 2002. Every year the Worldwatch Institute publishes a progress report on the movement toward a sustainable society. These reports focus on environmental issues. The Worldwatch Institute also publishes other resources.

Corson-Finnerty, Adam Daniel, *World Citizen: Action for Global Justice.* Maryknoll, N.Y.: Orbis Books, 1982. Although this book is dated and now out of print, it is included in the list because it serves as a model for this book. It is still worth reading.

Crocker, Chester A., Fen Osler Hampson, with Pamela Aall, eds., *Turbulent Peace: The Challenges of Managing International Conflict.* Washington, D.C.: United States Institute of Peace, 2001; and *Managing Global Chaos.* Washington, D.C.: United States Institute of Peace, 1996. Comprehensive collections of essays by respected researchers on global conflict and its resolution.

Duffey, Michael, K., *Sowing Justice, Reaping Peace.* Kansas City: Sheed and Ward, 2001. Duffey ably analyzes nine cases of global conflict and efforts at healing, including the Middle East, the Balkans, Northern Ireland, and race relations in the United States.

Friedman, Thomas L., *The Lexus and the Olive Tree: Understanding Globalization.* New York: Anchor Books, 2000. *New York Times* foreign affairs columnist has produced a best-selling account of and argument for globalization.

Goldstein, Joshua S., *International Relations*. Fifth Edition. New York: Longman, 2003. Perhaps the best of the texts in international relations. It is clear, informative, and concerned about humanity.

Himes, Michael J. and Kenneth R. Himes, *Fullness of Faith: The Public Significance of Theology*. New York: Paulist Press, 1993. A creative theological reflection on public policy themes.

Kegley, Charles W., and Eugene R. Wittkopf, *World Politics: Trend and Transformation*. Eighth Edition. New York: Wadsworth Publishing, 2001. A clear and comprehensive text on international relations.

Kennedy, Paul, *Preparing for the Twenty-first Century*. New York: Random House, 1993. Kennedy, a historian and a best-selling author, has written a thoughtful, well-researched, and provocative overview of the global situation as humanity enters a new millennium.

Klare, Michael T., Yogesh Chandrani, and Daniel C. Thomas, eds., *World Security: Challenges for a New Century*. Third Edition. New York: Palgrave Macmillan, 1997. An excellent collection of essays by top scholars in the field on global issues.

O'Brien, David J. and Thomas A. Shannon, eds., *Catholic Social Thought: The Documentary Heritage*. Maryknoll, N.Y.: Orbis Books, 1992. A collection of documents of the Catholic Church that comprise a hundred years of Catholic social teaching.

Powers, Gerard F., Drew Christiansen, and Robert T. Hennemeyer, eds., *Peacemaking: Moral and Policy Choices for a New World*. Washington, D.C.: United States Catholic Conference, 1994. This book includes the National Conference of Catholic Bishops' statement *The Harvest of Justice Is Sown in Peace*, which reflects on international relations in the post-Cold War world, and scholarly but readable reflections on the various issues.

Russett, Bruce, Harvey Starr, and David Kinsella, *World Politics: The Menu for Choice*. Sixth Edition. New York: Wadsworth Publishing, 1999. A clear textbook on international relations that offers some constructive proposals for social transformation.

Todaro, Michael P., *Economic Development*. Eighth Edition. Reading, Mass.: Addison-Wesley, 2002. A clear and comprehensive textbook on economic development.

United Nations Development Programme, *Human Development Report 2002*. New York: Oxford University Press, 2002. A thoughtful and statistic-filled *annual* report on global progress toward human development (see www.undp.org).

World Resources Institute, *World Resources 2000–2001*. New York: Oxford University Press, 2001. A regularly published comprehensive guide to the global environment (see www.wri.org). Available also in a CD-ROM format.

Web Sites

The first edition of this book contained an appendix that included three comprehensive tables giving characteristics of the countries of the world. It included historical and demographic information, economic and social indicators, and both the Human Development Index and the Gender Development Index. Although it is convenient to have this information right at hand, data quickly become dated. Such information is now widely available on the internet. It makes more sense to tell the reader where to find up-to-date information, rather than to reproduce it here.

The internet provides an embarrassment of riches in information about our world and its social, economic, and political conditions. One difficulty is sorting out the gems from the garbage; another is finding what you want. David Ettinger has produced a helpful bibliographic essay, "International Relations Resources on the World Wide Web," in the April 2002 issue of *Choice* (pp. 1353–72) that annotates over a hundred sites. My much more limited goal is to direct readers to sources of demographic information and social and economic indicators for the countries of the world.

A wealth of information is found in the annual *Human Development Report;* the entire report, including the Human Development Index, the Gender Development Index, and other tables, is available online at www.undp.org. Similarly the various publications of the World Bank, including world development indicators, are available at www.worldbank.org. The CIA World Factbook is an excellent source of information on the various countries of the world (www.odci.gov/cia/publications/factbook/), and www.globastat.com compiles and ranks countries based on World Factbook data for 140 categories including population, population density, GDP, GDP per capita, debt, economic aid, life expectancy, literacy, and year of independence from colonial powers.

The Economist Intelligence Unit (eiu.com) is a commercial site that offers excellent country-specific information, but much of this data is available free from Economist.com Country Briefings at www.economist.com/countries.

Amnesty International's annual human rights reports are available at www.amnesty.org. Data on international security and military expenditure can be found at two sites associated with the Stockholm International Peace Research Institute (SIPRI) at www.sipri.se and Facts on International Relations and Security Trends (FIRST) at http://first.sipri.org. Environmental data can be found at EarthTrends, http://earthtrends.wri.org, which is maintained by the World Resources Institute (www.wri.org).

Excellent maps, which are not subject to any copyright restriction, can be found at the Perry-Castaneda Library Map Collection at the University of Texas: www.lib.utexas.edu/maps/. Among the best meta-sites, which provide links to resources in all of the above categories, is the WWW Virtual Library for International Resources created by Wayne A. Selcher of Elizabethtown College at www.etown.edu/vl/.

STUDY QUESTIONS

1. In what ways could you simplify your life? Would these steps improve you? Would they be beneficial for the poor and for the earth?
2. Is responsible citizenship an obligation for disciples of Christ? What strategies can be used in advocating for the poor in public policy discussions? Can civil disobedience sometimes be justified? Sometimes be required?
3. What are the responsibilities of a justice seeker and a peacemaker in the contemporary world?
4. How will you integrate the call to be a justice seeker and a peacemaker into your vocation or career?
5. How do you think the church should speak to society on issues of public policy? Does the separation of church and state mean that the church is excluded from public policy discussions?
6. Do you vote? What is your experience of lobbying your elected representative?
7. Which organizations have you decided to join?

Notes

INTRODUCTION

1. National Conference of Catholic Bishops (NCCB), *The Challenge of Peace: God's Promise and Our Response* (1983) in David J. O'Brien and Thomas A. Shannon, eds., *Catholic Social Thought: The Documentary Heritage* (Maryknoll, N.Y.: Orbis Books, 1992), #68. References to official documents of the Catholic Church will use the paragraph or section numbers, rather than page numbers.

2. NCCB, *Economic Justice for All* (1986) in O'Brien and Shannon, eds., *Catholic Social Thought,* #8 in the introductory message. These two opening quotes indicate at least a description (rather than a definition) of peace and justice from a Christian perspective. Peace is not merely the absence of war, but the presence of justice and community. A society is just when every person has his or her basic needs met and the opportunity to flourish, to realize his or her human potential. The litmus test of the justice of a society is the condition of the poor and the marginalized people (#38, #123). The U.S. bishops present a fuller description of justice in *Economic Justice for All,* #68–95. See also Daniel C. Maguire, "The Primacy of Justice in Moral Theology," *Horizons* 10 (Spring 1983), pp. 72–85.

3. The idea of a "starter" and "getting started" book comes from Adam Daniel Corson-Finnerty, *World Citizen: Action for Global Justice* (Maryknoll, N.Y.: Orbis), 1982. Corson-Finnerty's book informed and transformed my students in a course on "Christianity and Social Justice" for several years in the way I hope this book can. *World Citizen* is now out of date and out of print.

4. These sentences paraphrase ideas found in NCCB, *Economic Justice for All,* passim.

5. Daniel C. Maguire, *The Moral Choice* (Minneapolis, Minn.: Winston Press, 1978), chap. 5.

6. Quoted in Michael True, *Justice Seekers and Peace Makers: 32 Portraits in Courage* (Mystic, Conn.: Twenty-Third Publications, 1985), p. 96.

7. Fred Kammer, *Doing Faithjustice: An Introduction to Catholic Social Thought* (New York: Paulist Press), 1991, p. 73.

8. In analyzing the obstacles to justice and peace in the current world situation, this book takes up the task of developing a theology of peace as described by the U.S. bishops in *The Challenge of Peace:* "A theology of peace should ground the task of peacemaking solidly in the biblical vision of the kingdom of God, then place it centrally in the ministry of the Church. It should specify the obstacles in the way of peace, as these are understood theologically and in the social and political sciences. It should both identify the specific contributions a community of faith can make to the work of peace and relate these to the wider work of peace pursued by other groups and institutions in society. Finally, a theology of peace must include a message of hope" (#25).

1. THE TWENTY-FIRST CENTURY: HOW DID WE GET HERE?

1. National Conference of Catholic Bishops (NCCB), *The Harvest of Justice Is Sown in Peace* (Nov. 17, 1993) in Gerard F. Powers et al., eds., *Peacemaking: Moral*

and Policy Challenges for a New World (Washington, D.C.: United States Catholic Conference, 1994), p. 345.

2. In David S. Reynolds, "American Heritages," a book review of Edward Countryman's, *Americans: A Collision of Histories* (New York: Hill & Wang, 1996), *New York Times Book Review* (June 30, 1996), p. 31, quoting Mr. Countryman.

3. A few others could be added to this list, such as Ethiopia, which defeated Italian invaders, and Liberia, which had close ties to the United States, and some of the countries in the Persian Gulf. See George Thomas Kurian, ed., *Encyclopedia of the Third World* (New York: Facts on File, Fourth Edition, 1992), Vol. 3, Appendix I, p. 2233.

4. Adam Daniel Corson-Finnerty, *World Citizen: Action for Global Justice* (Maryknoll, N.Y.: Orbis Books, 1982), p. 9.

5. Ibid., p. 10. Corson-Finnerty is relying on D. K. Fieldhouse, *The Colonial Empires* (New York: Delacorte Press, 1967), p. 178.

6. This account relies on the summaries in Corson-Finnerty, *World Citizen,* chap. 1, and Paul Vallely, *Bad Samaritans: First World Ethics and Third World Debt* (Maryknoll, N.Y.: Orbis Books, 1990), pp. 85–105.

7. Ross Gandy, *A Short History of Mexico: From the Olmecs to the PRI* (Cuernavaca: The Center for Bilingual Multicultural Studies, 1987), p. 5. This account relies on Gandy and on Corson-Finnerty.

8. Corson-Finnerty, *World Citizen,* p. 12. See Gandy, *A Short History of Mexico,* pp. 6–7. Gandy counts the population of Mexico and Guatemala as 30 million when Cortez arrived, and agrees that it was reduced to 1 million by the end of the sixteenth century.

9. Gandy, *A Short History of Mexico,* p. 7.

10. Joseph Collins, "World Hunger: A Scarcity of Food or a Scarcity of Democracy," in Michael T. Klare and Daniel C. Thomas, eds., *World Security: Challenges for a New Century* (New York: St. Martin's Press, Second Edition, 1994), p. 360. Collins cites World Bank, *Assault on Poverty* (Washington, D.C.: World Bank, 1975), p. 244; and refers to Milton J. Esman, *Landlessness and Near Landlessness in Developing Countries* (Ithaca, N.Y.: Cornell University, Center for International Studies, 1978). Jessica Tuchman Matthews says that "In 1975, 7 percent of landowners in Latin America possessed 93 percent of all the arable land in this vast region. . . . These large holdings generally include the most desirable land and are often inefficiently used or not used at all" ("The Environment and International Security," in Klare and Thomas, eds., *World Security,* p. 278).

11. Gandy, *A Short History of Mexico,* pp. 8–9.

12. Corson-Finnerty, *World Citizen,* p. 11.

13. Vallely, *Bad Samaritans,* p. 88, quoting Paul Harrison, *Inside the Third World* (London: Penguin Books, 1979).

14. Corson-Finnerty, *World Citizen,* p. 17. Cf. Vallely, *Bad Samaritans,* p. 91.

15. Elizabeth Morgan, *Global Poverty and Personal Responsibility* (New York: Paulist Press, 1989), pp. 70–71.

16. Vallely, *Bad Samaritans,* p. 91; Corson-Finnerty, *World Citizen,* p. 16.

17. Corson-Finnerty, *World Citizen,* p. 14; Vallely, *Bad Samaritans,* p. 96. Chapter 5 examines ethnic conflict.

18. Corson-Finnerty, *World Citizen,* p. 16. Corson-Finnerty relies on Richard D. Wolff, *The Economics of Colonialism—Britain and Kenya, 1870–1930* (New Haven, Conn.: Yale University Press, 1974). The films *Out of Africa* (dir. by Sydney Pollack, starring Meryl Streep and Robert Redford, 1985), and *Mister Johnson* (dir. by Bruce Beresford, 1991) dramatize British colonization in Africa. *Mister Johnson* is especially recommended.

19. Vallely, *Bad Samaritans,* p. 96.

20. Corson-Finnerty, *World Citizen,* p. 17; Vallely, *Bad Samaritans,* pp. 93–94.

21. The film *Black Robe* (dir. by Bruce Beresford, 1991) addresses this issue very well. It is set in French Canada. The film contains some very violent scenes.

22. Vallely, *Bad Samaritans,* p. 99.

23. Ibid., p. 97.

24. The film *Mister Johnson* illustrates this point well.

25. Louis Fischer, *Gandhi: His Life and Message to the World* (New York: New American Library, 1954), pp. 65–67. This massacre is also depicted in the film *Gandhi* (dir. by Richard Attenborough, starring Ben Kingsley, 1982). General Dyer's Indian troops fired 1,650 bullets at unarmed civilians who were trapped in an enclosed area, causing 1,516 casualties and 379 deaths.

26. See Stanley Karnow, *In Our Image: America's Empire in the Philippines* (New York: Ballantine Books, 1989), chaps. 4–7, for a detailed account of this war and its political background.

27. Charles S. Olcott, *The Life of William McKinley* (Boston: Houghton Mifflin, Vol. 2, 1916), p. 110.

28. Karnow, *In Our Image,* p. 198. William Howard Taft, the first American governor of the Philippines, condescendingly referred to Filipinos as "little brown brothers" (p. 174). The term captures some of the air of superiority, racism, and self-deceptive benevolence that white Americans brought to their control of the Philippines.

29. Larry Rohter, "Remembering the Past; Repeating It Anyway," *New York Times* (July 24, 1994), pp. 1, 3. Mr. Rohter refers to the study of American intervention in the Caribbean basin from 1898–1989 by Ivan Musicant titled *The Banana Wars* (New York: Macmillan, 1990). See also Michael Duffey, *Sowing Justice, Reaping Peace* (Franklin, Wis.: Sheed & Ward, 2001), chap. 1.

30. Ibid.

31. Arthur Simon, *Bread for the World* (New York: Paulist Press, 1975), pp. 74–75, 90.

32. While my memory of this cultural exhibit might be fuzzy on the details, the overall impression is correct.

33. *Rerum Novarum* can be found in *Catholic Social Thought: The Documentary Heritage,* ed. David J. O'Brien and Thomas A. Shannon (Maryknoll, N.Y.: Orbis Books, 1992), pp. 14–39.

34. Paul Kennedy, *Preparing for the Twenty-First Century* (New York: Random House, 1993), pp. 4–5. My account of Malthus and population is drawn from Kennedy, pp. 3–13.

35. Kennedy, *Preparing,* p. 8. The three escape hatches are discussed on pp. 6–10.

36. Ibid., p. 9.

37. Ibid., pp. 10–11.

38. Quoted in Alvin Toffler, *Future Shock* (New York: Bantam Books, 1970), p. 13.

39. Ibid., chaps. 1 and 2. See also Richard P. McBrien, *Catholicism* (San Francisco: HarperCollins, 1994), pp. 80–85.

40. This history is common knowledge, but see Joshua S. Goldstein, *International Relations* (New York: HarperCollins, 1996), pp. 26–39, for a lucid summary.

41. Barbara Crossette, "Globally, Majority Rules," *New York Times* (August 4, 1996), pp. E1, E6. It is also worth noting that by January 1997 the world was at relative peace: "There are civil wars, drugs wars, gang wars and trade wars. But riproaring, sound-the-trumpet, bang-the-drum wars of national aggression seem to have gone out of fashion" (Simon Jenkins, "At Long Last, Peace in Our Time," *The Times of London* [Jan. 1, 1997], op. ed., p. 14).

42. See Raymond Bonner, *Waltzing with a Dictator* (New York: Times Books, 1987) for an insightful account of these events.

2. POVERTY AND DEVELOPMENT

1. National Conference of Catholic Bishops, *Economic Justice for All* (1986) in David J. O'Brien and Thomas A. Shannon, eds., *Catholic Social Thought: The Documentary Heritage* (Maryknoll, N.Y.: Orbis Books, 1992), #38, #123.

2. Negros is a relatively large island in the Visayas, a group of islands that make up the middle section of the Philippines. Bacolod is the capital city. Father Niall O'Brien, a Columban Irish missionary to the Philippines, has written the moving story of Negros during this period in *Revolution from the Heart* (New York: Oxford, 1987) and in *Island of Tears, Island of Hope* (Maryknoll, N.Y.: Orbis Books, 1993). Gerald and Janice Vanderhaar have written a briefer account in *The Philippines: Agony and Hope* (Erie, Penn.: Pax Christi USA, 1989).

3. United Nations Development Programme, *Human Development Report 2001* (New York: Oxford University Press, 2001), p. 9.

4. Joshua Goldstein, *International Relations* (New York: Harper Collins, 1996), p. 467. *Human Development Report 2001* says, "And 11 million children under age five die each year from preventable causes—equivalent to more than 30,000 a day" (p. 9).

5. Michael P. Todaro, *Economic Development* (Reading, Mass.: Addison-Wesley, Sixth Edition, 1997), pp. 16–18, at p. 16. Todaro indicates that three-fourths of the Earth's nearly 6 billion people experience poverty (p. 3). For an integral concept of human development see also Pope Paul VI, *On the Development of Peoples* (*Populorum Progessio*) (1967) in O'Brien and Shannon, eds., *Catholic Social Thought*, #6, #14–21.

6. Goldstein, *International Relations*, pp. 18–22.

7. High-income countries had a Gross National Product (GNP) per capita of $9,266 in 1999; middle-income countries had a GNP per capita ranging from $756 to $9,265; low-income below $756. These figures reflect a GNP per capita based on Purchasing Power Parity (PPP) rather than simply the exchange rate. See *Human Development Report 2001*, p. 258.

8. Ibid., p. 145.

9. *Human Development Report 1999*, pp. 3, 36–39. It is not surprising that the gap between the rich and the poor is increasing. Indeed it would take phenomenal growth in the developing countries and a radical redistribution of wealth to make it otherwise. "These trends stem from the already large gaps in per capita GDP and the relatively low average incomes in many developing countries, such that even rapid per capita GDP growth in poor countries cannot add annual increments of per capita income as large as those in rich countries." The World Resources Institute, et al., *World Resources: 1996–97* (New York: Oxford University Press, 1996), p. 162. In other words, if your annual income is $1,000, and you experience a 1 percent increase, you receive $1,010. If my annual income is $100, and I experience a 2 percent increase, twice your increase, I have $102. My economic growth is double yours, yet the gap between us has widened, not lessened. If the comparison is between countries instead of individuals, then population growth also has to be factored in. If a country has a 2 percent economic growth, but a 3 percent population growth, its per capita GDP decreases.

10. *Human Development Report 1999*, p. 37.

11. Martin Ravillion and Shaohua Chen, *What Can New Survey Data Tell Us*

About Recent Changes in Living Standards in Developing and Transitional Economies? (Washington, D.C.: The World Bank, 1996), pp. 1–8, passim.

12. Edward N. Wolff, *Top Heavy: The Increasing Inequality of Wealth in America and What Can Be Done About It* (New York: New Press and Twentieth Century Fund, 1995, 1996), p. 13. Wolff is writing about the increasing inequality of wealth in the United States. He points out that between 1983 and 1989 the already high Gini coefficient for the U.S. increased from 0.80 to 0.84, an almost unprecedented increase in wealth inequality. According to the *Human Development Report 1996*, a similar increase in wealth inequality has occurred in the formerly Communist countries of Eastern Europe and the republics of the Soviet Union in the period from 1989 to 1994, but the Gini coefficient there rose from a low 0.25 to a still low 0.30 (p. 17). *Human Development Report 2001* says that inequality remains on the rise in Eastern Europe and the former Soviet states and is consistently high in many Latin American countries and in Africa. The United States has the highest income inequality of the OECD countries (pp. 17–18, 182–85.)

13. *World Resources: 1996–97,* pp. 159–67; *Human Development Report 2001,* p. 20.

14. *Human Development Report 2001,* pp. 141–44. Vincent Ferraro and Melissa Rosser, "Global Debt and Third World Development," in Michael T. Klare and Daniel C. Thomas, *World Security: Challenges for a New Century* (New York: St. Martin's Press, 1994), pp. 335–36, make a similar point using older data.

15. Thomas L. Friedman, *The Lexus and the Olive Tree* (New York: Farrar, Straus, Giroux, 1999), p. xiv.

16. *Human Development Report 1996,* p. 5.

17. *Human Development Report 1999,* p. 1. "Globalization with a Human Face" is the subtitle for the *Human Development Report 1999*.

18. Friedman, *Lexus and Olive Tree,* p. 85–86, xviii.

19. Ibid., p. xv.

20. Ibid., pp. 86–87. It is worth noting that some of the economic policies of the Bush administration in 2002 break these golden rules: the Bush tax cut and increased military spending is resulting in deficit rather than balanced federal budgets, and Bush imposed tariffs to protect the steel industry in politically key states and approved farm subsidies, again with the hope of political gain. Corruption by American multinational corporations with the collusion of accounting firms also undermines the health of the economy.

21. Ibid., p. 87.

22. Ibid., p. 161.

23. *Human Development Report 1999,* p. 2.

24. Friedman, *Lexus and Olive Tree,* chapter 11, pp. 219–46. Market-based solutions, however, are no panacea. Eco-tourism, for example, might not provide enough jobs or jobs with adequate compensation, and tourism itself raises environmental concerns. See Lisa Mastny, "Redirecting International Tourism," in Christopher Flavin, et. al., *State of the World 2002* (New York: W.W. Norton & Company, 2002), pp. 101–26.

25. Ibid., pp. 291–93; *Human Development Report 1999,* pp. 5–6. The International Campaign to Ban Landmines was successful in having 90 countries sign a Mine Ban Treaty in Ottawa, Canada, in December 1997. Various NGOs helped halt the secretive OECD negotiations for a Multilateral Agreement on Investment that would have constructed international rules that favored corporations over citizens in 1998.

26. NCCB, *Economic Justice for All* (1986), #24.

27. Ibid., #1, 5, passim.

28. Bob Herbert, "Nike's Pyramid Scheme," *New York Times* (June 10, 1996), op-ed page.

29. Kathy McAfee, "Why the Third World Goes Hungry: Selling Cheap, Buying Dear," *Commonweal* 117 (June 15, 1990), p. 380.

30. James B. McGinnis, *Bread and Justice: Toward a New International Economic Order* (New York: Paulist Press, 1979), chaps. 8–12. E. F. Schumacher, *Small Is Beautiful: Economics As If People Mattered* (New York: Harper & Row, 1973). Todaro, *Economic Development,* pp. 537–43.

31. Nancy Gibbs, "Cause Celeb," *Time* (June 17, 1996), pp. 28–30. The *New York Times* columnist Bob Herbert has repeatedly addressed this issue and has been especially critical of Michael Jordan and Nike. See his op-ed page columns June 10, June 14, June 24, July 12, and Nov. 1, 1996, and March 28, March 31, and April 14, 1997. See also Seth Mydans, "For Indonesian Workers at Nike Plant: Just Do It," *New York Times* (August 9, 1996), p. A4; and Cynthia Enloe, "The Globetrotting Sneaker," *Ms.* (March/April, 1995), pp. 10–15.

32. Jim Sessions, "Cross-border Blues," *Forum for Applied Research and Public Policy* 14 (Spring, 1999): 58–64; David Schilling, "*Maquiladora* Workers Deserve a Sustainable Living Wage," *Interfaith Center on Corporate Responsibility Brief* 23, no. 10 (1995), p. 3B. Schilling is drawing on the research of Ruth Rosenbaum, *Market Basket Survey: A Comparison of the Buying Power of Maquiladora Workers in Mexico and UAW Assembly Workers in GM Plants in the U.S.* (F. L. Putnam Securities, Sept., 1994). Sam Dillon, "At U.S. Door, Huddled Masses Yearn for Better Pay," *New York Times* (Dec. 4, 1995), p. A4.

33. Bob Herbert, "Nike's Boot Camps," *New York Times* (March 31, 1997), op-ed page.

34. Andrew Julien, "Garment Workers Allege Exploitation," *Hartford Courant* (July 12, 1995), p. F1. Seth Mydans, "For Indonesian Workers," p. A4.

35. Schilling, "*Maquiladora* Workers," p. 3C. Schilling relies on Sarah Anderson et al., *Workers Lose, CEOs Win II,* Institute for Policies Study, April 29, 1995.

36. Philip Knight, "Nike Pays Good Wages to Foreign Workers," *New York Times* (June 24, 1996), letter to the editor.

37. Enloe, "The Globetrotting Sneaker," pp. 10, 12, 13. For a sneaker that retails for $70, less than $1.70 goes for the labor that produced the shoes.

38. Larry Rohter, "To U.S. Critics, a Sweatshop; To Hondurans, a Better Life," *New York Times* (July 18, 1996), pp. A1, A14. This may be a commentary on the injustice attendant to agricultural labor in much of Latin America.

39. Abigail McCarthy, "By the Sweat of Kids' Brows," *Commonweal* 123 (June 1, 1996), p. 8. See Bob Herbert, "A Sweatshop Victory," *New York Times* (Dec. 22, 1995), op-ed page.

40. Felicity Lawrence, "The Sweatshop Generation," *The Guardian* (June 12, 2002), p. 17.

41. Abigail McCarthy, "By the Sweat of Kids' Brows," pp. 7–8. Steven Greenhouse, "Sporting Goods Concerns Agree to Combat Sale of Soccer Balls Made by Children," *New York Times* (Feb. 14, 1997), p. A12.

42. Larry Rohter, "To U.S. Critics," p. A14. Kaushik Basu, "The Poor Need Child Labor," *New York Times* (Nov. 29, 1994), op-ed page.

43. David Moberg, "Bringing Down Niketown," *Nation* 268 (June 7, 1999), pp. 15–19; Steven Greenhouse, "Voluntary Rules on Apparel Labor Proving Elusive," *New York Times* (Feb.1, 1997), pp. 1, 7; Steven Greenhouse, "Accord To Combat

Sweatshop Labor Faces Obstacles," ibid. (Apr. 13, 1997), pp. 1, 20; Bob Herbert, "A Good Start," ibid. (Apr. 14, 1997), op-ed page; "A Modest Start on Sweatshops," ibid. (Apr. 16, 1997), editorial; Abigail McCarthy, "Kinder, Gentler Sweatshops," *Commonweal* 124 (June 6, 1997), pp. 6–7.

44. Jeffrey C. Isaac, "Thinking about the Anti-Sweatshop Movement," *Dissent* 36 (Fall 2001), 100–08; Dana O'Rourke, "Sweatshops 101," *Dollars and Sense* 237 (Sept./Oct., 2001), pp. 14–19.

45. Jim Hightower, "Dressed for Success," *Nation* 274 (June 24, 2002), pp. 8–9.

46. Moberg, "Bringing Down Niketown," p. 18.

47. Steven Greenhouse, "Foreign Aid: Under Siege in the Budget Wars," *New York Times* (April 30, 1995), p. E4. Don Noel, "Foreign Aid: Less Costly, More Effective Than Most Think," *Hartford Courant* (June 12, 1995), op-ed page. The poll was conducted by the Program on International Policy Attitudes at the University of Maryland in January, 1995.

48. *Human Development Report 2002*, p. 202.

49. "U.S. Drops to 4th in Aid to Developing Countries," *Hartford Courant* (June 18, 1996), reporting on an OECD report.

50. *Human Development Report 2002*, pp. 30, 202.

51. Arthur Simon, *Bread for the World* (New York: Paulist Press, 1975), pp. 136–37.

52. Steven Greenhouse, "Foreign Aid," p. E4.

53. Blaine Harden, *Africa: Dispatches from a Fragile Continent* (New York: W.W. Norton, 1990), chap. 5, pp. 177–81. It should be noted that the Scandinavian countries are not only more generous with foreign aid, but generally target it on genuine development of the poor.

54. "How To Make Aid Work," *Economist* 351 (June 26, 1999), pp. 23–26. In March 2002, the Bush administration announced "The Millennium Challenge Account," a $5 billion increase in U.S. development assistance over the following three years. This account will be targeted on the world's poorest nations, but only if they have a demonstrated commitment to the rule of law and to sound fiscal policies. See David E. Sanger, "Bush Plan Ties Foreign Aid to Free Market and Civic Rule," *New York Times* (November 26, 2002), p. A12.

55. See Jeffrey D. Sachs, "When Foreign Aid Makes a Difference," *New York Times* (Feb. 3, 1997), op-ed page. A current problem regarding development assistance is the tension between the needs of developing countries, especially the least developed ones, and the needs of the transition economies of the former Soviet empire. See Todaro, *Economic Development,* p. 658.

56. Todaro, *Economic Development,* chap. 13.

57. Ibid., p. 481. It should be noted that this situational approach implies that the "golden straitjacket" may not fit every case.

58. Ibid., pp. 480, 489–90.

59. Based on Todaro, *Economic Development,* pp. 480–90.

60. *Human Development Report 2002*, p. 33.

61. McGinnis, *Bread and Justice,* pp. 89–91.

62. *Human Development Report 2002*, p. 33.

63. J. Milburn Thompson, "Progressive Christians Should Not Oppose the Expansion of NAFTA," *Journal for Peace and Justice Studies* 10 (2000): 1–27.

64. Lori Wallach and Michelle Sforza, "NAFTA at Five," *The Nation* 268 (Jan. 25, 1999), pp. 7–8.

65. Peter Morici, "Grasping the Benefits of NAFTA," *Current History* 92 (Feb., 1993), pp. 52–53.

66. Wallach and Sforza, "NAFTA at Five," pp. 7–8.

67. Based on a comparison of the data in *Human Development Report 1999*, p. 146 and *Human Development Report 2001*, p. 149.

68. Felipe A.M. de la Balze, "Finding Allies in the Back Yard: NAFTA and the Southern Cone," *Foreign Affairs* 80 (July/Aug., 2001): 7–12.

69. *Human Development Report 1999*, pp. 193–95.

70. Ferraro and Rosser, "Global Debt," pp. 337–39; Joseph Collins, "World Hunger: A Scarcity of Food or a Scarcity of Democracy?" in Michael T. Klare and Daniel C. Thomas, eds., *World Security: Challenges for a New Century* (New York: St. Martins Press, 1994), p. 363.

71. Collins, "World Hunger," p. 364.

72. M. A. Thomas, "Getting Debt Relief Right," *Foreign Affairs* 80 (Sept./Oct., 2001), p. 36.

73. The United States was the most indebted country, but it also has the world's largest GNP. Thus the clumsy HIPC (pronounced Hippic) acronym.

74. "Can Debt Relief Make a Difference?" *Economist* 357 (Nov. 18, 2000), p. 85.

75. Ibid.; Thomas, "Getting Debt Relief Right," pp. 36–46; and Robert Snyder, "Proclaiming Jubilee—For Whom?" *Christian Century* 116 (June 30, 1999), pp. 682–85.

76. Thomas, "Getting Debt Relief Right," documents this point with considerable detail. See also David Malin Roodman, "Ending the Debt Crisis," in Lester R. Brown, et. al., *State of the World 2001* (New York: W.W. Norton & Company, 2001), p. 163.

77. Friedman, *Lexus and Olive Tree*, chap. 12, pp. 247–63.

78. *Human Development Report 1996*, p. 5. "Short-term advances in human development are possible—but they will not be sustainable without further growth. Conversely, economic growth is not sustainable without human development." See Peter Passell, "Asia's Path to More Equality and More Money for All," *New York Times* (August 25, 1996), E5.

79. Diana Jean Schemo, "Brazil's Chief Acts to Take Land to Give to the Poor," *New York Times* (Nov. 13, 1995), p. A9. Although the land reform hinted at by this article's title is a good idea, the article also suggests that this is a small step, even a token, in the right direction. In Zimbabwe, 0.5 percent of the population (whites) own 70 percent of the land. See Brian Halweil, "Farming in the Public Interest," in *State of the World 2002*, p. 62.

80. *Human Development Report 2001*, p. 17.

81. *Human Development Report 1996*, p. 16.

82. Ibid., pp. 5–6.

83. Based on *Human Development Report 1996*, pp. 6–8.

84. Ibid., p. 80; Paul Kennedy, *Preparing for the Twenty-First Century* (New York: Random House, 1993), pp. 197–98.

85. *Human Development Report 1996*, p. 8.

86. The land reform initiated by President Robert Mugabe in Zimbabwe in the summer of 2002 suggests the importance of how land reform is accomplished. There is no doubt that white British settlers confiscated the land during colonization in the nineteenth century. But when Mugabe prohibited white farmers from planting crops during a time of drought and scarcity, he increased the hunger and suffering of the people.

87. Patrick E. Tyler, "Star at Conference on Women: Banker Who Lends to the Poor," *New York Times* (Sept. 14, 1995), p. A6; Paul Lewis, "Small Loans May Be

Key To Helping Third World," ibid. (Jan. 26, 1997), p. 4; "Micro-Loans for the Very Poor," ibid. (Jan. 16, 1997), editorial; Teresa Puente, "Tiny Loans Help Entrepreneurs Battle Poverty in Africa, Asia, and Latin America," *Chicago Tribune* (Nov. 23, 2001).

88. *Human Development Report 2001*, p. 3. "Making New Technologies Work for Human Development" is the subtitle and theme of this edition of the *HDR*.

89. Goldstein, *International Relations*, pp. 493–94. *Human Development Report 1996*, pp. 32–36, discussing the "gender-related development index" and the "gender empowerment measure."

90. Corruption is a serious obstacle to development. An organization called Transparency International has developed a corruption index that ranks countries on a scale of 0 to 10. See Barbara Crossette, "A Global Gauge of Greased Palms," *New York Times* (August 20, 1995), p. E3; and Raymond Bonner, "The Worldly Business of Bribes: Quiet Battle Is Joined," *New York Times* (July 8, 1996), p. A3. Recently the 26 members of the OECD committed themselves to re-write tax laws so that bribes will not be tax deductible. See Marlise Simons, "U.S. Enlists Rich Nations in Move to End Business Bribes," *New York Times* (April 12, 1996), p. A10. See also Goldstein, *International Relations*, pp. 525–27, on the problem in general.

91. John Kenneth Galbraith, *The Good Society: The Humane Agenda* (Boston: Houghton Mifflin Company, 1996), chap. 17.

92. *Human Development Report 2001*, p. 17.

93. Larry Elliott, "Africa Betrayed: The Aid Workers' Verdict," *The Guardian* (June 28, 2002), p. A1. The Group of 8 includes the world's most powerful countries—the United States, Japan, Great Britain, Germany, France, Canada, Italy, and Russia.

94. *Human Development Report 1999*, p. 38.

95. This quote from Gandhi is found on an Oxfam poster on the environment. I have not been able to find the exact quote in Gandhi's extensive writings, but it is certainly true to his spirit. He says, for example, "The rich have a superfluous store of things which they do not need, and which are therefore neglected and wasted; while millions are starved to death for want of sustenance. If each retained possession only of what he needed, no one would be in want, and all would live in contentment. As it is the rich are discontented no less than the poor." M. K. Gandhi, *Non-Violent Resistance* (New York: Schocken Books, 1951), p. 46.

96. *Human Development Report 2002*, pp. 16–35.

97. *Human Development Report 2001*, p. 178.

98. Edward N. Wolff, "The Rich Get Richer . . . and Why the Poor Don't," *The American Prospect* 12 (Feb. 12, 2001), pp. 15–16.

99. Paul Krugman, "For Richer: How the Permissive Capitalism of the Boom Destroyed American Equality," *New York Times Magazine* (October 20, 2002), pp. 64–65.

100. Ibid., p. 64.

101. Ibid., p. 64.

102. Robert Pear, "Number of People Living in Poverty Increases in U.S.: Census Bureau Report Also Says That Income of the Middle Class Fell for the First Time Since '91," *New York Times* (September 25, 2002), pp. A1, A19.

103. See Goldstein, *International Relations*, pp. 368–71. Kennedy, *Preparing for the Twenty-First Century*, pp. 290–302.

104. Crime rates are actually down across the United States, but fear of crime is not. See Richard Lacayo, "Law and Order," *Time* (January 15, 1996), pp. 48–56.

105. See Joseph Califano, "It's Drugs, Stupid," *New York Times Magazine* (January 29, 1995), pp. 40–41, for an argument about the centrality of drugs to American social problems.

106. Kennedy, *Preparing for the Twenty-First Century,* pp. 302–11. The Scholastic Aptitude Test (S.A.T.) scores for 1996, however, continued the upward trend that began in 1990. Karen W. Arenson, "Students Continue to Improve, College Board Says," *New York Times* (August 23, 1996), p. A16.

107. See Philip S. Keane, *Health Care Reform* (New York: Paulist Press, 1993), chapters 1 and 2 for a good overview of the problem.

108. Robert Pear, "After Decline, The Number of Uninsured Rose in 2001," *New York Times* (September 30, 2002), p. A21; Craig Whitney, "Rising Health Costs Threaten Generous Benefits in Europe," *New York Times* (August 6, 1996), pp. A1, A4.

109. Robin Toner and Sheryl Gay Stolberg, "Decade after Health Crisis, Soaring Costs Bring New Strains," *New York Times* (August 11, 2002), p. A18.

110. Quoted in George J. Church, "Ripping Up Welfare," *Time* (August 12, 1996), p. 20.

111. Michael Anft, "Weighing in on Welfare," *Chronicle of Philanthropy* 13 (Aug. 9, 2001): 1–6.

112. Isabel V. Sawhill, "The Perils of Early Motherhood," *The Public Interest* 146 (Winter 2002): 74–85.

113. Susan Mayer and Christopher Jencks, "War on Poverty: No Apologies, Please," *New York Times* (Nov. 9, 1995), op-ed page.

114. "The Working from Poverty to Promise Act," Bread for the World Background Paper #159 (May, 2002); David Beckman, "Welfare Reform," *Commonweal* (June 14, 2002), pp. 8–9; Patricia Ann Lamoureux, "Improving Welfare Reform," *America* (April 8, 2002), pp. 12–15; Peter Edelman, "Reforming Welfare—Take Two," *The Nation* (Feb. 4, 2002), pp. 16–20.

115. *Human Development Report 1996,* p. 26. Goldstein, *International Relations,* pp. 494–505.

116. Helder Camara, *Spiral of Violence* (London: Sheed & Ward, 1971).

117. Eileen Egan, "The Beatitudes, the Works of Mercy, and Pacifism," in Thomas Shannon, ed., *War or Peace?* (Maryknoll, N.Y.: Orbis Books, 1980), pp. 173–75.

3. POPULATION EXPLOSION, RESOURCE DEPLETION, AND ENVIRONMENTAL DESTRUCTION

1. John Paul II, "Peace with God the Creator, Peace with All of Creation," *Origins* 19 (January 1, 1990), p. 467.

2. United Nations Development Programme, *Human Development Report 1996* (New York: Oxford University Press, 1996), pp. 5–6, passim.

3. Jim MacNeil, "Strategies for Sustainable Economic Development," *Scientific American* 261 (September 1989), p. 155. This issue of *Scientific American* is devoted to environmental issues.

4. Lynn White, "The Historical Roots of the Ecological Crisis," *Science* 155 (March 10, 1967), pp. 1203–07.

5. Genesis 1:28. See also Genesis 9:1–7, where God repeats the admonition to subdue the earth and gives humanity the animals to eat as well.

6. See, for example, Mary Evelyn Jegen and Bruno V. Manno, eds., *The Earth Is the Lord's: Essays on Stewardship* (New York: Paulist Press, 1978); and Carolyn Thomas, *Gift and Response: A Biblical Spirituality for Contemporary Christians* (New York: Paulist Press, 1994), pp. 10–12.

7. Michael J. Himes and Kenneth R. Himes, *Fullness of Faith: The Public Significance of Theology* (New York: Paulist Press, 1993), chap. 5.

8. See James A. Nash, *Loving Nature: Ecological Integrity and Christian Responsibility* (Nashville: Abingdon Press, 1991), chap. 3, for a discussion of the claim against Christianity, and chaps. 4 and 5, for a constructive theological response; H. Paul Santmire, *The Travail of Nature: The Ambiguous Ecological Promise of Christian Theology* (Minneapolis: Fortress Press, 1985), and *Nature Reborn: The Ecological and Cosmic Promise of Christian Theology* (Minneapolis: Fortress Press, 2000); Sean McDonagh, *To Care for the Earth: A Call to a New Theology* (Santa Fe: Bear & Co., 1986); and Larry L. Rasmussen, *Earth Community Earth Ethics* (Maryknoll, N.Y.: Orbis Books, 1996), among others, also offer constructive theological responses.

9. Thomas Berry, *The Dream of the Earth* (San Francisco: Sierra Club Books, 1988).

10. See Bill Davis and George Sessions, *Deep Ecology: Living as if Nature Mattered* (Salt Lake City: Gibbs Smith, 1985); and Arne Naess, "Sustained Development and Deep Ecology," in J. Ronald Engel and Joan Gibb Engel, eds., *Ethics of Environment and Development: Global Challenge, International Response* (Tucson: University of Arizona Press, 1990). The "Deep Ecology" perspective rejects an anthropocentric approach that seeks to reform human behavior toward the environment; it advocates a more radical view that recognizes the unity of humans, plants, animals, and the earth. It calls for a new ecological consciousness, a change in human understanding of the relationship of humans and the ecosystem. The ecosystem itself becomes the primary value.

11. See Drew Christiansen, "Ecology, Justice, and Development," *Theological Studies* 51 (March 1990), pp. 76–79. See also Pamela Smith, *What Are They Saying about Environmental Ethics* (New York: Paulist Press, 1997) for an excellent overview of these diverse positions.

12. This statement of values and perspective depends on Himes and Himes, *Fullness of Faith*, chap. 5.

13. Joshua Goldstein, *International Relations* (New York: HarperCollins, 1996), p. 451. Current projections suggest that sometime around mid-century global population will stabilize.

14. Paul Kennedy, *Preparing for the Twenty-First Century* (New York: Random House, 1993), p. 22; Dennis Pirages, "Demographic Change and Ecological Security," in Michael T. Klare and Daniel C. Thomas, ed., *World Security: Challenges for a New Century* (New York: St. Martin's Press, 1994), p. 316. Amartya Sen describes the growth of population this way: "It took the world population millions of years to reach the first billion, then 123 years to get to the second, 33 years to the third, 14 years to the fourth, 13 years to the fifth billion, with the sixth billion to come, according to one U.N. projection, in another 11 years" ("Population: Delusion and Reality," *The New York Review of Books* [September 22, 1994], p. 62).

15. Joel E. Cohen, "Ten Myths of Population," *Discover* 17 (April 1996), p. 42.

16. World Resources Institute, *World Resources 2000–2001* (New York: Oxford University Press, 2001), p. 28.

17. Bruce Russett and Harvey Starr, *World Politics: The Menu for Choice*, 5th ed. (New York: W. H. Freeman and Co., 1996), p. 437.

18. Robert Engelman, Brian Halweil, and Danielle Nierenberg, "Rethinking Population, Improving Lives," in Christopher Flavin et al., *State of the World 2002: A Worldwatch Institute Report on Progress Toward a Sustainable Society* (New York: W. W. Norton & Company, 2002), p. 129.

19. Nathan Keyfitz, "The Growing Human Population," *Scientific American* 261 (September 1989), p. 122.

20. The World Resources Institute, *World Resources 1996–97* (New York: Oxford University Press, 1996), pp. 173–74.

21. Ibid., p. 174; *World Resources 2001–2002*, pp. 296–97.

22. Barbara Crossette, "U.N. Is Facing Angry Debate on Population," *New York Times* (September 4, 1994), p. A16.

23. *World Resources 1996–97*, p. 175. Richard W. Mansbach, *The Global Puzzle: Issues and Actors in World Politics* (Boston: Houghton Mifflin, 1994), p. 514: "More people live in Asia than in the rest of the world combined."

24. Sen, "Population: Delusion and Reality," p. 62.

25. Kennedy, *Preparing for the Twenty-First Century*, p. 24.

26. Sen, "Population: Delusion or Reality," p. 63.

27. *World Resources 1996–97*, p. 175; *World Resources 2001–2002*, p. 297. Lester R. Brown, "The Acceleration of History," in Lester R. Brown et al., *State of the World 1996* (New York: W. W. Norton, 1996), pp. 12–13. Brown lists the thirty countries that have reached a stable population.

28. Kennedy, *Preparing for the Twenty-First Century*, pp. 32–33.

29. Russett and Starr, *World Politics*, pp. 450–51.

30. Mansbach, *The Global Puzzle*, p. 514.

31. John F. Burns, "Bangladesh, Still Poor, Cuts Birth Rate Sharply," *New York Times* (September 13, 1994), p. A10.

32. *World Resources 2001–2002*, p. 28.

33. Mansbach, *The Global Puzzle*, p. 515.

34. Pirages, "Demographic Change and Ecological Security," p. 320.

35. Ibid., pp. 318–22; Engelman et al., "Rethinking Population," pp. 130–31.

36. *World Resources 1996–97*, chaps. 1–6.

37. Pirages, "Demographic Change and Ecological Security," pp. 319, 322.

38. Sen, "Population: Delusion and Reality," pp. 62–63.

39. Tas Papathanasis, "Population Debate Misses the Real Issue," *Hartford Courant* (September 30, 1994), op-ed page. See also *World Resources 2001–2002*, pp. 26–27.

40. Russett and Starr, *World Politics*, p. 450.

41. Paul Erlich and Anne Erlich, "Population, Plenty, and Poverty," *National Geographic* 174 (December 1988), p. 916.

42. Goldstein, *International Relations*, pp. 452–53.

43. Ibid., p. 453.

44. William K. Stevens, "Poor Lands' Success in Cutting Birth Rate Upsets Old Theories," *New York Times* (January 2, 1994), pp. 1, 8.

45. Anastasia Toufexis, "Too Many Mouths," *Time* (January 2, 1989), p. 50. This issue of *Time* was devoted to the ecological crisis by recognizing the earth as "Planet of the Year."

46. John F. Burns, "Bangladesh, Still Poor, Cuts Birth Rate Sharply," p. A10. Sen ("Population: Delusion and Reality," p. 71) wonders if economic and social development will not be necessary for Bangladesh to lower its fertility rate to around 2, which would begin to stabilize its population.

47. Bill Keller, "Zimbabwe Taking a Lead in Promoting Birth Control," *New York Times* (September 4, 1994), p. 16.

48. Goldstein, *International Relations*, pp. 454–55.

49. Sen, "Population: Delusion or Reality," pp. 63–64. Sen suggests that the dire predictions of eco-pessimists such as Paul Erlich (*The Population Bomb* [New York:

Ballantine, 1968]), in the tradition of Malthus, leave them open to supporting coercive measures to limit population growth. He argues against coercion and for the proven effectiveness of a collaborative approach that focuses on economic development and empowering women. For a succinct debate on this issue, see Charles F. Westoff, "Finally, Control Population," and Ellen Chesler, "Stop Coercing Women," in *New York Times Magazine* (February 6, 1994), pp. 30–33.

50. See Charles E. Curran, "Population Control: Methods and Morality," in his *Issues in Sexual and Medical Ethics* (University of Notre Dame Press, 1978), pp. 168–97; and Charles E. Curran, ed., *Contraception: Authority and Dissent* (New York: Herder and Herder, 1969). In general, the Christian churches in the Protestant or Reformed traditions do not oppose contraception or birth control, although most do oppose abortion. It is interesting to note that in Italy the prevalence of contraception exceeds 90 percent and the fertility rate is 1.2, among the lowest in the world. See Engelman et al., "Rethinking Population," p. 138.

51. Neil MacFarquhar, "With Iran Population Boom, Vasectomy Receives Blessing," *New York Times* (September 8, 1996), pp. 1, 14. See Burns, "Bangladesh, Still Poor, Cuts Birth Rate Sharply," p. A10; and Engelman et al., "Rethinking Population," pp. 141–42.

52. Toufexis, "Too Many Mouths," p. 50. See Goldstein, *International Relations*, pp. 455–56.

53. Engelman et al., "Rethinking Population," pp. 137–47.

54. See Julian Simon, *The Ultimate Resource* (Princeton: Princeton University Press, 1981) and *The Ultimate Resource II* (Princeton: Princeton University Press, 1996). Professor Simon died in 1998. Another deflator of doomsayers is Bjorn Lomborg, *The Skeptical Environmentalist* (New York: Cambridge University Press, 1998), a Danish statistician who makes some good points, but who may be as guilty of exaggeration and selectivity as those he criticizes. See Andrew Goldstein, "Danish Darts," *Time* 160 (August 26, 2002), p. A60; and "Misleading Math about the Earth," *Scientific American* 286 (January, 2002), pp. 61–71 with essays by Stephen Schneider, John P. Holdren, John Bongaart, and Thomas Lovejoy.

55. See Paul R. Erlich and Anne H. Erlich, *The Population Explosion* (New York: Simon & Schuster, 1990).

56. John Tierney, "Betting the Planet," *New York Times Magazine* (December 2, 1990), p. 81. This description is based on Tierney's article.

57. Ibid.

58. Russett and Starr, *World Politics*, p. 450.

59. Goldstein, *International Relations*, p. 443.

60. John H. Gibbons, Peter D. Blair, and Holly L. Gwin, "Strategies for Energy Use," *Scientific American* 261 (September 1989), p. 136. This article says that fossil fuels account for 88 percent of energy consumption.

61. *World Resources 1996–97*, p. 273.

62. Russett and Starr, *World Politics*, p. 449.

63. *World Resources 1996–97*, p. 275.

64. See Colin J. Campbell and Jean H. Laherrere, "The End of Cheap Oil," *Scientific American* 278 (March 1998), pp. 78–84.

65. William C. Clark, "Managing Planet Earth," *Scientific American* 261 (September 1989), p. 47. *World Resources 1996–97*, p. 274.

66. Joshua S. Goldstein, *International Relations: Brief Edition* (New York: Longman, 2002), p. 425. Goldstein bases his calculations on the United Nations, *1995 Energy Statistics Yearbook* (New York: United Nations, 1997).

67. Nathan Keyfitz, "The Growing Human Population," p. 121. The special issue of *Scientific American* 262 (September 1990) was devoted to "Energy for Planet Earth."

68. *World Resources 1996–97*, pp. 274–78.

69. Goldstein, *International Relations* (1996), pp. 445–46.

70. Paula Gonzalez, "Facing the Challenge of Global Warming," *Network* (July/August, 1996), pp. 10–11. Gibbons et al., "Strategies for Energy Use," p. 142.

71. Agis Salpukas, "Suburbia Can't Kick the Nozzle," *New York Times* (July 23, 1996), pp. D1, D5. See Keith Bradsher, "What Not to Drive to the Recycling Center," *New York Times* (July 28, 1996), p. E2, and *High and Mighty: SUVs—The World's Most Dangerous Vehicles and How They Got That* Way (New York: Public Affairs, 2002) on the U.S. fascination with the environmentally harmful sports utility vehicle (SUV) that gets about 15 miles to the gallon.

72. Lester Brown, "The Acceleration of History," pp. 14–16. "What the U.S. Should Do," *Time* (January 2, 1989), p. 65.

73. Russett and Starr, *World Politics*, p. 449. See Donella H. Meadows et al., *The Limits to Growth: A Report for the Club of Rome's Project on the Predicament of Mankind* (New York: New American Library, 1972) for similar sorts of projections made a decade earlier. The message of the Club of Rome was quite controversial, but, like that of other environmental prophets, it deserves critical attention. See also Campbell and Laherrere, "The End of Cheap Oil."

74. Jessica Tuchman Matthews, "The Environment and International Security," in Klare and Thomas, *World Security*, p. 276.

75. Eugene Linden, "The Death of Birth," *Time* (January 2, 1989), p. 32.

76. Edward O. Wilson, "Threats to Biodiversity," *Scientific American* 261 (September 1989), p. 111.

77. *World Resources 2001–2002*, p. 90, although the challenge of calculating deforestation rates should be noted.

78. See Linden, "The Death of Birth," p. 32.

79. Wilson, "Threats to Biodiversity," p. 113.

80. *World Resources 1996–97*, p. 201.

81. Linden, "The Death of Birth," p. 32.

82. Wilson, "Threats to Biodiversity," p. 108.

83. *World Resources 1996–97*, p. 247.

84. Wilson, "Threats to Biodiversity," p. 112; Linden, "The Death of Birth," p. 32.

85. Linden, "The Death of Birth," p. 33. This phenomenon is dramatized in two films: "Medicine Man" (1992) and "The Emerald Forest" (1985). The latter focuses on the plight of indigenous people who live in tropical forests.

86. Wilson, "Threats to Biodiversity," p. 114.

87. Samuel Taylor Coleridge, "The Rime of the Ancient Mariner," in *The Complete Poetical Works of Samuel Taylor Coleridge*, ed. Ernest Hartley Coleridge, vol. 1 (Oxford: Clarendon Press, 1912, 1957), line 120, p. 191. This is a paraphrase of the line from Coleridge's poem.

88. Russett and Starr, *World Politics*, p. 450. J. W. Maurits la Riviere ("Threats to the World's Water," *Scientific American* 261 [September 1989], p. 80) puts the figure at .01 percent.

89. Sandra Postel, "Forging a Sustainable Water Strategy," in Brown et al., *State of the World 1996*, p. 41.

90. Russett and Starr, *World Politics*, p. 450.

91. Maurits la Riviere, "Threats to the World's Water," p. 80.

92. Postel, "Forging a Sustainable Water Strategy," pp. 42–47. Aquifers can be irreparably damaged because the pores and spaces that hold water can collapse when they are empty.

93. Ibid., p. 40.

94. Goldstein, *International Relations* (2002), p. 430.

95. Payal Sampat, "Uncovering Groundwater Pollution," in Lester R. Brown et al., *State of the World 2001* (New York: W. W. Norton & Company, 2001), pp. 21–22.

96. Barry Commoner, *The Closing Circle* (New York: Bantam Books, 1971), chap. 6.

97. "The Rebirth of a River," *New York Times* (June 16, 1996), editorial. This editorial summed up a two-part series written by the *Times*' William Stevens and Andrew Revkin, published the previous week.

98. James C. McKinley, Jr., "An Amazon Weed Clogs an African Lake," *New York Times* (August 5, 1996), p. A5.

99. See Chris Bright, "Understanding the Threat of Bioinvasions," in Brown et al., *State of the World 1996*, pp. 95–113, for many examples of this phenomenon and its economic and health cost; Gina Maranto, "In Nature vs. Nature, Nature May Not Win," *New York Times* (April 27, 1997), p. E6; and Mireya Navarro, "U.S. Dispatches an Army of Tree-Hungry Beetles to Fight Everglades Menace," ibid. (May 4, 1997), p. 22.

100. United Nations Development Program, *Human Development Report 2002* (New York: Oxford University Press, 2002), p. 29.

101. "There are several avenues to raising water productivity, but the key is pricing water at its market value, a step that leads to systemic advances in efficiency" (Lester R. Brown, "Eradicating Hunger: A Growing Challenge," in Brown et al., *State of the World 2001*, p. 54).

102. *World Resources 1996–97*, pp. 301–02.

103. Postel, "Forging a Sustainable Water Strategy," pp. 55–59; *World Resources 1996–97*, p. 303.

104. Postel, "Forging a Sustainable Water Strategy," pp. 49–51; Peter Theroux, "The Imperiled Nile Delta," *National Geographic* 191 (January 1997), pp. 2–35; Somini Sengupta, "In Israel and Lebanon, Talk of War over Water," *New York Times* (October 16, 2002), p. A10.

105. *World Resources 2000–2001*, p. 79.

106. Brown, "The Acceleration of History," p. 9. See Terry McCarthy, "Fishy Business," *Time* 160 (November 25, 2002), pp. A8–A16 for a discussion of environmental and economic concerns in aquaculture.

107. *World Resources 2000–2001*, p. 78.

108. Craig S. Smith, "North Sea Cod Crisis Brings Call for Nations to Act," *New York Times* (November 7, 2002), p. A3.

109. *World Resources 2000–2001*, pp. 76, 78; *World Resources 1996–97*, pp. 297–98.

110. Goldstein, *International Relations* (2002), pp. 420.

111. Joel E. Cohen has reflected and written extensively on the complex question of the carrying capacity of Earth. See *How Many People Can Earth Support?* (New York: W. W. Norton & Co., 1995); an article by the same title in *The Sciences* (November/December 1995), pp. 18–23; and "Population Growth and Earth's Human Carrying Capacity," *Science* 296 (July 21, 1995), pp. 341–46. Cohen's book was reviewed by William D. Nordhaus, "Elbow Room," *New York Times Book Review* (January 14, 1996), pp. 12–13.

112. Brown, "The Acceleration of History," pp. 7–11, 16–17; Lester R. Brown, "Facing the Prospect of Food Scarcity," in *State of the World 1997,* pp. 23–41; and *Tough Choices: Facing the Challenge of Food Scarcity* (New York: W. W. Norton & Co., 1996); and *World Resources 1996–97,* pp. 228–29.

113. Brown, "The Acceleration of History," p. 8.

114. *World Resources 1996–97,* p. 225; Brown, "Eradicating Hunger," p. 51.

115. Kennedy, *Preparing for the Twenty-First Century,* p. 67.

116. *World Resources 1996–97,* pp. 226–27.

117. Brown, "Eradicating Hunger," p. 49. Brown points out that hungry people are concentrated on the Indian subcontinent (India, Pakistan, and Bangladesh) and in Africa (p. 44).

118. Matthews, "The Environment and International Security," p. 277; *World Resources 1996–97,* pp. 230–33.

119. Brown, "Eradicating Hunger," p. 52.

120. Ibid.; and Brian Halweil, "Farming in the Public Interest," in *State of the World* (2002), p. 58. For a discussion of genetically modified foods see the special section "Genetically Modified Foods: Are They Safe?" *Scientific American* 284 (April 2001), pp. 50–65. Europeans and much of the rest of the world seem more critical and cautious about "frankenfoods" than are Americans. Countries facing famine in southern Africa have even refused American food aid that was genetically modified.

121. Kennedy, *Preparing for the Twenty-First Century,* pp. 70–81. Sen argues that food production is likely to keep up with population growth, despite the predictions of doomsayers; that Asia, in particular, has made dramatic advances in food production recently; but that Africa may be an exception ("Population: Delusions and Reality," pp. 66–67).

122. Brown, "Eradicating Hunger," pp. 59–62.

123. Michael D. Lemonick, "Deadly Danger in a Spray Can," *Time* (January 2, 1989), p. 42.

124. Ibid.; Goldstein, *International Relations* (2002) pp. 415–17; Mathews, "The Environment and International Security," p. 283.

125. *World Resources 1996–97,* p. 316.

126. Ibid.; Russett and Starr, *World Politics,* p. 454.

127. Goldstein, *International Relations* (2002), pp. 415–17.

128. Michael D. Lemonick, "Feeling the Heat," *Time* (January 2, 1989), p. 38. Thomas E. Graedel and Paul J. Crutzen, "The Changing Atmosphere," *Scientific American* 261 (September 1989), pp. 58–68.

129. Trees absorb carbon dioxide, and when a tree dies it releases the carbon dioxide whether it rots or burns. Lemonick, "Feeling the Heat," p. 38.

130. Christopher Flavin, "Facing Up to the Risks of Climate Change," in Lester Brown et al., *State of the World 1996,* p. 29. Carbon dioxide is about 4 times heavier than carbon. Thus, "In 1992, global emissions of carbon dioxide . . . amounted to 26.4 billion metric tons per year, of which 84 percent (22.3 billion metric tons) was from industrial activity" (*World Resources 1996,* p. 316). As one who is not a scientist, I am amazed at these figures of *billions* of metric tons of carbon released into the atmosphere. Forests and oceans absorb about 3 billion tons of carbon per year. Any amount over that adds to the carbon accumulating in the atmosphere.

131. Lemonick, "Feeling the Heat," p. 38. *World Resources 1996–97,* p. 320. Seth Dunn and Christopher Flavin, "Moving the Climate Change Agenda Forward," *State of the World 2002,* p. 28.

132. Bill McKibben, "Not So Fast," *New York Times Magazine* (July 23, 1995), p. 24.

133. Dunn and Flavin, "Moving the Climate Change Agenda Forward," p. 34.

134. Ibid., pp. 34–35.

135. *World Resources 1996–97*, pp. 316–18. The U.S. per capita emission of carbon is 5.26 tons per year (Flavin, "Facing Up to the Risks of Climate Change," p. 29).

136. Russett and Starr, *World Politics*, p. 454. Stephen H. Schneider, "The Changing Climate," *Scientific American* 261 (September 1989), pp. 70–79. Estimates vary on how much and how fast global temperature may rise. Dunn and Flavin ("Moving the Climate Change Agenda Forward," p. 28) say, "Global average temperature is due to increase by 1.4–5.8 degrees Celsius between 1990 and 2100." They also point out that, "Even after greenhouse gas concentrations are stabilized, climate change will persist for many centuries, with surface temperature and sea level continuing to rise in response to past emissions" (p. 28).

137. Dunn and Flavin, "Moving the Climate Change Agenda Forward," p. 26, based on the third report (2001) of the authoritative Intergovernmental Panel on Climate Change (IPCC), sponsored by the World Meteorological Association and the United Nations, which Dunn and Flavin suggest has laid to rest any doubts about the reality of human-induced global warming.

138. John Noble Wilford, "Ages-Old Icecap at North Pole Is Now Liquid, Scientists Find," *New York Times* (August 19, 2000), pp. A1, A13. As is typical of the *New York Times,* this story gave no indication whether Santa and the reindeer could swim. See also Eugene Linden, "The Big Meltdown," *Time* (September 4, 2000), pp. 52–56.

139. Flavin, "Facing Up to the Risks of Climate Change," pp. 22–23; Bill McKibben, "The Earth Does a Slow Burn," *New York Times* (May 3, 1997), op-ed page; Juan Forero, "As Andean Glaciers Shrink, Water Worries Grow," *New York Times* (November 24, 2002), p. A3.

140. C. Drew Harvell et al., "Climate Warming and Disease Risks for Terrestrial and Marine Biota," *Science* 296 (June 21, 2002), pp. 2158–62.

141. *World Resources 1996–97*, p. 322. See Dunn and Flavin, "Moving the Climate Change Agenda Forward," p. 29; and David Wirth, "Catastrophic Climate Change," in Klare and Thomas, *World Security*, pp. 386–90.

142. Kennedy, *Preparing for the Twenty-First Century*, pp. 108–13. Michael D. Lemonick, "Heading For Apocalypse?" *Time* (October 2, 1995), pp. 54–55.

143. See, for example, Celia W. Dugger, "A Cruel Choice in New Delhi: Jobs vs. a Safer Environment," *New York Times* (November 24, 2000), pp. A1, A12. Dunn and Flavin, "Moving the Climate Change Agenda Forward," pp. 30–50, discuss the economics and politics of reducing carbon emissions and suggest it might not be prohibitively costly to the economy.

144. Flavin, "Facing Up to the Risks of Climate Change," pp. 29–31.

145. See the special section "How to Preserve the Planet and Make This a Green Century," *Time* 160 (August 26, 2002), A1–A62, for practical "green" ideas.

146. McKibben, "Not So Fast," p. 25. On strategies for reducing carbon emissions, see also Flavin, "Facing Up to the Risks of Climate Change," pp. 31–33; *World Resources 1996–97*, p. 324; Brown, "The Acceleration of History," pp. 15–16; Wirth, "Catastrophic Climate Change," pp. 390–96; Lemonick, "Heading For Apocalypse?" p. 55.

147. Flavin, "Facing Up to the Risks of Climate Change," p. 33. It is also a moral and spiritual challenge.

148. Goldstein, *International Relations* (2002), pp. 414–15; Flavin, "Facing Up to the Risks of Climate Change," p. 21; Wirth, "Catastrophic Climate Change," pp. 395–96.

149. Dunn and Flavin, "Moving the Climate Agenda Forward," p. 27.

150. Andrew C. Revkin, "Climate Talks Shift Focus to How to Deal With Changes," *New York Times* (November 3, 2002), p. A10.

151. Lemonick, "Heading For Apocalypse?" expresses skepticism that the developed countries will be willing to undergo such a radical transformation of their societies and lifestyles and be willing to subsidize the transformation of poorer countries. He thinks the world will have to adapt to global warming, rather than be able to prevent it.

152. Eugene Linden, "Condition Critical," *Time* 155 (April–May, 2000), p. 20, in a special Earth Day 2000 edition.

153. Helen Caldicott, *Nuclear Madness* (Brookline, Mass.: Autumn Press, 1978), p. 65 and passim. Russett and Starr, *World Politics*, p. 453.

154. Eric Pooley, "Nuclear Warriors," *Time* (March 4, 1996), p. 50.

155. Ibid, pp. 47–54. This account of a whistle blower's concern about safety and the resistance of both Northeast Utilities and the NRC is worth reading. It is an unsettling story, especially if you live near a nuclear power plant.

156. Matthew L. Wald, "Demolition of Nuclear Plant Illustrates Problems Involved," *New York Times* (May 14, 2002), p. A16.

157. Pooley, "Nuclear Warriors," p. 49.

158. John Langone, "A Stinking Mess," *Time* (January 2, 1989), p. 44; Goldstein, *International Relations* (1996), p. 441.

159. Amal Kumar Naj, "Private Industry Could Clean Up Toxic Waste," in Neal Bernards, ed., *The Environmental Crisis: Opposing Viewpoints* (San Diego: Greenhaven Press, 1991), p. 173. Reprinted from the *Wall Street Journal* (Sept. 15, 1988). Chapter 4 of this book debates toxic waste disposal.

160. Langone, "A Stinking Mess," p. 45.

161. Goldstein, *International Relations* (2002), p. 423–24.

162. Ivan Amato, "Can We Make Garbage Disappear?" *Time* (November 8, 1999), p. 116. Statistics for 1997. See also National Solid Wastes Management Association (NSWMA), "New Landfills Can Solve the Garbage Crisis," in *The Environmental Crisis*, p. 123; Langone, "A Stinking Mess," p. 45.

163. NSWMA, "New Landfills," p. 123.

164. John Tierney, "Recycling Is Garbage," *New York Times Magazine* (June 10, 1996), pp. 28, 51.

165. Brent Staples, "Life in the Toxic Zone: Environmental Justice in Chester, Pa.," *New York Times* (September 15, 1996), editorial page.

166. Tierney, "Recycling Is Garbage," pp. 26–27.

167. "Recycling Without Tears," *New York Times* (July 29, 1996), editorial. It should be noted that Mayor Michael Bloomberg moved at the end of 2002 to end New York City's recyling program because of the budget restraints.

168. Ibid.; Barry Commoner, "Recycling More, Spending Less," *New York Times* (July 6, 1996), op-ed page; Tierney, "Recycling Is Garbage," pp. 29, 41.

169. Tierney, "Recycling Is Garbage," pp. 48, 51; Langone, "A Stinking Mess," p. 45.

170. Amato, "Can We Make Garbage Disappear?" p, 116; and Eric Roston, "New War on Waste," *Time* (August 26, 2002), pp. A28–31.

171. Michael T. Klare., *Resource Wars: The New Landscape of Global Conflict* (New York: Metropolitan Books, Henry Holt and Company, 2001), pp. 1–9.

172. Ibid., p. 25.

173. Thomas Homer-Dixon, "Environmental Scarcity and Intergroup Conflict," in Michael T. Klare and Daniel C. Thomas, eds., *World Security*, pp. 351–52.

174. Michael Renner, "Breaking the Link Between Resources and Repression,"

State of the World 2002, pp. 149–73, especially p. 150; and Michael Renner, *The Anatomy of Resource Wars* (Worldwatch Paper 162, October 2002).

175. Thomas F. Homer-Dixon, Jeffrey H. Boutwell, and George W. Rathjens, "Environmental Change and Violent Conflict," *Scientific American* 268 (February 1993), p. 38. These three co-authors are also co-directors of the "Environmental Change and Acute Conflict" research project, jointly sponsored by the University of Toronto and the American Academy of Arts and Sciences. Thomas Homer-Dixon has published the following related articles on this topic: "On the Threshold: Environmental Changes As Causes of Acute Conflict," *International Security* 16 (Fall 1991), pp. 76–116; "Destruction and Death," *New York Times* (January 31, 1993), op-ed page; and "Environmental Security and Intergroup Conflict," in Michael T. Klare and Daniel C. Thomas, eds., *World Security*, pp. 290–313; and in the 3rd edition, 1998, pp. 342–65. There is a great deal of overlap among these articles. See also Thomas Homer-Dixon, *Environment, Scarcity, and Violence* (Princeton: Princeton University Press, 2001).

176. Steven Greenhouse, "The Greening of U.S. Diplomacy: Focus on Ecology," *New York Times* (October 9, 1996), p. A6; Matthews, "The Environment and International Security," pp. 288–89.

177. Goldstein, *International Relations* (2002), pp. 430–32.

178. Harvell et al., "Climate Warming and Disease Risks," pp. 2158–62.

179. See Anne R. Platt, "Confronting Infectious Diseases," in Brown et al., *State of the World 1996*, pp. 114–132; Eugene Linden, "Global Fever," *Time* (July 8, 1996), pp. 56–57; Gregg Easterbrook, "Forget PCB's. Radon. Alar.: The World's Greatest Environmental Dangers Are Dung Smoke and Dirty Water," *New York Times Magazine* (Sept. 11, 1994), pp. 60–63; Pirages, "Demographic Change and Ecological Insecurity," p. 322.

180. Commoner, *The Closing Circle*, pp. 29–42.

181. Thomas Berry, *The Dream of the Earth* (San Francisco: Sierra Club Books, 1988), pp. 206–07.

182. *Human Development Report 1996*, pp. 5–6, and passim.

183. Jeffrey Kluger and Andrea Dorfman, "The Challenges We Face," *Time* 160 (August 26, 2002), p. A7.

184. Goldstein, *International Relations* (1996) p. 428; Clark, "Managing Planet Earth," p. 47.

185. Russett and Starr, *World Politics*, p. 460. This section depends on Russett and Starr.

186. Ibid.

187. Ibid., p. 462.

188. Nash, *Loving Nature*, pp. 200–02; Goldstein, *International Relations* (1996) pp. 428–29.

189. Bill McKibben, "Buzzless Buzzword," *New York Times* (April 10, 1996), op-ed page. McKibben argues that "sustainability," while it is a word that is tossed around often, has not effectively stabilized economic growth. He wonders if "maturity" might not be a better buzzword, since it implies inner development rather than outer growth, and requires restraint, self-discipline, and other-directedness.

4. HUMAN RIGHTS

1. Pope John XXIII, *Peace on Earth* (Pacem in Terris) (1963), in David J. O'Brien and Thomas A. Shannon, eds., *Catholic Social Thought: The Documentary Heritage* (Maryknoll, N.Y: Orbis Books, 1992), #9.

2. Malcolm Linton, "War Wounds," *Time* 154 (Sept. 13, 1999), pp. 36–39.

3. Jack Donnelly, *International Human Rights* (Boulder, Col.: Westview Press, 1993), p. 177, note 2.

4. Originally these were envisioned to be one document, but the United States insisted that they be divided into two. Although ready by 1953, they were tabled until 1966, when they were finally issued. As with any treaty, governments first sign the treaty, then formally ratify it according to their constitutions. Because of concerns about sovereignty, the United States has only ratified the Covenant on Civil and Political Rights and that in 1992. Although the U.S. generally abides by the provisions of these covenants, it refuses to subject itself to outside scrutiny. See Donnelly, *International Human Rights,* pp. 10, 100–103, 182.

5. See Stephen P. Marks, "Promoting Human Rights," in Michael T. Klare and Daniel C. Thomas, eds., *World Security: Trends and Challenges at Century's End* (New York: St. Martin's Press, 1991), pp. 297–99, for a comparable list.

6. See Michael Hovey, "Interceding at the United Nations: The Human Right to Conscientious Objection," in *Transnational Social Movements and Global Politics* (Syracuse University Press, 1997), and Jose de Sousa e Brito, "Political Minorities and the Right to Tolerance: The Development of a Right to Conscientious Objection in Constitutional Law," *Brigham Young University Law Review* 1999 (1999): 607–34.

7. Donnelly, *International Human Rights,* pp. 57–82.

8. Oliver Burkman and Richard Norton-Taylor, "Newborn World Court Fights For Survival," *The Guardian* (July 1, 2002), p. 15.

9. Jack Donnelly, "International Human Rights After the Cold War," in Michael T. Klare and Daniel C. Thomas, eds., *World Security: Challenges for a New Century,* 2nd ed. (New York: St. Martin's Press, 1994), p. 237.

10. Barbara Crossette, "U.N. Reports Latin America Suffers Fewer 'Disappeared'," *New York Times* (May 25, 1997), p. 4.

11. Donnelly, *International Human Rights,* p. 150.

12. Donnelly, "International Human Rights and After the Cold War," p. 241.

13. See Nicholas Kristoff, "Let Them be P.O.W.s," *New York Times* (Jan. 29, 2002). op-ed page, for an insightful discussion of this issue.

14. Donnelly, *International Human Rights,* p. 101. Donnelly calls this an attitude of "American exceptionalism."

15. Ibid., p. 238.

16. David Hollenbach, "Global Human Rights: An Interpretation of the Contemporary Catholic Understanding," in his *Justice, Peace, and Human Rights: American Catholic Social Ethics in a Pluralistic World* (New York: Crossroad, 1988), p. 91. Originally in Alfred T. Hennelly and John Langan, eds., *Human Rights in the Americas* (Washington, D.C.: Georgetown University Press, 1982). See also Mary Ann Glendon, "Catholicism and Human Rights," Marianist Award Lecture 2001, The University of Dayton; and Glendon's *A World Made New: Eleanor Roosevelt and the Universal Declaration of Human Rights* (New York: Random House, 2001); and Avery Dulles, *Human Rights: The United Nations and Papal Teaching* (New York: Fordham University Press, 1999).

17. Michael J. Himes and Kenneth R. Himes, *Fullness of Faith: The Public Significance of Theology* (New York: Paulist Press, 1993), p. 64.

18. Donnelly, *International Human Rights,* pp. 19–28. Natural Law and Kantian philosophies would logically provide stronger bases for human rights than utilitarian or Marxist philosophies.

19. National Conference of Catholic Bishops (NCCB), *Economic Justice for All* in O'Brien and Shannon, eds., *Catholic Social Thought,* #25 (p. 15), and passim.

"This tradition [of Catholic social thought] insists that human dignity, realized in community with others and with the whole of God's creation, is the norm against which every social institution must be measured."

20. Himes and Himes, *Fullness of Faith*, chap. 3, "The Trinity and Human Rights," pp. 55–73.

21. Richard W. Mansbach, *The Global Puzzle: Issues and Actors in World Politics* (Boston: Houghton Mifflin, 1994), p. 539.

22. David Hollenbach, *Claims in Conflict: Retrieving and Renewing the Catholic Human Rights Tradition* (New York: Paulist Press, 1979), p. 95. This section depends on Hollenbach, pp. 89–100.

23. Ibid., p. 97.

24. Ibid., p. 203. Also see pp. 195–207.

25. Ibid., p. 204.

26. Donnelly, *International Human Rights,* pp. 37–38. This section depends on Donnelly.

27. The whole idea of human rights is inimical to a strong conception of cultural relativism. This is, however, a much debated philosophical issue. It should be noted that Catholic theology has little difficulty with the idea of universal moral norms and principles, but there is much discussion of their interpretation and implementation.

28. "Prostituted Children," *New York Times* (Aug. 26, 1996), editorial; and Barbara Crossette, "U.N. Is Urged To Combat Sex Abuse of Children," *New York Times* (Sept. 25, 1996), p. A7.

29. Donnelly, *International Human Rights,* p. 38. "The New Attack on Human Rights," *New York Times* (Dec. 10, 1995), editorial, which concludes, "On Human Rights Day, let it be affirmed again that some truths are globally self-evident, and that a society deserves to be judged by its treatment of those least able to defend themselves, and by the degree to which rulers govern by consent and persuasion, rather than by terror."

30. See the gender-related development index table in the United Nations Development Programme, *Human Development Report 2001* (New York: Oxford University Press, 2001), pp. 210–13.

31. *Human Development Report 1996,* pp. 32–34. These same points are confirmed in *Human Development Report 2001,* pp. 15–16.

32. *Human Development Report 2001,* pp. 214–17, Gender Empowerment Measure Table.

33. Ibid., p. 16. The good news is that most countries have higher GDI and GEM scores in 2001 than in 1996.

34. Adam Daniel Corson-Finnerty, *World Citizen: Action for Global Justice* (Maryknoll, N.Y.: Orbis Books, 1982), pp. 76–77.

35. Owen R. Jackson, *Dignity and Solidarity: An Introduction to Peace and Justice Education* (Chicago: Loyola University Press, 1985, 1990), p. 178. NCCB, *Economic Justice For All,* #178–80.

36. Saint Joseph College, the women's college where I taught from 1982–2001, was founded in 1932 by the Sisters of Mercy because there was no opportunity for women to acquire a college education in the area at that time.

37. Women hold less than 6 percent of the seats in these countries' parliaments (*Human Development Report 2001,* pp. 214–17).

38. Paul Lewis, "In the World's Parliaments, Women Are Still a Small Minority," *New York Times* (March 16, 1997), p. 10.

39. Carole J. Sheffield, "Sexual Terrorism," in Jo Freeman, ed., *Woman: A Feminist Perspective* (Mountain View, Calif.: Mayfield, 1989), pp. 3–19; Charlotte Bunch and Roxanna Carrillo, "Global Violence Against Women: The Challenge to Human Rights and Development," in Michael T. Klare and Daniel C. Thomas, eds., *World Security: Challenges for a New Century* (New York: St. Martin's Press, 1994), p. 261; Marie M. Fortune, *Sexual Violence: The Unmentionable Sin* (New York: Pilgrim Press, 1983).

40. Celia W. Dugger, "African Ritual Pain: Genital Cutting," *New York Times* (Oct. 5, 1996), pp. 1, 6, 7.

41. Xavier Bosch, "Female Genital Mutilation in Developed Countries," *The Lancet* 358 (Oct. 6, 2001): 1177.

42. Dugger, "African Ritual Pain," p. 6; Corson-Finnerty, *World Citizen*, p. 79.

43. "Egyptian Girl Dies After Genital Mutilation," *New York Times* (Aug. 25, 1996), p. A18. This girl was the second known to have bled to death in two months after the procedure in Egypt. See also Howard W. French, "The Ritual: Disfiguring, Hurtful, Wildly Festive," ibid. (Jan. 31, 1997), p. A4; and "Africa's Culture War: Old Customs, New Values," ibid. (Feb. 2, 1997), p. E1. For an argument that this cultural practice should be tolerated, see Richard A. Shweder, "What About 'Female Genital Mutilation'? and Why Understanding Culture Matters in the First Place," *Daedalus* 129 (Fall, 2000): 209–32.

44. Dugger, "African Ritual Pain," p. 6.

45. Neil MacFaquar, "Mutilation of Egyptian Girls, Despite Ban, It Goes On," *New York Times* (Aug. 8, 1996), p. A3.

46. Celia W. Dugger, "A Refugee's Body Is Intact But Her Family Is Torn," *New York Times* (Sept. 11, 1996), pp. A1, B6–7.

47. Corson-Finnerty, *World Citizen*, p. 78; Howard W. French, "The Ritual Slaves of Ghana," *New York Times* (Jan. 20, 1997), pp. A1, A5.

48. Ellen Goodman, "Outlaw Female Genital Mutilation Before Girls Are Harmed," *Hartford Courant* (October 20, 1995), op-ed page; Barbara Crossette, "Female Genital Mutilation by Immigrants Is Becoming Cause for Concern in the U.S.," *New York Times* (Dec. 10, 1995), p. 18.

49. Celia W. Dugger, "New Law Bans Genital Cutting in United States," *New York Times* (Oct. 12, 1996), pp. 1, 28.

50. Bunch and Carrillo, "Global Violence Against Women," p. 256.

51. For example, women often suffer from harsh discrimination in Islamic societies, but many scholars of Islam argue that the Koran can be interpreted to support the equality of women. See Elaine Sciolino, "The Many Faces of Islamic Law," *New York Times* (Oct. 13, 1996), p. E4; and Riffat Hassan, "Women in Islam and Christianity: A Comparison," *Concilium* (1994/3): 18–22.

The Catholic Church affirms the equality of women and men and condemns discrimination against women. See Pope John XXIII, *Pacem in Terris*, #41, and the National Conference of Catholic Bishops, "To Live in Christ Jesus: A Pastoral Reflection on the Moral Life" (Washington, D.C.: United States Catholic Conference, 1976), pp. 24–25. Many Catholic theologians disagree with the Catholic Church's prohibition on the ordination of women, in part, precisely on human rights grounds. See Jackson, *Dignity and Solidarity*, p. 177.

52. Jackson, *Dignity and Solidarity*, p. 187.

53. Corson-Finnerty, *World Citizen*, p. 67.

54. Dee Brown, *Bury My Heart at Wounded Knee: An Indian History of the American West* (New York: Bantam Books, 1970).

55. Ibid., pp. 86–89. Some recent films dramatize this tragic history, for example, *Little Big Man,* directed by Arthur Penn and starring Dustin Hoffman (1970), and *Dances with Wolves,* directed by and starring Kevin Costner (1990).

56. Jackson, *Dignity and Solidarity,* pp. 188–89. See Alex Haley, *Roots* (Garden City, New York: Doubleday, 1976), and the made-for-TV movie based on this book for a good insight into the reality of slavery in the southern United States.

57. See John Howard Griffin, *Black Like Me* (New York: New American Library, 1960, 1961) for a moving account of the daily life of blacks in the segregated South.

58. See Taylor Branch, *Parting the Waters: America in the King Years 1954–63* (New York: Simon & Schuster, 1988) for a thorough account of the early Civil Rights movement, or David J. Garrow, *Bearing the Cross: Martin Luther King, Jr. and the Southern Christian Leadership Conference* (New York: William Morrow, 1986). Both books won the Pulitzer Prize. The PBS series "Eyes on the Prize," (1986) and "Eyes on the Prize II," (1989) (Boston: Blackside, Inc.) are excellent video documentaries of the Civil Rights movement.

59. For example, over 100 churches with predominantly black congregations, mainly in the South, were burned between January 1995 and the end of summer, 1996. About 20 percent of these arsons appear to have been racially motivated. Officials of the U.S. Commission on Civil Rights, which held community forums on the church arsons, discovered evidence of deep racial divisions in southern states. See "Church Fire Probe Finds Rise in Racial Tensions," *Hartford Courant* (October 10, 1996), p. A4.

Gordon Witkin and Jeannye Thornton ("Pride and Prejudice," *U.S. News and World Report* [July 15/22, 1996]: 74–76) discuss the rise of hate crimes and the resurgence of racism in the U.S.

60. Corson-Finnerty, *World Citizen,* pp. 68–69; Donnelly, *International Human Rights,* pp. 70–75, 121–25; H. Paul Santmire, *South African Testament* (Grand Rapids, Mich.: Wm. B. Eerdmans, 1987), pp. 6–11, passim; and Oliver Williams, *The Apartheid Crisis* (San Francisco: Harper & Row, 1986), especially chaps. 1 and 2. There are several good films that dramatize apartheid in South Africa: *A Dry White Season* (1989), directed by Euzhan Palcy; *A World Apart* (1988), directed by Chris Menges; *Mandela* (1987), directed by Philip Saville; *Master Harold and the Boys* (1986), directed by Michael Lindsay-Hogg.

61. See Ted Robert Gurr and Barbara Harff, *Ethnic Conflict in World Politics* (Boulder, Col.: Westview Press, 1994), pp. 65–75; Marlise Simons, "Tangier, a Magnet for Africans Slipping into Spain," *New York Times* (Aug. 26, 1996), p. A2. Judy Mayotte, *Disposable People? The Plight of Refugees* (Maryknoll, N.Y.: Orbis Books, 1992) discusses the situation of refugees in Cambodia, Afghanistan, Eritrea, and Sudan.

62. Corson-Finnerty, *World Citizen,* p. 66.

63. Calvin Sims, "For Blacks in Peru, There's No Room At the Top," *New York Times* (Aug. 17, 1996), p. A2.

64. Corson-Finnerty, *World Citizen,* p. 67.

65. There is voluminous literature on the Holocaust. See Jackson, *Dignity and Solidarity,* chap. 17; and Elie Wiesel, *Night* (New York: Bantam Books, 1960). The movie *Schindler's List,* directed by Steven Spielberg and starring Liam Neeson (1993), conveys the horror well.

66. Corson-Finnerty, *World Citizen,* pp. 69–70.

5. CONFLICT AND WAR

1. National Conference of Catholic Bishops (NCCB), "The Harvest of Justice is Sown in Peace," in *Peacemaking: Moral and Policy Challenges for a New World*, ed. Gerard F. Powers et al. (Washington, D.C.: United States Catholic Conference, 1994), pp. 329, 331.

2. This refrain is repeated several times in the conclusion of John Paul II's "Message for World Peace Day, Jan. 1, 2002," in the aftermath of the September 11 terrorist attacks (*America* [January 7–14, 2002], pp. 7–11, at 11).

3. See Lisa Sowle Cahill, *Love Your Enemies: Discipleship, Pacifism, and Just War Theory* (Minneapolis: Fortress Press, 1994); and Thomas A. Shannon, ed., *War or Peace? The Search for New Answers* (Maryknoll, N.Y.: Orbis Books, 1980).

4. See Glen H. Stassen, *Just Peacemaking: Transforming Initiatives for Justice and Peace* (Louisville: Westminster/John Knox Press, 1992); and Glen Stassen, ed., *Just Peacemaking: Ten Practices for Abolishing War* (Cleveland: Pilgrim Press, 1998).

5. This phrase is from Michael T. Klare, *Resource Wars: The New Landscape of Global Conflict* (New York: Metropolitan Books, Henry Holt & Co., 2001).

6. Francis Fukuyama, "The End of History," *The National Interest* (Summer, 1989), pp. 3–18.

7. Rodolfo Stavenhagen, "Ethnic Conflicts and Their Impact on International Society," *International Social Science Journal* 43 (February, 1991), pp. 118–19; James Lee Ray, *Global Politics* (Boston: Houghton Mifflin, 1995), pp. 112–14.

8. Ted Robert Gurr and Barbara Harff, *Ethnic Conflict in World Politics* (Boulder: Westview Press, 1994), p. 5.

9. Ibid., p. 144, see also pp. 18–26; Gidon Gottlieb, *Nation Against State: A New Approach to Ethnic Conflicts and the Decline of Sovereignty* (New York: Council on Foreign Relations, 1993), p. xii. Most often the nation lives in the territory it claims as its homeland, as with the Slovenes and Croats in the former Yugoslavia, or the Kurds in parts of Turkey, Iraq, Iran, and Syria. But the claim can also be primarily historical as with the Jews toward Israel prior to 1948.

10. Walker Connor, "From Tribe to Nation?" *History of European Ideas* 13 (1991), p. 6. Walker Connor, "The Specter of Ethno-Nationalist Movements Today," *PAWSS Perspectives* 1 (April, 1991), p. 2.

11. Connor, "From Tribe to Nation," p. 9.

12. Walker Connor, "Beyond Reason: The Nature of the Ethnonational Bond," *Ethnic and Racial Studies* 16 (July, 1993), p. 382.

13. Walker Connor, "When Is a Nation?" *Ethnic and Racial Studies* 13 (January, 1990), pp. 97–98.

14. Connor, "The Specter of Ethno-Nationalist Movements Today," p. 4.

15. Michael Ignatieff, *Blood and Belonging: Journeys Into the New Nationalism* (New York: Farrar, Straus and Giroux, 1993), pp. 37–38.

16. Bruce Russett and Harvey Starr, *World Politics* (New York: W. H. Freeman and Company, 1996), p. 54; Ray, *Global Politics*, p. 168.

17. Connor, "Beyond Reason," pp. 374–75; Connor, "The Specter of Ethno-Nationalist Movements Today," p. 3.

18. Gurr and Harff, *Ethnic Conflict in World Politics*, p. 5.

19. Gottlieb, *Nation Against State*, p. 78, referring to the Genocide Convention of 1948.

20. Joshua S. Goldstein, *International Relations* (New York: Harper-Collins, 1996), pp. 201–2.

21. Gottlieb, *Nation Against State,* p. 35.

22. Ted Robert Gurr, "Minorities and Nationalists: Managing Ethnopolitical Conflict in the New Century," in *Turbulent Peace: The Challenges of Managing International Conflict,* ed. Chester A. Crocker et al. (Washington, D.C.: United States Institute of Peace, 2001), pp. 164–66; and Gurr, *Peoples versus States: Minorities at Risk in the New Century* (Washington, D.C.: United States Institute of Peace, 2000), pp. 9–13. For figures in 1993 and 1994, see Ted Robert Gurr, "Communal Conflicts and Global Security," *Current History* 94 (May, 1995), pp. 212–14; and Gurr, *Minorities at Risk: A Global View of Ethnopolitical Conflicts* (Washington, D.C.: United States Institute of Peace Press, 1993); and the Appendix in Gurr and Harff, *Ethnic Conflict in World Politics,* pp. 159–65.

23. Gurr and Harff, *Ethnic Conflict in World Politics,* p. 17.

24. This section depends on Michael J. Himes and Kenneth R. Himes, *Fullness of Faith: The Public Significance of Theology* (Mahwah, N.J.: Paulist Press, 1993), Chapter 6, "Incarnation and Patriotism," pp. 125–56, and Chapter 7, "The Communion of Saints and an Ethic of Solidarity," pp. 157–83.

25. Ibid., p. 130.

26. John Paul II, "On Social Concern" (*Sollicitudo Rei Socialis,* December 30, 1987) in *Catholic Social Thought: The Documentary Heritage,* ed. David J. O'Brien and Thomas A. Shannon (Maryknoll, N.Y.: Orbis, 1992), #38, p. 421.

27. Himes and Himes, *Fullness of Faith,* p. 146.

28. Ignatieff, *Blood and Belonging,* pp. 6–8.

29. Jean Bethke Elshtain, "Identity, Sovereignty, and Self-Determination," in *Peacemaking,* ed. Powers et al., pp. 101–104.

30. Gurr and Harff, *Ethnic Conflict in World Politics,* pp. 139–44; Gottlieb, *Nation Against State,* p. 31, passim.

31. Goldstein, *International Relations,* p. 204; David Little, "Religious Nationalism and Human Rights," in *Peacemaking,* ed. Powers et al., pp. 88–89.

32. David Little, *Sri Lanka: The Invention of Enmity* (Washington, D.C.: United States Institute of Peace Press, 1994), pp. 103–07; Mark Juergensmeyer, "Religious Nationalism: A Global Threat?" *Current History* 95 (November, 1996), pp. 372–76.

33. Gurr, "Communal Conflicts and Global Security," p. 214; Douglas M. Johnston, "Religion and Conflict Resolution," *The Fletcher Forum of World Affairs* 20 (Winter, 1996), p. 53.

34. NCCB, "The Harvest of Justice Is Sown in Peace," in *Peacemaking,* ed. Powers et al., p. 329. Quote is from John Paul II, "To Build Peace, Respect Minorities," 1989 World Day of Peace Message, *Origins* 18 (December 29, 1988), p. 469. See also NCCB, "The Harvest of Justice Is Sown in Peace," p. 330, which says that authentic religion is the proper response to religiously authorized ethnic hatred. See Gerard F. Powers, "Conclusion: The Power of Virtue and the Virtue of Belief in Foreign Policy," in *Peacemaking,* ed. Powers et al., pp. 301–04; Gregory Baum and Harold Wells, eds., *The Reconciliation of Peoples: Challenge to the Churches* (Maryknoll, N.Y.: Orbis Books, 1997); and Johnston, "Religion and Conflict Resolution," pp. 53–60.

35. See Michael K. Duffey, *Sowing Justice, Reaping Peace: Case Studies of Racial, Religious, and Ethnic Healing Around the World* (Chicago: Sheed & Ward, 2001); and Mark Juergensmeyer, *Terror in the Mind of God: The Global Rise of Religious Violence* (Berkeley: University of California Press, 2000).

36. Gurr, *People versus States,* p. xiii.

37. No one knows this better than an author who is trying to write a book such

as this, hoping it will be of service in college courses for several years. In the first edition of this book I consciously did not address the Persian Gulf War of 1991. The conflict seemed resolved. The first time I used the book myself, in the spring of 1998, the big news story was Saddam Hussein throwing U.N. weapons inspectors out of Iraq, and the book had no background information on this conflict.

The first edition of this book included fairly detailed descriptions of five eth-nonationalist conflicts: Bosnia, Rwanda, Sri Lanka, Northern Ireland, and the Kurds. I have chosen breadth over depth in this edition.

38. John W. Mulhall, *America and the Founding of Israel: An Investigation of the Morality of America's Role* (Los Angeles: Deshon Press, 1995), pp. 60–72.

39. Ibid., pp. 137–62.

40. Ibid., pp. 163–66.

41. Duffey, *Sowing Justice, Reaping Peace*, pp. 118–23.

42. Ibid., pp. 127, 130–31. As of January 2003, more than 700 Israeli and 2000 Palestinians have been killed in this second *intifada*. See Thomas L. Friedman, "The New Math," *New York Times* (January 15, 2003), op. ed.

43. *New York Times* columnist Thomas R. Friedman has consistently taken this position.

44. Sara Roy, "Why Peace Failed: An Oslo Autopsy," *Current History* 101 (January, 2002), pp. 8–16.

45. George A. Lopez, "The Sanctions Dilemma," *Commonweal* (September 11, 1998), p. 12.

46. Mark Thompson, "The Forgotten War," *Time* (September 23, 2002), pp. 43–44.

47. Dan Morgan and Daid Ottaway, "Saddam's Ouster Could Mean Windfall for U.S. Petroleum Companies," *Courier-Journal* (September 16, 2002), p. A4.

48. Daniel Benjamin, "Saddam Hussein and Al Qaeda Are Not Allies," *New York Times* (September 30, 2002), op-ed page.

49. Gurr and Harff, *Ethnic Conflict in World Politics*, p. 30.

50. Ibid., p. 31; Ignatieff, *Blood and Belonging*, p. 179.

51. Marvin Zonis, "The Dispossessed: A Review of *A Modern History of the Kurds* by David McDowall (New York: I.B. Tauris/St. Martin's Press, 1996)," *New York Times Book Review* (March 10, 1996), p. 15.

52. Ignatieff, *Blood and Belonging*, pp. 194–98; Zonis, "The Dispossessed," p. 15.

53. Celestine Bohlen, "War on Rebel Kurds Puts Turkey's Ideals to Test," *New York Times* (July 16, 1995), p. 3; Celestine Bohlen, "In Turkey, Open Discussion of Kurds Is Casualty of Effort to Confront War," *New York Times* (October 29, 1995), p. 20; Ignatieff, *Blood and Belonging*, pp. 199–212; Zonis, "The Dispossessed," p. 14.

54. Tim Pat Coogan, *The Troubles: Ireland's Ordeal 1966–1996 and the Search for Peace* (Boulder: Roberts Rinehart Publishers, 1996), pp. 12–25. The film "Michael Collins" (1996), directed by Neil Jordan and with Liam Neeson in the title role, depicts the period from 1916–1922 in Irish history, but there is scant attention paid to Ulster. The neglect of Ulster at the time of the establishment of the Republic of Ireland seems to be historically accurate.

55. Michael MacDonald, *Children of Wrath: Political Violence in Northern Ireland* (Cambridge, England: Polity Press, 1986), p. 54.

56. See Ignatieff, *Blood and Belonging*, chap. 6. Although Ulster is commonly used to designate Northern Ireland, actually only six of its nine counties comprise Northern Ireland.

57. MacDonald, *Children of Wrath*, p. 25.

58. MacDonald, *Children of Wrath*, pp. 75–79; Ronnie Munck, "The Making of the Troubles," *Journal of Contemporary History* 27 (April, 1992), pp. 215–28; Sabine Wichert, "The Role of Nationalism in the Northern Ireland Conflict," *History of European Ideas* 16 (January, 1993), pp. 110–14.

59. James F. Clarity, "In What Passes for Peace in Ulster, Anxiety Still," *New York Times* (September 1, 1995), p. A3.

60. John Darnton, "After a Massacre in Ulster, Another Season of Fear," *New York Times* (November 1, 1993), pp. A1, A12.

61. Daniel Patrick Moynihan, *Pandaemonium: Ethnicity in International Politics* (New York: Oxford University Press, 1993), p. 15. See Ignatieff, *Blood and Belonging*, pp. 21–22.

62. This history is based primarily on Bill Weinberg and Dorie Wilsnak, *War at the Crossroads: An Historical Guide Through the Balkan Labyrinth* (New York: War Resister's League pamphlet, 1993).

63. Ignatieff, *Blood and Belonging*, pp. 22–23.

64. Josef Joffe, "Bosnia: The Return of History," *Commentary* 94 (October, 1992), p. 25.

65. Lenard J. Cohen, "Bosnia and Herzegovina: Fragile Peace in a Segmented State," *Current History* 95 (March, 1996), pp. 103, 111–12.

66. Marsha A. Hewitt, "Neither Bread Nor Roses: Women, War, & Intervention in the Balkans," *The Ecumenist* (May/June, 1994), p. 57.

67. James M. B. Lyon, "Will Bosnia Survive Dayton?" *Current History* (March 2000), pp. 110–16.

68. Roy Gutman, "Tragedy of Errors," *The New Republic* (October 26, 1998), pp. 17–18.

69. Ibid., p. 18; Howard Clark, "Kosovo's Distinctive History," *Fellowship* (July/August, 1999), pp. 4–6.

70. Lenard J. Cohen, "Kosovo: 'Nobody's Country,'" *Current History* (March, 2000), pp. 117–23.

71. Gurr, *People versus States*, pp. xiii–xiv.

72. Tariq Yasin, "Chechen Chagrin," *Harvard International Review* 24 (Spring, 2002), p. 7; Vera Tolz, "The War in Cechnya," *Current History* 95 (October, 1996), pp. 316–21; Anatol Lieven, "Chechnya: History as Nightmare," *New York Times* (November 3, 2002), p. wk3.

73. Yasin, "Chechen Chagrin," pp. 6–7; Masha Gessen, "Putin's War," *U. S. News and World Report* 132 (May 27, 2002), p. 24; Steven Lee Myers, "Russia Recasts Bog in Caucasus as War on Terror," *New York Times* (October 5, 2002), pp. A1, A6; Yevgenia Albats, "The Chechen War Comes Home," ibid. (October 26, 2002), op-ed page.

74. Christian Caryl, "Dispatches From Hell," *Newsweek* (May 27, 2002), p. 24; Myers, "Russia Recasts Bog," pp. A1, A6.

75. This section primarily relies on: David Little, *Sri Lanka: The Invention of Enmity* (Washington, D.C.: United States Institute of Peace Press, 1994); Kalpana Isaac, "Sri Lanka's Ethnic Divide," *Current History* 95 (April, 1996), pp. 177–79; and Lucinda Kaye, "Chances for Peace in Sri Lanka," *Peacework* 260 (February, 1996), pp. 7–11. See also Priit J. Vesilind, "Sri Lanka," *National Geographic* 191 (Jan., 1997), pp. 111–33.

76. See the following articles by John F. Burns in the *New York Times*: "A Corner of Sri Lanka Tires of Living Under Siege" (October 16, 1994); "After the Sri Lanka Violence: A Sense of Despair" (October 30, 1994); "Sri Lankans Hear Details of

Decade of Slaughter" (May 21, 1995); "Torn by War, Sri Lanka Faces Deepening Despair" (January 19, 1997).

77. Seth Mydans, "Sri Lankan Rebels in Talks with Government Say Autonomy Is Not Linked to Separate State," *New York Times* (September 19, 2002), p. A14.

78. "A Path to Peace in Kashmir," *New York Times* (November 24, 2000), editorial; Barry Bearak, "Kashmir a Crushed Jewel Caught in a Vise of Hatred," ibid. (August 12, 1999), pp. A1, A6.

79. Celia W. Dugger, "India Ends Kashmir Truce; Seeks Top-Level Pakistan Meeting," *New York Times* (May 24, 2001), p. A12.

80. Alex De Waal and Rakiya Omaar, "The Genocide in Rwanda and the International Response," *Current History* 94 (April 1995), p. 156.

81. The number of Tutsi killed is disputed. The *New York Times* now consistently reports that at least 500,000 Tutsi were killed during this period. See, for example, James C. McKinley Jr., "Old Revolutionary Is New Power to Be Reckoned With in Central Africa," *New York Times* (November 27, 1996), p. A12. De Waal and Omaar ("The Genocide in Rwanda," p. 156) put the number at 750,000 people slaughtered. Ann Rall ("Genocide in Rwanda—A Western-Made Massacre," *Peacework* 260 [February, 1996] says as many as one million were killed, including 300,000 children (p. 2). Whether the number is 500,000 or twice that, the massacre is an act of genocide. The estimate of the number of refugees resulting from this event (mostly Hutu) likewise varies from one million to two million.

82. Howard W. French, "The Anatomy of Autocracy: Mobutuism's Three Decades," *New York Times* (May 17, 1997), pp. 1, 7; and Nicholas D. Kristof, "In Congo, a New Era with Old Burdens," ibid. (May 29, 1997), pp. A1, A10.

83. Michela Wrong, "The Congo That Never Was," *New York Times* (January 29, 2001), op-ed page. See Ian Fisher et al., "Many Armies Ravage Rich Land in the 'First World War' of Africa," ibid. (February 6, 2000), pp. A1, A10–11.

84. James Astill, "Congo: An Everyday Story of Horror and Grief," *The Guardian* (July 24, 2002), p. 15.

85. Unless otherwise noted, Fisher, "Many Armies Ravage Rich Land," pp. A1, A10–11, is the source of what follows.

86. See the film "Black Hawk Down" (2001) for a sense of the fighting that occurred there.

87. "Eritreans and Ethiopians Sign Treaty to End Their Border War," *New York Times* (December 13, 2000), p. A12.

88. Norimitsu Onishi, "In Ruined Liberia, Its Despoiler Sits Pretty," *New York Times* (December 7, 2000), p. A1, A20.

89. John F. Burns, "Unforeseen Strife Eases for Algeria," *New York Times* (March 7, 1999), pp. A1, A6.

90. Duffey, *Sowing Justice, Reaping Peace*, pp. 11–18.

91. NCCB, *The Harvest of Justice Is Sown in Peace*, p. 336.

92. J. Bryan Hehir, "Intervention: From Theories to Cases," *Ethics and International Affairs* 9 (1995), pp. 3–6; Kenneth R. Himes, "The Morality of Humanitarian Intervention," *Theological Studies* 55 (1994), pp. 84–85, 92–93.

93. Hehir, "Intervention," p. 8; Himes, "The Morality of Humanitarian Intervention," p. 97.

94. Hehir, "Intervention," p. 13.

95. Himes, "The Morality of Humanitarian Intervention," p. 97.

96. See J. Milburn Thompson, "Purposeful Intervention, Christian Ethics, and the Case of Haiti," *Journal for the Study of Peace and Conflict* (1997–98), pp. 65–77.

97. Kenneth R. Himes, "Catholic Social Thought and Humanitarian Intervention," in *Peacemaking,* ed. Powers et al., pp. 218–20; NCCB, *The Harvest of Justice Is Sown in Peace,* p. 337.

98. NCCB, *The Challenge of Peace* (1983) in *Catholic Social Thought,* ed. O'Brien and Shannon, #66–121.

99. See Richard B. Miller, "Casuistry, Pacifism, and the Just War Tradition in the Post-Cold War Era," in *Peacemaking,* ed. Powers et al., pp. 205–09; Robert Phillips and Duane L. Cady, *Humanitarian Intervention: Just War vs. Pacifism* (Lanham, Md.: Rowman & Littlefield, 1996). Cady explicates the position of a philosophical pacifist; and Himes, "Catholic Social Thought and Humanitarian Intervention," pp. 224–35.

100. Hehir, "Intervention," pp. 7–8; Cady, *Humanitarian Intervention,* pp. 61–62; NCCB, *The Harvest of Justice Is Sown in Peace,* p. 337.

101. Hehir, "Intervention," p. 8.

102. See Hehir, "Intervention," pp. 9, 11–13; Himes, "The Morality of Humanitarian Intervention," pp. 100–1.

103. Hehir, "Intervention," p. 9; Himes, "The Morality of Humanitarian Intervention," pp. 98–100.

104. This is the argument of Robert Phillips in *Humanitarian Intervention.* See also J. Milburn Thompson, "Why Send in the Troops? Christian Ethics and Humanitarian Intervention," *Theology: Expanding the Borders: The Annual of the College Theology Society,* Vol. 43, ed. Maria Pilar Aquino and Roberto S. Goizueta (Mystic, Conn.: Twenty-Third Publications, 1998), pp. 320–33.

105. Himes, "Catholic Social Teaching and Humanitarian Intervention," p. 227.

106. Himes, "The Morality of Humanitarian Intervention," pp. 101–4; Hehir, "Intervention," p. 13.

107. Hehir, "Intervention," pp. 10–11; Himes, "The Morality of Humanitarian Intervention," pp. 101–2.

108. Glen H. Stassen, *Just Peacemaking: Transforming Initiatives for Justice and Peace* (Louisville: Westminster/John Knox Press, 1992); and Glen H. Stassen, ed., *Just Peacemaking: Ten Practices for Abolishing War* (Cleveland: Pilgrim Press, 1998).

109. Stassen, *Just Peacemaking: Transforming Initiatives,* pp. 89–113.

110. J. Milburn Thompson, "Humanitarian Intervention, Just Peacemaking, and the United Nations," *Concilium, 2001/2: The Return of the Just War,* ed. Maria Pilar Aquino and Dietmar Mieth (London: SCM Press, 2001), pp. 83–93.

111. "Text of President Bush's Speech," *Courier-Journal* (September 21, 2001), op-ed page.

112. John Paul II, "Message for World Peace Day, January 1, 2002," *America* 186 (January 7–14, 2002), p. 8.

113. James Burtchaell, "A Moral Response to Terrorism," in his *The Giving and Taking of Life: Essays Ethical* (South Bend, Ind.: University of Notre Dame Press, 1989), pp. 213–16. This section depends heavily on this essay, which was originally published in *Fighting Back: Winning the War against Terrorism,* ed. Neil Livingstone and Terrell Arnold (Lanham, Md.: Lexington Books, 1986).

114. Burtchaell says, "But for whoever must respond morally to a terrorist act, it surely makes a difference whether it is the work of a tyrant or of the tyrant's victims" ("A Moral Response to Terrorism," p. 216).

115. "The discernment of justice will be sensitive to whether the terrorists are a group that attempts to manipulate a larger people or a group that has been manhandled" (ibid., p. 227).

116. In 1986, Burtchaell wrote, "The history of the State of Israel is the world's best contemporary example of how incessant resistance to injustice cannot be repressed by reprisals" (ibid., p. 228).

117. In this regard, Ishai Menuchin, a major in the Israel Defense Forces Reserves and a leader of the soldiers' movement for selective refusal, wrote in an essay in the *New York Times,* "After 35 years of Israel's occupation of the West Bank and Gaza, the two sides seem only to have grown accustomed to assassinations, bombings, terrorist attacks, and house demolitions. Each side characterizes its own soldiers as either 'defense forces' or 'freedom fighters' when in truth these soldiers take part in war crimes on a daily basis" ("Saying No to Israel's Occupation," [March 9, 2002], op-ed page). Menuchin and others, while continuing to serve in Israel's defense forces, are selectively refusing to obey orders to go into the West Bank or Gaza or to commit what they judge to be war crimes.

118. John Kelsay, "Bin Laden's Reasons," *The Christian Century* (February 27–March 6, 2002), p. 26.

119. Ibid., p. 29. This chilling quote is taken directly from the February 23, 1998, statement, "Jihad Against Jews and Crusaders," by the World Islamic Front, which is reprinted in the article in *The Christian Century*. Kelsay points out how this *fatwa* twists and misinterprets the Qur'an.

120. Burtchaell, "A Moral Response to Terrorism," p. 228.

121. Richard Falk, "A Just Response," *The Nation* 273 (October 8, 2001), pp. 11–15; J. Bryan Hehir, "What Can Be Done? What Should Be Done?" *America* 185 (October 8, 2001), pp. 9–12; Susan Sontag, "Real Battles and Empty Metaphors," *New York Times* (September 10, 2002), op-ed page; Paul Krugman, "The Long Haul," ibid.

122. Thomas L. Friedman, "Better Late Than . . .," *New York Times* (March 17, 2002), op-ed page.

123. Glen H. Stassen, "Turning Attention to Just Peacemaking Initiatives That Prevent Terrorism," *Bulletin of the Council of Societies for the Study of Religion* 31 (September, 2002), p. 61.

124. The pastoral message of the United States Conference of Catholic Bishops titled, "Living with Faith and Hope after September 11" (November 14, 2001, available at www.usccb.org), while affirming the right of the state to defend itself, stresses the importance of spreading the benefits of globalization to all and especially to the poor and of working for the global common good through constructive diplomacy in the Israeli-Palestinian conflict, by removing economic sanctions on Iraq, by affirming human rights, by reversing the spread of weapons of mass destruction and reducing the U.S. role in the arms trade, and by strengthening the U.N. and other international institutions.

125. Gottlieb, in *Nation against State,* suggests new ideas and institutions.

6. WEAPONS AND DISARMAMENT

1. National Conference of Catholic Bishops, *The Challenge of Peace* (1986) in David J. O'Brien and Thomas A. Shannon, eds., *Catholic Social Thought: The Documentary Heritage* (Maryknoll, N.Y.: Orbis Books, 1992), #219. Quote from John Paul II, "Homily at Bagington Airport," Coventry, England, #2, *Origins* 12 (1982): 55.

2. Michael T. Klare, "Deadly Convergence: The Arms Trade, Nuclear/Chemical/ Missile Proliferation, and Regional Conflict in the 1990s," in *World Security: Trends*

and Challenges at Century's End, ed. Michael Klare and Daniel Thomas (New York: St. Martin's Press, 1991), pp. 170–196.

3. Rakiya Omaar, "Somalia: At War with Itself," *Current History* 91 (October 1991), p. 231.

4. It needs to be remembered that nuclear terrorism was a way for the West to stand against the terrorism represented by the totalitarian Communist system. Thus, with the end of the Cold War, the people of the West could shed their fear of an attack from the East and of imminent nuclear holocaust, and the people of the East could shed their fear of a midnight knock on the door and of imminent nuclear holocaust.

5. This description is based on Ronald Sider and Richard Taylor, *Nuclear Holocaust & Christian Hope* (Downers Grove, Ill.: InterVarsity Press, 1982), chap. 1; Richard McSorley, *Kill? For Peace?* (Washington, D.C.: Georgetown University, Center for Peace Studies, 1977), chap. 1; John Hershey, *Hiroshima* (New York: Bantam, 1956); and informational material from Physicians for Social Responsibility, including the film *The Last Epidemic: Medical Consequences of Nuclear Weapons and Nuclear War*.

6. Jonathan Schell, *The Fate of the Earth* (New York: Knopf, 1982), pp. 181–82. Originally published in *The New Yorker* (February 15, 1982), p. 45.

7. The film *Crimson Tide* (1995) (directed by Tony Scott, starring Denzel Washington and Gene Hackman) dramatizes both the possibility of a change for the worse in Russia and the power of the captain of a nuclear submarine.

8. See Bill Keller, "Nuclear Nightmares," *New York Times Magazine* (May 26, 2002), pp. 22–29, 51, 54–57.

9. On the controversy about using the atomic bomb, see Guy Alperovitz, "Use of the Atomic Bomb Was Not Inevitable," *The Hartford Courant* (October 23, 1994), pp. C1, C4; Ronald Takaki, *Hiroshima: Why America Dropped the Atomic Bomb* (Boston: Little, Brown and Company, 1995).

10. "Belarus Gives Up Last Nuclear Missile," *The Hartford Courant* (November 1996), p. A7; Jane Perlez, "Sunflower Seeds Replace Ukraine's Old Missile Sites," *New York Times* (June 5, 1996), p. A5.

11. "Nuclear Breakthrough in Korea," *New York Times* editorial (October 19, 1994); "North Korea Nuclear Plan Gains," *New York Times* (September 30, 1996), p. A8.

12. Joseph Cirincione, "The Non-Proliferation Treaty and the Nuclear Balance," *Current History* 94 (May 1995), pp. 201–06; Barbara Crossette, "Discord over Renewing Pact on Spread of Nuclear Arms," *New York Times* (April 17, 1995), p. A1; Zachary S. Davis, "Nuclear Proliferation and Nonproliferation Policy in the 1990s," in *World Security*, ed. Klare and Thomas, pp. 106–33; "A Nuclear Milestone," *New York Times* editorial (May 12, 1995).

13. Paul Walker, *Seizing the Initiative: First Steps to Disarmament* (Philadelphia: American Friends Service Committee, 1983), pp. 8–16; Joshua Goldstein, *International Relations*, 2nd ed. (New York: HarperCollins, 1996), pp. 259–62.

14. Allan S. Krass, "Death and Transfiguration: Nuclear Arms Control in the 1980s and 1990s," in *World Security*, ed. Klare and Thomas, pp. 75–79.

Strategic nuclear weapons are those that can be delivered from one superpower to the other. *Intermediate* nuclear weapons have a shorter, yet significant range. They could be fired from France to Russia, for example, or from Russia to China. *Tactical* nuclear weapons are designed for battlefield use. Their range is shorter and they have less power, although there is no such thing as a nuclear weapon that is genuinely limited in its blast effect, or truly discriminate in its target or effect.

15. Allen Krass, "The Second Nuclear Era," in Klare and Thomas, *World Society*, pp. 92–93.

16. Peter Gray, *Briefing Book on U.S. Leadership and the Future of Nuclear Arsenals* (Washington, D.C.: Council for a Livable World Education Fund, 1996), p. 12; Steven Erlanger, "After 3-Year Wait, START II Wins Senate Approval But Still Faces Russian Opposition," *New York Times* (January 27, 1996), p. 5; Mikhail Gorbachev, "NATO's Plans Threaten START II," *New York Times* (February 10, 1996), op-ed page; David Hoffman, "Future of Arms Limitations Cloudy in Wake of Helsinki Summit," *New York Times* (March 23, 1997), p. A15; Thomas L. Friedman, "It's Unclear," *New York Times* (June 2, 1997), op-ed page.

17. "Russia, Iran and the Bomb," *New York Times* editorial (Feb. 26, 1995). In 1996 Russia was also selling weapons-grade material to France and Germany, despite a U.S.-imposed embargo on such sales (Paul Leventhal, "The Nuclear End Run," *New York Times* [June 5, 1996], op-ed page).

18. Michael R. Gordon, "Russia Struggles in Long Race to Prevent an Atomic Theft," *New York Times* (April 20, 1996), pp. 1, 4; Philip Shenon, "Ex-Soviet A-Bomb Fuel an Easy Target for Terrorists, U.S. Says," *New York Times* (March 13, 1996), p. A5; Tim Zimmerman and Alan Cooperman, "The Russian Connection," *U.S. News & World Report* 119 (October 23, 1995), pp. 56–67; Jane Perlez, "Tracing a Nuclear Risk: Stolen Enriched Uranium," *New York Times* (February 15, 1995); Craig R. Whitney, "Germans Seize 3rd Atom Sample, Smuggled by Plane From Russia," *New York Times* (August 14, 1994), p. 1; Michael R. Gordon and Matthew L. Wald, "Russian Controls on Bomb Material Are Leaky," *New York Times* (August 18, 1994), p. 1; and Matthew L. Wald and Michael R. Gordon, "Russia Treasures Plutonium, But U.S. Wants to Destroy It," *New York Times* (August 19, 1994), p. 1; Bruce W. Nelan, "Formula For Terror," *Time* (August 29, 1994), pp. 47–51.

19. Russia is clearly the cause of most concern in this regard. Yet when the U.S. made public the records of all the plutonium that ever passed through federal hands, Washington disclosed that it had shipped three-quarters of a ton of plutonium to 39 countries under the Atoms for Peace program. All of these transfers were legal; many of them involved small amounts; and none of the plutonium was of bomb-grade quality. Nevertheless, experts say that these peaceful transfers undoubtedly aided the development of nuclear arms in some cases (William J. Broad, "U.S. Sent Ton of Plutonium to 39 Countries," *New York Times* [February 6, 1996], p. A10). China provokes anxiety on this matter as well (Patrick E. Tyler, "China Raises Nuclear Stakes on the Subcontinent," *New York Times* [August 27, 1996], p. A6); A. M. Rosenthal, "The Nuclear Gamble," *New York Times* (October 11, 1996), op-ed page.

20. Matthew L. Wald, "Nuclear Lapses Raise Questions of Safety," *New York Times* (June 26, 1996), pp. A1, A16.

21. Peter Passell, "Profit Motive Clouding Effort to Buy Up A-Bomb Material," *New York Times* (August 28, 1996), p. A1, D3; William J. Broad, "Deal for U.S. to Buy Bomb Fuel From Russia Said to Be in Peril," *New York Times* (June 12, 1995), p. 1.

22. On the above problems, see Krass, "The Second Nuclear Era," pp. 85–105; Matthew L. Wald, "Agency to Pursue 2 Plans to Shrink Plutonium Supply," *New York Times* (December 10, 1996), pp. A1, B8; Peter Passell, "U.S. Set to Allow Reactors to Use Plutonium from Disarmed Bombs," *New York Times* (November 22, 1996), pp. A1, D18; Matthew L. Wald, "Factory Set to Process Dangerous Nuclear Waste," *New York Times* (March 13, 1996), p. A16; Matthew L. Wald, "Plan for Managing Nuclear Arms Leaves a Tough Issue Unresolved," *New York*

Times (February 29, 1996), p. A18; Matthew L. Wald, "Today's Drama: The Twilight of the Nukes," *New York Times* (July 16, 1995), p. E5.

23. Matthew L. Wald, "Big Price Tag for A-Bombs, Study Finds: 50 Year Cost to U.S. Is Almost $4 Trillion," *New York Times* (July 12, 1995); Stephen I. Schwartz, "Atomic Audit: What the U.S. Nuclear Arsenal Has Cost," *The Brookings Review* (Fall 1995): 14–17.

24. *The Pastoral Constitution on the Church in the Modern World*, in *The Documents of Vatican II*, ed. Walter Abbott, trans. Joseph Gallagher (London: Geoffrey Chapman, 1966), # 81.

25. Matthew L. Wald ("Study Finds Destruction in the Making of A-Bombs," *New York Times* [July 26, 1995], p. A12) reports on a study produced over six years by the International Physicians for the Prevention of Nuclear War, winners of the Nobel Peace Prize in 1985, on the environmental damage from the nuclear weapons program. See Arjun Makhijani and Katherine Yih, eds., *Nuclear Wastelands: A Global Guide to Nuclear Weapons Production and Its Health and Environmental Effects* (Cambridge, Mass.: MIT Press, 1995).

26. Jessica Stern, "Preventing Portable Nukes," *New York Times* (April 10, 1996), op-ed page.

27. Goldstein, *International Relations*, pp. 245–47.

28. These church documents are available from the United States Catholic Conference in Washington, D.C. *The Challenge of Peace* and *Peace on Earth* can also be found in *Catholic Social Thought*, ed. O'Brien and Shannon, and *The Harvest of Justice Is Sown in Peace* is included in *Peacemaking: Moral and Policy Challenges for a New World*, ed. Gerard F. Powers et al. (Washington, D.C.: U.S.C.C., 1994), reference at p. 333.

29. Cirincione, "The Non-Proliferation Treaty and the Nuclear Balance," p. 205. See Selig S. Harrison, "Zero Nuclear Weapons. Zero," *New York Times* (February 15, 1995), op-ed page; Gray, *Briefing Book on U.S. Leadership and the Future of Nuclear Arsenals*, which presents the debate about deterrence or disarmament and argues for the latter. See Richard N. Haass, "It's Dangerous to Disarm," *New York Times* (December 11, 1996), op-ed page, for a dissenting view.

30. Cirincione, "The Non-Proliferation Treaty and the Nuclear Balance," p. 205; "General Suggests U.S. Get Rid of Nuclear Arms," *The Hartford Courant* (July 16, 1994).

31. "Nuclear Commitments," *New York Times* editorial (June 12, 1995).

32. Tim Weiner, "Huge Chemical Arms Plant Near Completion in Libya, U.S. Says," *New York Times* (February 25, 1996), p. 8; A. M. Rosenthal, "Shall We Wait and See?" ibid. (February 27, 1996), op-ed page.

33. Goldstein, *International Relations*, pp. 250–51.

34. Jonathon B. Tucker, "The Chemical Weapons Convention: Has It Enhanced U.S. Security?" *Arms Control Today* 31 (April 2001): 8–12.

35. Jon Kyl, "A Treaty That Deserved to Die," *New York Times* (Sept. 13, 1996), op-ed page; George F. Will, "A Piece of Paper Won't Stop Evildoers," *The Hartford Courant* (September 9, 1996), op-ed page; and "A Flawed Pact That Won't Limit Chemical Weapons," ibid. (May 1, 1997), op-ed page.

36. Tucker, "The Chemical Weapons Convention."

37. Ibid.

38. Seth Grugger, "U.S. to Miss Chemical Weapons Convention Deadline," *Arms Control Today* 31 (November 2001), p. 24.

39. James Brooke, "At Utah Plant, Safety Debate Rages," *New York Times* (November 28, 1996), p. A4. See Jill Smolowe, "Chemical Time Bombs," *Time* 147 (February 12, 1996), pp. 42–43.

40. Barbara Crossette, "A Russian Scientist Cautions Chemical Arms Safety Is Lax," *New York Times* (October 1, 1995), p. 12.

41. Michael Crowley, "Combating Biological Weapons," *UN Chronicle* 39 (June–August 2002): 73–75.

42. Jonathan B. Tucker, "Putting Teeth In the Biological Weapons Convention," *Issues in Science and Technology* 18 (Spring 2002): 71–77; Susan Wright, "U.S. Vetoes Verification," *Bulletin of the Atomic Scientists* 58 (March/April 2002): 24–26.

43. Goldstein, *International Relations*, pp. 251–52.

44. Anne Goldfield and Holly Nyers, "Declare a Moratorium on the Use of Land Mines," *The Hartford Courant* (July 21, 1995), op-ed page.

45. "Ottawa Convention States Meet," *Arms Control Today* 31 (October 2001): 24; and Kevin Fedarko, "Land Mines: Cheap, Deadly and Cruel," *Time* 147 (May 13, 1996), p. 54.

46. "The Land Mine Wars," *National Geographic* 201 (May, 2002), pp. 20–22; and Christopher S. Wren, "Everywhere, Weapons That Keep on Killing," *New York Times* (October 8, 1995), p. E3.

47. Goldfield and Nyers, "Declare a Moratorium on the Use of Land Mines."

48. Bernard E. Trainor, "Land Mines Saved My Life," *New York Times* (March 27, 1996), op-ed page.

49. Barbara Crossette, "Pact on Land Mines Stops Short of Total Ban," *New York Times* (May 4, 1996), p. 4.

50. "Bush Team Shies From Clinton Landmine Policy," *Arms Control Today* 31 (September 2001): 38.

51. Gill Donovan, "Report Cites Global Progress in Eliminating Land Mines," *National Catholic Reporter* (September 28, 2001), p. 11, and "Ottawa Convention States Meet," p. 24.

52. Michael T. Klare, "Adding Fuel to the Fire: The Conventional Arms Trade in the 1990s," in *World Security*, ed. Klare and Thomas, pp. 134–54, at 147.

53. Klare, "Adding Fuel to the Fire," pp. 147–48; Klare, "Deadly Convergence," pp. 186–87.

54. Mark R. Amstutz, *International Conflict and Cooperation: An Introduction to World Politics* (Madison, Wis.: Brown & Benchmark, 1995), p. 383.

55. Charles M. Sennott, "Armed for Profit: The Selling of U.S. Weapons," *Boston Globe* (February 11, 1996), A Special Report, p. B2.

56. Klare, "Adding Fuel to the Fire," pp. 134, 139; and Michael T. Klare and Lora Lumpe, "Fanning the Flames of War: Conventional Arms Transfers in the 1990s," in *World Security*, ed. Michael T. Klare and Yogesh Chandrani, 3rd ed. (New York: St. Martin's Press, 1998), pp. 166–67.

57. Klare, "Adding Fuel to the Fire," pp. 139–42.

58. Sennott, "Armed for Profit," p. B2; Klare and Lumpe, "Fanning the Flames of War," p. 172.

59. Sennott, "Armed for Profit," p. B11, also B7; see James Sterngold, "A Swift Transformation," *New York Times* (December 16, 1996), pp. A1, D14.

60. Sennott, "Armed for Profit," p. B12. The salaries of the next four highest paid CEOs ranged from $1.6 to $4.6 million.

61. Klare, "Adding Fuel to the Fire," p. 138.

62. Klare, "Adding Fuel to the Fire," pp. 134–36.

63. Klare and Lumpe, "Fanning the Flames of War," pp. 170–71.

64. Jeffrey Boutwell and Michael T. Klare, eds. *Light Weapons and Civil Conflict: Controlling the Tools of Violence* (New York: Rowman and Littlefield, 1999). This

book was supported by the Carnegie Commission on Preventing Deadly Conflict and the American Academy of Arts and Sciences and contains excellent essays and bibliographies on this issue.

65. Sennott, "Armed for Profit," pp. B6, B8.

66. Ibid., p. B6.

67. Klare and Lumpe, "Fanning the Flames of War," pp. 161–63.

68. Klare, "Adding Fuel to the Fire," pp. 148–51; Klare and Lumpe, "Fanning the Flames of War," pp. 172–76. Regarding the control of light weapons, see Jeffrey Boutwell and Michael T. Klare, "Light Weapons and Civil Conflict: Policy Options for the International Community," in their *Light Weapons and Civil Conflict*, chap. 14, pp. 217–30.

69. Sennott, "Armed for Profit," p. B4. Although the amount of military spending held steady, as a percentage of GDP military spending decreased by nearly half, from 6.3 percent of GDP in 1986 to 3.6 percent in 1996. The number of personnel in uniform declined by about 25 percent in the 1990s.

70. Michael T. Klare, "Endless Military Superiority," *The Nation* 275 (July 15, 2002), pp. 12–16.

71. "Military Spending Threatens Nation's Priorities," *The National Catholic Reporter* (January 18, 2002), p. 20.

72. Goldstein, *International Relations*, pp. 224–26; Bruce Russett and Harvey Starr, *World Politics: The Menu for Choice* (New York: W. H. Freeman, 1996), pp. 295–96.

73. Klare, "Endless Military Superiority."

7. PEACE AND SECURITY IN THE TWENTY-FIRST CENTURY

1. National Conference of Catholic Bishops (NCCB), *The Harvest of Justice Is Sown in Peace* (Nov. 17, 1993) in Gerard F. Powers et al., eds., *Peacemaking: Moral and Policy Challenges for a New World* (Washington, D.C.: United States Catholic Conference, 1994), pp. 340–41.

2. Leslie H. Gelb, "Fresh Faces," *New York Times Magazine* (Dec. 8, 1991), pp. 50–54. Gelb suggests that the new thinking needed in foreign policy requires "fresh faces" making policy and decisions.

3. George Weigel, "Back to Basics: Moral Reasoning and Foreign Policy 'After Containment,'" in Powers et al., eds., *Peacemaking*, pp. 57–60.

4. Joshua S. Goldstein, *International Relations* (New York: HarperCollins, 1996), pp. 52–53; Pierre de Senarclens, "The 'Realist' Paradigm and International Conflicts," *International Social Science Journal* 43 (February 1991): 5–6; Richard Falk, "Theory, Realism, and World Security," in Michael Klare and Daniel Thomas, eds., *World Security: Trends and Challenges at Century's End* (New York: St. Martin's Press, 1991), pp. 10–17.

5. Besides the sources in the previous note, see Michael Klare and Daniel Thomas, "Introduction: Thinking About World Security," in their *World Security: Challenges for a New Century*, 2nd. ed. (New York: St. Martin's Press, 1994), p. 2; Seyom Brown, "World Interests and the Changing Dimensions of Security," *World Security*, pp. 10–12; and Charles W. Kegley, Jr. and Eugene R. Wittkopf, *World Politics: Trend and Transformation*, 6th ed. (New York: St. Martin's Press, 1997), pp. 22–25.

6. de Senarclens, "The 'Realist' Paradigm and International Conflicts," p. 9.

7. Ibid., p. 17.

8. Brown, "World Interests and the Changing Dimensions of Security," pp. 10–26; Falk, "Theory, Realism, and World Security," pp. 19–21; Goldstein, *International Relations,* p. 96.

9. Klare and Thomas, "Introduction: Thinking About World Security," pp. 2–3.

10. See Robert C. Johansen, "Building World Security: The Need for Strengthened International Institutions," in Klare and Thomas, eds., *World Security: Challenges For a New Century,* pp. 374–76; Charles W. Kegley, Jr., "The New Global Order: The Power of Principle in a Pluralistic World," in Joel H. Rosenthal, ed., *Ethics and International Affairs: A Reader* (Washington, D.C.: Georgetown University Press, 1995), p. 123; Gerard F. Powers, "Conclusion: The Power of Virtue, the Virtue of Belief in Foreign Policy," in Powers et al., eds., *Peacemaking,* p. 305; Goldstein, *International Relations,* pp. 104–08.

11. Goldstein, *International Relations,* pp. 104–06. See David C. Hendrickson, "The Ethics of Collective Security," in Rosenthal, ed., *Ethics and International Affairs,* pp. 197–212, for a critical discussion of collective security.

12. Michael T. Klare, "Redefining Security: The New Global Schisms," *Current History* 95 (November 1996): 353–58, at 358.

13. Chester A. Crocker and Fen Osler Hampson, with Pamela Aall, eds., *Managing Global Chaos: Sources of and Responses to International Conflict* (Washington, D.C.: United States Institute of Peace, 1996); cf. Klare, "Redefining Security," pp. 353–58.

14. Crocker, Hampson, and Aall, eds., *Managing Global Chaos,* "Conclusion," pp. 624–26.

15. Chester A. Crocker, Fen Osler Hampson, and Pamela Aall, eds., *Turbulent Peace: The Challenges of Managing International Conflict* (Washington, D.C.: United States Institute of Peace, 2001), "Introduction," pp. xv–xvii.

16. Johansen, "Building World Security," p. 376.

17. This analysis is primarily drawn from Michael Klare, *Rogue States and Nuclear Outlaws: America's Search for a New Foreign Policy* (New York: Hill & Wang, 1995), chap. 7, "Beyond the Rogues: Military Doctrine in a World of Chaos"; and Johansen, "Building World Security," pp. 372–97.

18. See, for example, Mark Juergensmeyer, *Fighting Fair: A Nonviolent Strategy for Resolving Everyday Conflicts* (San Francisco: Harper & Row, 1986); Glen H. Stassen, *Just Peacemaking: Transforming Initiatives for Justice and Peace* (Louisville: Westminster/John Knox Press, 1992); and Roger Fisher and William Ury, with Bruce Patton, *Getting to Yes: Negotiating Agreement Without Giving In* (New York: Penguin Books, 1983).

19. Kegley, "The New Global Order," p. 121. Although Kegley emphasizes reciprocity, toward the end of his article he seems to reduce the Golden Rule to "Let's leave one another alone." Reciprocity might be more effective when it is more active and more interventionist.

20. Johansen, "Building World Security," p. 377.

21. Klare, *Rogue States,* pp. 214–15.

22. *Human Development Report 2002: Deepening Democracy in a Fragmented World* (New York: Oxford University Press, 2002), p. 120.

23. Ibid., p. 215; NCCB, *The Harvest of Justice Is Sown in Peace,* p. 325; Johansen, "Building World Security," pp. 378, 389–91; Charles William Maynes, "Containing Ethnic Conflict," *Foreign Policy* (Spring 1993): 6–11; Brian Urquhart, "For a U.N. Volunteer Military Force," *New York Review of Books* (June 10, 1993); Brian Hall, "Blue Helmets, Empty Guns," *New York Times Magazine* (Jan.2, 1994),

pp. 19–28ff; Paul Lewis, "U.N. Panel Proposes Expanding Security Council to 24 Members," *New York Times* (March 21, 1997), p. A13.

24. See Michael Doyle, "War Making and Peace Making: The United Nations' Post-Cold War Record," in Crocker et al., eds., *Turbulent Peace*; Margaret P. Karns and Karen A. Mingst, "Maintaining International Peace and Security: UN Peacekeeping and Peacemaking," in Klare and Thomas, eds. *World Security: Challenges for a New Century,* pp. 188–215; and Alvaro de Soto, "Strengthening Global Institutions," in Powers et al., eds., *Peacemaking,* pp. 149–64.

25. Klare, *Rogue States,* p. 215; NCCB, *The Harvest of Justice Is Sown in Peace,* p. 325.

26. NCCB, *The Harvest of Justice Is Sown in Peace,* p. 327.

27. Johansen, "Building World Security," pp. 379–81. Johansen analyzes separately the principles of "equity" and "sustainability." See Klare, *Rogue States,* p. 217.

28. Thomas L. Friedman, *The Lexus and the Olive Tree* (New York: Farrar, Straus and Giroux, 1999), chapter 10. Since his book was published there has been one exception to his theory—the NATO bombing of Belgrade, Serbia (which had a McDonald's), but Friedman has argued that this exception confirms his point.

29. Johansen, "Building World Security," pp. 379–82.

30. Johansen, "Building World Security," pp. 385–86; NCCB, *The Harvest of Justice Is Sown in Peace,* p. 326.

31. Bruce Russett, "Peace and the Moral Imperative of Democracy," in Powers et al., eds, *Peacemaking,* pp. 105–15, at 107.

32. *Human Development Report 2002: Deepening Democracy in a Fragmented World,* pp. 1, 2, 14–15, passim.

33. Russett, "Peace and the Moral Imperative of Democracy," p. 107.

34. Johansen, "Building World Security," p. 384.

35. Ibid., p. 387.

36. Klare, *Rogue States,* p. 217. Chapter 6 outlines a regime for reducing the arms trade.

37. The following updates the elegant argument in Klare, *Rogue States.*

38. See Chris Hedges "Studying Bosnia's U.S. 'Prisoners of Peace'," *New York Times* (March 30, 1997), p. 11 for a discussion of the morale and psychological problems that arise when troops trained for combat are used for peacekeeping missions, such as in Bosnia.

39. "School of Dictators," *New York Times* (Sept. 28, 1996), editorial; "Be All You Can Be: Your Future as an Extortionist," *New York Times* (Oct. 6, 1996), p. E9; Dana Priest, "U.S. Instructed Latins on Executions, Torture," *Washington Post* (Sept. 21, 1996), pp. A1, A9; and Jack Nelson-Pallmeyer, *School of Assassins: Guns, Greed, and Globalization,* rev. ed. (Maryknoll, N.Y.: Orbis Books, 2001). Father Roy Bourgeois, a Maryknoll priest who lived and worked with the poor in Bolivia, has established "School of the Americas (SOA) Watch" (PO Box 4566, Washington, D.C. 20017; 202 234-3440; www.soaw.org) to educate Americans about the SOA and to lobby Congress to close it. An educational film titled "School of Assassins" is available from Maryknoll, New York 10545.

8. CHRISTIAN FAITH, JESUS, AND CATHOLIC SOCIAL TEACHING

1. National Conference of Catholic Bishops (NCCB), *The Challenge of Peace: God's Promise and Our Response* in David J. O'Brien and Thomas A. Shannon, eds., *Catholic Social Thought: The Documentary Heritage* (Maryknoll, N.Y.: Orbis Books, 1992), #276, pp. 551–52.

2. See chapter 5 of the Song of Solomon in the Hebrew Scriptures where the female lover wearies her friends with talk of her beloved.

3. Marcus J. Borg, *Meeting Jesus Again for the First Time* (San Francisco: HarperSanFrancisco, 1994), pp. 31–32. This section on Jesus as a spirit person relies on Borg, pp. 30–39.

4. All three synoptic Gospels—Matthew, Mark, and Luke—have accounts of these visions by Jesus.

5. Borg, *Meeting Jesus Again*, p. 46. This section depends on chapter 3, "Jesus, Compassion, and Politics," in Borg and on Donald P. McNeill, Douglas A. Morrison, and Henri J. M. Nouwen, *Compassion: A Reflection on the Christian Life* (Garden City, N.Y.: Doubleday Image Book, 1982), Part One.

6. The New Revised Standard Version of the Bible uses the term merciful instead of compassionate, which is found in the Jerusalem Bible and the New English Bible. Borg argues persuasively that compassion is a better translation, pp. 47–48.

7. Richard Gula, *Reason Informed by Faith* (New York: Paulist Press, 1989), p. 185. By this expression Gula means to indicate that Jesus is God's fullest revelation of the invitation of divine love to us and the fullest human response to God.

8. McNeill et al., *Compassion*, pp. 15–16.

9. Borg, *Meeting Jesus Again*, pp. 47–49; McNeill et al., *Compassion*, pp. 15–17. See John Shea, *Stories of Faith* (Chicago: Thomas More Press, 1980), chapter 6 for a poetic account of Jesus, the "Son Who Must Die."

10. Borg, *Meeting Jesus Again*, p. 49. This section on the politics of compassion versus the politics of purity depends on Borg, pp. 49–61.

11. Borg, *Meeting Jesus Again*, pp. 51–52.

12. Mt 23:23; Lk 11:42. Borg, *Meeting Jesus Again*, p. 54.

13. See also Isaiah 1:10–15. Ronald J. Sider, *Rich Christians in an Age of Hunger: A Biblical Study* (New York: Paulist Press, 1977), pp. 80–81, makes this point well.

14. Borg, *Meeting Jesus Again*, pp. 55–57.

15. See also Acts 4:32–37.

16. Sider, *Rich Christians in an Age of Hunger*, p. 101.

17. Ibid., pp. 101–10, quote at p. 106.

18. See Jack Nelson-Pallmeyer, *Brave New World Order* (Maryknoll, N.Y.: Orbis Books, 1992), chapter 8, "Mark, Jesus, and the Kingdom: Confronting World Orders, Old and New"; and Ched Myers, *Binding the Strong Man: A Political Reading of Mark's Story of Jesus* (Maryknoll, N. Y.: Orbis Books, 1988).

19. The Zealots emerge clearly only at the time of the 70 A.D. revolt against the Romans that led to the destruction of the Temple by the Romans, but their brand of militant nationalism was surely around in Jesus' time. They are mentioned indirectly in the Gospels. The Essenes were a sort of monastic community who retreated to the desert to lead a holy and pure and faithful religious life. The Pharisees, who are prominent in the Gospels, become Jesus' adversaries. See Donald Senior, *Jesus: A Gospel Portrait* (Cincinnati: Pflaum Standard, 1975), chapter 2, "The World of Jesus."

20. Ibid., pp. 47–48.

21. Ms. Egan said this in a personal conversation. For a sense of what she had in mind see her "The Beatitudes, the Works of Mercy, and Pacifism," in Thomas A. Shannon, ed., *War or Peace?* (Maryknoll, N.Y.: Orbis Books, 1980), pp. 169–87.

22. Walter Wink, *Violence and Nonviolence in South Africa: Jesus' Third Way* (Philadelphia: New Society Publishers, 1987), chapter 2.

23. Ibid., p. 15.

24. Two of the early scenes in the movie *Gandhi* (directed by Richard Attenborough, starring Ben Kingsley, 1982) illustrate this point well. Both take place in

South Africa. In the first, Gandhi is beaten by a police officer while taking part in a protest where Indians burn their passbooks. Gandhi's defiant but nonviolent resistance both provokes and puzzles the police officer. In the second, Gandhi meets an American minister and is challenged by some young white thugs as they walk to Gandhi's office. The minister wants to walk around the Sermon on the Mount, but Gandhi decides to walk through it.

25. Wink, *Violence and Nonviolence in South Africa*, p. 17.

26. Luke's slightly different version of this saying ends with "Be compassionate as your Father is compassionate," the verse that Borg finds so central to the message of Jesus.

27. Jesus' rejection of dominating power is a key to understanding Jesus and discipleship according to Richard Gula, *Reason Informed by Faith*, pp. 189–97.

28. Mark 1:14–15; Matthew 4:17.

29. For a theological discussion of the notion of transformation that is rooted in H. Richard Niebuhr's classic work, *Christ and Culture* (New York: Harper, 1951) see Glen H. Stassen, D. M. Yeager, and John Howard Yoder, *Authentic Transformation* (Nashville: Abingdon Press, 1996).

30. Charles E. Curran, "Conversion: The Central Moral Message of Jesus," in his *A New Look at Christian Morality* (Notre Dame, Ind.: Fides, 1968), p. 65. See also James P. Hanigan, "Conversion and Christian Ethics," *Theology Today* 40 (April 1983): 33–34.

31. See Roland Bainton, *Christian Attitudes Toward War and Peace* (Nashville: Abingdon Press, 1960), chapter 5; and John Helgeland, Robert J. Daly, and J. Patout Burns, *Christians and the Military: The Early Experience* (Philadelphia: Fortress Press, 1985).

32. See Suzanne Toton, *World Hunger* (Maryknoll, N.Y.: Orbis Books, 1982), pp. 115–21; and Donal Dorr, *The Social Justice Agenda* (Maryknoll, N.Y.: Orbis Books, 1991).

33. There is no official canon for Catholic social teaching. In Catholic ecclesiastical polity, the official teachings of councils of the whole Church (Vatican II), of the popes (social encyclicals), and of Vatican synods carry more weight and authority than that of National Conferences of Bishops or of individual bishops, yet all of these documents could be considered official Catholic teaching that in some degree should bind or guide a Catholic. For a listing of the papal, conciliar, and synod documents, see Charles Curran, "A Century of Catholic Social Teaching," *Theology Today* 48 (July 1991): 154, n. 2. David J. O'Brien and Thomas A. Shannon have produced two very helpful collections of documents associated with Catholic social teaching: *Renewing the Earth: Catholic Documents on Peace, Justice, and Liberation* (Garden City, N.Y.: Image Books, Doubleday & Co., 1977); and *Catholic Social Thought: The Documentary Heritage* (Maryknoll, N.Y.: Orbis Books, 1992).

34. Peter J. Henriot, Edward P. DeBerri, and Michael J. Schultheis, *Catholic Social Teaching: Our Best Kept Secret* (Maryknoll, N.Y.: Orbis Books, 1988). In his *Responses to 101 Questions on Catholic Social Teaching* (Mahwah, N.J.: Paulist Press, 2001), Kenneth Himes suggests that this perception may be changing.

35. See for example: Charles E. Curran, *Catholic Social Teaching 1891—Present: A Historical and Theological Analysis* (Washington, D.C.: Georgetown University Press, 2002); Himes, *Responses to 101 Questions on Catholic Social Teaching*; Thomas Massaro, *Living Justice: Catholic Social Teaching in Action* (Kansas City, Mo.: Sheed & Ward, 2000); Marvin L Krier Mich, *Catholic Social Teaching and Movements* (Mystic, Conn.: Twenty-Third Publications, 1998); Philip S. Land, *Catholic Social Teaching: As I Have Lived, Loathed, and Loved It* (Chicago: Loyola

Press, 1996); John A. Coleman, ed., *One Hundred Years of Catholic Social Thought: Celebration and Challenge* (Maryknoll, N.Y.: Orbis Books, 1991); Fred Kammer, *Doing Faithjustice: An Introduction to Catholic Social Thought* (New York: Paulist Press, 1991); Gregory Baum, *Compassion and Solidarity: The Church for Others* (New York: Paulist Press, 1990); Charles E. Curran and Richard A. McCormick, eds., *Readings in Moral Theology No. 5: Official Catholic Social Teaching* (New York: Paulist Press, 1986); Donal Dorr, *Option for the Poor: A Hundred Years of Vatican Social Teaching* (Maryknoll, N.Y.: Orbis Books, 1983); and John C. Haughey, ed., *The Faith That Does Justice* (New York: Paulist Press, 1977).

36. In O'Brien and Shannon, *Catholic Social Teaching*, p. 289.

37. National Conference of Catholic Bishops (NCCB), *Economic Justice for All* (1986), in O'Brien and Shannon, *Catholic Social Thought*, Introduction, #25.

38. NCCB, *Economic Justice for All*, #35–36.

39. Ibid, #36; see Kammer, *Doing Faithjustice*, pp. 22–24; and Sider, *Rich Christians*, pp. 88–93.

40. Sider, *Rich Christians*, pp. 60–65. On the biblical concept of justice, see Daniel A. Maguire, "The Primacy of Justice in Moral Theology," *Horizons* 10 (Spring 1983): 72–85; Stephen Charles Mott, *Biblical Ethics and Social Change* (New York: Oxford University Press, 1982); and John R. Donahue, "Biblical Perspectives on Justice," in Haughey, *The Faith That Does Justice*, pp. 68–112. On the spiritual consciousness and experience of the prophets see Abraham Heschel, *The Prophets* (New York: Harper & Row, 1962), pp. 12–37, 223–31, 307–19, 483–86.

41. I have chosen to quote consistently from the prophet Micah in this section, but similar quotes could be taken from any of the prophetic books, such as Amos, Hosea, Isaiah, Jeremiah, or Ezekiel.

42. See NCCB, *Economic Justice for All*, #123.

43. Pope John XXIII, *Peace on Earth (Pacem in Terris)*, in O'Brien and Shannon, *Catholic Social Thought*, pp. 131–62. See also Pope John Paul II, *On the Hundredth Anniversary of "Rerum Novarum" (Centesimus Annus)*, ibid., #47, for a sort of summary statement of human rights.

44. See NCCB, *Economic Justice for All*, #79–85; David Hollenbach, "Global Human Rights: An Interpretation of Contemporary Catholic Understanding," in Curran and McCormick, *Readings in Moral Theology No. 5*, pp. 366–83; and John Langan, "Human Rights in Roman Catholicism," ibid., pp. 110–29.

45. Pope John Paul II, *On Social Concern (Sollicitudo Rei Socialis)* (1987), in O'Brien and Shannon, *Catholic Social Thought*, #36.

46. Ibid., #37.

47. See Synod of Bishops, *Justice in the World*, in O'Brien and Shannon, *Catholic Social Thought*, pp. 290–91, passim; Pope Paul VI, *Evangelization in the Modern World (Evangelii Nuntiandi)*, ibid., #31, 36; Kammer, *Doing Faithjustice*, chapter 5.

48. Pope John Paul II, *On Social Concern*, #38. See Jacques Delcourt, "The New Status of Solidarity in the Social Teaching of the Catholic Church," in Samuel M. Natale and Francis P. McHugh, eds., *Proceedings of the First International Conference on Social Values*, held at St. Edmond's College, University of Cambridge, vol. I (New Rochelle, N.Y.: Iona College, 1991), pp. 189–96.

49. Pope John Paul II, *On Social Concern*, #39; NCCB, *Economic Justice for All*, #66, and chapter IV, "A New American Experiment: Partnership for the Public Good."

50. The principle of participation is developed in Pope Paul VI, *A Call to Action (Octogesima Adveniens)* (1971), #22, 24; Synod of Bishops, *Justice in the World*,

pp. 291, 298–99; John Paul II, *On the Hundredth Anniversary,* #43, 46–48; and throughout NCCB, *Economic Justice for All.* Theological reflection on participation would include: John Donaghy, "Justice as Participation: An Emerging Understanding," in Natale and McHugh, *Proceedings of the First International Conference on Social Values,* vol. II (1991), pp. 61–79; George Weigel, "Catholicism and Democracy," *Washington Quarterly* 12 (Autumn 1989): 5–28; and David Hollenbach, *Justice, Peace, and Human Rights: American Catholic Social Ethics in a Pluralistic Context* (New York: Crossroad Publishing, 1988).

51. NCCB, *Economic Justice for All,* #71.

52. Pope John Paul II, *On the Hundredth Anniversary,* #46–48; NCCB, *Economic Justice for All,* #77, passim; and Canadian Conference of Catholic Bishops, *Ethical Choices and Political Challenges: Ethical Reflections on the Future of Canada's Socioeconomic Order* in David M. Byers, ed., *Justice in the Marketplace: Collected Statements of the Vatican and the U.S. Catholic Bishops on Economic Policy, 1891–1984* (Washington, D.C.: United States Catholic Conference, 1985), p. 485.

53. Synod of Bishops, *Justice in the World,* pp. 298–99.

54. The principle of subsidiarity was first articulated by Pope Pius XI, *After Forty Years (Quadragesimo Anno,* 1931) in O'Brien and Shannon, *Catholic Social Thought,* #79–80. See also John Paul II, *On the Hundredth Anniversary,* #48; and NCCB, *Economic Justice for All,* #99, 124.

55. Pope John XXIII, *Christianity and Social Progress (Mater et Magistra)* (1961) in O'Brien and Shannon, *Catholic Social Thought,* #51–67; NCCB, *Economic Justice for All,* #124. See Kammer, *Doing Faithjustice,* pp. 80, 83.

56. NCCB, *Economic Justice for All,* 52, 85–91, passim.

57. Ibid., #24.

58. Vatican II, *Pastoral Constitution on the Church in the Modern World* (1965) in O'Brien and Shannon, *Catholic Social Thought,* #4.

59. The pertinent Medellín Conference Documents can be found in O'Brien and Shannon, *Renewing the Earth,* pp. 549–84. The Puebla Conference Documents can be found in John Eagleson and Philip Sharper, eds., *Puebla and Beyond: Documentation and Commentary,* trans. John Drury (Maryknoll, N.Y.: Orbis Books, 1979).

60. These documents are in O'Brien and Shannon, *Catholic Social Thought.* Pope John Paul II returns to the question of development and the "social mortgage" on private property in his encyclical, *On the Hundredth Anniversary,* #30–46. See also Pope Paul VI, *A Call to Action,* #23.

61. Peter J. Henriot, *Opting for the Poor: A Challenge for North Americans* (Washington, D.C.: Center for Concern, 1990), p. 24.

62. NCCB, *Economic Justice for All,* #86. Henriot, *Opting for the Poor,* p. 25, distinguishes between the "needy" and the poor. The needy, of course, should not be neglected, but the poor require our committed attention and action.

63. Henriot, *Opting for the Poor,* p. 26.

64. This is Kammer's preferred description of this principle (Kammer, *Doing Faithjustice,* chap. 4).

65. This is the critical question raised in Ronald Sider's book *Rich Christians in a Hungry World.* It is based primarily on the parable of the rich man who overlooked a poor beggar at his gate (Lk 16:19–31) and secondarily in the parable of the rich fool (Lk 12:13–21). In chap. 5 Sider explores a "Biblical attitude toward property and wealth." He concludes that, according to Scripture, possessions, although not innately evil, are "positively dangerous because they often encourage unconcern for the poor, because they lead to strife and war, and because they seduce people into forsaking God" (p. 122).

66. NCCB, *The Challenge of Peace,* in O'Brien and Shannon, *Catholic Social Thought,* #71–78, 111–21. See NCCB, *The Harvest of Justice Is Sown in Peace* in Gerard F. Powers et al., eds., *Peacemaking: Moral and Policy Challenges for a New World* (Washington, D.C.: United States Catholic Conference, 1994), pp. 317–19.

67. Paul VI, *On the Development of Peoples,* #87, 76–77. John Paul II, *On Social Concern,* #39, and *On the Hundredth Anniversary,* #52.

68. See Vatican II, *The Pastoral Constitution on the Church in the Modern World,* #85; and NCCB, *The Harvest of Justice Is Sown in Peace,* pp. 316–17.

69. John Paul II, "World Day of Peace Message (Jan. 1, 2002)" in *America* (Jan. 7/14, 2002), p. 8, passim. The Pope uses justice and forgiveness as a repeated refrain in this post-September 11 message.

70. Vatican II, *The Pastoral Constitution on the Church in the Modern World,* #80.

71. NCCB, *The Challenge of Peace,* #160–61, 188, passim.

72. Ibid., #186, 188.

73. This is not to conclude, however, that the Persian Gulf War was morally justified or that it was conducted justly. See, for example, Thomas C. Fox, *Iraq: Military Victory, Moral Defeat* (Kansas City, Mo.: Sheed & Ward, 1991); and Kenneth L. Vaux, *Ethics and the Gulf War* (Boulder, Col.: Westview Press, 1992). The U.S. bishops themselves differed on these questions.

74. See, for example, *On the Hundredth Anniversary,* #52. This has been a constant theme of his World Day of Peace statements and of his talks and homilies on his various journeys. In my opinion, however, the Pope missed an important opportunity in not highlighting violence and war, along with capital punishment, abortion, and euthanasia, in his encyclical *The Gospel of Life* (*Origins* 24 [April 6, 1995], pp. 690–727).

75. Vatican II, *The Pastoral Constitution on the Church in the Modern World,* #81. See also John Paul II, *On Social Concern,* #23–24.

76. See Vatican II, *The Pastoral Constitution on the Church in the Modern World,* #82; NCCB, *The Challenge of Peace,* #235–244; John Paul II, *On Social Concern,* #41–45; NCCB, *The Harvest of Justice Is Sown in Peace,* p. 325, passim.

77. See John Paul II, *On Social Concern,* #25, 26, 34; *On the Hundredth Anniversary,* #37; "Peace with All Creation," *Origins* 19 (1990): 465–68. The most recent statement of the U.S. Bishops' Conference is "Global Climate Change: A Plea for Dialogue, Prudence, and the Common Good," June 15, 2001. Previous statements include "Stewardship: A Disciple's Response," in 1993 and "Renewing the Earth: An Invitation to Reflection and Action on the Environment in Light of Catholic Social Teaching" (1992). Drew Christiansen, "Ecology, Justice, and Development," *Theological Studies* 51 (1990): 68–71, indicates that the Pope's treatment of the issue in *On Social Concern* is significant. While it is certainly good that the Pope is aware of the issue and addresses it in the context of development, I do not think the Pope gives the issue the attention it deserves. There is no encyclical on the topic, nor have the U.S. bishops produced a pastoral letter on the issue. The Philippine Bishops' Conference has issued a very thoughtful pastoral letter on ecology titled "What Is Happening to Our Beautiful Land?" (1988) but it is not widely available. See Mich, *Catholic Social Teaching and Movements,* chap. 9, for an overview of church teaching on the environment.

78. Orbis Books, for example, has a series of publications on theology and ecology.

79. See, for example, Pax Christi's Peacemaker Pamphlet Series and Mary Ann Luke, ed., *Pilgrims and Seekers: Saints Without Pedestals* (Erie, Penn.: Pax Christi USA,

1995); and Michael True, *Justice Seekers, Peace Makers: 32 Portraits in Courage* (Mystic, Conn.: Twenty-Third Publications, 1985) and *To Construct Peace: 30 More Justice Seekers and Peace Makers* (Mystic, Conn.: Twenty-Third Publications, 1992).

9. CHRISTIAN CITIZENSHIP AND RESOURCES FOR INVOLVEMENT

1. See James W. Douglass, *Resistance and Contemplation: The Way of Liberation* (New York: Dell Publishing, 1972); and Robert H. King, *Thomas Merton and Thich Nhat Hanh: Engaged Spirituality in an Age of Globalization* (New York: Continuum, 2001).

2. See 1 Kings 3:3–15 where Solomon asks God for the gift of wisdom.

3. Charles E. Curran, "Conversion: The Central Moral Message of Jesus," in his *A New Look at Christian Morality* (Notre Dame, Ind.: Fides, 1968), pp. 50–52.

4. See John F. Kavanaugh, *Following Christ in a Consumer Society: The Spirituality of Cultural Resistance,* rev. ed. (Maryknoll, N.Y.: Orbis Books, 1991).

5. Adam Daniel Finnerty, *No More Plastic Jesus: Global Justice and Christian Lifestyle* (Maryknoll, N.Y.: Orbis Books, 1977), p. 97.

6. Ronald J. Sider, *Rich Christians in an Age of Hunger: A Biblical Study* (New York: Paulist Press, 1977), pp. 92–93.

7. National Conference of Catholic Bishops, *Economic Justice for All,* #97–98; John Paul II, *On Human Work* (*Laborens Exercens*) in David J. O'Brien and Thomas A. Shannon, eds., *Catholic Social Thought: The Documentary Heritage* (Maryknoll, N.Y.: Orbis Books, 1992), #6, 9, 10.

8. NCCB, *Economic Justice for All,* #92.

9. See the films *A Civil Action* (1998), directed by Steven Zaillian, starring John Travolta; and *Erin Brockovich* (2000), directed by Steven Soderbergh, starring Julia Roberts.

10. See Joseph A. Grassi, *Broken Bread and Broken Bodies: The Lord's Supper and World Hunger* (Maryknoll, N.Y.: Orbis Books, 1985); and Monica K. Hellwig, *The Eucharist and the Hunger of the World,* 2nd rev. ed. (Kansas City: Sheed & Ward, 1992).

11. "While the Church is bound to give witness to justice, she recognizes that everyone who ventures to speak to people about justice must first be just in their eyes. Hence we must undertake an examination of the modes of acting and of the possessions and lifestyle found within the Church herself." Synod of Bishops, *Justice in the World* in O'Brien and Shannon, *Catholic Social Thought,* p. 295.

12. Arthur Simon, *Christian Faith and Public Policy: No Grounds for Divorce* (Grand Rapids: Eerdmans Publishing, 1987), p. 12 and chap. 5.

13. See J. Milburn Thompson, "A Theological Perspective on Church and Politics in the United States," in Samuel M. Natale and Francis P. McHugh, eds., *Proceedings of the First International Conference on Social Values,* vol. 2 (New Rochelle, N.Y.: Iona College, 1991), pp. 37–44, at 39–41.

14. See Simon, *Christian Faith and Public Policy,* pp. 104–13. Arthur Simon is a founding member and past executive director of Bread for the World.

15. The sample letter is based upon "Jesse Helms Mocks the Senate," *New York Times* (Feb. 10, 1997), editorial. See www.fns.usda.gov/wic/ for more information about the WIC program.

16. See Gene Sharp, *The Politics of Nonviolent Action,* 3 vols., esp. vol. 2, *The Methods of Nonviolent Action* (Boston: Porter Sargent Publishers, 1973); and Elizabeth Morgan, *Global Poverty and Personal Responsibility* (New York: Paulist Press, 1989), pp. 148–53.

Index